McGRAW-HILL MATHEMATIC

Math in my World

Douglas H. Clements

Kenneth W. Jones

Lois Gordon Moseley

Linda Schulman

McGraw-Hill School Division

New York Farmington

PROGRAM AUTHORS

Dr. Douglas H. Clements

Kenneth W. Jones

Lois Gordon Moseley

Dr. Linda Schulman

CONTRIBUTING AUTHORS

Dr. Liana Forest

Christine A. Fernsler

Dr. Kathleen Kelly-Benjamin

Maria R. Marolda

Dr. Richard H. Moyer

Dr. Walter G. Secada

CONSULTANTS

Multicultural and Educational Consultants

Rim An

Sue Cantrell

Mordessa Corbin

Dr. Carlos Diaz

Carl Downing

Linda Ferreira

Judythe M. Hazel

Roger Larson

Josie Robles

Veronica Rogers

Telkia Rutherford

Sharon Searcy

Elizabeth Sinor

Michael Wallpe

Claudia Zaslavsky

COVER PHOTOGRAPHY Jade Albert for MMSD; m. Superstock; l. MMSD.

PHOTOGRAPHY All photographs are by the McGraw-Hill School Division (MMSD), Ken Karp for MMSD, Ken Lax for MMSD and Scott Harvey for MMSD except as noted below.
Table of Contents • Superstock, Inc. : iii t. • Tom and Pat Leeson/Photo Researchers : iii m. • John Yurka/The Picture Cube : iv m. • J.D. Bartlett/Bruce Coleman Inc. : v t. • Index Stock : v b. • Nancy Sheehan/The Picture Cube : vi t. • Bob Daemmrich : vi m. • Bob Daemmrich/Stock Boston : vii t. • Gary Retherford/Photo Researchers : vii b. • Jason Green/Liaison Int'l. : vii m. b. • Superstock, Inc. : ix t. • Bob Daemmrich/Stock Boston : x m. • Richard Hutchings/Photo Edit : 1 t.r. • Lawrence Migdale : 1 b.r. • **Chapter 1** • Tom & Pat Leeson/Photo Researchers : 3 • Superstock, Inc. : 7 • Fletcher & Baylis/Photo Researchers : 19 • Gregory Dimijian/Photo Researchers : 21 • Cindy Karp/National Geographic Society : 30 • John M. Roberts/The Stock Market : 32 • **Chapter 2** • Lawrence Migdale : 45 r. • T. Tracy/FPG Int'l : 48 • Richard Paisley/Stock Boston, Inc. : 53 r. • Louise Gubb/The Image Works : 62 l. • Ben Simmons/Stock Market : 62 r. • Buffalo Bill Historical Center, Cody, Wy : 66 • **Chapter 3** • John Yurka/Picture Cube.: 85 • M.W.F. Tweedie/Photo Researchers : 107 t.r. • Renee Lynn/Photo Researchers : 112 b.m. • L. West/Photo Researchers : 117 r. • Gregory K. Scott/Photo Researchers : 117 m. • J & D Bartlett/Bruce Coleman, Inc. : 117 l. • Bob Daemmrich/Stock Boston, Inc.: 123 • Henley and Savage/Uniphoto : 128 • **Chapter 5** • Lawrence Migdale/Stock Boston, Inc. : 170 t.m. • Henley and Savage/The Stock Market : 170 t.r. • Lee Boltin Picture Library : 176 • Index Stock : 182 t.r. • Anne Heimann/The Stock Market: 189 • Michael Busselle/Tony Stone Images : 190 • Nancy Sheehan/The Picture Cube : 191 • M. Eastcott/The Image Works : 194 • Robert Kristofik/The Image Bank : 196 t. • Spencer Jones/FPG International : 196 b. • **Chapter 6** • John Feingersh/The Stock Market : 201 • Jacob Taposchaner/FPG Int'l : 204 • Bob Daemmrich: 211 • John Lei for MMSD : 221 l. • Anne Nielsen for MMSD : 221 r. • Abe Rezny/The Image Works : 230 • **Chapter 7** • Index Stock Photography, Inc. : 237 • Photo Researchers: 238 • The Stock Market : 238 b. • Robert Ginn/Unicorn Stock Photos : 238 t. l. • Courtesy of June Acker Myers: 253 m. • The Granger Collection: 262 • Jonathan A. Meyers/FPG International: 263 t.r. • Jerry Jacka : 263 b.r. • Bob Daemmrich/Stock Boston, Inc.: 268 • **Chapter 8** • Lori Adamski Peek/Tony Stone Images : 273 • M.H. Sharp/Photo Researchers : 281 t.r. • Bill Ivy/Tony Stone Worldwide : 281 l. • Larry West/FPG International : 281 b. • Gary Retherford/Photo Researchers : 282 r. • Jason Green/Gamma Liaison : 282 l. • Grace Davies/Omni Photo Communications : 284 • Comstock : 286 b. • Patti Murray/Animals Animals : 287 t. • Clyde Smith/FPG International : 287 b. • Rolf Bettner : 296 • Stephen Simpson/FPG International : 297 t. • Erwin & Peggy Bauer/Natural Selection : 299 • Frans Lanting/Photo Researchers : 301 • **Chapter 9** • photographed courtesy permission Museum of Modern Art, New York, New York/ Pablo Picasso, "Bull," 1958 c. Estate of Pablo Picasso/Artists Rights Society, New York : 311 • Jimmy Ernst, "Another Silence," oil painting 6' x 10'3", courtesy The Rimrock Foundation : 322 • Paul Gauguin, "Still Life With Three Puppies" c. 1888 oil on wood 36 1/8" x 24 5/8" Museum of Modern Art, Mrs. Simon Guggenheim Fund : 335 • **Chapter 10** • Superstock, Inc. : 349 • Kim Robbie/The Stock Market : 356 • R. Rathe/FPG: 365 • Bob Daemmrich/Stock Boston, Inc. : 366 • Superstock, Inc.: 384 • **Chapter 11** • Bob Daemmrich/Uniphoto : 389 • Bonnie Kamin/Photo Edit : 395 • The Granger Collection : 398 b.r. • Kindra Clineff/The Picture Cube : 405 • E. Crews/The Image Works : 425 • Michael Newman/Photo Edit : 429 • Wayne Hay/The Picture Cube : 430 • **Chapter 12** • Richard Hutchings/PhotoEdit: 443 • Superstock, Inc. : 444 • John Running/Stock Boston Inc. : 447 • Lawrence Migdale : 449 • Bob Daemmrich/Stock Boston, Inc.: 452 • Ken Kerbs for MMSD : 459 t.

ILLUSTRATION Winky Adam: 2, 3, 44, 45, 84, 85, 134, 135, 166, 167, 200, 201, 236, 237, 272, 273, 310, 311, 348, 349, 388, 389, 442, 443 • Jo Lynn Alcorn: 259, 261, 350, 364 • Bob Barner: 95, 123, 207, 208, 225, 226, 230, 232, 456, 458, 472, 474, 476 • Sue Bialecki: 398 • Ken Bowser: 29, 358, 362, 381, 385 • Hal Brooks: 46, 47, 56, 57, 64, 133, 209, 210, 224, 260 • Roger Chandler: 402 • Randy Chewning: 290 • Genevieve Claire: 335, 336, 339 • Betsy Day: 103, 401 • Daniel Del Valle: 75, 120, 121, 122, 184, 337 • Eldon Doty: 399, 410 • Brian Dugan: 82 • Doreen Gay-Kassel: 4, 11, 20, 23, 24, 25, 34, 168, 442, 446, 447, 448, 450, 463 • Annie Gusman: 404, 428 • Robert Hynes: 86, 108 • Stanford Kay: 28 • Jim Kelly: 56, 65, 68, 73, 74 • Rita Lascaro, 88, 130, 136, 141, 142, 150, 156, 160, 161, 202, 218, 222, 293, 473 • Tom Leonard: 283, 284, 288, 298, 301, 302 • Claude Martinot: 295, 306 • Hatley Mason: 422, 427, 431, 432, 433, 438 • Bonnie Matthews: 252 • Paul Meisel: 40 • Jonathan Milne: 9, 10, 22, 36 • Jim Paillot: 67, 143, 144, 145, 157, 179 • Hima Pamoedjo: 41, 54, 257, 271, 313, 322, 325, 331, 339, 340, 344, 346 • Miles Parnell: 182, 185, 190, 193 • Brenda Pepper: 33, 42, 175, 177, 285, 286, 315 • Mary Power:178, 180, 186, 193 • Victoria Raymond: 240, 333, 334 • Andy San Diego: 155 • Audrey Schorr: 170, 325 • Bob Shein: 7, 8, 21, 30, 394, 400, 403, 404, 416, 420, 424, 429, 430, 440 • Michael Sloan: 91, 92, 93, 94, 102, 109, 114, 119 • Matt Straub: 86, 97, 98, 100, 104, 106, 113, 119, 213, 215, 231 • Susan Swan: 146, 149, 250, 251, 256, 258, 266, 267, 453, 454, 457, 466, 469 • Peggy Tagel: 171, 173, 174, 181, 465 • Don Tate: 352, 354, 356, 373, 375, 376, 379 • Terry Taylor: 101 • TCA Graphics: 97, 98, 100, 104, 106, 119, 120, 121, 122, 123, 126, 132, 174, 187, 188, 189, 190, 191, 194, 195, 197, 199, 441 • Dale Verzaal: 15, 16, 31, 115, 116, 120 • Nina Wallace: 235, 309, 365, 368, 370, 378, 382, 383, 477 • Matt Wawiorka: 293, 294, 407, 408 • Rebecca Wildsmith: 18, 278, 308.

ACKNOWLEDGMENTS "Ten Puppies (Diez Perritos)" from THE SPECTRUM OF MUSIC, Grade 1, Mary Val Marsh, Carroll Rinehart, and Edith Savage, Authors. Copyright (c) 1983 Macmillan/McGraw-Hill School Publishing Company. • Unabridged text of "Rope Rhyme" from HONEY, I LOVE by Eloise Greenfield. Text copyright (c) 1978 by Eloise Greenfield. Selection reprinted by permission of HarperCollins Publishers.

McGraw-Hill School Division

A Division of The McGraw-Hill Companies

McGraw-Hill School Division
1221 Avenue of the Americas
New York, New York 10020

Printed in the United States of America
ISBN 0-02-110317-8 / 2
10 11 12 13 14 15 043/073 09 08 07 06 05 04

Contents

1 Understanding Addition and Subtraction

THEME: In the Rain Forest

2 Addition and Subtraction Strategies

THEME: Pen Pals

These lessons develop, practice, or apply algebraic thinking through the study of patterns, relationships and functions, properties, equations, formulas, and inequalities.

3 Place Value and Graphing

THEME: Our Backyard

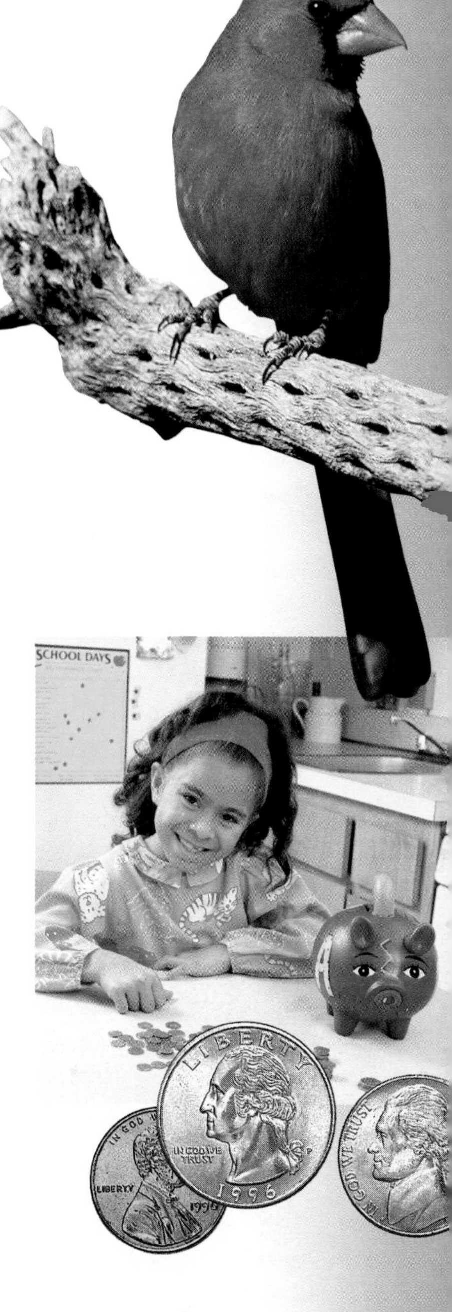

4 Money

THEME: Saving and Spending

5 Telling Time

THEME: Apple Pie Time

These lessons develop, practice, or apply algebraic thinking through the study of patterns, relationships and functions, properties, equations, formulas, and inequalities.

6 Exploring 2-Digit Addition and Subtraction

THEME: Fun and Games

7 Adding 2-Digit Numbers

THEME: Fun at the Fair

8 Subtracting 2-Digit Numbers

THEME: Animals on the Move

These lessons develop, practice, or apply algebraic thinking through the study of patterns, relationships and functions, properties, equations, formulas, and inequalities.

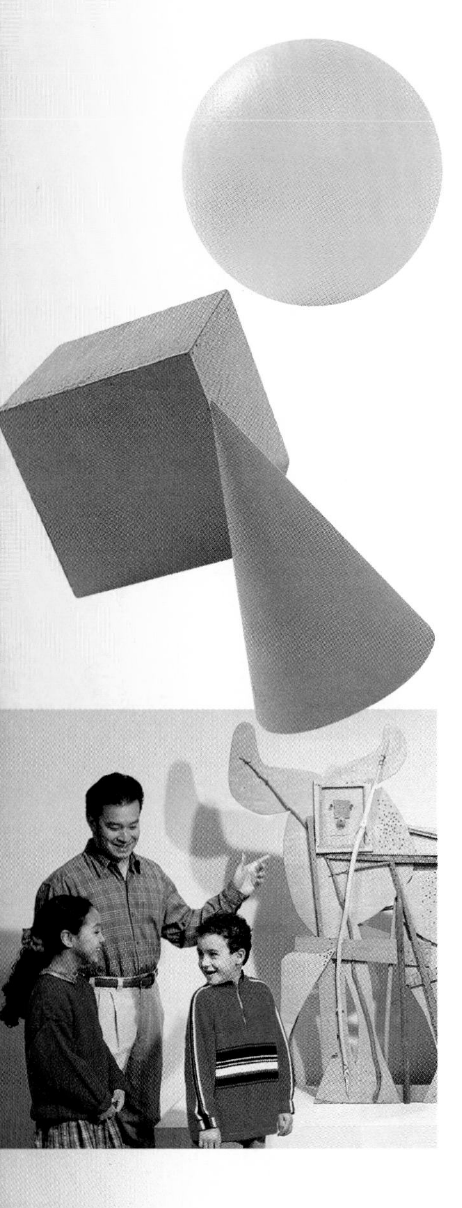

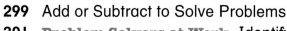

9 Geometry and Fractions

THEME: Shapes in Art

10 Measurement

THEME: Mapping Adventures

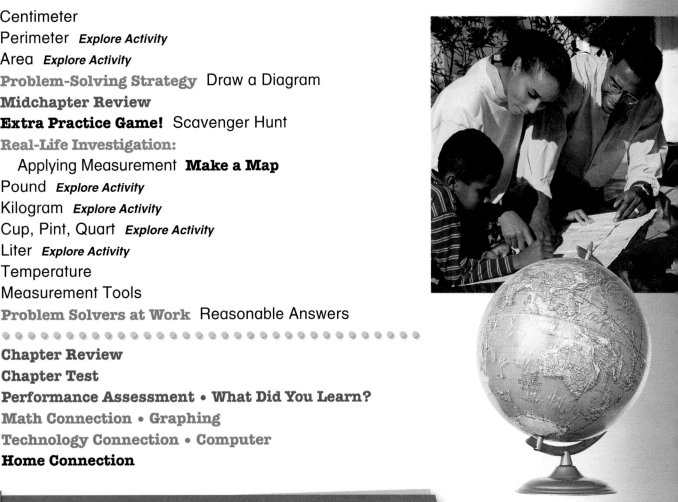

11 Numbers to 1,000—Adding and Subtracting

THEME: Math and Music

These lessons develop, practice, or apply algebraic thinking through the study of patterns, relationships and functions, properties, equations, formulas, and inequalities.

12 Exploring Multiplication and Division

THEME: Vegetables

These lessons develop, practice, or apply algebraic thinking through the study of patterns, relationships and functions, properties, equations, formulas, and inequalities.

Welcome to your new math book!

This year you will learn about many ways to use math in your world.

How many in each bunch?

How long to bake?

How many letters?

At Home

Dear Family,

I am beginning the first chapter in my new mathematics book. During the next few weeks I will be learning to use strategies to add and subtract.

I will also be talking about rain forests and the animals and plants that live in them.

Learning About Rain Forests

Let's talk about what kinds of animals might live in a rain forest. We can make a list of different animals.

My Math Words

I am going to use these and other math words in this chapter.

Please help me make word cards for the math words. I can use these word cards when I practice addition and subtraction.

- part
- total
- add
- addition sentence
- addend
- sum
- count on
- order
- related facts
- subtract
- subtraction sentence
- difference
- count back

Your child,

____

Signature

Understanding Addition and Subtraction

Theme: In the Rain Forest

CHAPTER 1

Reread You may have questions after you listen to a story. You can read or listen to the story again.

Listen to the story *In the Rain Forest.*

What facts can you tell about a toucan's beak? Go back to the story. Read to find out.

Name

What Do You Know?

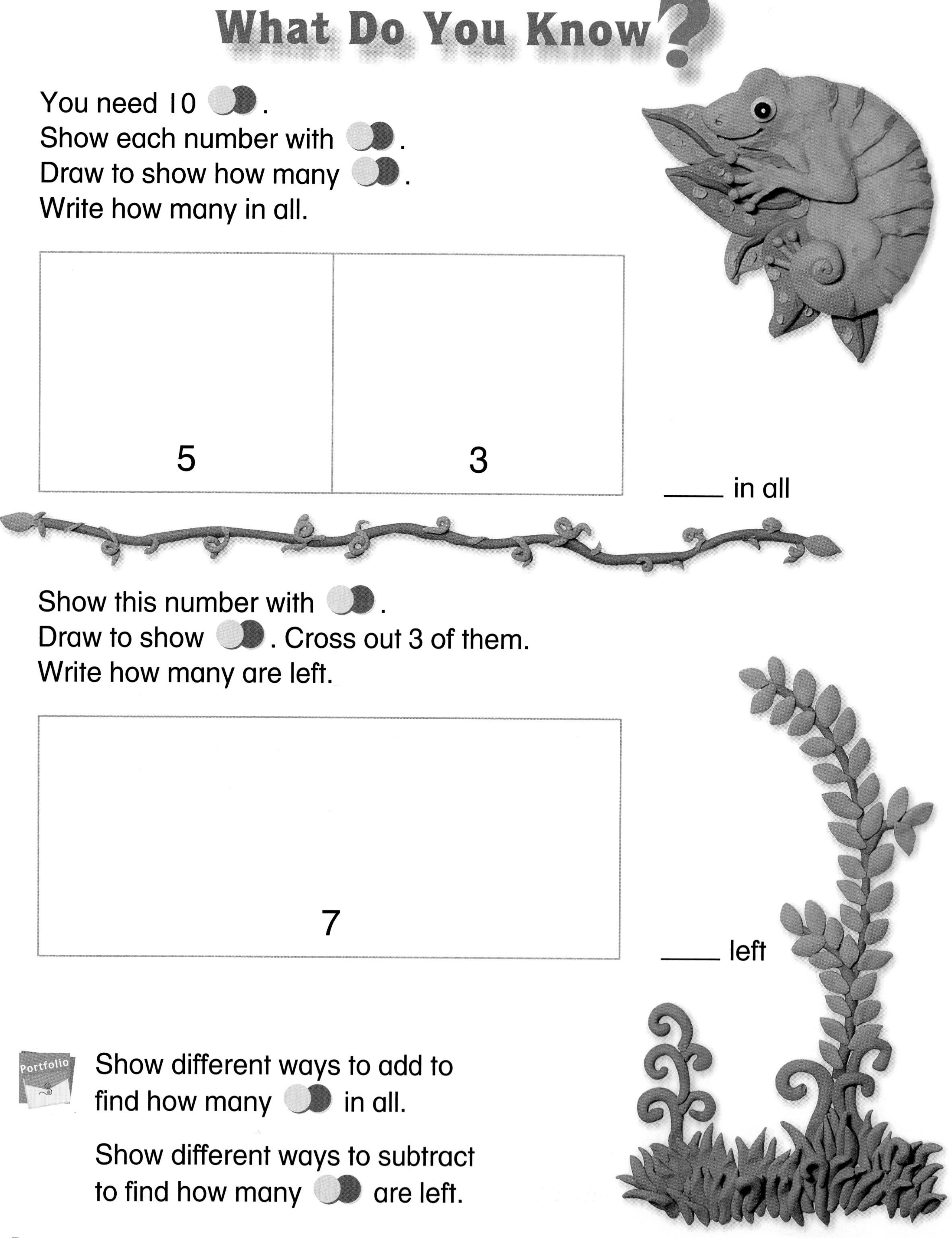

You need 10 ●.
Show each number with ●.
Draw to show how many ●.
Write how many in all.

5	3

____ in all

Show this number with ●.
Draw to show ●. Cross out 3 of them.
Write how many are left.

7

____ left

Portfolio

Show different ways to add to find how many ● in all.

Show different ways to subtract to find how many ● are left.

Name ______________________

Working Together

You and your partner need 10 cubes.
Take turns.

- Make a cube train for the **total**.
- Snap it into 2 **parts**.
- Write how many in each part.
- Find all the parts for the total.

TOTAL 3	
3	0
2	1

TOTAL 4	

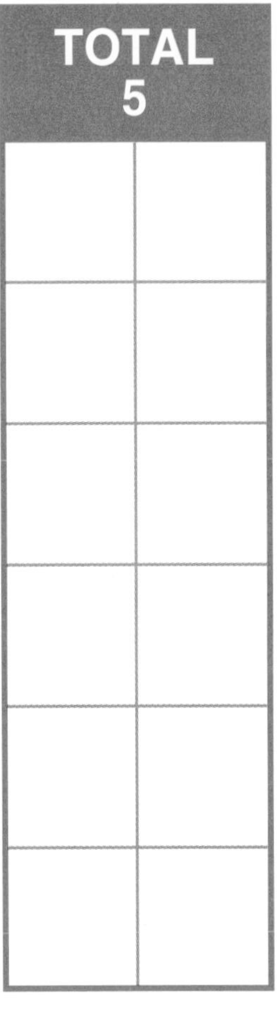

TOTAL 5	

TOTAL 6	

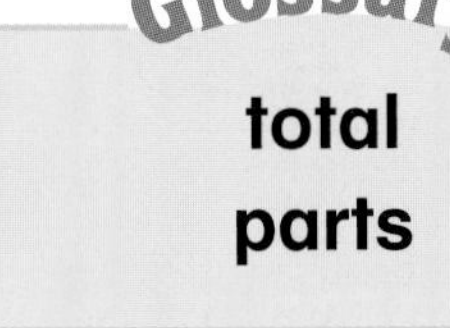

Look at the total 6. How are the parts the same?
How are they different?

Practice!

Find all the parts for the total.
Use cubes if you want to.

TOTAL 7	
7	0
6	1

TOTAL 8	

TOTAL 9	

TOTAL 10	

At Home: We found all the parts for totals. Ask your child to name parts for 11.

Name

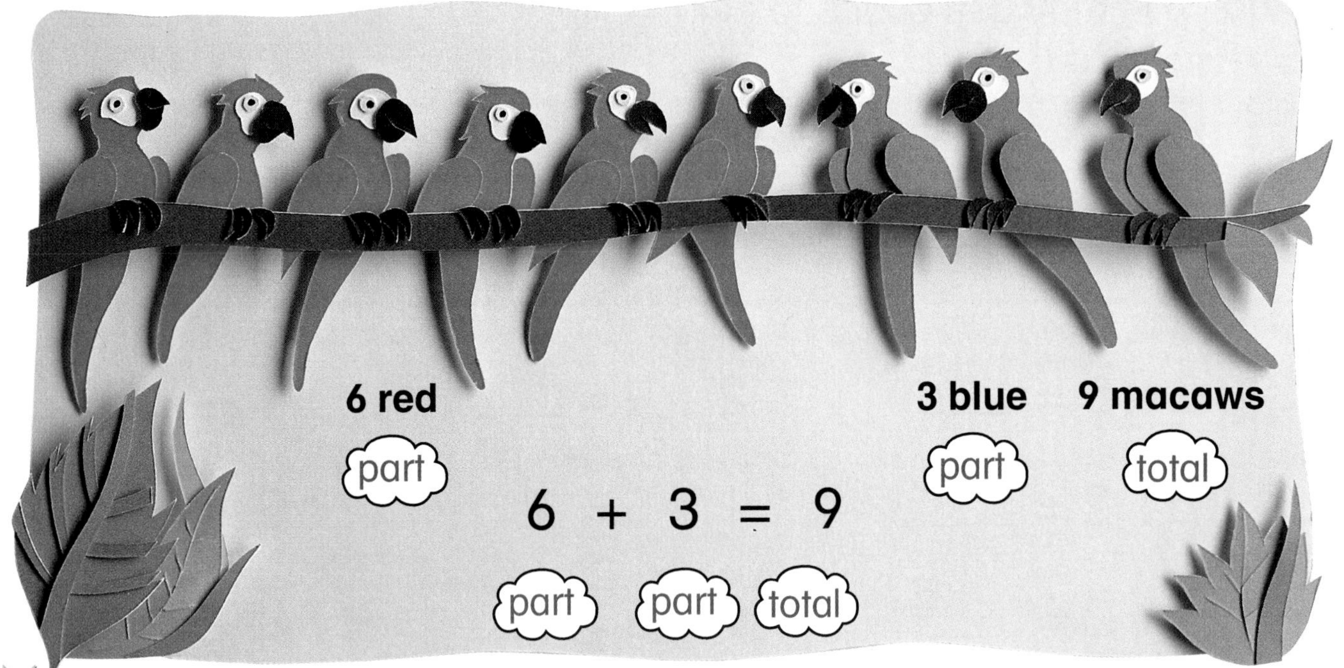

Working Together

You and your partner need 9 and 9.

Glossary
add
addition sentence

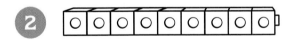

- Make a train to show parts.
- Color to show your parts.
- **Add**. Write the **addition sentence**.

1  3 + 4 = 7

2 ___ + ___ = ___

3 ___ + ___ = ___

4 ___ + ___ = ___

5 ___ + ___ = ___

6 ___ + ___ = ___

What does the addition sentence 6 + 4 = 10 mean?

Practice!

Add. You may use cubes to help.

1 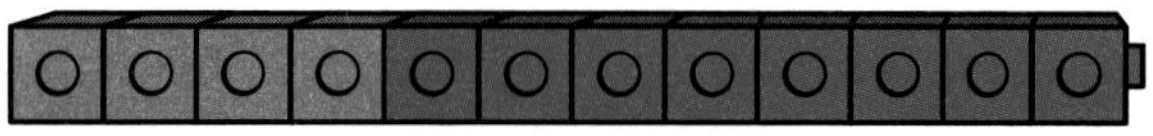

4 + 8 = 12

2 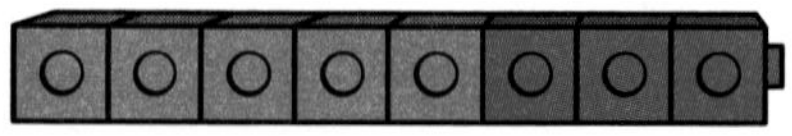

5 + 3 = ____

3	6 + 5 = ____	2 + 4 = ____	9 + 1 = ____
4	7 + 2 = ____	1 + 5 = ____	3 + 8 = ____
5	6 + 2 = ____	9 + 3 = ____	4 + 3 = ____
6	8 + 1 = ____	2 + 2 = ____	2 + 5 = ____
7	4 + 6 = ____	1 + 4 = ____	3 + 9 = ____
8	8 + 4 = ____	3 + 6 = ____	2 + 3 = ____

Mixed Review Test Preparation

9 Write the missing numbers.

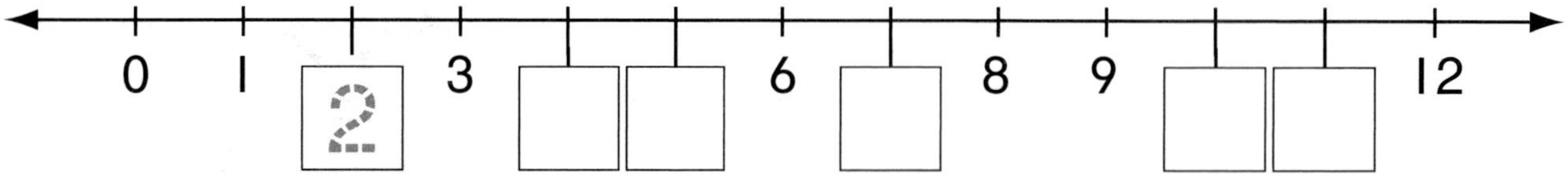

10 

2 + 5 = ____

3 + 9 = ____

At Home: We added and wrote addition sentences. Ask your child to tell how to add 4 + 8.

Name ____________________

Explore Activity

Addition Patterns

3 yellow   4 red   7 flowers

3 + 4 = 7
addend **addend** **sum**

Working Together

You and your partner need 12 .

- Use counters to show facts for 7.
- Color to match your counters.
- Write the addition sentences.

Glossary
addend
sum
pattern

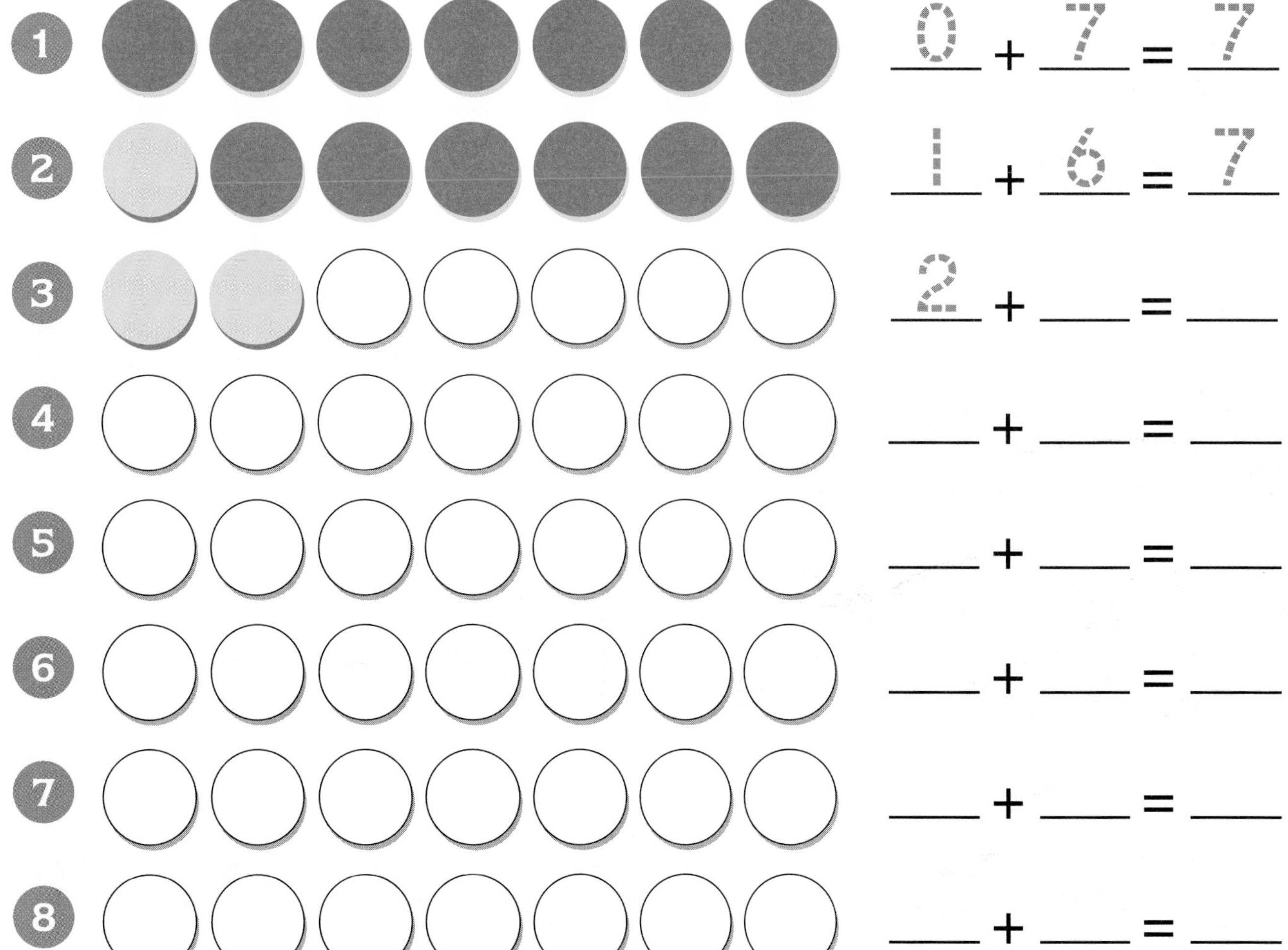

1. 0 + 7 = 7
2. 1 + 6 = 7
3. 2 + ___ = ___
4. ___ + ___ = ___
5. ___ + ___ = ___
6. ___ + ___ = ___
7. ___ + ___ = ___
8. ___ + ___ = ___

Algebra Critical Thinking **PATTERNS** What **pattern** do you see in facts for 7?

Practice!

PATTERNS Add. Use the patterns to help.

1

0	1	2	3	4
+ 9	+ 8	+ 7	+ 6	+ 5
9				

2

9	8	7	6	5	4	3
+ 3	+ 4	+ 5	+ 6	+ 7	+ 8	+ 9

3

0	1	2	3	4	5
+ 5	+ ☐	+ ☐	+ ☐	+ ☐	+ ☐
5	5	5	5	5	5

4

1	2	3	4	5	6
+ 9	+ ☐	+ ☐	+ ☐	+ ☐	+ ☐
10	10	10			

Write all the addition facts for 8.

5

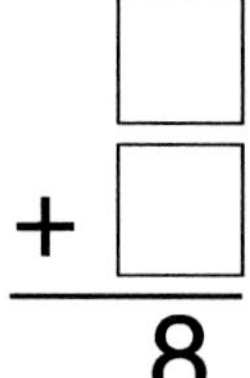

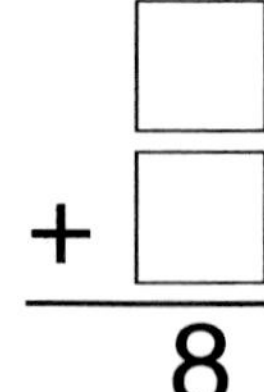

☐	☐	☐	☐
+ ☐	+ ☐	+ ☐	+ ☐
8	8	8	8

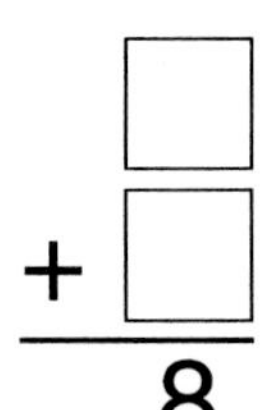

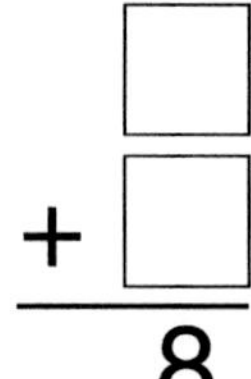

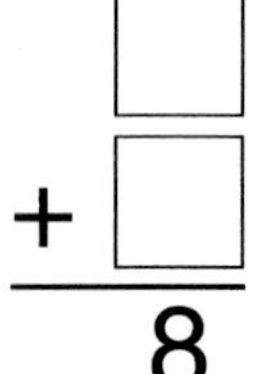

☐	☐	☐	☐	☐
+ ☐	+ ☐	+ ☐	+ ☐	+ ☐
8	8	8	8	8

How does a pattern help you find all the facts for a number?

At Home: We used patterns to help us add. Ask your child to tell you about the pattern in row 3 above.

Name ____________________

Count On

Find 7 + 2.

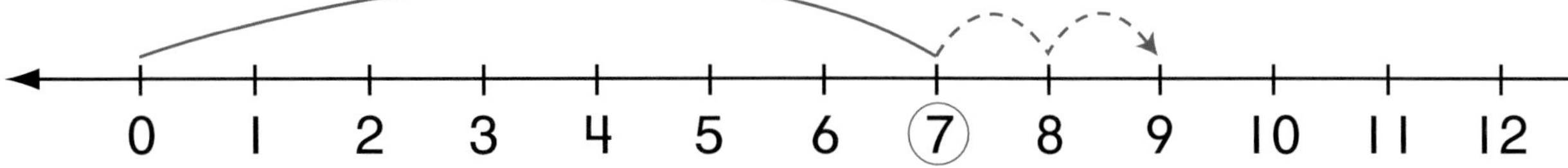

7 + 2 = 9

Glossary
count on
mental math
number line

Count on to add.
Use **mental math** or the **number line**.

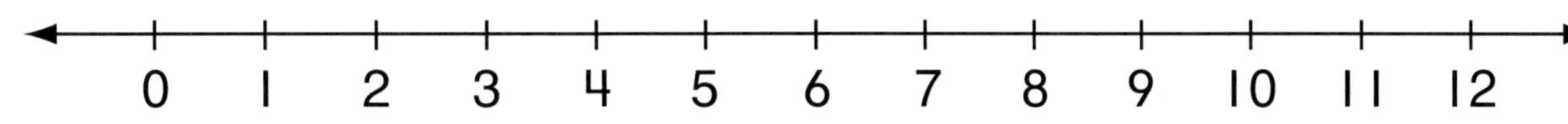

1. 5 + 3 = 8 (Say **5.** Count on 3. Say **6, 7, 8.**) | 1 + 4 = 5 (Say **4.** Count on 1. Say **5.**)

2. 2 + 6 = ____ | 3 + 1 = ____ | 9 + 3 = ____
3. 7 + 3 = ____ | 8 + 1 = ____ | 6 + 1 = ____
4. 3 + 2 = ____ | 5 + 1 = ____ | 3 + 6 = ____
5. 2 + 1 = ____ | 3 + 8 = ____ | 4 + 2 = ____
6. 4 + 3 = ____ | 9 + 2 = ____ | 1 + 7 = ____
7. 8 + 2 = ____ | 1 + 9 = ____ | 5 + 2 = ____

How could you count on to solve 17 + 2?

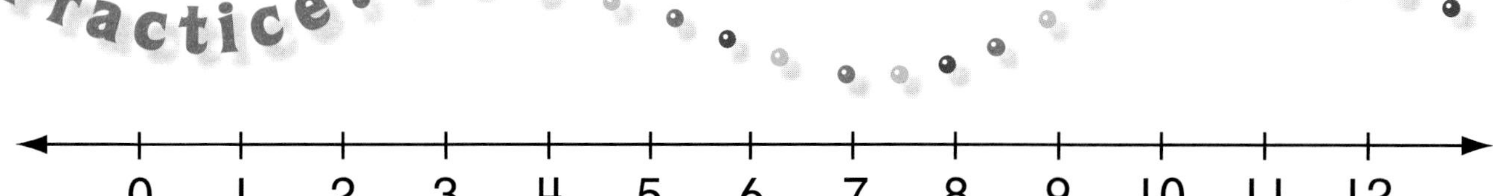

0 1 2 3 4 5 6 7 8 9 10 11 12

Count on to add.

1. $3 + 4 =$ 7 $\qquad 9 + 1 =$ ___ $\qquad 3 + 5 =$ ___
2. $2 + 7 =$ ___ $\qquad 8 + 3 =$ ___ $\qquad 9 + 3 =$ ___
3. $2 + 5 =$ ___ $\qquad 1 + 6 =$ ___ $\qquad 1 + 3 =$ ___
4. $\begin{array}{r} 1 \\ +\,8 \\ \hline \end{array}$ $\quad \begin{array}{r} 2 \\ +\,1 \\ \hline \end{array}$ $\quad \begin{array}{r} 4 \\ +\,2 \\ \hline \end{array}$ $\quad \begin{array}{r} 2 \\ +\,4 \\ \hline \end{array}$ $\quad \begin{array}{r} 6 \\ +\,2 \\ \hline \end{array}$ $\quad \begin{array}{r} 3 \\ +\,7 \\ \hline \end{array}$

Cultural Connection

Lakota Counting

The Lakota used fingers to show numbers.

1

2

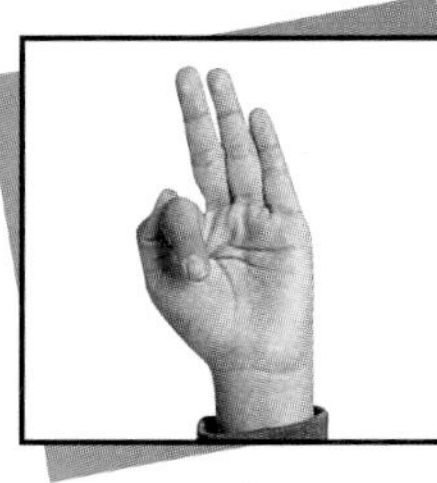
3

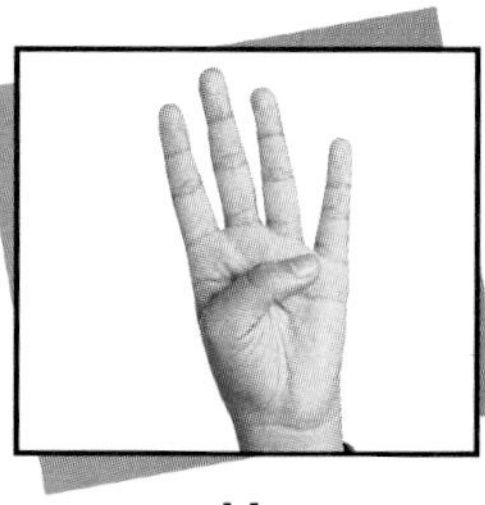
4

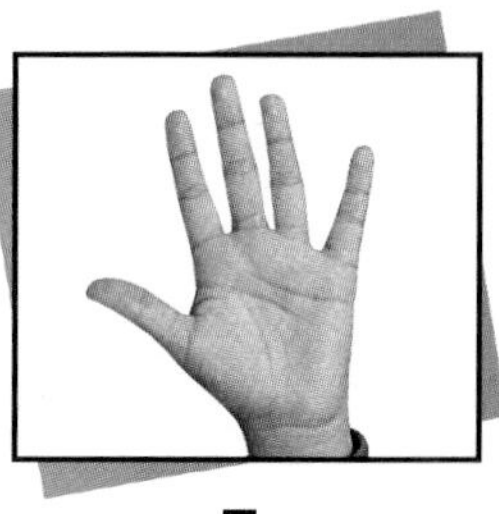
5

6

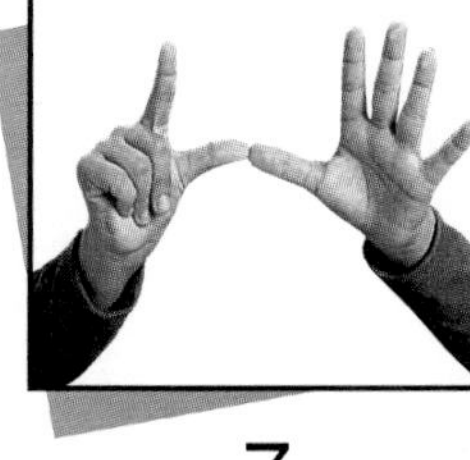
7

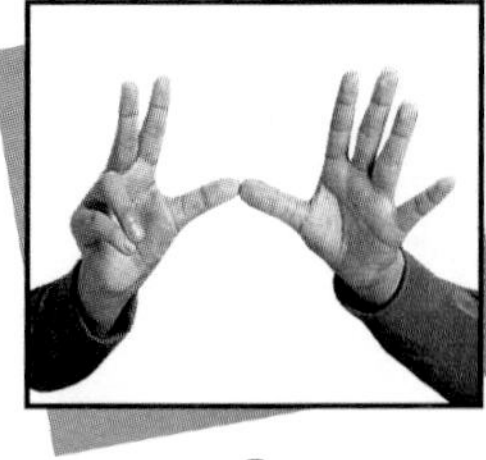
8

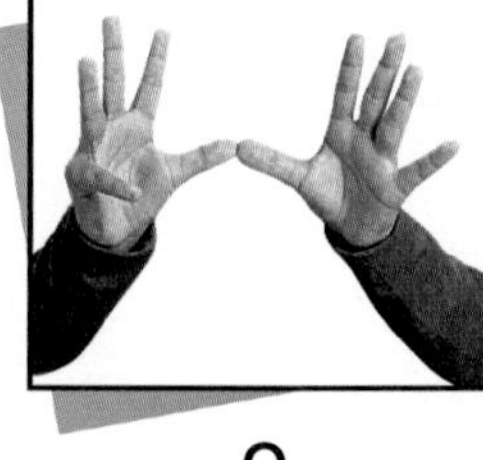
9

10

Show 6. Count on 3. How many? ___

At Home We used counting on to add 1, 2, or 3. Ask your child to explain how to count on to add 6 + 2.

Name

Related Addition Facts

The **order** of addends can change. These are **related facts**.

The sum is the same.

Glossary
order
related facts

5 + 3 = 8

addend addend sum

3 + 5 = 8

Algebra Add. You may use cubes to help.

1. 4 + 6 = 10
   6 + 4 = 10

2. 1 + 3 = ____
   3 + 1 = ____

3. 6 + 3 = ____ 7 + 4 = ____ 8 + 4 = ____
   3 + 6 = ____ 4 + 7 = ____ 4 + 8 = ____

4. $\begin{array}{r} 2 \\ +9 \\ \hline \end{array}$ $\begin{array}{r} 9 \\ +2 \\ \hline \end{array}$ $\begin{array}{r} 1 \\ +8 \\ \hline \end{array}$ $\begin{array}{r} 8 \\ +1 \\ \hline \end{array}$ $\begin{array}{r} 3 \\ +2 \\ \hline \end{array}$ $\begin{array}{r} 2 \\ +3 \\ \hline \end{array}$

5. $\begin{array}{r} 4 \\ +5 \\ \hline \end{array}$ $\begin{array}{r} 5 \\ +4 \\ \hline \end{array}$ $\begin{array}{r} 7 \\ +5 \\ \hline \end{array}$ $\begin{array}{r} 5 \\ +7 \\ \hline \end{array}$ $\begin{array}{r} 6 \\ +0 \\ \hline \end{array}$ $\begin{array}{r} 0 \\ +6 \\ \hline \end{array}$

Critical Thinking What do you notice about adding with zero?

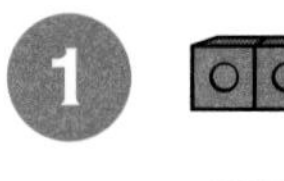

Practice!

Add.

1.

2	4
+ 4	+ 2
6	6

2.

7	2
+ 2	+ 7

3.

7	1	3	9	4	1
+ 1	+ 7	+ 9	+ 3	+ 1	+ 4

4.

1	9	2	8	0	9
+ 9	+ 1	+ 8	+ 2	+ 9	+ 0

More to Explore Algebra Sense

Use the numbers to write two addition sentences.

1 2 3

1 + 2 = 3

2 + 1 = 3

3 7 10

___ + ___ = ___

___ + ___ = ___

5 11 6

___ + ___ = ___

___ + ___ = ___

7 1 6

___ + ___ = ___

___ + ___ = ___

At Home: We learned that we can add in any order. Ask your child to tell another way to add 3 + 6 = 9.

Name ____________________

Canopy

Write an Addition Sentence

Read
Plan
Solve
Look Back

The rain forest has three levels.
Different kinds of animals live at each level.
The top level is called the *canopy.*

Glossary
strategy

Read Sue counted 8 birds in the canopy.
She counted 4 monkeys.
How many animals did she count?

What do you know? ____________________

____

Understory

What do you need to find out? ____________________

____

Plan You can use a **strategy** to find out. Write an addition sentence to solve the problem. $8 + 4 = \blacksquare$

Solve Carry out your plan.

____

What is the answer to the problem? ____________________

Look Back Does your answer make sense? ____________________

How do you know? ____________________

____

Ground

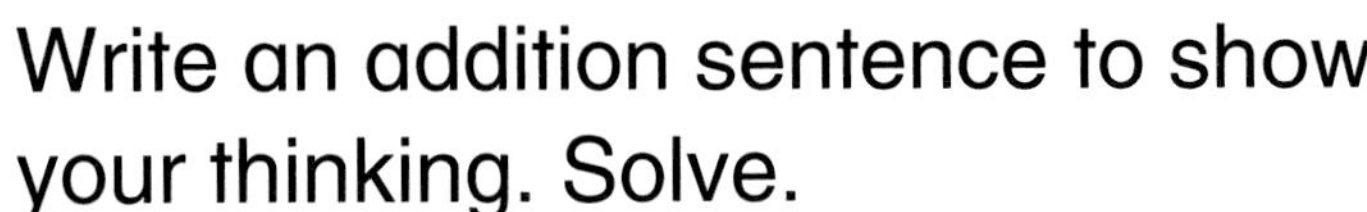

Write an addition sentence to show your thinking. Solve.

Workspace

1. 5 kinds of monkeys live in the canopy.
7 kinds of monkeys live in the understory.
How many kinds of monkeys live here?

____ kinds of monkeys

$5 + 7 = 12$

2. There were 6 monkeys in a tree.
5 more jumped on the tree.
How many monkeys were in the tree?

____ monkeys

3. Ann counted 8 tree frogs yesterday.
Today she counted 2 tree frogs.
How many tree frogs did Ann count?

____ tree frogs

4. Len took pictures of 7 kinds of birds and 3 kinds of butterflies.
How many kinds of flying animals did he take pictures of?

____ kinds of flying animals

At Home: We used addition sentences to solve problems. You may want to have your child make up his or her own problems.

Name

Midchapter Review

Do your best!

Add.

1. 3 + 4 = ____

2. 4 + 2 = ____

3. 5 + 4 = ____

4. $\begin{array}{r} 8 \\ +3 \\ \hline \end{array}$

5. $\begin{array}{r} 9 \\ +1 \\ \hline \end{array}$

6. $\begin{array}{r} 7 \\ +5 \\ \hline \end{array}$ $\begin{array}{r} 5 \\ +7 \\ \hline \end{array}$

7. $\begin{array}{r} 3 \\ +6 \\ \hline \end{array}$ $\begin{array}{r} 6 \\ +3 \\ \hline \end{array}$

Solve.

Workspace

8. 6 frogs are on one tree branch.
4 frogs are on another branch.
How many frogs are in the tree?

____ frogs

9. There were 5 toucans in a tree.
7 more toucans came along.
How many toucans are there in all?

____ toucans

10. How did you use a strategy to solve problem 9?

____

____

What are some ways to use addition?

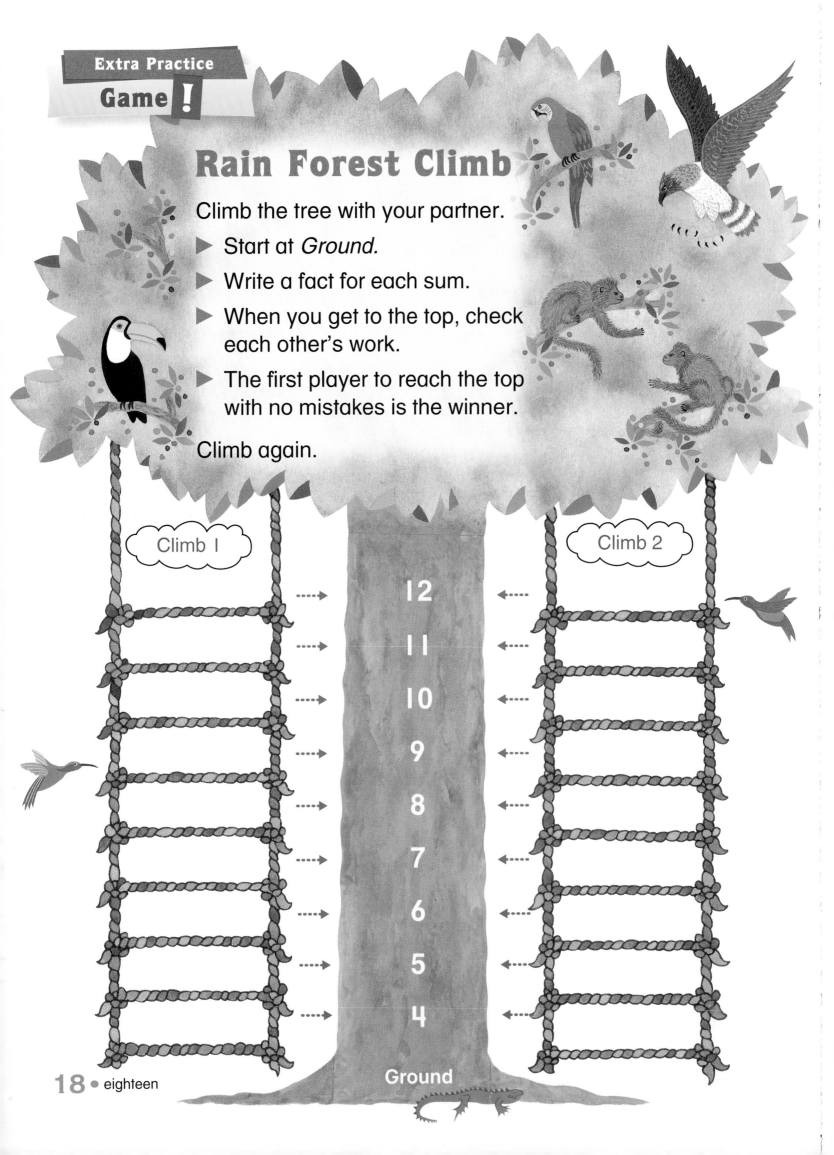

Extra Practice

Game!

Rain Forest Climb

Climb the tree with your partner.

- Start at *Ground.*
- Write a fact for each sum.
- When you get to the top, check each other's work.
- The first player to reach the top with no mistakes is the winner.

Climb again.

Climb 1

Climb 2

12

11

10

9

8

7

6

5

4

Ground

Name

Rain to Grow On

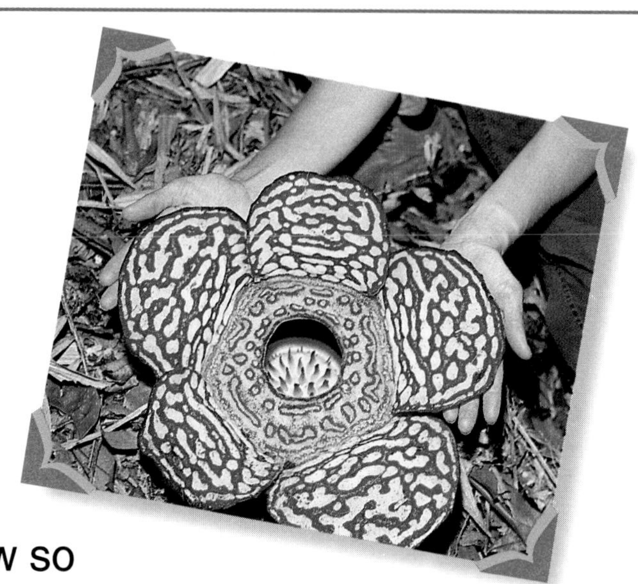

A rain forest can get more than 400 inches of rain in one year.

Many plants grow very large in the rain forest. This flower is about 2 feet across.

Why do you think plants grow so large in the rain forest?

Working Together

Find out what plants need to grow.

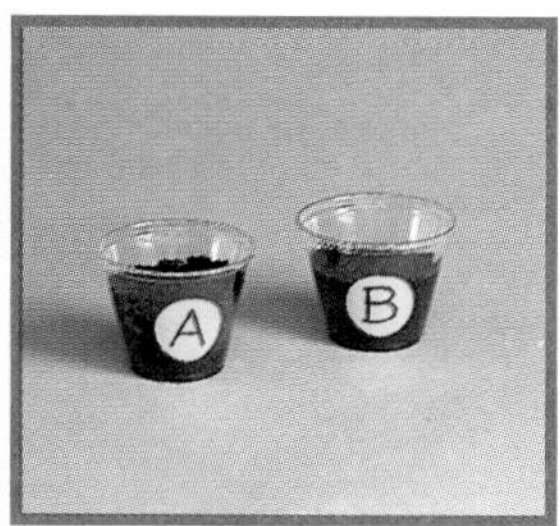

Put soil in two cups. Label them.

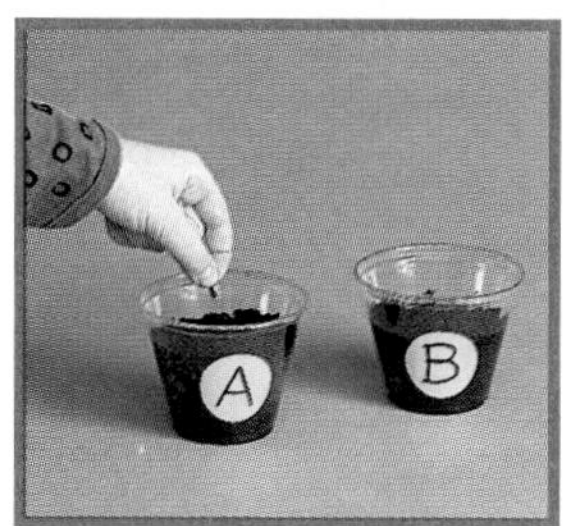

Plant a seed in each cup. Water them.

Place the cups in a sunny place.

Water cup A each day.

What do you think will happen?

- Measure how big the plant grows each week for three weeks.
- Show the data on a chart.

GROWTH OF PLANTS

Cup A	Cup B
Week 1	
Week 2	
Week 3	

Decision Making

1. Decide how to measure your plants. Explain your method.
2. How much did the plant in cup A grow during

   week 1? ________ week 2? ________ week 3? ________

3. How much did the plant in each cup grow altogether?

   Cup A: ________

   Cup B: ________

Write a report.

4. Tell what you learned about plants and water.
5. Tell how you found how much the plants grew each week.

More to Investigate

PREDICT Can a plant grow without light?

EXPLORE Plant more seeds. Water the seeds each day. Put one cup in a sunny place. Put one cup in a dark place.

FIND Find the total growth for each plant after three weeks. Then compare.

Name

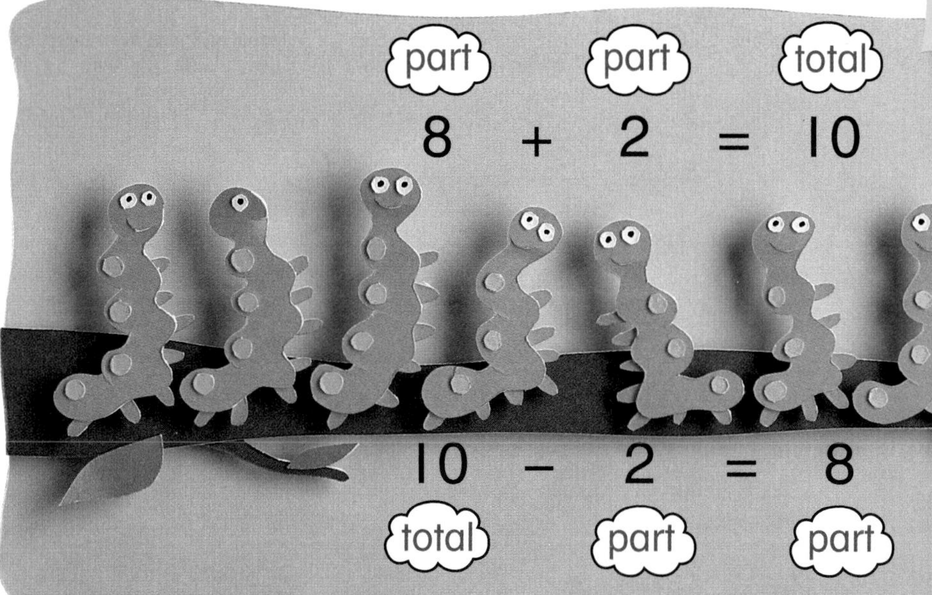

How can the same cube train show both addition and subtraction?

Working Together

You and your partner need 9 and 9 .

Glossary
subtract
subtraction sentence

- Make a train to show parts.
- Color to show your parts.
- **Subtract**. Write the **subtraction sentence**.

1.  5 − 1 = 4
2.  ___ − ___ = ___
3. ___ − ___ = ___
4. ___ − ___ = ___
5. ___ − ___ = ___
6. ___ − ___ = ___
7. ___ − ___ = ___

Subtract. You may use cubes to help.

1. 4 − 3 = 1

2. 11 − 7 = ____

3	12 − 5 = ____	10 − 3 = ____	7 − 2 = ____
4	5 − 2 = ____	9 − 3 = ____	11 − 6 = ____
5	8 − 4 = ____	12 − 9 = ____	8 − 7 = ____
6	6 − 3 = ____	9 − 7 = ____	7 − 4 = ____
7	9 − 1 = ____	8 − 5 = ____	12 − 6 = ____
8	7 − 6 = ____	10 − 8 = ____	6 − 4 = ____
9	11 − 9 = ____	5 − 1 = ____	10 − 5 = ____

Mixed Review Test Preparation

Add.

10. 3 + 6 = ____

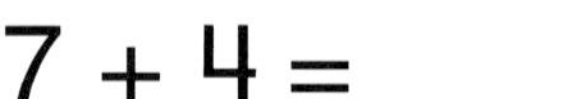

11. 7 + 4 = ____

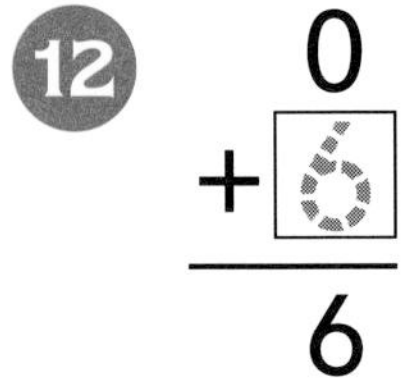

12.

0	1	2	3	4	5
+ 6	+ □	+ □	+ □	+ □	+ □
6	6	6	6	6	6

At Home: We subtracted and wrote subtraction sentences. Ask your child to explain how to subtract 7 − 3.

Name ________________________

Explore Activity

Subtraction Patterns

6 frogs
2 are yellow.
4 are red.

$6 - 2 = 4$

difference

Glossary

difference

Working Together

You and your partner need 12 .

PATTERNS

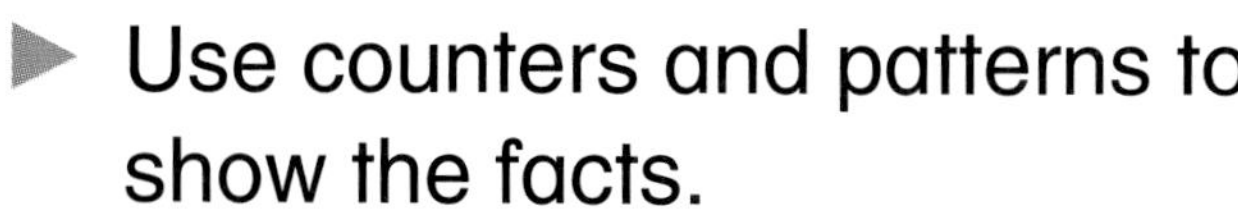

- Use counters and patterns to show the facts.
- Color to match your counters.
- Write the subtraction sentence.

1.  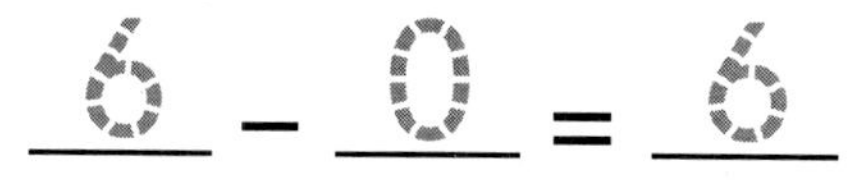 6 – 0 = 6
2.  6 – 1 = 5
3.  ___ – ___ = ___
4. 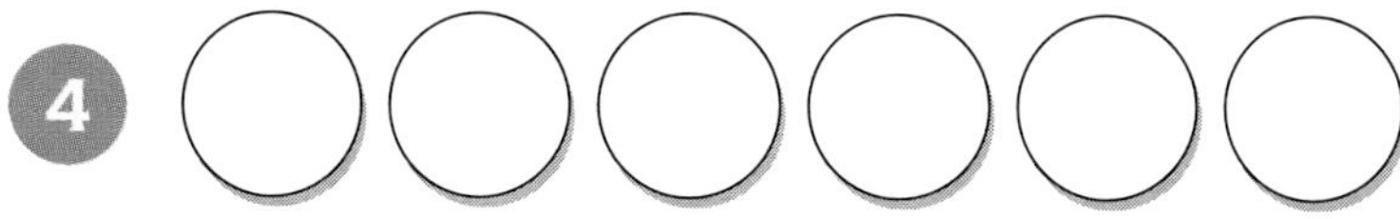 ___ – ___ = ___
5.  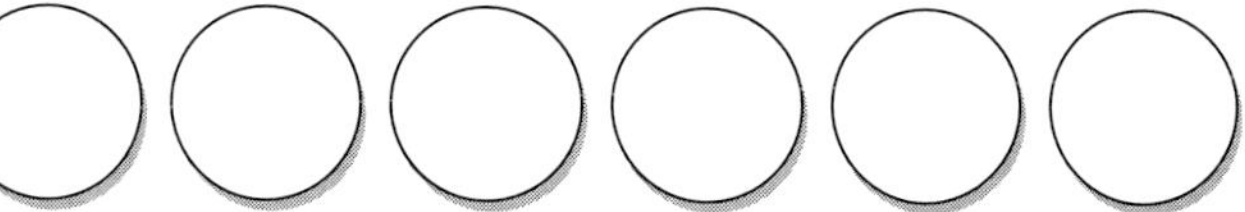 ___ – ___ = ___
6.  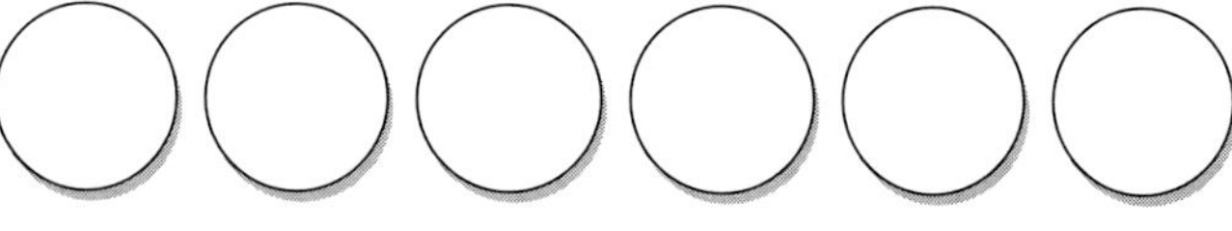 ___ – ___ = ___
7.  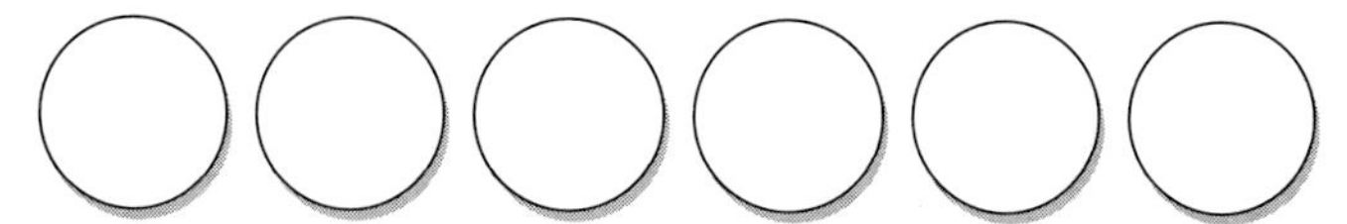 ___ – ___ = ___

Critical Thinking

Do you think there are more subtraction facts for 5 or for 6? How do you know?

Practice!

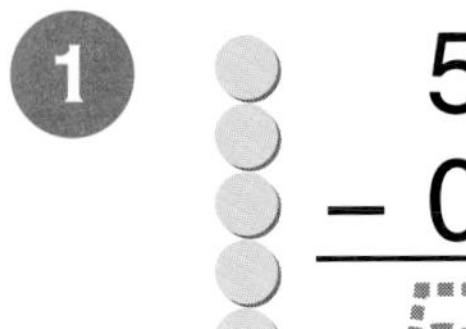

PATTERNS Subtract. Use the patterns to help.

1.

5	5	5	5	5
− 0	− 1	− 2	− 3	− 4
5				

2.

9	9	9	9	9	9
− 0	− 1	− 2	− 3	− 4	− 5

3.

11	11	11	11	11	11
− 9	− □	− □	− □	− □	− □
2	3	4	5	6	7

4.

10	10	10	10	10	10
− 4	− 5	− □	− □	− □	− □
6	5	4	□	□	□

Write all the subtraction facts for 8.

5.

8	8	8	8	
− 0	− □	− □	− □	
8	8	8	8	8
− □	− □	− □	− □	− □

How is a subtraction pattern like an addition pattern?

At Home: We used patterns to help us subtract. Ask your child to continue the pattern in row 2 above.

Name ____________________

Count Back

Find 11 − 3.

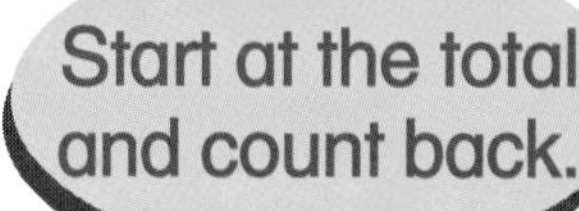

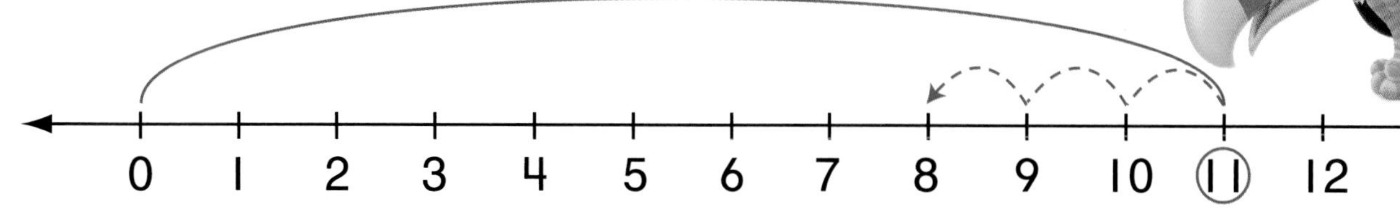

11 − 3 = 8

Glossary
count back

Count back to subtract.
Use mental math or the number line.

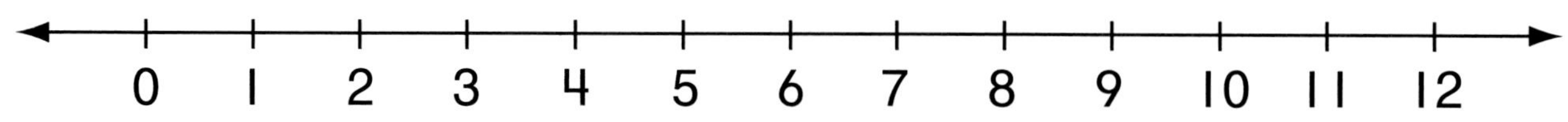

1. 7 − 1 = 6 (Say 7. Count back 1. Say 6.) 10 − 2 = 8 (Say 10. Count back 2. Say 9, 8.)
2. 12 − 3 = ___ 4 − 1 = ___ 6 − 2 = ___
3. 8 − 2 = ___ 6 − 3 = ___ 9 − 1 = ___
4. 9 − 3 = ___ 7 − 3 = ___ 4 − 2 = ___
5. 10 − 1 = ___ 5 − 2 = ___ 8 − 3 = ___
6. 5 − 3 = ___ 10 − 3 = ___ 7 − 2 = ___
7. 9 − 2 = ___ 4 − 3 = ___ 5 − 1 = ___

How could you count back to solve 17 − 2?

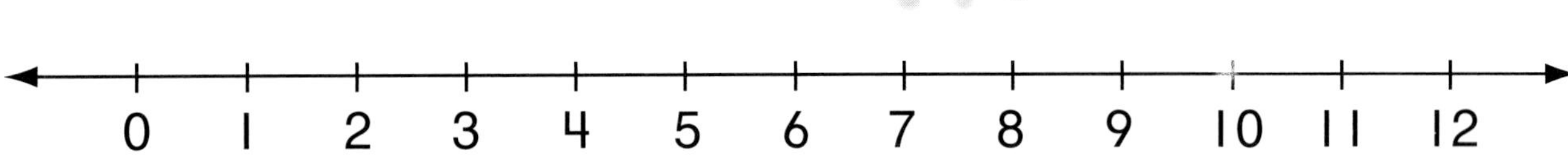

Count back to subtract.

1. $12 - 3 =$ 9 　 $5 - 1 =$ ___ 　 $9 - 2 =$ ___
2. $6 - 1 =$ ___ 　 $7 - 3 =$ ___ 　 $3 - 1 =$ ___
3. $\begin{array}{r} 7 \\ -1 \\ \hline 6 \end{array}$ 　 $\begin{array}{r} 4 \\ -3 \\ \hline \end{array}$ 　 $\begin{array}{r} 10 \\ -1 \\ \hline \end{array}$ 　 $\begin{array}{r} 3 \\ -2 \\ \hline \end{array}$ 　 $\begin{array}{r} 11 \\ -3 \\ \hline \end{array}$ 　 $\begin{array}{r} 9 \\ -3 \\ \hline \end{array}$
4. $\begin{array}{r} 10 \\ -3 \\ \hline \end{array}$ 　 $\begin{array}{r} 8 \\ -1 \\ \hline \end{array}$ 　 $\begin{array}{r} 6 \\ -2 \\ \hline \end{array}$ 　 $\begin{array}{r} 7 \\ -2 \\ \hline \end{array}$ 　 $\begin{array}{r} 8 \\ -3 \\ \hline \end{array}$ 　 $\begin{array}{r} 5 \\ -2 \\ \hline \end{array}$

Write the subtraction fact.

5. 

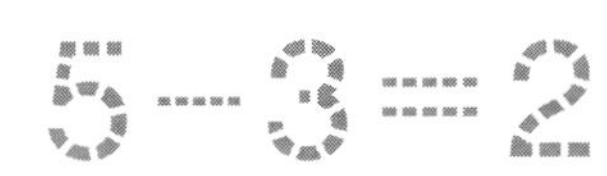

$5 - 3 = 2$

6. 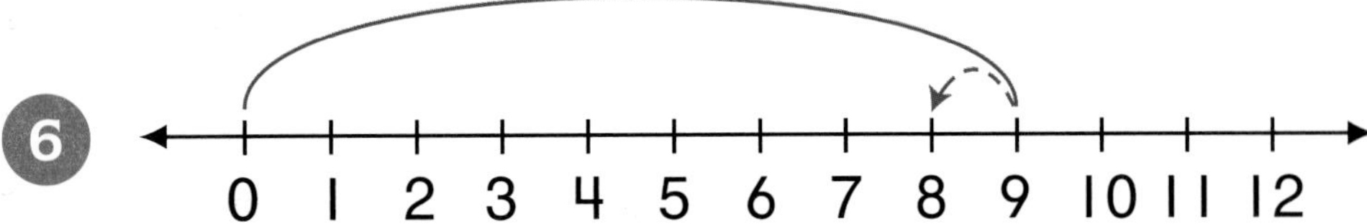

___

7. 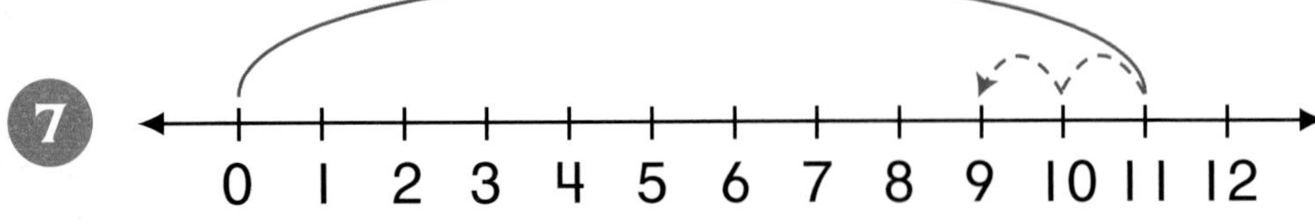

___

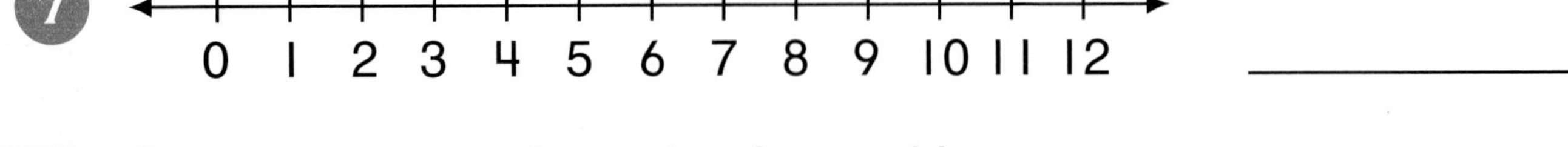

Compare your subtraction facts with a partner's facts. Talk about how they are the same or different.

At Home: We used counting back to subtract 1, 2, or 3. Have your child explain how to subtract $7 - 2$.

Name ____________________

Related Subtraction Facts

The same cube train can show two different subtraction sentences.

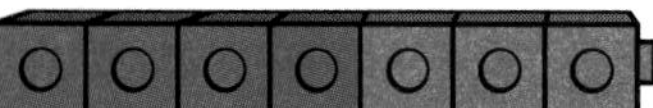

$7 - 4 = 3$ difference

$7 - 3 = 4$ difference

These are related facts.

Algebra

Subtract. You may use cubes to help.

1. $6 - 2 = \underline{4}$
   $6 - 4 = \underline{2}$

2. $5 - 3 =$ ____
   $5 - 2 =$ ____

3. $8 - 0 =$ ____ $12 - 9 =$ ____ $9 - 5 =$ ____
   $8 - 8 =$ ____ $12 - 3 =$ ____ $9 - 4 =$ ____

4. $\begin{array}{r} 11 \\ -\ 2 \\ \hline \end{array}$ $\begin{array}{r} 11 \\ -\ 9 \\ \hline \end{array}$ $\begin{array}{r} 6 \\ -\ 5 \\ \hline \end{array}$ $\begin{array}{r} 6 \\ -\ 1 \\ \hline \end{array}$ $\begin{array}{r} 9 \\ -\ 9 \\ \hline \end{array}$ $\begin{array}{r} 9 \\ -\ 0 \\ \hline \end{array}$

5. $\begin{array}{r} 4 \\ -\ 3 \\ \hline \end{array}$ $\begin{array}{r} 4 \\ -\ 1 \\ \hline \end{array}$ $\begin{array}{r} 12 \\ -\ 8 \\ \hline \end{array}$ $\begin{array}{r} 12 \\ -\ 4 \\ \hline \end{array}$ $\begin{array}{r} 7 \\ -\ 5 \\ \hline \end{array}$ $\begin{array}{r} 7 \\ -\ 2 \\ \hline \end{array}$

Critical Thinking

How does $11 - 6 = 5$ help you find $11 - 5$?

Practice!

Subtract.

1. 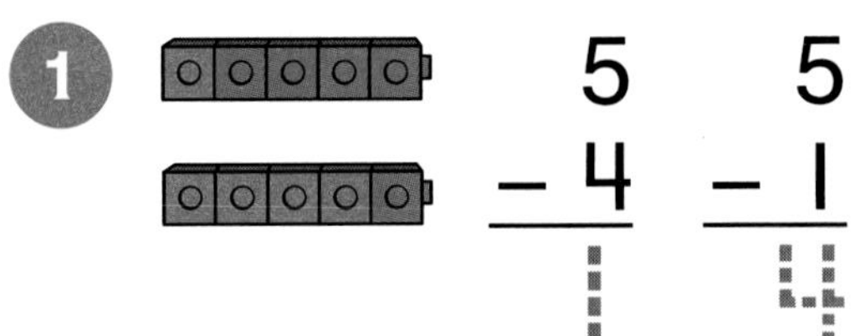

5	5
− 4	− 1
1	4

2.

8	8
− 6	− 2

3.

12	12	9	9	3	3
− 5	− 7	− 6	− 3	− 1	− 2

4.

10	10	7	7	11	11
− 9	− 1	− 0	− 7	− 3	− 8

5.

8	8	11	11	10	10
− 1	− 7	− 7	− 4	− 8	− 2

More to Explore

Algebra Sense

This machine subtracts 3 from any number.

Write the rule for these machines.

At Home We learned about related subtraction facts. Have your child give the related fact for 9 − 6 = 3.

Name ______________________

Problem-Solving Strategy

Write a Subtraction Sentence

Read · Plan · Solve · Look Back

Read

The rain-forest zoo has a big toucan.
11 children watched the bird eat.
3 children got tired and left.
How many children are still watching the toucan?

What do you know?  ______________________

____

What do you need to find out? ______________________

____

Plan

You can write a subtraction sentence to solve the problem. $11 - 3 = \blacksquare$

Solve

Carry out your plan.

____

What is the answer to the problem? __________

Look Back

Does your answer make sense? __________

How do you know? ______________________

____

____

____

Practice!

Write a subtraction sentence to show your thinking. Solve.

Workspace

1. Rita had 9 animal crackers left after lunch. She gave 3 crackers to Jesse. How many crackers does Rita have now?

$9 - 3 = 6$

_____ crackers

2. 8 children got on the zoo train. 3 children got off at the first stop. How many children are left on the train?

_____ children

3. Greg bought 10 rain-forest stickers. He gave 2 stickers to Lily. How many stickers does Greg still have?

_____ stickers

4. 12 friends went to the bird show. 3 left early. The rest stayed. How many of the friends stayed at the show?

_____ friends

We used subtraction sentences to solve problems. You may want to have your child make up his or her own problems.

Name ______________________________

Extra Practice
Activity !

What Do You See?

Add or subtract. Then color.

sums of 0 to 5	red	differences of 0 to 3	yellow
sums of 6 to 9	blue	differences of 4 to 6	black
sums of 10 to 12	orange	differences of 7 to 9	green

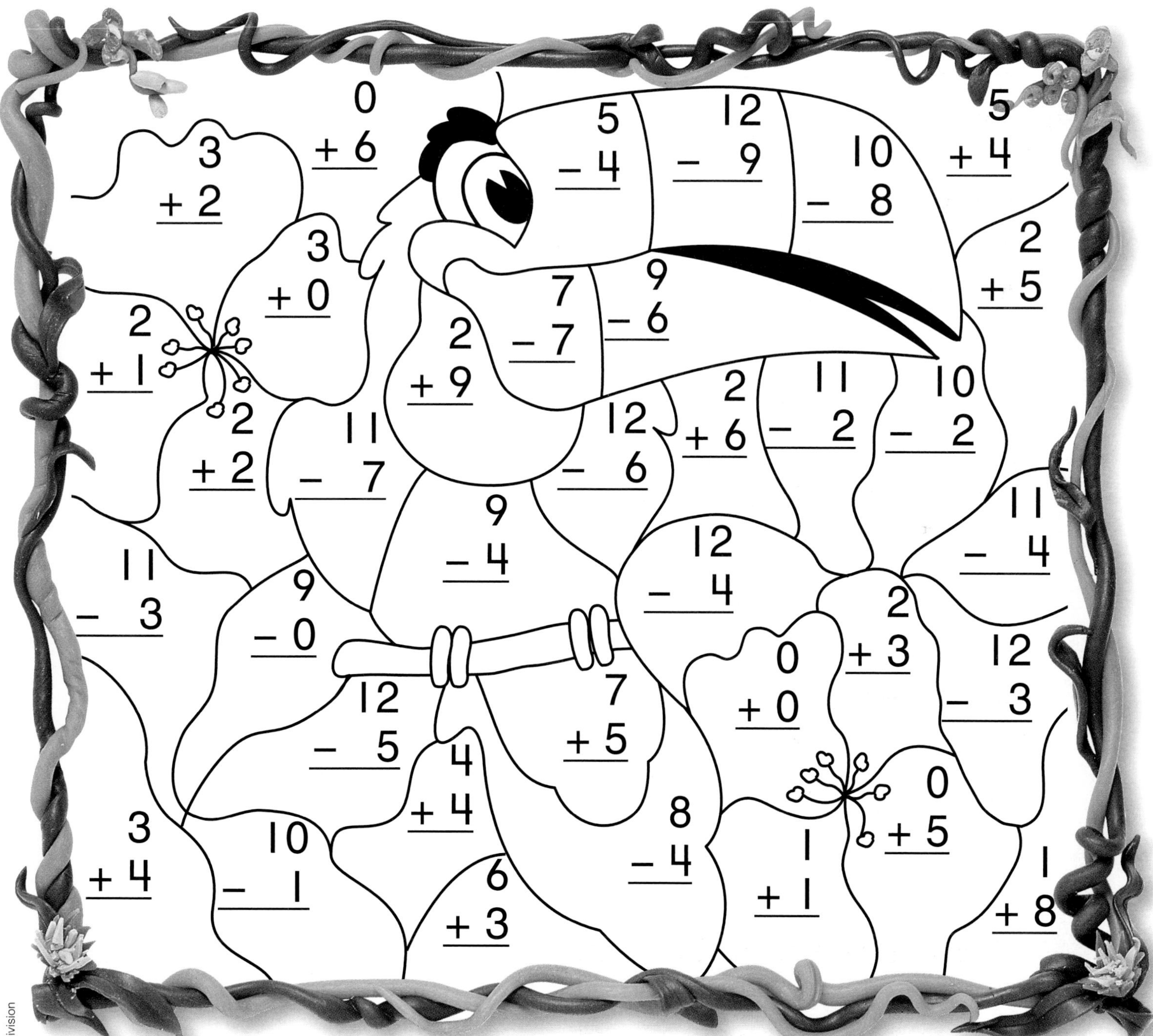

I see a ______________________.

Add or subtract.

1	$9 + 3 = 12$	$9 - 9$	$11 - 8$	$8 - 3$	$0 + 7$	$11 - 4$
2	$10 - 7$	$4 + 4$	$5 + 6$	$12 - 6$	$6 - 5$	$1 + 4$
3	$6 + 0$	$8 - 1$	$2 + 4$	$5 + 7$	$5 - 3$	$1 + 3$
4	$2 + 8$	$7 - 3$	$7 + 3$	$10 - 2$	$4 + 5$	$12 - 7$

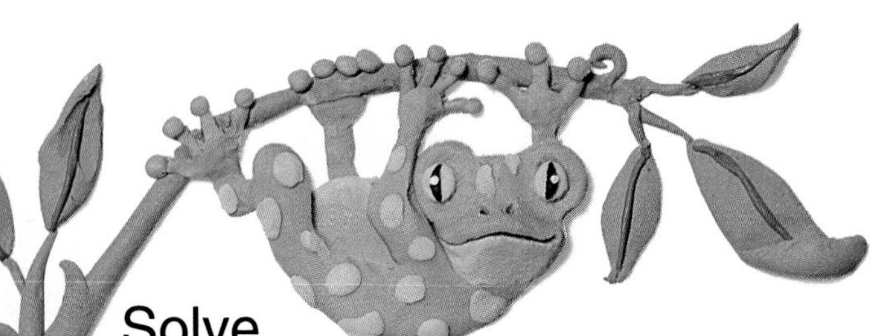

Solve.

Workspace

5 3 frogs sat in a puddle.
9 more frogs hopped in.
How many frogs are in the puddle now? ____ frogs

6 10 turtles sat on a log.
2 turtles fell off.
How many turtles are on the log now? ____ turtles

Name ______________________

Problem Solvers at Work

Read | Plan | Solve | Look Back

Read to Understand

Nino plans to take a trip to the rain forest.

1 Read the problem.

Nino packs 8 T-shirts.
He packs 6 pairs of shorts.
Does he pack more shorts or T-shirts?

What do you need to find out? ______________________

____

Can you add or subtract to solve? Explain.

Does Nino pack more shorts or T-shirts? ______________

Reread Read problem 1 again.

2 How many more shorts does Nino need to match each shirt with a pair of shorts? ____

3 Nino packs socks to match each shirt. How many pairs of socks does Nino pack? ____

Practice!

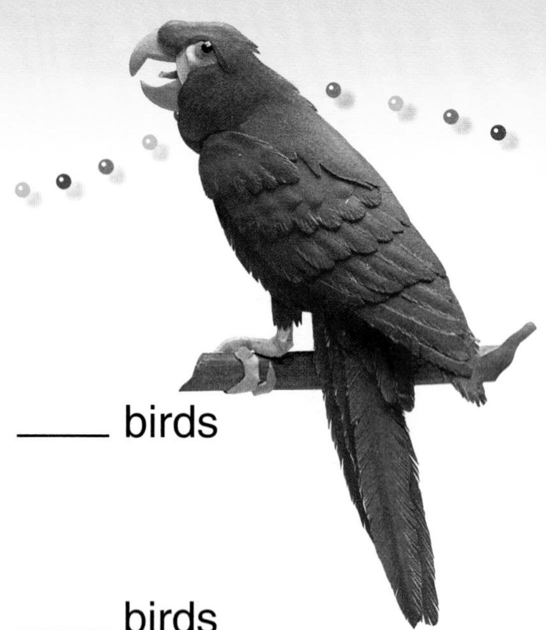

Solve.

1. Nino saw 6 toucans on Monday. He also saw 2 red parrots. How many birds did Nino see? ____ birds

2. What if Nino also saw 3 green parrots. How many birds would he have seen in all? ____ birds

Write and Share

Jessica Stranger
Hawthorne School
Indianapolis, Indiana

Jessica wrote this problem.

One day Sasha, Victoria, and Jenny went fishing. Sasha caught 7 fish. Victoria caught 6 fish. Jenny caught 5 fish. How many fish did they catch altogether?

3. Solve Jessica's problem. ________________

What strategy did you choose? ________________

____

4.  

Write a new question for Jessica's problem. Have a partner answer it.

Use your own paper.

What strategy did your partner use? ________________

What strategy would you use? ________________

Ask your child to tell you about the new question he or she wrote for problem 4.

Name ______________________

Chapter Review

Language and Mathematics

Choose the correct word to complete the sentence.

number line
sum
order
difference

1. You add 6 + 4 to find the ________.
2. You subtract 8 – 2 to find the ________.

Concepts and Skills

Add.

3. 4 + 1 = ____
4. 3 + 4 = ____
5. 5 + 5 = ____

Subtract.

6. 8 – 3 = ____
7. 7 – 5 = ____
8. 9 – 4 = ____

Add or subtract.

9. 6 + 5
10. 6 + 4
11. 6 + 3
12. 7 + 5   5 + 7
13. 10 – 7
14. 10 – 6
15. 10 – 5
16. 11 – 3   11 – 8

Problem Solving

Write an addition or subtraction sentence. Solve.

17 Len found 8 little frogs.
He found 3 big frogs.
How many frogs did Len find?

____

_____ frogs

---

18 Lily bought 10 cards.
She gave 2 cards away.
How many cards does Lily have now?

____

_____ cards

---

19 Nino had 12 crackers.
He ate 3 crackers.
How many crackers does Nino have left?

____

_____ crackers

Solve.

20 Kim put 6 buttons on her hat.
She put 5 buttons on her shirt.
Did she put more buttons on her hat or on her shirt?

____

What Do You Think?

Which strategy would you use to add 9 + 2?
☑ Check one.

☐ Patterns ☐ Number line ☐ Counting on ☐ 2 + 9

Why? ______________________________

Journal Write a list of ways you add and subtract.

Name ___

Chapter Test

Add.

1. 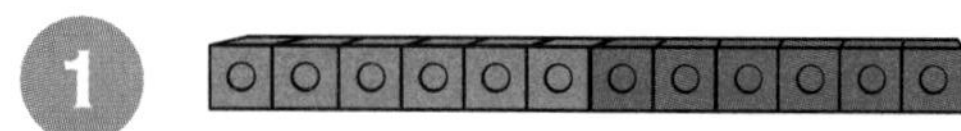

$6 + 6 =$ ___

2. $4 + 5 =$ ___

3. $\begin{array}{r} 5 \\ +\ 6 \\ \hline \end{array}$

4. $\begin{array}{r} 4 \\ +\ 8 \\ \hline \end{array}$

Subtract.

5. $9 - 0 =$ ___

6. $12 - 5 =$ ___

7. $\begin{array}{r} 11 \\ -\ \ 6 \\ \hline \end{array}$

8. $\begin{array}{r} 10 \\ -\ \ 8 \\ \hline \end{array}$

Write an addition sentence or subtraction sentence. Solve.

9. Ned saw 6 birds. Then he saw 4 more birds. How many birds did Ned see?

___

___ birds

10. Maria had 12 cookies. She ate 4 of them. How many cookies does Maria have left?

___

___ cookies

Performance Assessment

What Did You Learn?

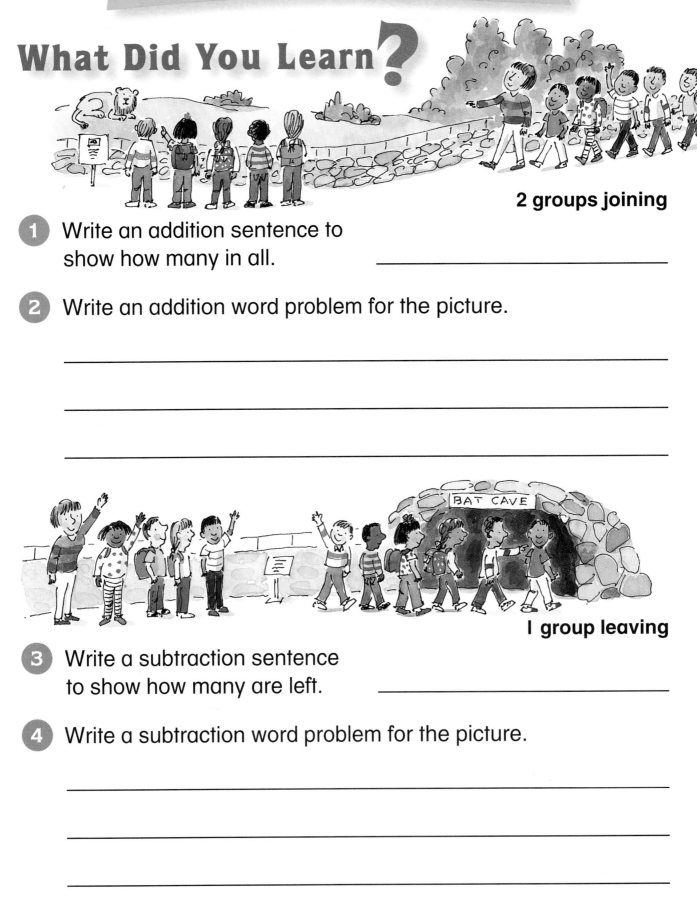

2 groups joining

1. Write an addition sentence to show how many in all. ______________________

2. Write an addition word problem for the picture.

____

____

____

I group leaving

3. Write a subtraction sentence to show how many are left. ______________________

4. Write a subtraction word problem for the picture.

____

____

____

You may want to put this page in your portfolio.

Math Connection
Probability

Name ________________________________

Number Race

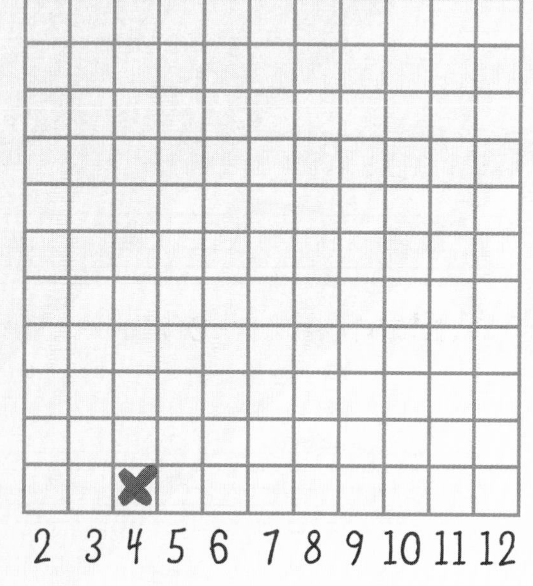

You and your partner need 2 number cubes and a graph form.

Take turns.

- Roll the number cubes. Add.
- Mark an X to show the sum.
- Play until one sum reaches the top of the graph form.

Predict the winning sum. ____

Now play.

Glossary
most likely
least likely

Talk: Why did you get one or two sums more than the others?

1. When you roll a pair of number cubes, which sums are **most likely** to show?

____

2. When you roll a pair of number cubes, which sums are **least likely** to show?

____

3. Which sums will never show when you roll a pair of number cubes?

____

Curriculum Connection

Music

Count Back

Sing this song from Puerto Rico.

Ten Puppies
(Diez Perritos)
1. Oh, I used to have ten pup - pies,
Yo te - ní - a diez pe - rri - tos,
yō te nē´ ä dyes pe rē´ tōs
Oh, I used to have ten pup - pies;
Yo te - ní - a diez pe - rri - tos;
yō te nē´ ä dyes pe rē´ tōs
One fell in the snow so fine,
U - no se ca yó en la nie - ve
oo´ nō sā kä yō´ en lä nye´ ve
Leav - ing me with on - ly nine.
ya - no mas me que dan nue - ve.
yä nō mäs mā kä´ dän nooe´ ve

Write a number sentence to show what happened to the puppies. ____________

If one more puppy goes away, how many puppies will be left? ____ puppies

Home Connection

Chapter 1 Wrap-Up

Name ______________________________

Tic-Tac-Toe Sums

PLAYERS 2

MATERIALS game markers in two colors

DIRECTIONS Each player chooses a color. The first player puts a marker on a number and names an addition fact for that sum. Then the other player takes a turn.

The winner is the first player to cover three numbers across, down, or diagonally.

7	9	6
5	2	1
8	3	4

Play this game to practice addition facts to 9. To practice subtraction facts, your child names a subtraction fact with that number as the difference.

Dear Family,

I am beginning another chapter in my mathematics book. During the next few weeks I will be learning new strategies for adding and subtracting and for solving problems.

We will also be talking about pen pals and writing letters.

Learning About Writing Letters

Let's talk about letters we write and receive. We can make a list.

My Math Words

I am going to use these math words in this chapter.

Please help me make word cards for the math words. I can use these word cards when I practice addition and subtraction strategies.

- doubles
- data
- chart
- equal parts
- count up
- fact family

Your child,

____

Signature

Addition and Subtraction Strategies

Theme: Pen Pals

CHAPTER 2

Set Purposes Before you listen to a story, decide what you want to find out.

Listen to the story *Dear Mr. Blueberry.*

Why did Mr. Blueberry write to Emily?

Tell about whales. What facts would you use?

What Do You Know?

Solve.

1. Nick wrote 9 letters to his pen pals.
He forgot to mail 2 of the letters.
How many letters did Nick mail? ______

Show or write about how you solved the problem.

____

____

2. Lily got 3 letters last month.
She got 6 letters this month.
Did she get more than 10 letters or fewer than 10 letters? ______

Show or write about how you solved the problem.

____

____

Write a word problem that uses addition or subtraction.
Show how to solve your problem.

Name

Working Together

You and your partner need 9 and 9 .
Take turns.

- Make a **doubles** fact with cubes.
- Your partner adds 1 more cube.
- Record the facts.

Glossary
doubles

	Double	Double Plus One
1	6 + 6 = 12	6 + 7 = 13
2	5 + 5 = 10	5 + 6 = 11
3	4 + 4 = 8	4 + 5 = 9
4	3 + 3 = 6	3 + 4 = 7
5	10 + 10 = 20	10 + 11 = 21
6	2 + 2 = 4	2 + 3 = 5
7	1 + 1 = 2	1 + 2 = 3
8	7 + 7 = 14	7 + 8 = 15
9	8 + 8 = 16	8 + 9 = 17

How can you find the sum of 10 + 11?

Practice!

Add.

1 5 + 6 = 11

Think: 5 + 5 = 10

2 3 + 4 = 7

Think: 3 + 3 = 6

3	8 + 7	6 + 6	2 + 1	8 + 8	4 + 5	3 + 3
4	7 + 6	2 + 2	9 + 8	5 + 5	2 + 3	4 + 4
5	4 + 3	7 + 7	6 + 5	1 + 1	7 + 8	6 + 7

Mixed Review Test Preparation

6	7 + 3	2 + 8	4 + 6	5 − 4	10 − 5	8 − 1

Write a subtraction fact.

7

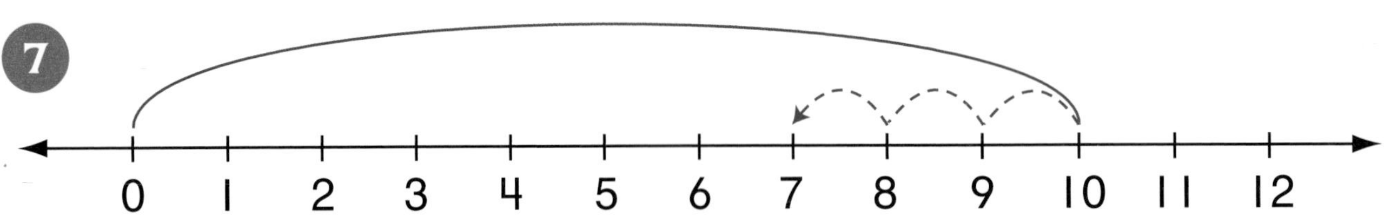

We explored adding doubles-plus-one facts. Ask your child to name the doubles fact that helps find 6 + 7.

Name

Working Together

You and your partner need a [10-frame], [spinner], and 18 [counters].

- Show 9 yellow counters in a 10-frame.
- Spin. Show the number with red counters.
- Move 1 red counter to make a 10.
- Draw and record the addition.

	Draw	Addition Fact	Total
1		9 + 6	15
2		9 + 2	11
3		9 + 4	13
4		9 + 8	17

Practice!

Add. Make a 10 if you forget a fact.

1

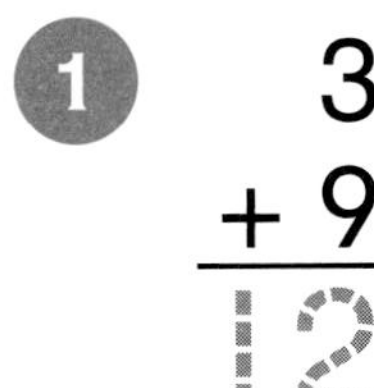

$$\begin{array}{r} 3 \\ +\,9 \\ \hline 12 \end{array}$$

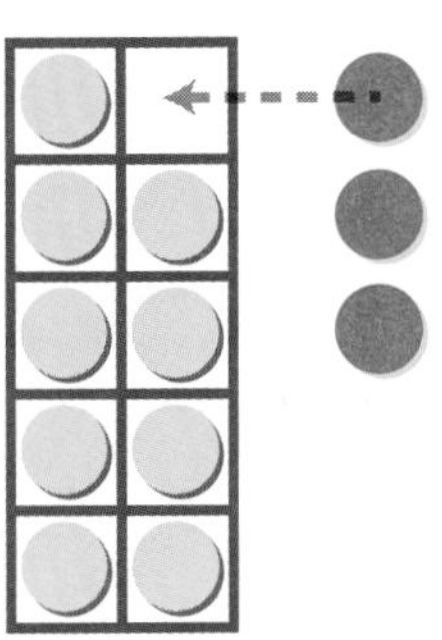

2

$$\begin{array}{r} 9 \\ +\,5 \\ \hline 14 \end{array}$$

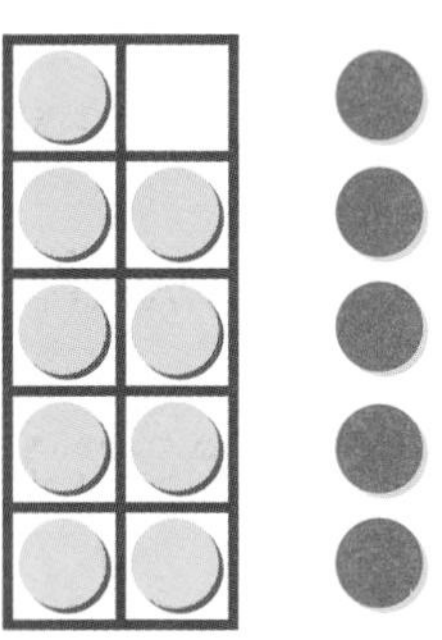

3

$\begin{array}{r} 1 \\ +\,9 \\ \hline 10 \end{array}$	$\begin{array}{r} 9 \\ +\,8 \\ \hline 17 \end{array}$	$\begin{array}{r} 9 \\ +\,3 \\ \hline 12 \end{array}$	$\begin{array}{r} 4 \\ +\,9 \\ \hline 13 \end{array}$	$\begin{array}{r} 9 \\ +\,7 \\ \hline 16 \end{array}$	$\begin{array}{r} 9 \\ +\,9 \\ \hline 18 \end{array}$

4

$\begin{array}{r} 7 \\ +\,9 \\ \hline 16 \end{array}$	$\begin{array}{r} 5 \\ +\,9 \\ \hline 14 \end{array}$	$\begin{array}{r} 9 \\ +\,6 \\ \hline 15 \end{array}$	$\begin{array}{r} 9 \\ +\,1 \\ \hline 10 \end{array}$	$\begin{array}{r} 2 \\ +\,9 \\ \hline 11 \end{array}$	$\begin{array}{r} 8 \\ +\,9 \\ \hline 17 \end{array}$

More to Explore Number Sense

Another way to add with 9 is to think of the 10 fact. Then find 1 less.

$$\begin{array}{r} 9 \\ +\,5 \\ \hline 14 \end{array}$$

Think: 10 + 5 = 15
1 less than 15 is 14.
9 + 5 = 14

Add. Think of the 10 fact. Then find 1 less.

$\begin{array}{r} 9 \\ +\,8 \\ \hline 17 \end{array}$	$\begin{array}{r} 3 \\ +\,9 \\ \hline 12 \end{array}$	$\begin{array}{r} 9 \\ +\,6 \\ \hline 15 \end{array}$	$\begin{array}{r} 7 \\ +\,9 \\ \hline 16 \end{array}$	$\begin{array}{r} 8 \\ +\,9 \\ \hline 17 \end{array}$	$\begin{array}{r} 4 \\ +\,9 \\ \hline 13 \end{array}$

At Home We learned a strategy for adding 9. Ask your child to explain exercises 1 and 2 above.

Name

Make a 10

Abby has 7 stamps from Brazil.
Then she buys 5 more.
How many Brazilian stamps
does she have?

7 + 5
7 + 3 = 10
2 more is 12.

Abby has 12 Brazilian stamps.

Draw arrows to make a 10. Add.

1. 8 + 3 = 11

2. 7 + 4 = 11

3. 7 + 6 = 13

4. 9 + 6 = 15

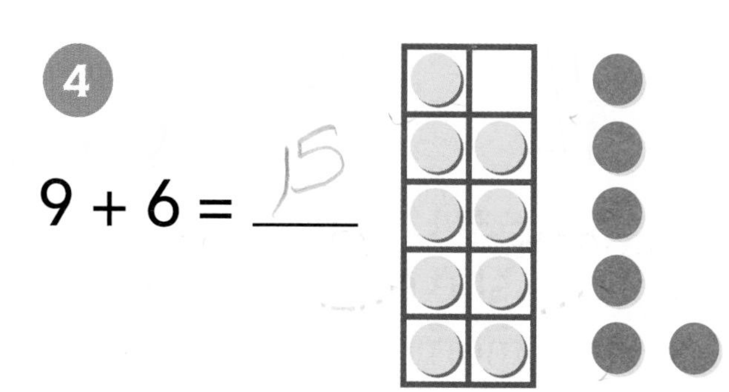

5. 8 + 4 = 12

6. 8 + 6 = 14

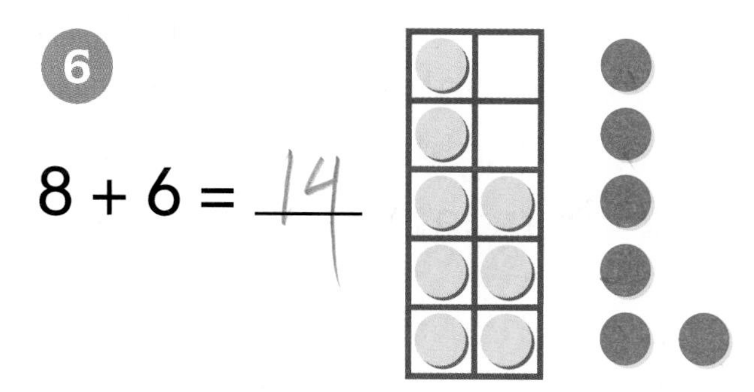

Critical Thinking How can you use mental math to find 8 plus 4?

Practice!

Add.

1. $\begin{array}{r} 8 \\ +5 \\ \hline 13 \end{array}$

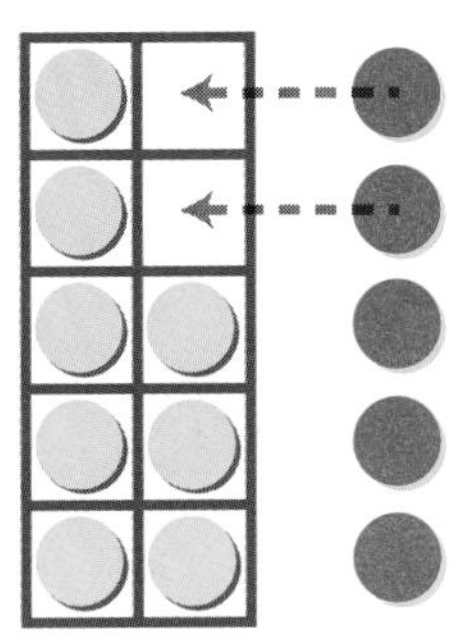

2. $\begin{array}{r} 7 \\ +9 \\ \hline 16 \end{array}$

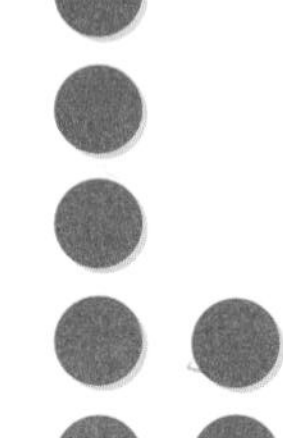

3. $\begin{array}{r} 7 \\ +8 \\ \hline 15 \end{array}$ $\begin{array}{r} 8 \\ +9 \\ \hline 17 \end{array}$ $\begin{array}{r} 7 \\ +6 \\ \hline 13 \end{array}$ $\begin{array}{r} 8 \\ +5 \\ \hline 13 \end{array}$ $\begin{array}{r} 7 \\ +4 \\ \hline 11 \end{array}$ $\begin{array}{r} 8 \\ +7 \\ \hline 15 \end{array}$

4. $\begin{array}{r} 8 \\ +3 \\ \hline 11 \end{array}$ $\begin{array}{r} 9 \\ +7 \\ \hline 16 \end{array}$ $\begin{array}{r} 8 \\ +6 \\ \hline 14 \end{array}$ $\begin{array}{r} 7 \\ +5 \\ \hline 12 \end{array}$ $\begin{array}{r} 8 \\ +4 \\ \hline 12 \end{array}$ $\begin{array}{r} 9 \\ +8 \\ \hline 17 \end{array}$

Solve.

Workspace

5. Sam sent 8 letters to her pen pal. Then she sent 6 more. How many letters did Sam send in all?

14 letters

6. Ty bought 4 flag stamps. He bought 9 bird stamps. How many stamps did he buy?

13 stamps

Write 7 + 5 = ? Write about the strategy you used to find the sum.

At Home: We solved addition facts by making a 10. Have your child explain how to find 8 + 6.

Name ______________________________

Three or More Addends

You can find out how many cards Miko has.

Which addition strategies could you use?

$$\begin{array}{r} 2 \\ 8 \\ +\,2 \\ \hline \end{array} \quad 2 + 8 = 10$$

Look for a 10 fact.

10 + 2 = 12

or

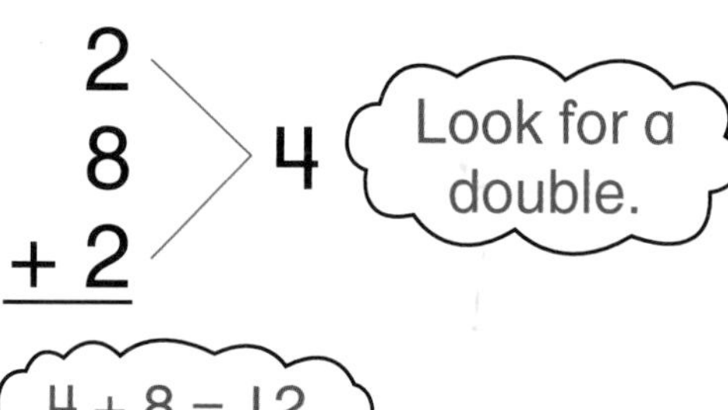

$$\begin{array}{r} 2 \\ 8 \\ +\,2 \\ \hline \end{array} \quad 2 + 2 = 4$$

Look for a double.

4 + 8 = 12

How many cards does Miko have? 12

Add.

$$\begin{array}{r} 1 \\ 3 \\ +\,7 \\ \hline 11 \end{array} \quad \begin{array}{r} 5 \\ 4 \\ +\,1 \\ \hline \end{array} \quad \begin{array}{r} 9 \\ 2 \\ +\,2 \\ \hline \end{array} \quad \begin{array}{r} 8 \\ 3 \\ +\,0 \\ \hline \end{array} \quad \begin{array}{r} 3 \\ 3 \\ +\,2 \\ \hline \end{array}$$

(3 + 7 = 10)

$$\begin{array}{r} 3 \\ 7 \\ 1 \\ +\,1 \\ \hline 12 \end{array} \quad \begin{array}{r} 1 \\ 2 \\ 2 \\ +\,8 \\ \hline \end{array} \quad \begin{array}{r} 2 \\ 4 \\ 1 \\ +\,6 \\ \hline \end{array} \quad \begin{array}{r} 0 \\ 3 \\ 3 \\ +\,5 \\ \hline \end{array} \quad \begin{array}{r} 7 \\ 4 \\ 3 \\ +\,4 \\ \hline \end{array}$$

Why is it easier to use a strategy than just to add the numbers in order?

Practice!

Add.

1

$$\begin{array}{r} 8 \\ 3 \\ +\ 1 \\ \hline 12 \end{array}$$

8 and 3 → 11 (Count on.)

2

$$\begin{array}{r} 6 \\ 3 \\ 3 \\ +\ 4 \\ \hline \end{array}$$

3 and 3 → 6; 6 and 4 → 10 (Use doubles and look for a 10 fact.)

3

3	4	3	9	5	7
1	8	4	0	5	3
+ 2	+ 0	+ 3	+ 7	+ 5	+ 2

4

4	3	2	1	5	3
4	0	3	2	1	7
4	8	5	0	1	3
+ 4	+ 2	+ 5	+ 8	+ 5	+ 3

Cultural Connection

Chinese Magic Squares

Magic squares were used in China long ago.
Numbers are added in any direction.
The sum is always the same.

Complete the magic square.

What is the sum? ____

5	6	
0	4	
	2	3

At Home: Today we added three and four numbers. Ask your child to explain how to add 3 + 6 + 4.

Name

Midchapter Review

Do your best!

Add.

1.
$$\begin{array}{r} 9 \\ +\,9 \\ \hline \end{array}$$

2.
$$\begin{array}{r} 5 \\ +\,6 \\ \hline \end{array}$$

3.
$$\begin{array}{r} 7 \\ +\,9 \\ \hline \end{array}$$

4.
$$\begin{array}{r} 8 \\ +\,5 \\ \hline \end{array}$$

5.
$$\begin{array}{r} 9 \\ 1 \\ +\,3 \\ \hline \end{array}$$

6.
$$\begin{array}{r} 2 \\ 5 \\ +\,7 \\ \hline \end{array}$$

7.
$$\begin{array}{r} 3 \\ 0 \\ 2 \\ +\,2 \\ \hline \end{array}$$

8.
$$\begin{array}{r} 4 \\ 3 \\ 3 \\ +\,4 \\ \hline \end{array}$$

Solve.

9. Tara mailed 9 letters.
Then she mailed 5 more letters.
How many letters did Tara mail?

____ letters

10. How did you add for exercise 8?

____

____

____

What are different strategies for adding?
Which do you like best? Why?

Mailbox Drop

You and your partner need 2 counters.

Take turns.

4	9
7	4
5	8
8	5
6	7
9	6

- Drop both counters on the mailboxes.

- Add the two numbers.
- Find the sum below and write the addition under it.
- Play until you get all the sums.

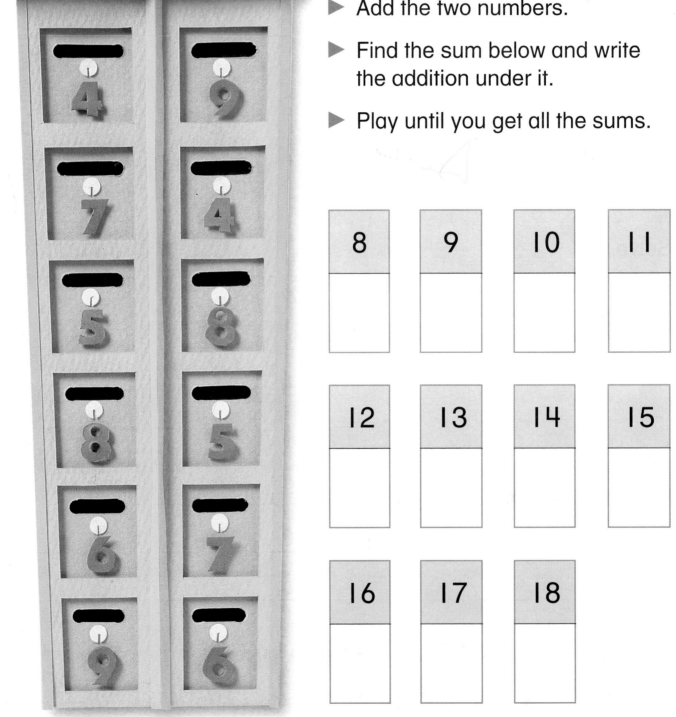

8	9	10	11

12	13	14	15

16	17	18

Name

What's in the Mail?

How many letters did Emily and Mr. Blueberry write? Listen to *Dear Mr. Blueberry.*

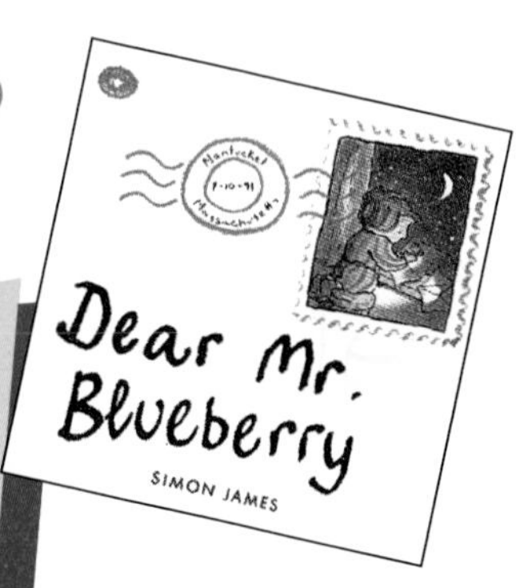

Do you know how much mail comes to your home?

- Sort the mail with your family for 2 days.
- Fill in the **data**. Write the numbers for each day on the **chart**.

Glossary
data
chart

FAMILY MAIL CHART						
	Magazines	**Cards and Letters**	**Catalogs**	**Newspapers**	**Other**	**Total**
Day 1						
Day 2						
Total						

- Find the total for each day.
- Find the total for each kind of mail.

1. Which kind of mail did your family get most? ____________

2. How much mail did your family get in 2 days? ____ pieces

What can you tell from the data you collected?

Decision Making

1 Decide what kind of chart to make to display the class's data. Make it.

Look at the class display. What do you notice about the totals for each kind of mail?

Write a report.

2 Tell how you sorted and counted your family's mail.

3 Tell how the totals in your chart compare with the totals in the class chart.

More to Investigate

PREDICT How many pieces of mail will come to your home over 7 days?

EXPLORE Try it. Sort and count the mail with your family for 5 more days. Find the new total for each kind of mail.

FIND How did the data change over 7 days? What patterns do you see?

Name ______________________

Explore Activity

Subtract with Doubles

Working Together

You and your partner need 9 and 9 .

Take turns.

- Show a doubles fact with cubes.
- Your partner snaps the cubes into 2 **equal parts**.
- Record the facts.

Glossary
equal parts

	Addition	Subtraction
1	3 + 3 = 6	6 − 3 = 3
2	4 + 4 = 8	8 − 4 = 4
3	2 + 2 = 4	4 − 2 = 2
4	5 + 5 = 10	10 − 5 = 5
5	6 + 6 = 12	12 − 6 = 6
6	7 + 7 = 14	14 − 7 = 7
7	8 + 8 = 16	16 − 8 = [illegible]
8	9 + 9 = 18	18 − 9 = 9
9	1 + 1 = 2	2 − 1 = 1

Practice!

Solve.

Workspace

1. Clint got 4 letters on Monday.
He got 4 letters on Tuesday.
How many letters did he get in all?

8 letters

$$\begin{array}{r} 4 \\ +\ 4 \\ \hline 8 \end{array}$$

2. 4 of Clint's letters were from his pen pals. How many were not from his pen pals?

____ letters

3. Mindy bought 6 postcards.
She also bought 6 birthday cards.
How many cards did she buy?

____ cards

4. Mindy mailed 6 of the cards she bought. How many cards does she have left?

____ cards

5. Ming has 8 stamps. He buys 8 more. How many stamps does Ming have now?

____ stamps

6. Write Write a subtraction problem about Ming.

____

____

At Home: We learned to use doubles to subtract. Ask your child to tell about the problem he or she wrote.

Name

Count Up to Subtract

Sam put 9 pictures in his book. The book can hold 12 pictures. How many more pictures can go into the book?

You can **count up** to subtract. Start at 9. Count up to 12.

Glossary

count up

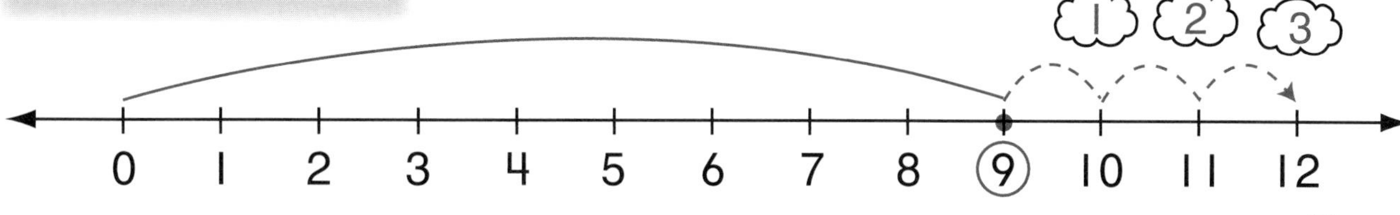

Sam can put 3 more pictures in his book.

Subtract. Use the number line if you want.

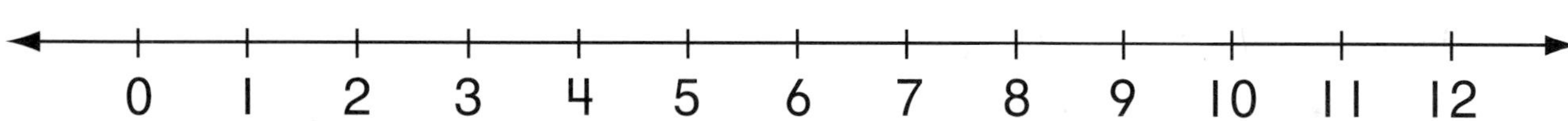

1. $11 - 8 =$ 3 (9, 10, 11) $9 - 7 =$ 2 (8, 9)

2. $8 - 5 =$ ____ $10 - 8 =$ ____

3. $7 - 5$ ____ $9 - 6$ ____ $8 - 6$ ____ $11 - 9$ ____ $9 - 8$ ____ $8 - 7$ ____

4. $10 - 9$ ____ $7 - 4$ ____ $5 - 4$ ____ $10 - 7$ ____ $6 - 5$ ____ $7 - 6$ ____

When would you count up to subtract?

Practice!

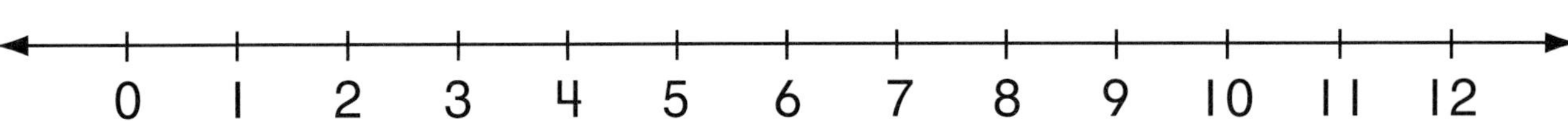

0 1 2 3 4 5 6 7 8 9 10 11 12

Subtract.
Count up if you forget a fact.

1

11	10	9	7	8	11
− 9	− 9	− 6	− 5	− 7	− 8
2					

2

12	4	7	10	5	9
− 9	− 2	− 6	− 8	− 3	− 7

3

5	10	8	6	9	7
− 4	− 7	− 6	− 4	− 8	− 4

Mixed Review Test Preparation

Add or subtract.

4

9	9	9	9	9	9
− □	− □	− □	− □	− □	− □
9	8	7	6	5	4

5 $9 + 3 =$ ____ $5 + 0 =$ ____ $6 + 3 =$ ____

$3 + 9 =$ ____ $0 + 5 =$ ____ $3 + 6 =$ ____

At Home: We learned how to count up to subtract. Have your child explain how to count up to solve 10 – 8.

Name ______________________

Subtract 9

Karen and her class wrote 15 letters to a pen-pal class in Canada.
The pen pals wrote 9 letters.
How many more letters did Karen and her class write?

Show 15. Subtract 9.

Karen and her class wrote __6__ more letters than the pen pals.

Cross out to show how to subtract 9.

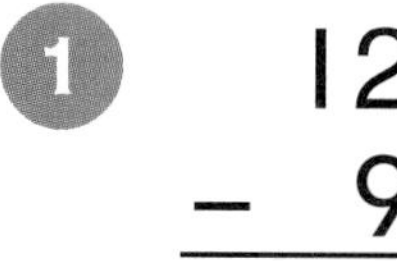

1

$$\begin{array}{r} 12 \\ -\ 9 \\ \hline 3 \end{array}$$

2

$$\begin{array}{r} 11 \\ -\ 9 \\ \hline \end{array}$$

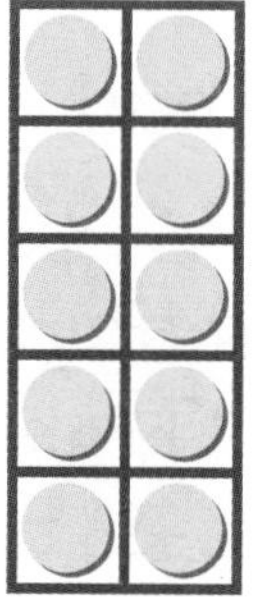

3

$$\begin{array}{r} 17 \\ -\ 9 \\ \hline \end{array}$$

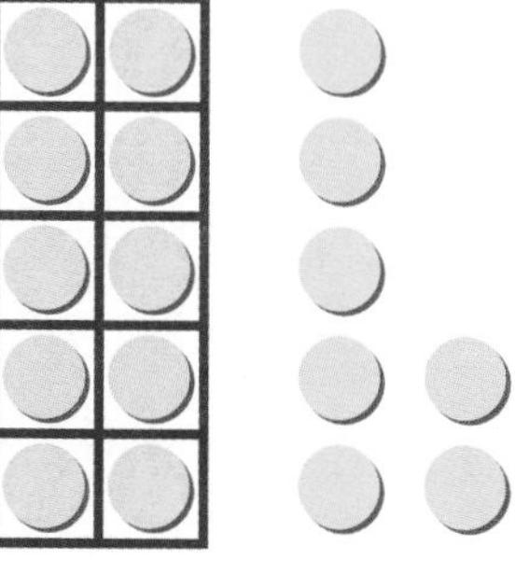

4

$$\begin{array}{r} 14 \\ -\ 9 \\ \hline \end{array}$$

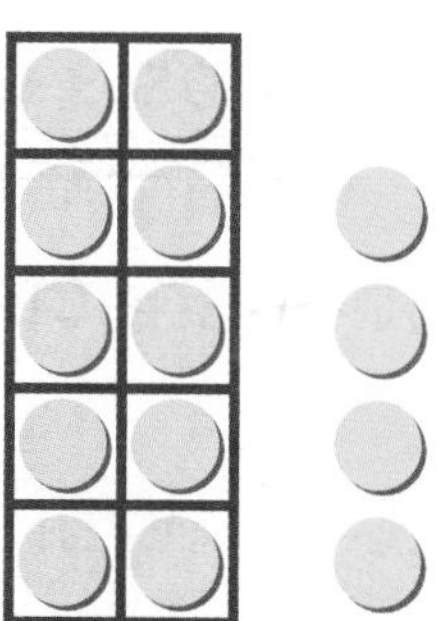

5

$$\begin{array}{r} 13 \\ -\ 9 \\ \hline \end{array}$$

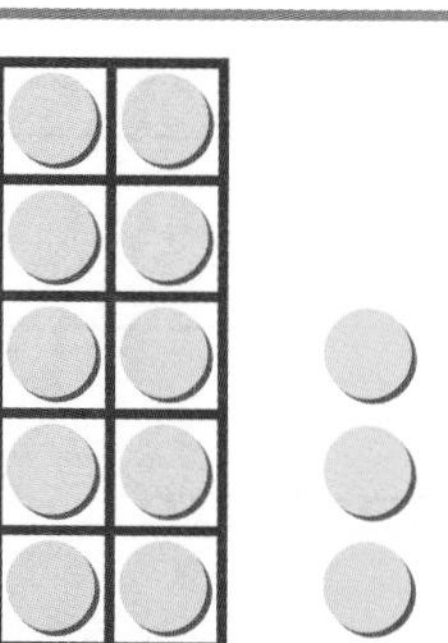

6

$$\begin{array}{r} 16 \\ -\ 9 \\ \hline \end{array}$$

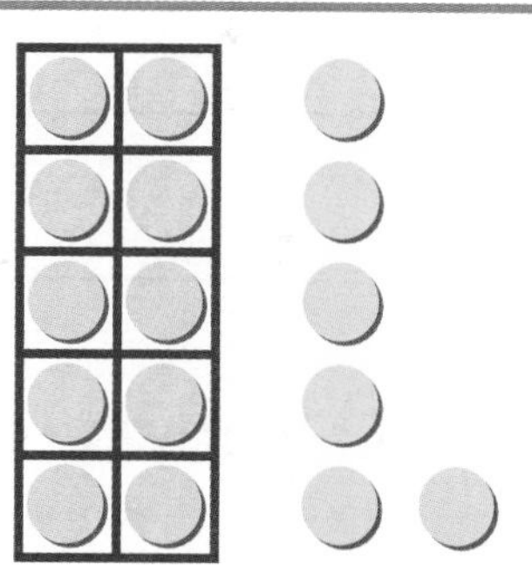

Practice!

Subtract. Use strategies if you need help.

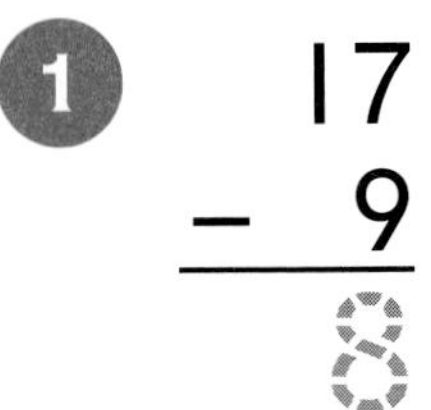

1. $17 - 9 = 8$ $12 - 9 =$ ___ $10 - 9 =$ ___ $14 - 9 =$ ___ $18 - 9 =$ ___

2. $15 - 9 =$ ___ $11 - 9 =$ ___ $13 - 9 =$ ___ $9 - 9 =$ ___ $16 - 9 =$ ___

Solve.

Workspace

3. Cobb had 18 postcards.
He used 9 of them.
How many postcards does
he still have? ____ postcards

4. Clara has to mail 16 cards.
She has 9 stamps.
How many more stamps
does she need? ____ stamps

5. 

Write a problem where you subtract 9.
Have a partner solve it.

____

____

Talk: Tell how you solved your partner's problem.

We studied subtracting 9. Talk with your child about how to solve the problem he or she wrote.

Name ________________________

Extra Practice
Activity!

Subtraction Postcards

PATTERNS Use a pattern to find the differences.
Write about the pattern.

1

13 – 4 = 9
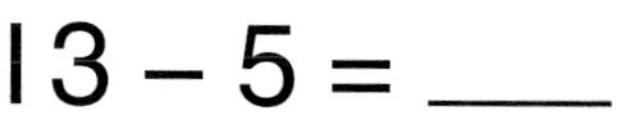
13 – 5 = ___
13 – 6 = ___
13 – 7 = ___
13 – 8 = ___

____
____
____
____

2

13 – 4 = 9
14 – 5 = ___
15 – 6 = ___
16 – 7 = ___
17 – 8 = ___

____
____
____
____

3

15 – 9 = 6
15 – 8 = ___
15 – 7 = ___
15 – 6 = ___

____
____
____
____

Add.

1. $9 + 6 = \_\_\_$ $5 + 9 = \_\_\_$ $9 + 7 = \_\_\_$

2. $8 + 5 = \_\_\_$ $7 + 5 = \_\_\_$ $6 + 8 = \_\_\_$

3. $\begin{array}{r} 6 \\ +\ 7 \\ \hline \end{array}$ $\begin{array}{r} 6 \\ +\ 6 \\ \hline \end{array}$ $\begin{array}{r} 8 \\ +\ 9 \\ \hline \end{array}$ $\begin{array}{r} 8 \\ +\ 8 \\ \hline \end{array}$ $\begin{array}{r} 7 \\ +\ 8 \\ \hline \end{array}$ $\begin{array}{r} 7 \\ +\ 7 \\ \hline \end{array}$

Subtract.

4. $17 - 9 = \_\_\_$ $12 - 9 = \_\_\_$ $16 - 9 = \_\_\_$

5. $11 - 8 = \_\_\_$ $14 - 7 = \_\_\_$ $17 - 8 = \_\_\_$

6. $\begin{array}{r} 16 \\ -\ 7 \\ \hline \end{array}$ $\begin{array}{r} 13 \\ -\ 5 \\ \hline \end{array}$ $\begin{array}{r} 15 \\ -\ 7 \\ \hline \end{array}$ $\begin{array}{r} 14 \\ -\ 5 \\ \hline \end{array}$ $\begin{array}{r} 13 \\ -\ 9 \\ \hline \end{array}$ $\begin{array}{r} 18 \\ -\ 9 \\ \hline \end{array}$

Set Purposes

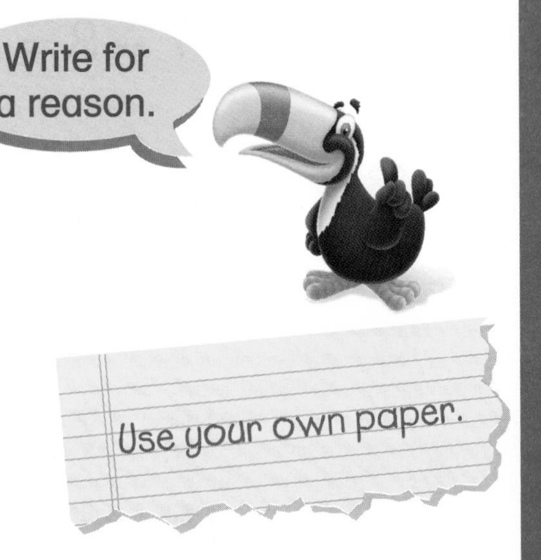

People write letters and postcards for different reasons. What if you put jokes and riddles on a postcard to your pen pal. What is your reason for writing?

Write a fun postcard. How many fun things did you write?

Name ____________________

Choose the Operation

Read Sal mailed 9 letters
He mailed 7 cards.
How many items did he mail?

Plan Add or subtract? (9 + 7) 9 – 7

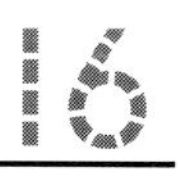

Solve 16 items mailed.

Look Back Does your answer make sense? Yes.

Read A mail truck has 9 bags of mail.
7 bags are for the city.
How many bags are not for the city?

Plan Add or subtract? 9 + 7 9 – 7

Solve ____ bags are not for the city.

Look Back Does your answer make sense? ______

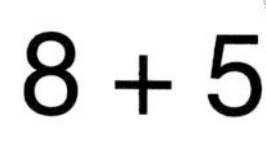

Choose addition or subtraction. Solve.

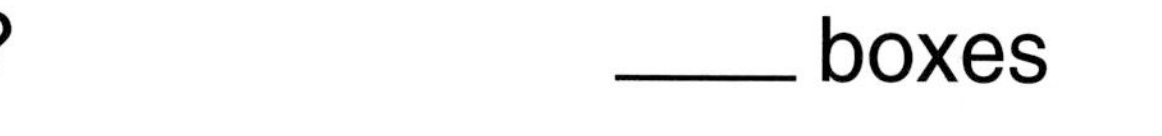

1. Gary had 8 boxes to mail. He mailed 5 of the boxes. How many boxes still have to be mailed? ____ boxes

   8 + 5

   8 – 5

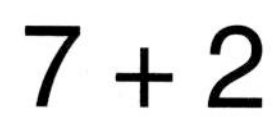

2. Ellie got 7 letters and 2 boxes in the mail this week. How many pieces of mail did Ellie get? ____ pieces

   7 + 2

   7 – 2

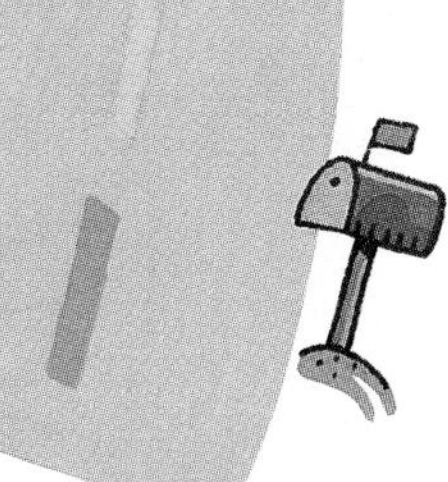

Practice!

Choose addition or subtraction.
Solve.

1. Jenna gave birthday presents to 9 people. She got 4 thank-you notes. How many people did not send a note?

   $9 + 4$

   $9 - 4$

   ____ people

---

2. May has 14 stamps. She uses 8 of them. How many stamps are left?

   $14 + 8$

   $14 - 8$

   ____ stamps

---

3. Hank sent for 8 Yankees' autographs. He sent for 6 Mets' autographs. How many autographs did Hank send for?

   $8 + 6$

   $8 - 6$

   ____ autographs

---

4. Justin wrote 7 letters. His brother wrote 4 letters. How many letters did they write in all?

   $7 + 4$

   $7 - 4$

   ____ letters

---

5. Betsy wrote 11 letters. Her brother wrote 8 letters. How many more letters did Betsy write?

   $11 + 8$

   $11 - 8$

   ____ letters

Today we decided whether to add or subtract to solve a problem. Ask your child to explain how he or she solved problems 4 and 5 above.

Name ______________________________

Related Facts

These are called related facts.

6 + 8 = 14 14 − 8 = 6

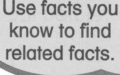

Use facts you know to find related facts.

Why do you think these facts are related?

Add and subtract.

1 8 + 9 = 17 17 − 9 = 8	2 9 + 7 = ___ 16 − 7 = ___	3 0 + 8 = ___ 8 − 8 = ___
4 9 + 9 = ___ 18 − 9 = ___	5 8 + 8 = ___ 16 − 8 = ___	6 6 + 9 = ___ 15 − 9 = ___
7 7 + 4 = ___ 11 − 4 = ___	8 5 + 9 = ___ 14 − 9 = ___	9 7 + 6 = ___ 13 − 6 = ___
10 9 + 6 = ___ 15 − 6 = ___	11 5 + 7 = ___ 12 − 7 = ___	12 8 + 5 = ___ 13 − 5 = ___

Are 8 + 6 and 8 − 6 related facts? Why or why not?

Practice!

Add and subtract.
Then match the related facts.

1

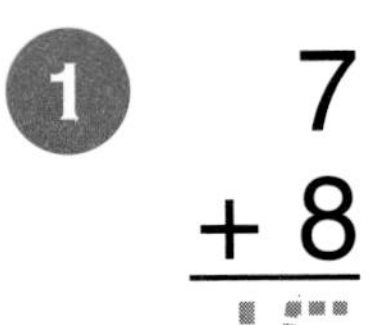

$7 + 8 = 15$	$11 - 6 =$
$9 + 4 =$	$15 - 8 = 7$
$5 + 6 =$	$13 - 5 =$
$9 + 7 =$	$16 - 7 =$
$8 + 5 =$	$13 - 4 =$

2

$6 + 6 =$	$17 - 8 =$
$8 + 6 =$	$12 - 6 =$
$9 + 8 =$	$14 - 6 =$
$7 + 3 =$	$13 - 7 =$
$6 + 7 =$	$10 - 3 =$

More to Explore Algebra Sense

Find the missing numbers.

$16 - \boxed{8} = 8$	$11 - \square = 5$	$12 - \square = 4$
$8 + \square = 16$	$5 + \square = 11$	$4 + \square = 12$

At Home: We learned about adding and subtracting related facts today. Ask your child to give the related addition fact for $15 - 6 = 9$.

Name ______________________

Working Together

You and your partner need 9 and 9 .

- Make a two-color cube train.
- Color to show your train.
- Write 2 addition sentences and 2 subtraction sentences for the train.

6 + 5 = 11

5 + 6 = 11

11 − 5 = 6

11 − 6 = 5

These four facts make a **fact family**.

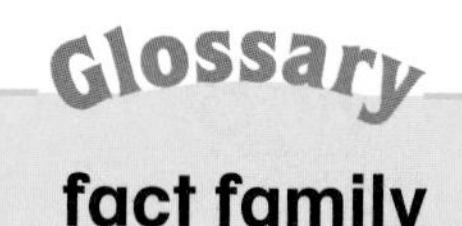

fact family

1. ______________ ______________
   ______________ ______________

2. ______________ ______________
   ______________ ______________

How many facts are in the 6 + 6 = 12 family? Why?

Complete the fact family.

1 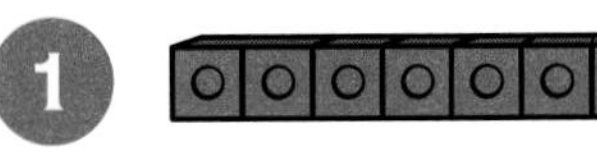

$\begin{array}{r} 8 \\ +\ 2 \\ \hline 10 \end{array}$ $\quad$ $\begin{array}{r} 2 \\ +\ 8 \\ \hline \end{array}$ $\quad$ $\begin{array}{r} 10 \\ -\ 2 \\ \hline 8 \end{array}$ $\quad$ $\begin{array}{r} 10 \\ -\ 8 \\ \hline \end{array}$

2
$\begin{array}{r} 9 \\ +\ 5 \\ \hline \end{array}$ $\quad$ $\begin{array}{r} 5 \\ +\ 9 \\ \hline \end{array}$

$\begin{array}{r} 14 \\ -\ 5 \\ \hline \end{array}$ $\quad$ $\begin{array}{r} 14 \\ -\ 9 \\ \hline \end{array}$

3
$\begin{array}{r} 7 \\ +\ 4 \\ \hline \end{array}$ $\quad$ $\begin{array}{r} 4 \\ +\ 7 \\ \hline \end{array}$

$\begin{array}{r} 11 \\ -\ 4 \\ \hline \end{array}$ $\quad$ $\begin{array}{r} 11 \\ -\ 7 \\ \hline \end{array}$

4
$\begin{array}{r} 8 \\ +\ 9 \\ \hline \end{array}$ $\quad$ $\begin{array}{r} 9 \\ +\ 8 \\ \hline \end{array}$

$\begin{array}{r} 17 \\ -\ 9 \\ \hline \end{array}$ $\quad$ $\begin{array}{r} 17 \\ -\ 8 \\ \hline \end{array}$

5
$\begin{array}{r} 4 \\ +\ 8 \\ \hline \end{array}$ $\quad$ $\begin{array}{r} 8 \\ +\ 4 \\ \hline \end{array}$

$\begin{array}{r} 12 \\ -\ 8 \\ \hline \end{array}$ $\quad$ $\begin{array}{r} 12 \\ -\ 4 \\ \hline \end{array}$

$\begin{array}{r} 8 \\ +\ 7 \\ \hline \end{array}$ $\quad$ $\begin{array}{r} 7 \\ +\ 8 \\ \hline \end{array}$

$\begin{array}{r} 15 \\ -\ 7 \\ \hline \end{array}$ $\quad$ $\begin{array}{r} 15 \\ -\ 8 \\ \hline \end{array}$

7
$\begin{array}{r} 7 \\ +\ 9 \\ \hline \end{array}$ $\quad$ $\begin{array}{r} 9 \\ +\ 7 \\ \hline \end{array}$

$\begin{array}{r} 16 \\ -\ 9 \\ \hline \end{array}$ $\quad$ $\begin{array}{r} 16 \\ -\ 7 \\ \hline \end{array}$

Write your own fact family.

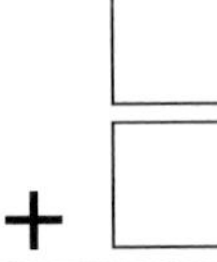 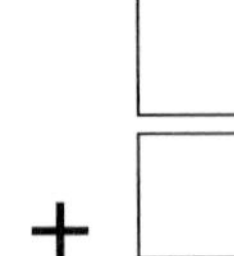 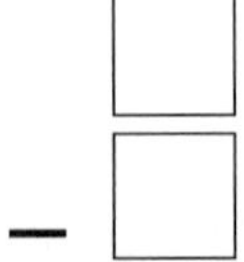 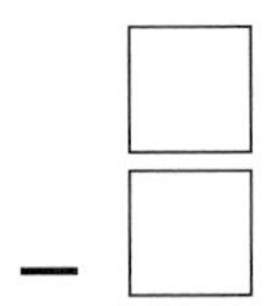

What is a fact family?
How can it help you to add and subtract?

At Home

We learned about fact families. Have your child write the fact family for 7, 6, and 13.

Name ____________________

Extra Practice

Activity !

Secret Message

- Add or subtract.
- Circle the facts that belong to each fact family.
- Write the letters in order for those facts. Use the letters to find the secret message.

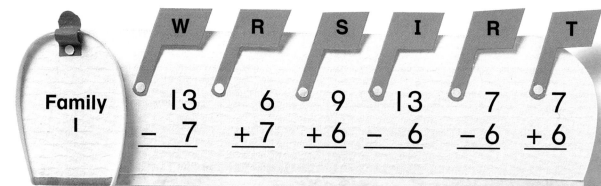

Family 1

W	R	S	I	R	T
13 − 7	6 + 7	9 + 6	13 − 6	7 − 6	7 + 6

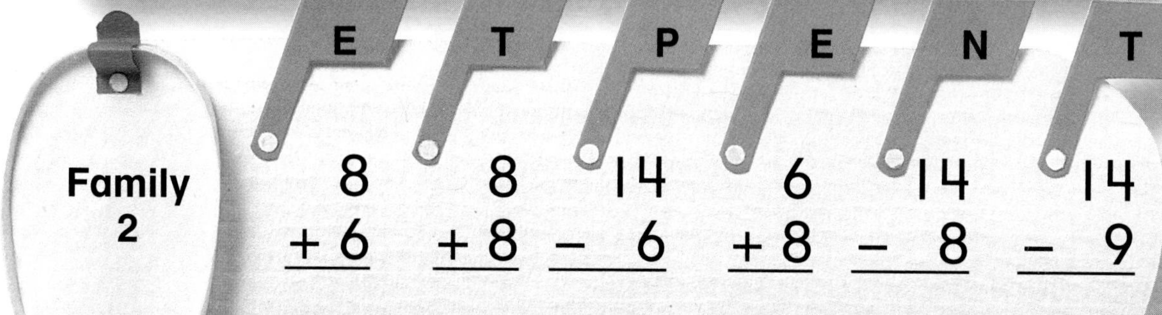

Family 2

E	T	P	E	N	T
8 + 6	8 + 8	14 − 6	6 + 8	14 − 8	14 − 9

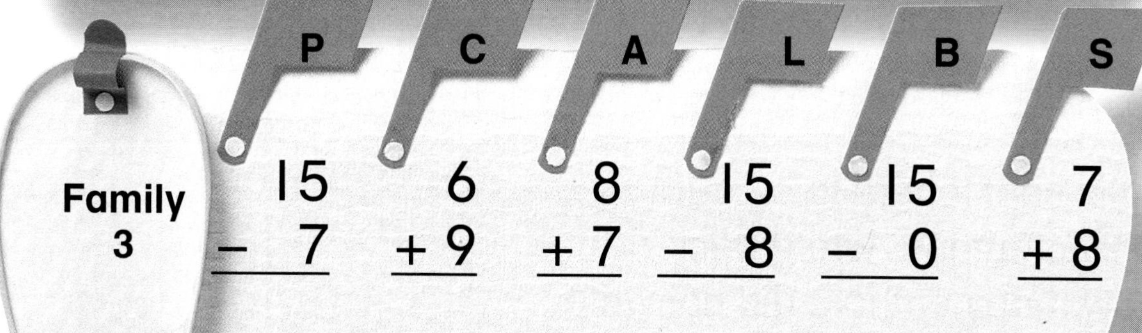

Family 3

P	C	A	L	B	S
15 − 7	6 + 9	8 + 7	15 − 8	15 − 0	7 + 8

Message:

___ ___ ___ ___ ___

___ ___ ___   ___ ___ ___ ___

Add or subtract.

1

9	16	8	18	5	13
+ 6	− 7	+ 8	− 9	+ 9	− 9
15					

2

8	17	9	14	5	15
+ 9	− 8	+ 9	− 9	+ 7	− 6

3

9	16	9	17	8	16
+ 8	− 9	+ 7	− 9	+ 5	− 8

Solve.

4 Lucas sent 6 packages by mail boat. He sent 7 by airplane. How many packages did Lucas send?

____ packages

5 Felix sent letters to 12 authors. Only 6 authors wrote back. How many authors did not write to Felix?

____ authors

6 Sofia read 4 books one week. She read 9 books the next week. What was the total number of books Sofia read?

____ books

Name ______________________________

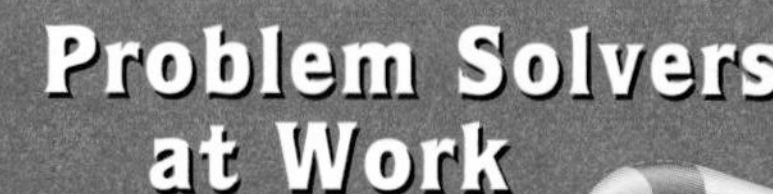

Choose a Strategy

Read
Plan
Solve
Look Back

Show how you solve this problem.

Jill made 15 cards.
Jack made 8 cards.
Who made more cards? ____

How many more cards? ____ cards

Explain your strategy. ______________________________

____

Solve.

1. Alana has 7 cards to mail. She has 4 boxes to mail. Does she have more boxes or cards to mail? __________

2. READING ARITHMETIC WRITING **Set Purposes** Alana made 7 cards. She made birthday cards, get well cards, and thank you cards.

Tell a reason for making each kind. Show how many of each kind Alana might have made.

Practice!

Workspace

Solve.

1. Betty wrote 10 letters last month.
Ted wrote 8 letters last month.
Who wrote more letters? ______

How many more letters? ____

2. Luis packed 14 boxes today.
Tomorrow he has to pack 9 boxes.
How many more boxes did he pack today than he will tomorrow? ______

Write and Share

Ashley wrote this problem.

I wrote 3 letters to Jessica in July. I wrote 5 more in August. How many letters did I write in all?

STUDENT TO STUDENT

Ashley Gruner
O'Rourke School
Mobile, Alabama

3. Solve Ashley's problem. ______________________

What strategy did you choose? ______________________

____

4. 

Write a problem about pen pals.
Have a partner solve it.

Use your own paper.

What strategy did your partner use? ______________

At Home: Ask your child to tell you about the problem he or she wrote.

Name

Chapter Review

Language and Mathematics

Choose the correct word to complete the sentence.

equal parts
count up
doubles
fact family

1. You can ______________ to subtract 6 – 4.
2. 5 + 2 = 7 and 2 + 5 = 7 belong to the same ______________.

Concepts and Skills

Add or subtract.

3. $\begin{array}{r} 7 \\ +8 \\ \hline \end{array}$
4. $\begin{array}{r} 9 \\ +5 \\ \hline \end{array}$
5. $\begin{array}{r} 8 \\ +9 \\ \hline \end{array}$
6. $\begin{array}{r} 7 \\ +6 \\ \hline \end{array}$
7. $\begin{array}{r} 5 \\ +8 \\ \hline \end{array}$
8. $\begin{array}{r} 18 \\ -\ 9 \\ \hline \end{array}$
9. $\begin{array}{r} 10 \\ -\ 7 \\ \hline \end{array}$
10. $\begin{array}{r} 9 \\ -8 \\ \hline \end{array}$
11. $\begin{array}{r} 16 \\ -\ 9 \\ \hline \end{array}$
12. $\begin{array}{r} 15 \\ -\ 6 \\ \hline \end{array}$
13. $\begin{array}{r} 1 \\ 2 \\ +7 \\ \hline \end{array}$
14. $\begin{array}{r} 4 \\ 3 \\ +7 \\ \hline \end{array}$
15. $\begin{array}{r} 2 \\ 6 \\ 2 \\ +6 \\ \hline \end{array}$
16. $\begin{array}{r} 8 \\ 1 \\ 2 \\ +1 \\ \hline \end{array}$
17. $\begin{array}{r} 6 \\ 4 \\ 2 \\ +2 \\ \hline \end{array}$
18. $\begin{array}{r} 17 \\ -\ 8 \\ \hline \end{array}$
19. $\begin{array}{r} 14 \\ -\ 8 \\ \hline \end{array}$
20. $\begin{array}{r} 15 \\ -\ 9 \\ \hline \end{array}$
21. $\begin{array}{r} 13 \\ -\ 8 \\ \hline \end{array}$
22. $\begin{array}{r} 16 \\ -\ 9 \\ \hline \end{array}$

Problem Solving

Choose addition or subtraction. Solve.

23 Billy mailed 9 cards. He mailed 12 boxes.
Did Billy mail more cards or boxes? ______

How many more? ____

---

24 Ling bought 6 stamps.
Jen bought 8 stamps.
How many stamps do they have in all?

$6 + 8$

$8 - 6$

____ stamps

Solve.

25 Lynn sent 15 letters.
Joe sent 9 letters.
How many more letters did Lynn send than Joe?

____ letters

What Do You Think?

Which strategy would you use to subtract $18 - 9$?
☑ Check one.

☐ Use doubles. ☐ Count up. ☐ Use a fact family. ☐ Subtract 9.

Why? ______________________________

Choose a fact family.
Write two word problems using two of the facts.

Name

Chapter Test

Add.

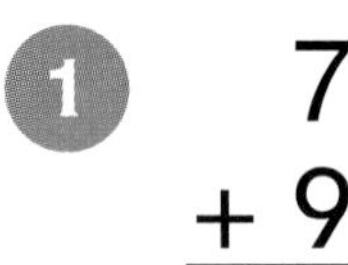

1. $7 + 9$

2. $9 + 8$

3. $1 + 3 + 6$

4. $3 + 7 + 6 + 2$

Subtract.

5. $14 - 9$

6. $10 - 8$

7. $11 - 7$

8. $17 - 9$

Choose addition or subtraction.
Solve.

9. Lu wrote 9 letters to Kim.
She wrote 6 letters to Robin.
How many more letters did she write to Kim than to Robin?

$9 + 6$

$9 - 6$

____ letters

10. George bought 9 postcards.
He also bought 6 birthday cards.
How many cards did George buy?

$9 + 6$

$9 - 6$

____ cards

Performance Assessment

What Did You Learn?

Make a train of 13 cubes.
Use two different colors.

Color to show the train you made.

Write two addition sentences for the train you made.

____

____

Write two subtraction sentences for the train you made.

____

____

Look at a partner's train.
How is it the same as your train?

How is it different? ____________________________

____

You may want to put this page in your portfolio.

Math Connection

Name ______________________

Variables

You can use related facts to find ■.

7 + ■ = 15

7 + 8 = 15

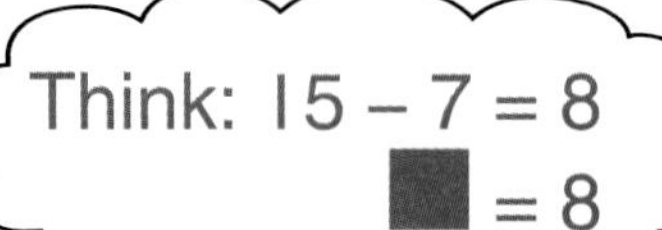

■ − 9 = 4

13 − 9 = 4

Add or subtract.
Find the missing numbers.

1	■ + 6 = 12 6 + 6 = 12	17 − ■ = 9 ______	5 + ■ = 12 ______
2	9 + ■ = 10 ______	■ − 5 = 9 ______	8 + 6 = ■ ______
3	16 − ■ = 8 ______	11 − 5 = ■ ______	■ + 8 = 8 ______

Write your own.

______________________ | ______________________

______________________ | ______________________

Technology Connection

Computer

Picture a Problem

How can making a picture help you write and solve a problem?

The screen shows a picture made with counter stamps.

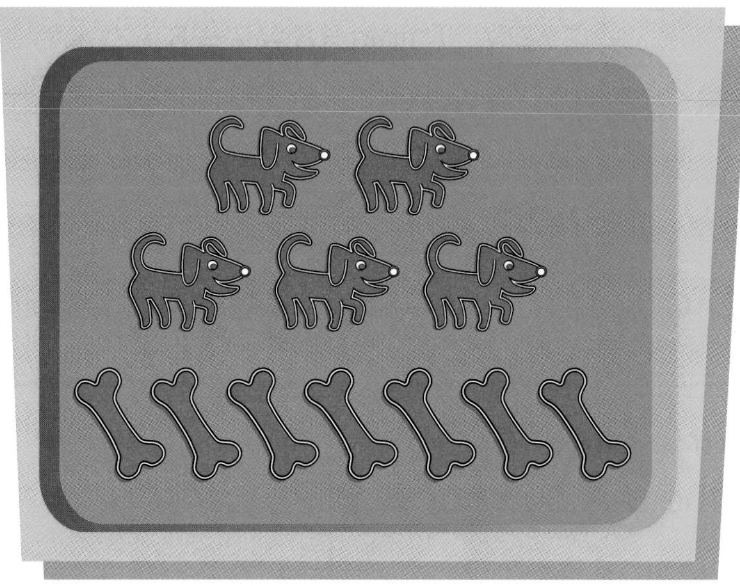

Use the picture to complete and solve.

Betsy has ____ dogs.

There are ____ bones.

How many more bones are there than dogs? ____ bones

At the Computer

1. Use counter stamps to make a picture.
2. Write an addition word problem for the picture. Solve it.
3. Write a subtraction word problem for the picture. Solve it.

Name ______________________________

Drop It!

PLAYERS 2

MATERIALS 2 pennies or counters

DIRECTIONS Take turns. Drop the 2 pennies or counters on the board below. Add the two numbers.

0	3	7	5	4	2
8	5	1	7	6	9
8	7	6	4	2	6
4	9	1	8	3	0
0	9	3	2	5	1

Play this game to help your child practice basic addition facts. To practice subtraction facts, choose a number from 11 to 18. Take turns dropping 1 penny on the game board. Then subtract that number from the number chosen.

Dear Family,

My new chapter in mathematics will be about place value and graphing. I will learn more about numbers to 100 and how to make graphs.

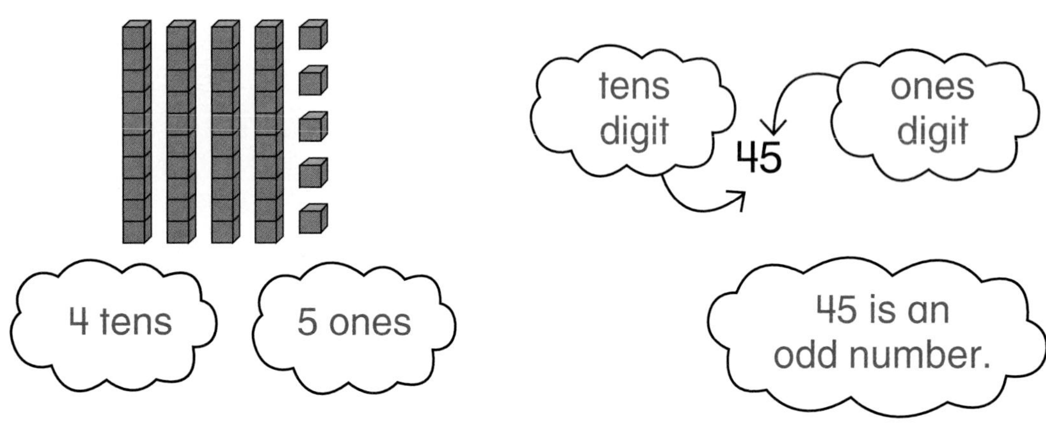

I will also be talking about things to count outside.

Learning About Our Backyard

Let's talk about different things that live outside. We can make a list of things to count.

My Math Words

I am going to use these and other math words in this chapter.

Please help me make word cards for the math words. I can use these word cards when I practice place value and graphing.

tens
estimate
ones
digit
order
after
before
between
skip-count
even
odd
is less than
is greater than

Your child,

____

Signature

Place Value and Graphing

Theme: Our Backyard

CHAPTER 3

Graph Listen to *The Icky Bug Counting Book.* Make a list of bugs you see pictured on trees in the book. Write how many of each kind you see.

Tell about your list of bugs. Use *more than 10* and *less than 10.*

Name

What Do You Know?

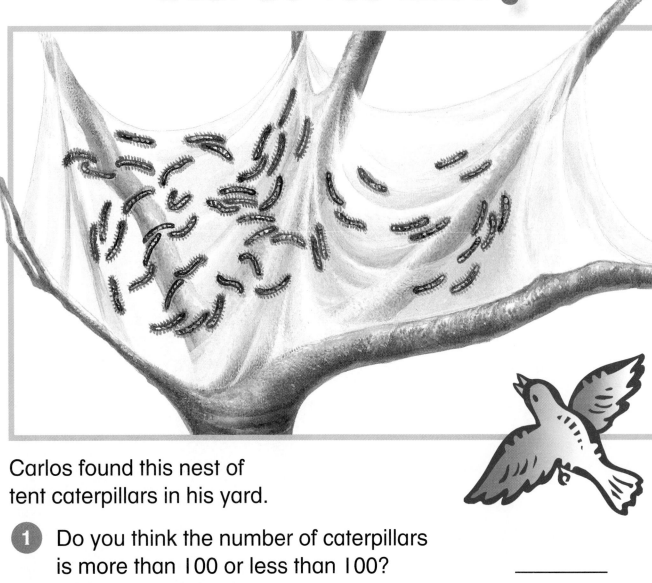

Carlos found this nest of tent caterpillars in his yard.

1. Do you think the number of caterpillars is more than 100 or less than 100? ________

2. Estimate how many. Estimate: ____

   Then count the number of caterpillars. Count: ____

3. Was your estimate more or less than the number you counted? ________

Explain how you counted to find the number of caterpillars. How could you find the number a different way?

Name ___

Explore Activity

Tens

Working Together

You and your partners need 100 ▢.

- Use cubes to make **tens**.
- Show one more ten each time.
- Write how many tens.
- Write the numbers.

Show.	Write.		Read.
|	1 ten	10	ten
||	2 tens	20	twenty
|||	___	___	thirty
	___	___	forty
	___	___	fifty
	___	___	sixty
	___	___	seventy
	___	___	eighty
	___	___	ninety
	10 tens	100	one hundred

PATTERNS What pattern do you see?

Glossary
tens

Practice!

Ring groups of ten.
Write how many tens. Write the number.

1 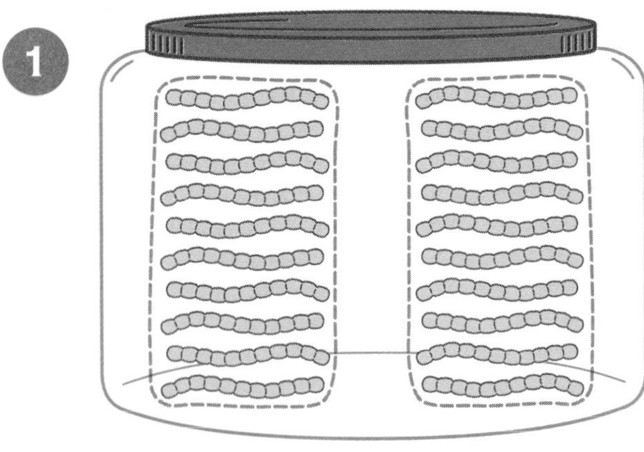

2 tens 20

2 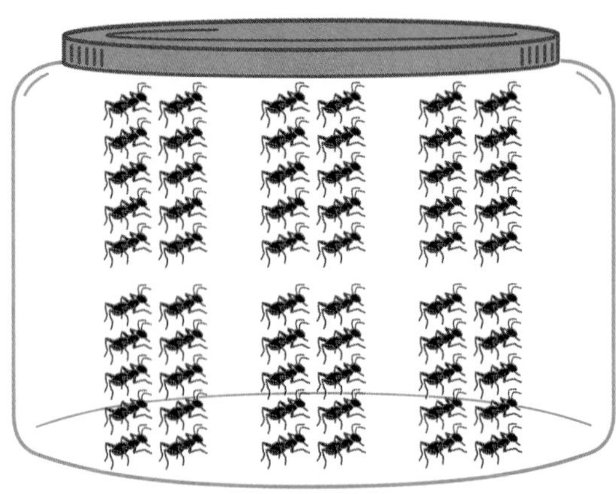

_______ _______

3 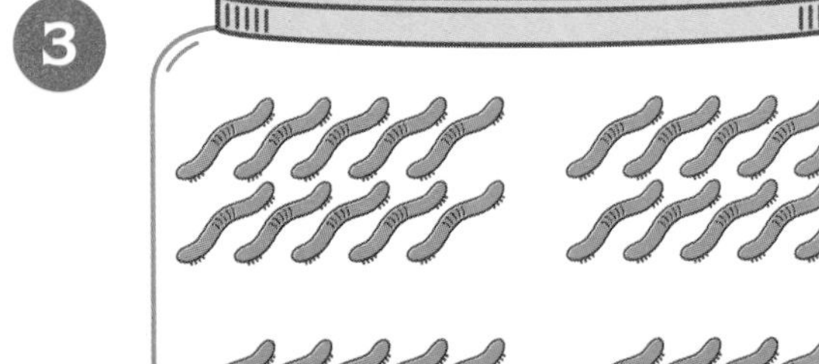

_______ _______

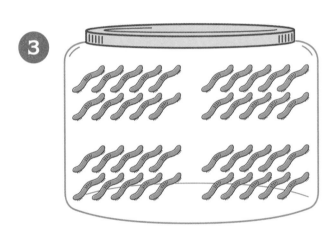

4 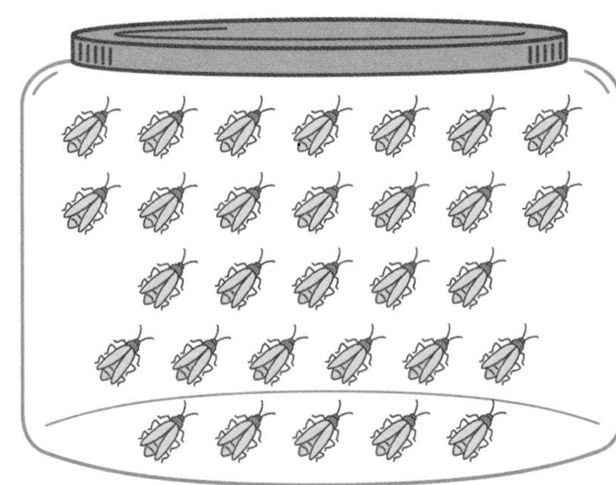

_______ _______

5 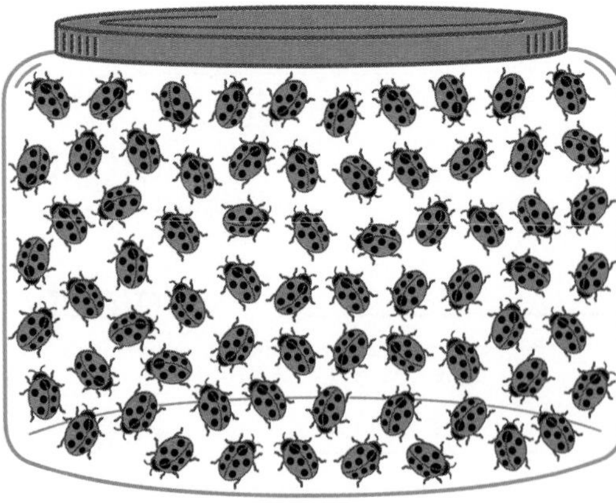

_______ _______

6 

_______ _______

At Home We grouped things in tens. Have your child tell you about making tens.

Name ____________________

Working Together

You and your partner need 40 ▢.

- Use two hands to take a bunch of cubes.
- **Estimate** how many cubes. Count.
- Make tens. Count again.
- Write how many tens and **ones**.
  Write the number.

1. 3 tens 2 ones 32
2. ____ tens ____ ones ____
3. ____ tens ____ ones ____
4. ____ tens ____ ones ____
5. ____ tens ____ ones ____

Which is easier to count: 40 cubes or 4 trains of 10? Explain.

Glossary
estimate
ones

Practice!

Write how many tens and ones.
Write the number.

1 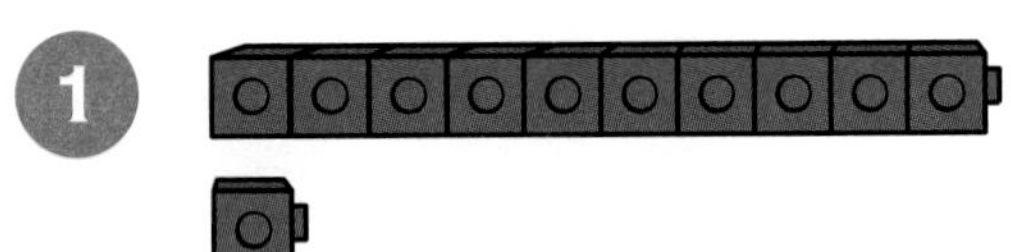
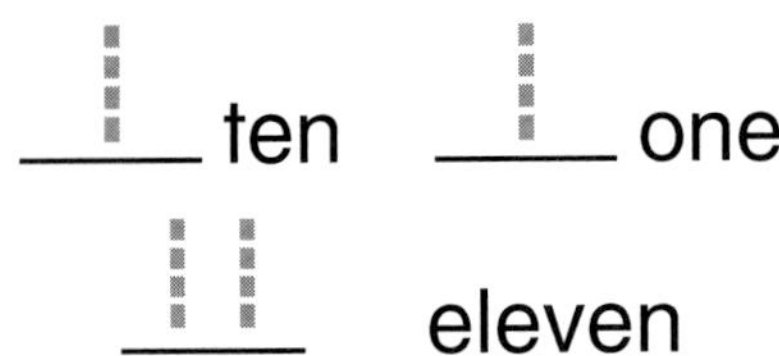

1 ten 1 one

11 eleven

2 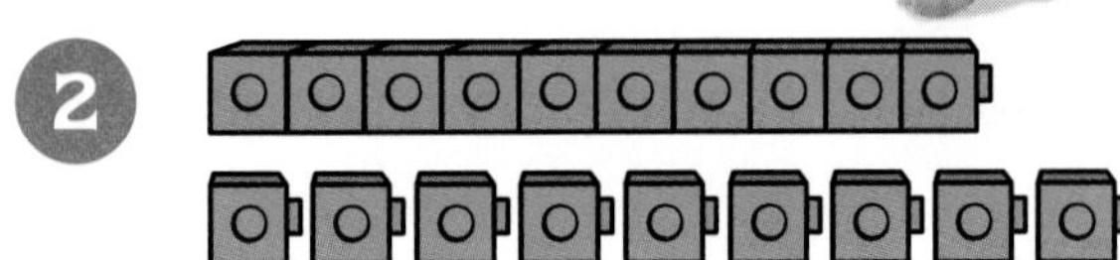

____ ten ____ ones

____ nineteen

3 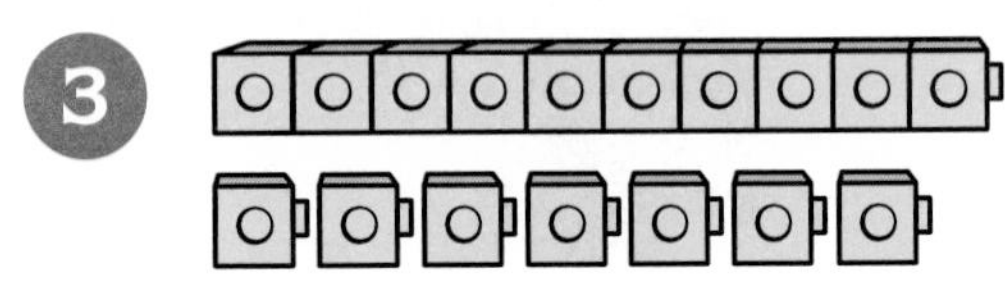

____ ten ____ ones

____ seventeen

4 

____ ten ____ ones

____ sixteen

5 

____ ten ____ ones

____ fifteen

6 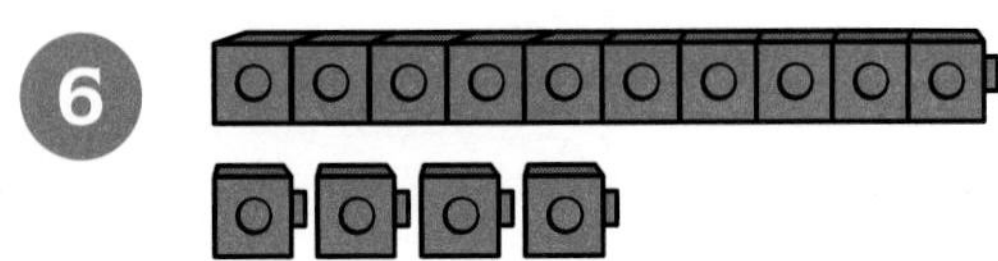

____ ten ____ ones

____ fourteen

7 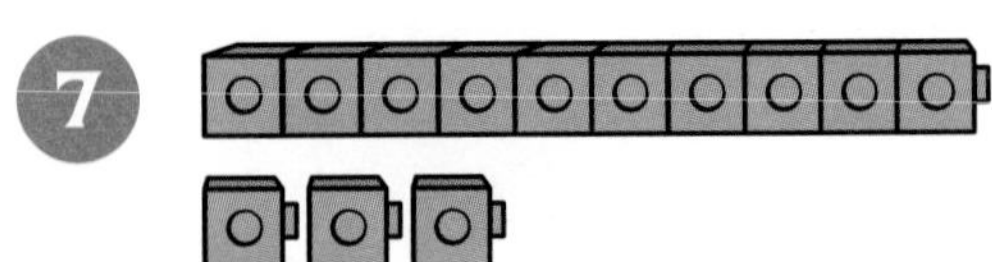

____ ten ____ ones

____ thirteen

8 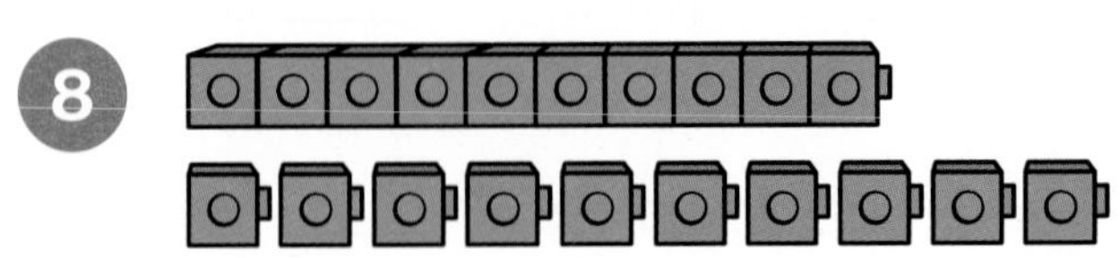

____ tens ____ ones

____ twenty

At Home: Today we learned about tens and ones. Have your child tell the number of tens and ones in 16 and in 36.

Name

Explore Activity

Numbers to 50

The **digit** 3 means 30.
The **digit** 2 means 2.
32
3 tens
2 ones

Working Together

You and your partner need 5 [tens rod], 9 [ones cube], and a [tens and ones mat].

Glossary

digit

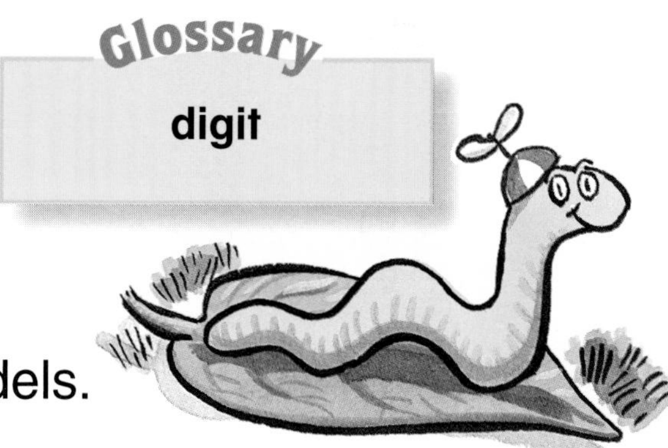

Take turns.

- You show the tens and ones with models.
- Your partner writes the number.

1. 4 tens 7 ones 47
2. 2 tens 1 one ____
3. 1 ten 9 ones ____
4. 4 tens 8 ones ____
5. 0 tens 6 ones ____
6. 4 tens 0 ones ____
7. 3 tens 5 ones ____
8. 0 tens 9 ones ____
9. 1 ten 3 ones ____
10. 2 tens 6 ones ____
11. 2 tens 4 ones ____
12. 4 tens 5 ones ____

Critical Thinking

What is the value of the 4 in 43?

Practice!

Count. Write how many tens and ones.
Write the number.

1

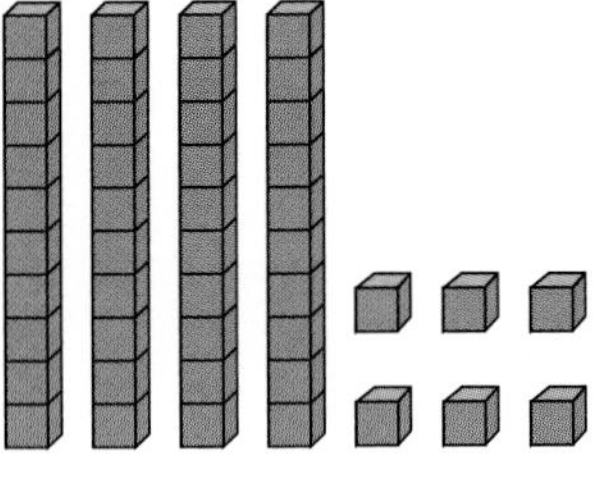

4 tens 6 ones

2

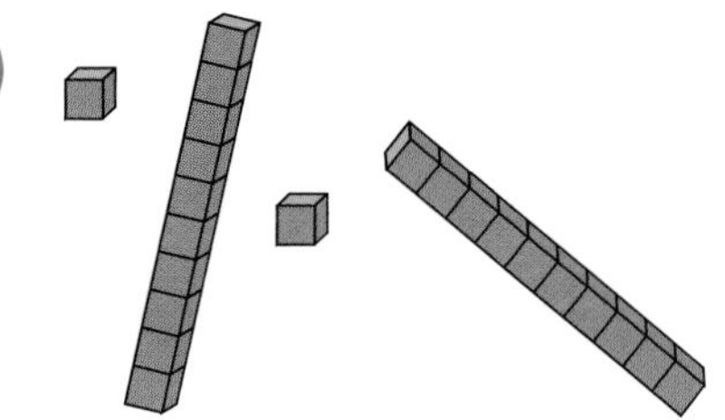

____ tens ____ ones

____

3

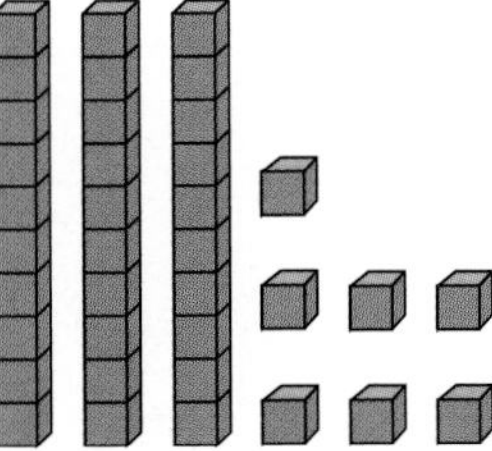

____ tens ____ ones

____

4

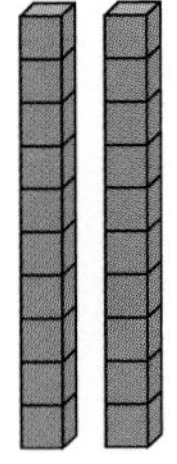

____ tens ____ ones

____

Write how many tens and ones.

5 29 2 tens 9 ones

6 34 ____ tens ____ ones

7 50 ____ tens ____ ones

8 12 ____ tens ____ ones

9 43 ____ tens ____ ones

10 38 ____ tens ____ ones

11 17 ____ tens ____ ones

12 25 ____ tens ____ ones

At Home

We identified tens and ones in numbers to 50. Ask your child how many tens and ones are in the number 40.

Name ________________

Explore Activity

Numbers to 100

The digit 6 means 60.
67
The digit 7 means 7.
6 tens
7 ones

Working Together

You and your partner need 9 ,

9 ▫, and a ▭.

Take turns.

▶ You show the tens and ones with models.

▶ Your partner writes the number.

1. 5 tens 4 ones 54
2. 8 tens 1 one ____
3. 9 tens 6 ones ____
4. 6 tens 9 ones ____
5. 5 tens 8 ones ____
6. 8 tens 4 ones ____
7. 7 tens 0 ones ____
8. 3 tens 7 ones ____
9. 6 tens 5 ones ____
10. 5 tens 2 ones ____
11. 9 tens 3 ones ____
12. 4 tens 3 ones ____

What is the value of the 4 in 74?

Practice!

Count. Write how many tens and ones.
Write the number.

1 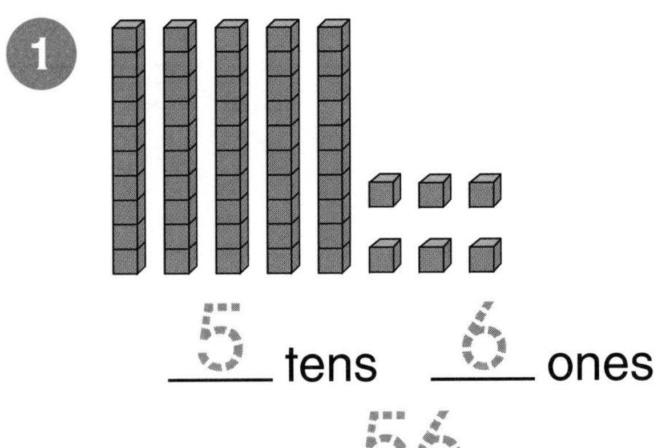

5 tens 6 ones

56

2 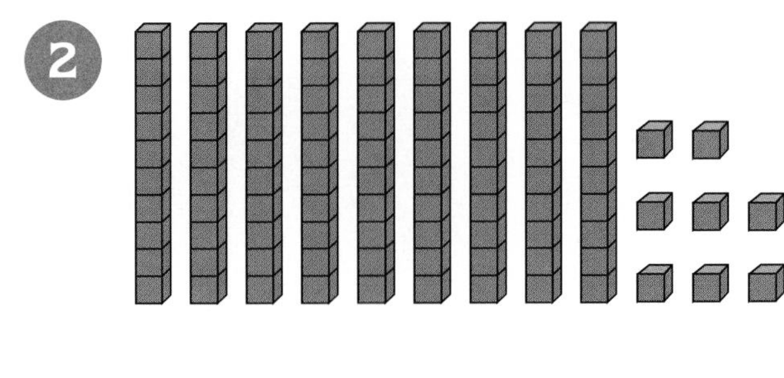

____ tens ____ ones

____

3 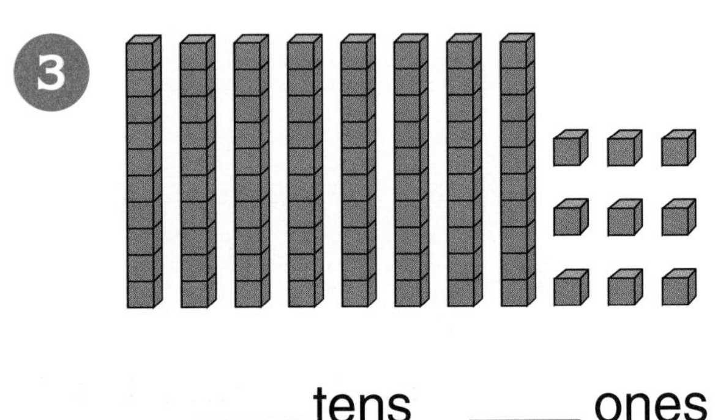

____ tens ____ ones

____

4 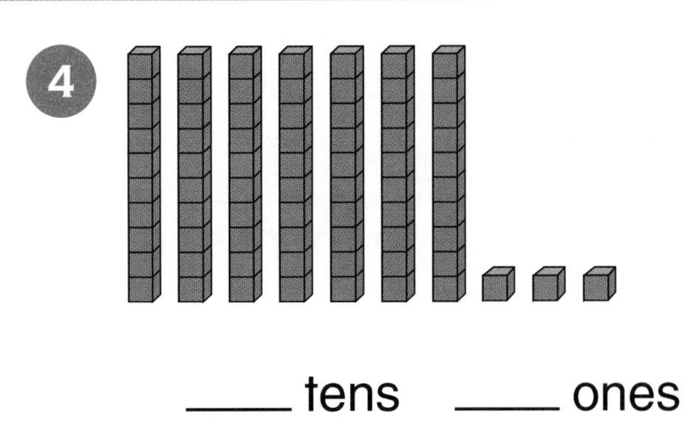

____ tens ____ ones

____

5 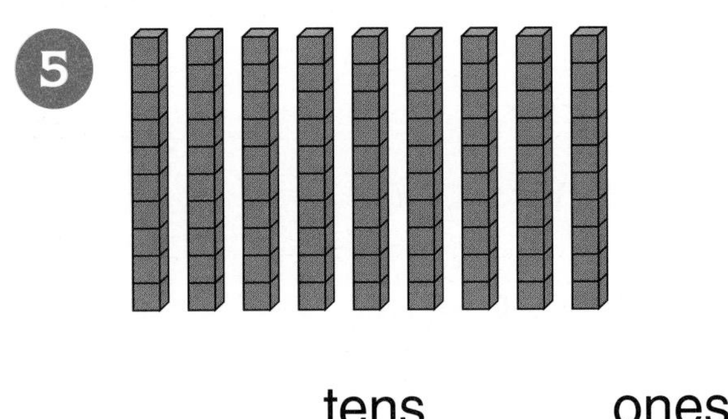

____ tens ____ ones

____

6 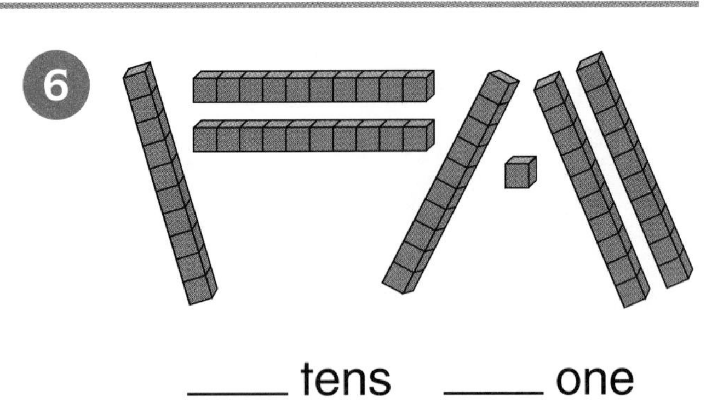

____ tens ____ one

____

Write how many tens and ones.

7 85 8 tens 5 ones

8 68 ____ tens ____ ones

9 99 ____ tens ____ ones

10 77 ____ tens ____ ones

At Home: We identified tens and ones in numbers to 100. Ask your child to tell what the 4 means in the numbers 42 and 34.

Name ______________________

Extra Practice
Game!

Schoolyard Numbers

You and your partner need a and 60 .

Take turns.

- Drop the on the board.
- Pick up that many cubes.
- For each turn, add more cubes to your set.
- Make a ten when you can.
- Write how many tens and ones after each turn.

Be the first to reach 30!

Total	
____ tens	____ ones
____ tens	____ ones
____ tens	____ ones
____ tens	____ ones
____ tens	____ ones
____ tens	____ ones
____ tens	____ ones
____ tens	____ ones
____ tens	____ ones
____ tens	____ ones

Write the number.

1 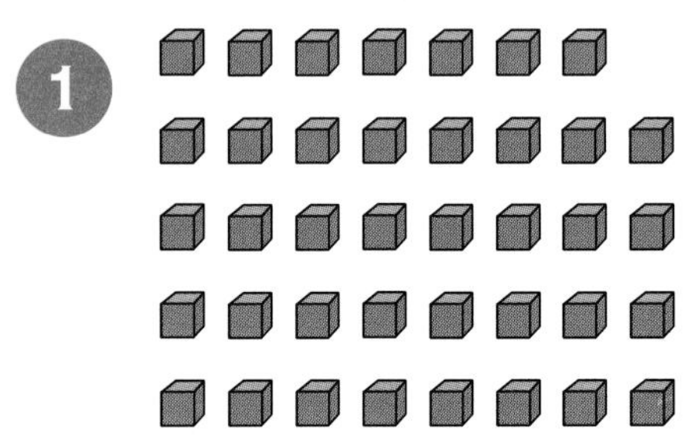
39

2 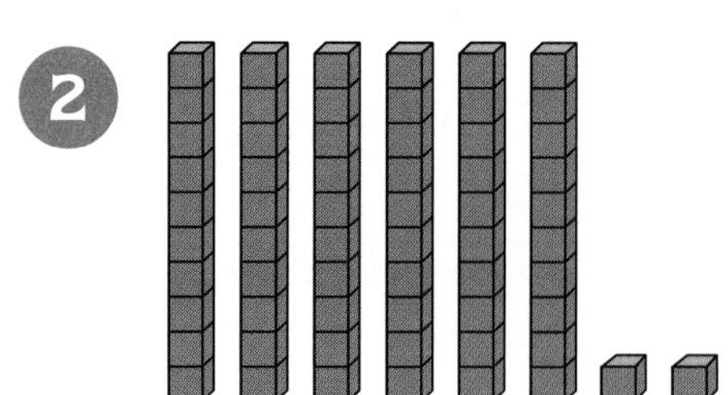
____

3 
____

4 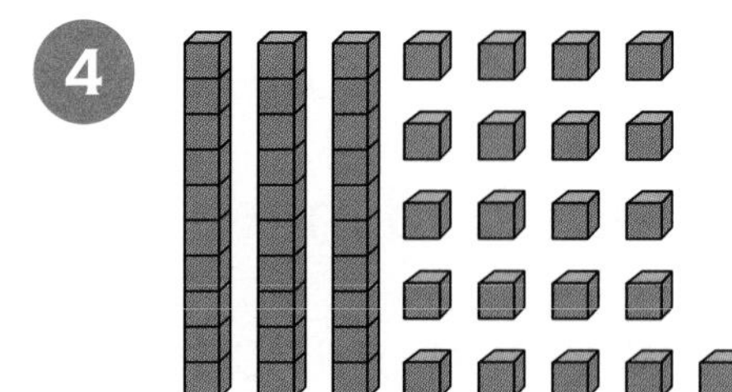
____

5 2 tens 5 ones ____

6 1 ten 3 ones ____

7 0 tens 8 ones ____

8 5 tens 6 ones ____

9 8 tens 8 ones ____

10 4 tens 1 one ____

Write how many tens and ones.

11 68 6 tens 8 ones

12 94 ____ tens ____ ones

13 12 ____ tens ____ ones

14 43 ____ tens ____ ones

15 35 ____ tens ____ ones

16 90 ____ tens ____ ones

17 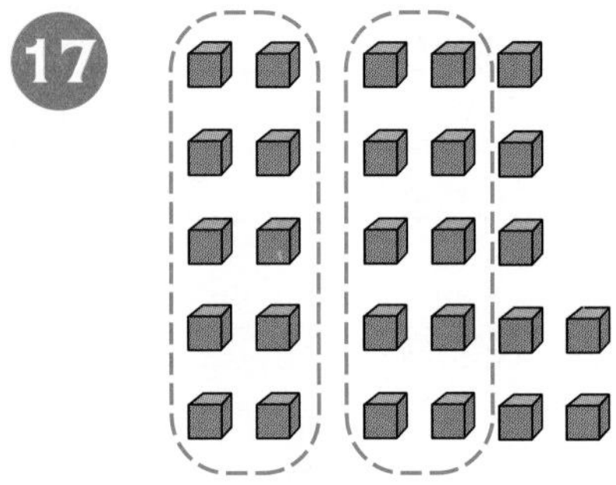

____ tens ____ ones

18 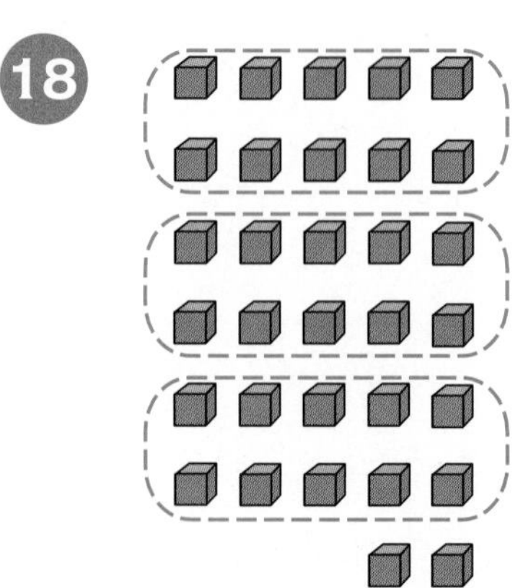

____ tens ____ ones

Name ______________________________

Order to 100

Write the numbers in **order**.

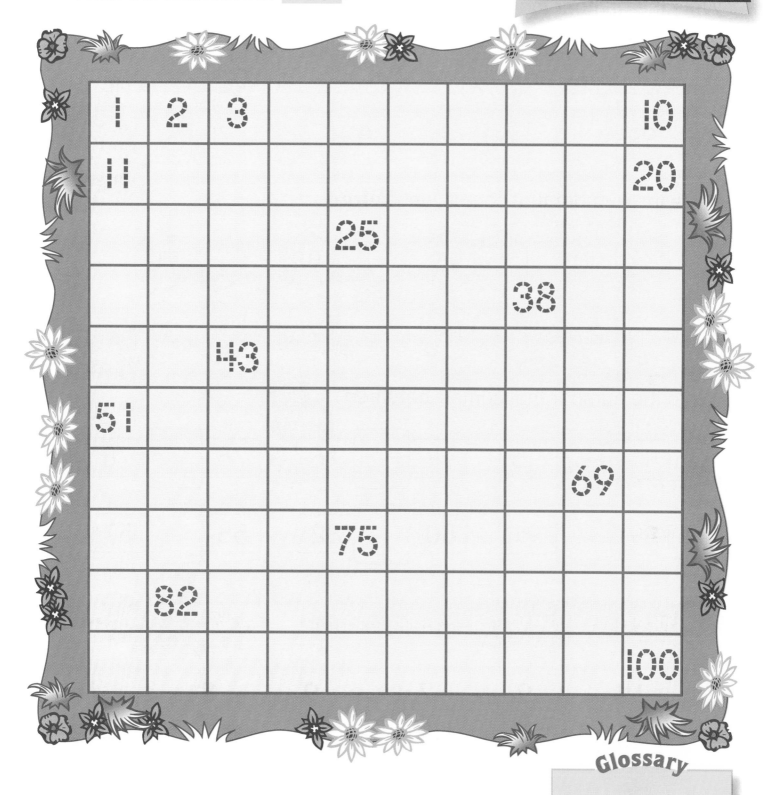

1	2	3							10
11									20
				25					
							38		
		43							
51									
								69	
				75					
	82								
									100

Glossary

order
after
before
between

Algebra Critical Thinking

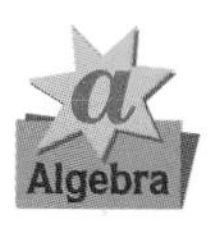

PATTERNS What is the number pattern going →?
What is the number pattern going ↓ ?
What is the number pattern going ←?

Practice!

Write the number that comes just **after**.

1. 21 22 | 93 ___ | 56 ___ | 39 ___

2. 99 ___ | 60 ___ | 85 ___ | 72 ___

Write the number that comes just **before**.

3.  39 40 | ___ 95 |  ___ 48 |  ___ 70

4.  ___ 21 |  ___ 89 |  ___ 76 | ___ 37

Write the number that comes **between**.

5. 41 42 43 | 14 ___ 16 | 76 ___ 78

6. 89 ___ 91 | 80 ___ 82 | 55 ___ 57

Mixed Review Test Preparation

7. $\begin{array}{r} 14 \\ -\ 8 \\ \hline \end{array}$ $\begin{array}{r} 9 \\ +9 \\ \hline \end{array}$ $\begin{array}{r} 7 \\ +6 \\ \hline \end{array}$ $\begin{array}{r} 9 \\ -1 \\ \hline \end{array}$ $\begin{array}{r} 8 \\ +7 \\ \hline \end{array}$ $\begin{array}{r} 16 \\ -\ 8 \\ \hline \end{array}$

8. $\begin{array}{r} 7 \\ -7 \\ \hline \end{array}$ $\begin{array}{r} 6 \\ +4 \\ \hline \end{array}$ $\begin{array}{r} 16 \\ -\ 9 \\ \hline \end{array}$ $\begin{array}{r} 5 \\ +8 \\ \hline \end{array}$ $\begin{array}{r} 15 \\ -\ 6 \\ \hline \end{array}$ $\begin{array}{r} 8 \\ +8 \\ \hline \end{array}$

At Home Ask your child to tell you a number that comes just after 60, a number between 43 and 45, and a number just before 93.

Name ______________________

Skip-Count by Fives and Tens

PATTERNS You can **skip-count** the coins by tens.

You can skip-count the coins by fives.

____¢

---

1. Skip-count by tens. Write the numbers.

   10, 20, 30, ____, ____, ____, ____, ____, ____, ____

2. Skip-count by fives. Write the numbers.

   5, 10, 15, 20, 25, 30, ____, ____, ____, ____, ____,

   ____, ____, ____, ____, ____, ____, ____, ____, ____

Practice!

Skip-count by tens. Write the numbers.

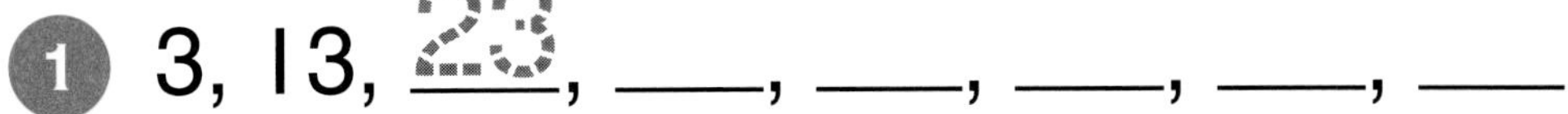

1. 3, 13, 23, ___, ___, ___, ___, ___
2. 16, 26, ___, ___, ___, ___, ___, ___
3. ___, ___, 28, 38, 48, ___, ___
4. ___, ___, ___, 62, ___, ___, ___

Skip-count by fives. Write the numbers.

5. 35, 40, 45, ___, ___, ___, ___, ___
6. 20, 25, ___, ___, ___, ___, ___, ___
7. ___, ___, 80, 85, 90, ___, ___
8. ___, ___, ___, 50, ___, ___, ___

More to Explore Patterns

Algebra **PATTERNS** Fill in the blanks. Use patterns to help.

21	22	23	24	25	26	27			
31									
							58		60

At Home We skip-counted by fives and tens to 100. Ask your child to skip-count by tens from 42.

Name ______________________

Skip-Count by Twos

PATTERNS What is an easy way to count the rabbit ears?

2, 4, 6, ___, ___, ___, ___

How many ears? ___

Skip-count by twos. Write the numbers.

1. How many spots? ___

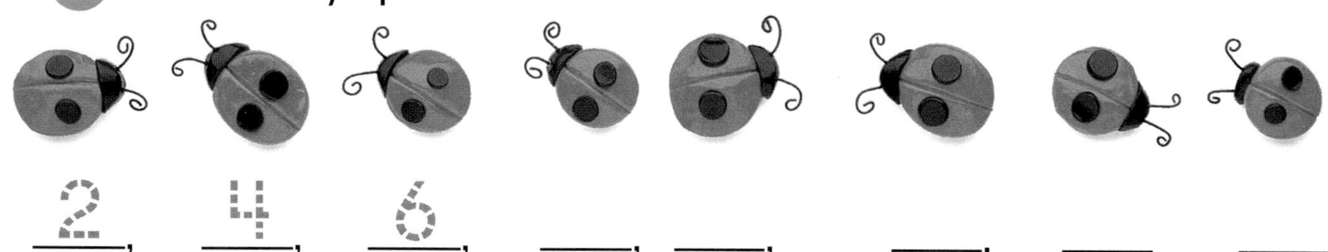

2, 4, 6, ___, ___, ___, ___ ___

2. How many eyes? ___

3. How many wings? ___

Practice!

Connect the dots. Skip-count by twos.

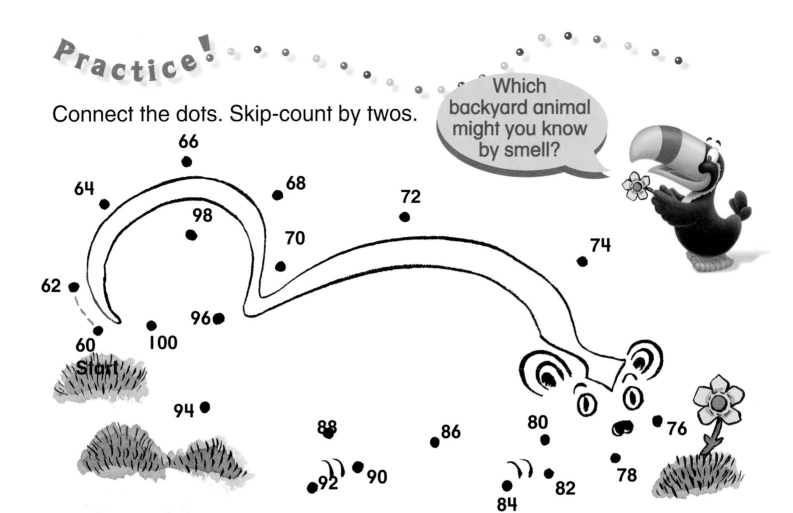

Which backyard animal might you know by smell?

60 Start, 62, 64, 66, 68, 70, 72, 74, 76, 78, 80, 82, 84, 86, 88, 90, 92, 94, 96, 98, 100

Cultural Connection

Numbers Around the World

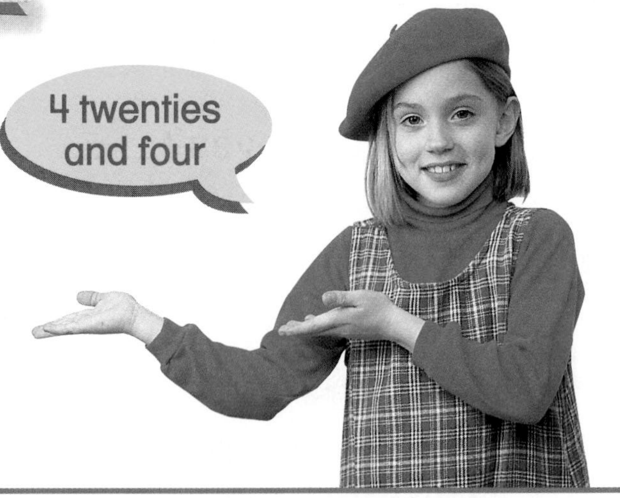

Numbers are said in different ways around the world. This is how 84 is said in some languages.

French	4 twenties and four	Arabic	four and eighty
Japanese	8 tens and four	Spanish	eight four

Can you say 84 in other languages? Try it with a partner.

We skip-counted by twos to 100. Ask your child to start at 48 and skip-count by twos to 80.

Name ______________________

Working Together

You and your partners need 55 cubes.

Build this tower of trains. Write the number of cubes.

1
2
___
___
___
___
___
___
___
___
___

1. Color the trains that can be split into 2 equal parts.

2. How many cubes are in trains with 2 equal parts?

2, 4, ___, ___, ___

3. How many cubes are in trains without 2 equal parts?

1,  3, ___, ___, ___

Glossary
even
odd

These numbers are **even** numbers.

These numbers are **odd** numbers.

Practice!

Write *odd* or *even* for each number.
You may use cubes to help.

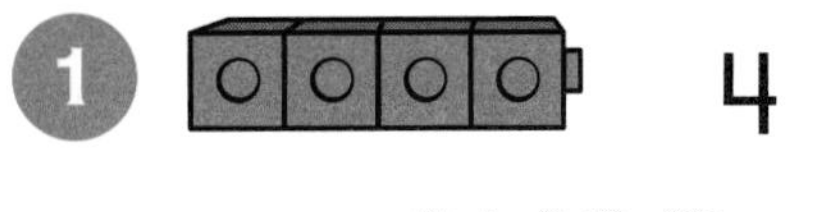

1. 4 even ______ 7 ______

2. 9 ______ 6 ______

3. 11 ______

4. 18 ______

5. Color the even numbers. Circle the tens.

1	2	3	4	5	6	7	8	9	10
11	12	13	14	15	16	17	18	19	20
21	22	23	24	25	26	27	28	29	30
31	32	33	34	35	36	37	38	39	40
41	42	43	44	45	46	47	48	49	50

Write about how you know when a number is odd or even.

We learned about odd and even numbers. Have your child name two odd numbers and two even numbers.

Name ___

Midchapter Review

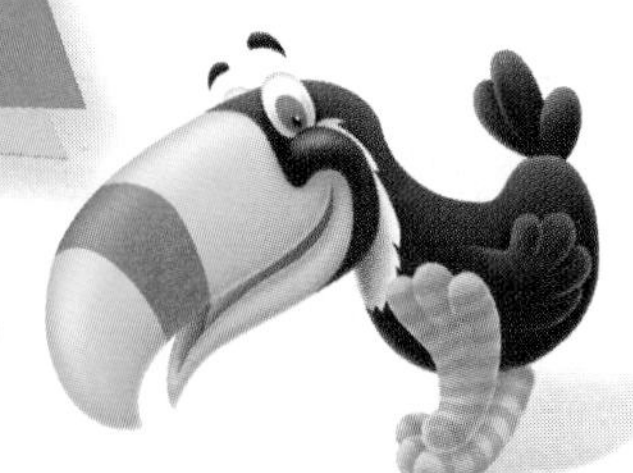

Write how many tens and ones.
Write the number.

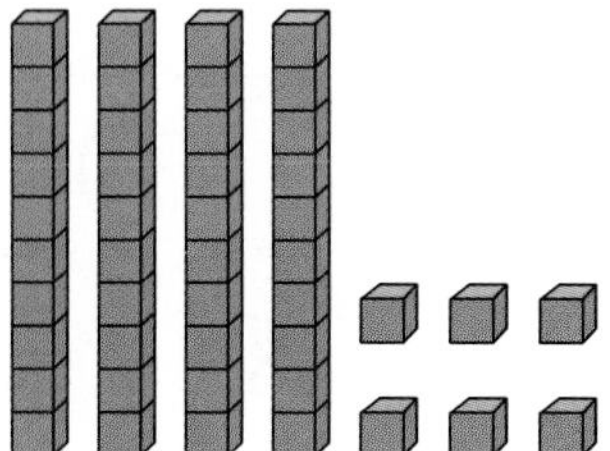

___ tens ___ ones

___

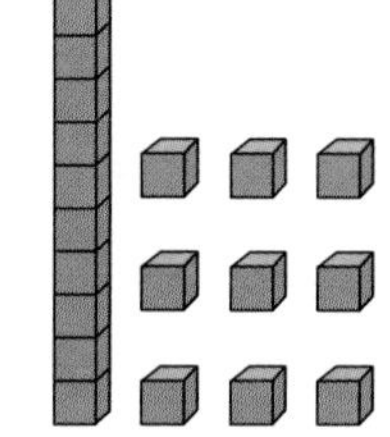

___ tens ___ ones

___

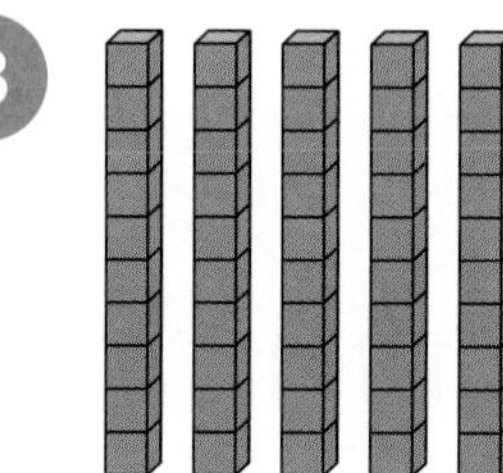

___ tens ___ ones

___

Write the number just before, between, or just after.

 ___, 30

 87, ___, 89

 74, ___

Skip-count. Write the numbers.

7. 10, 20, 30, ___, ___, ___, ___, ___

8. 30, 35, 40, ___, ___, ___, ___, ___

9. 66, 68, 70, ___, ___, ___, ___, ___

10. Is the number 5 even or odd? How can you tell?

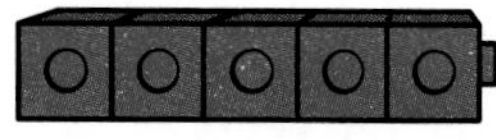

___

Write about skip-counting by tens, fives, and twos. Tell why you count this way.

Extra Practice

Game!

Count on the Bees

1	2	3	4	5	6	7	8	9	10
11	12	13	14	15	16	17	18	19	20
21	22	23	24	25	26	27	28	29	30
31	32	33	34	35	36	37	38	39	40
41	42	43	44	45	46	47	48	49	50
51	52	53	54	55	56	57	58	59	60
61	62	63	64	65	66	67	68	69	70
71	72	73	74	75	76	77	78	79	80
81	82	83	84	85	86	87	88	89	90
91	92	93	94	95	96	97	98	99	100

You and your partner need 5 .

PATTERNS Take turns.

- Look for a skip-counting pattern.
- Cover 5 numbers in the pattern.
- Your partner says the hidden numbers.
- Color 1 point for saying the pattern.

Points	1	2	3	4	5
Player 1					
Player 2					

Play until you reach 5 points.

Real-Life Investigation
Applying Numbers

Name

Backyard Bugs

Bugs, insects, and other creatures live everywhere. Some are easy to see. Some hide.

Cultural Note

Harvester ants store seeds in their nests. The Tuareg people of the Sahara Desert collect the ants' seeds.

Where could you find bugs, insects, and other creatures living in your backyard?

Working Together

- You and a partner need gloves, cups, some paper, and a pencil.
- Find a place to look for bugs, insects, and other creatures.
- Draw a picture of each kind of living thing you find.
- Keep a tally of how many of each living thing you find.
- Find the total for each living thing.

Decision Making

1. Decide how to show what you found. You can make a picture, a graph, or another kind of display.

2. How many bugs, insects, and other creatures did you find in all? ______________

3. Would you find the same living things three months from now? ______________

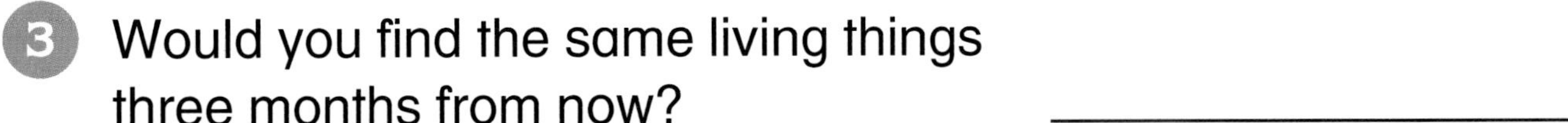

4. How might the numbers of living things change?

   Explain. ______________________________________

   ____

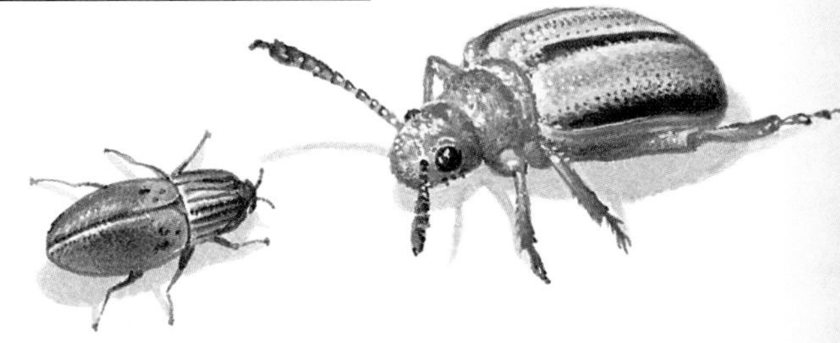

Write a report.

5. Tell what you learned about the numbers of living things you found.

6. Tell how you decided to show what you found.

More to Investigate

PREDICT Will the numbers or kinds of living things be different someplace else?

EXPLORE Look in another place. Record the new information.

FIND Find a library book about insects. Share what you learn with the class.

Greater and Less

Name ______________________

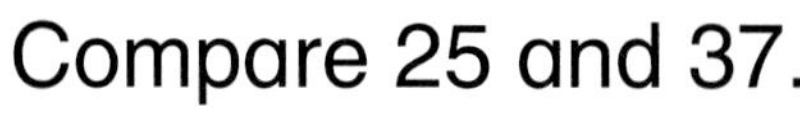

Compare 25 and 37.

I compare the tens to see which number is greater.

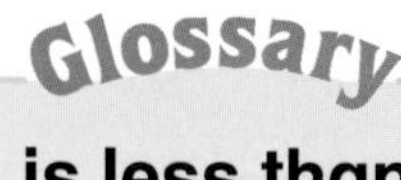

Glossary
is less than
is greater than

25 **is less than** 37. 37 **is greater than** 25.

How would you compare 25 and 27?

Working Together

You and your partner need 18 tens and 18 ones.

- You show one number with models.
- Your partner shows the other number.
- Compare.

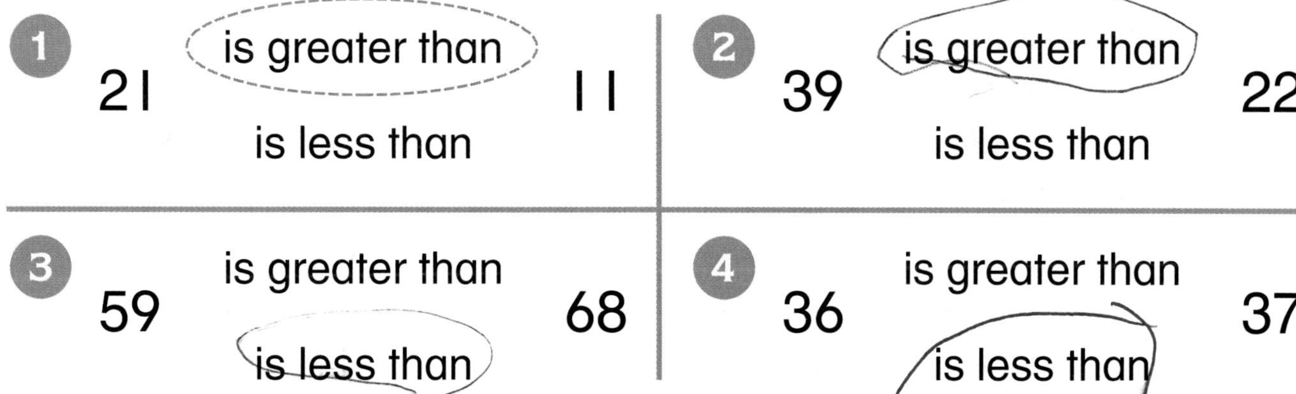

1	21	is greater than / is less than	11	2	39	is greater than / is less than	22
3	59	is greater than / is less than	68	4	36	is greater than / is less than	37

How would you compare 47 and 43 without models?

Compare.

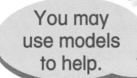

1 11	is greater than / is less than 21	2 41	is greater than / is less than 40
3 85	is greater than / is less than 25	4 53	is greater than / is less than 62
5 94	is greater than / is less than 98	6 92	is greater than / is less than 76

More to Explore Estimation

Choose the estimate you think is best.

The number of cars in a large parking lot.

greater than 100

less than 100

The number of books in a library.

greater than 100

less than 100

The number of children in your class.

greater than 100

less than 100

The number of pencils that you have.

greater than 25

less than 25

We compared numbers to 100. Ask your child to tell whether 45 is greater than or less than 29.

Name ______________________

Compare Numbers

Ernesto gathered 46 acorns and 64 pine cones. Which did he gather more of?

Compare 46 and 64 and find out.

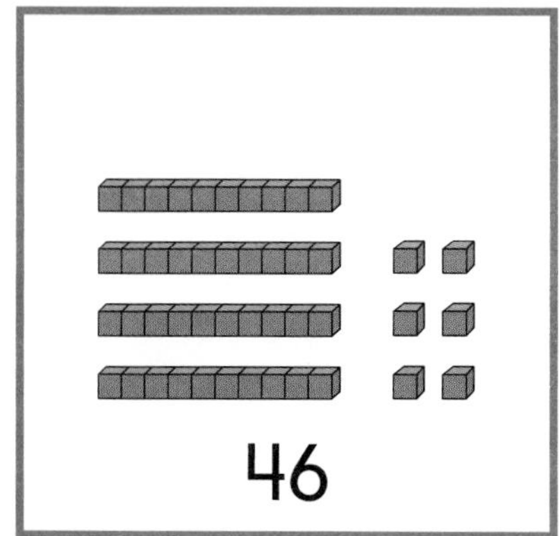

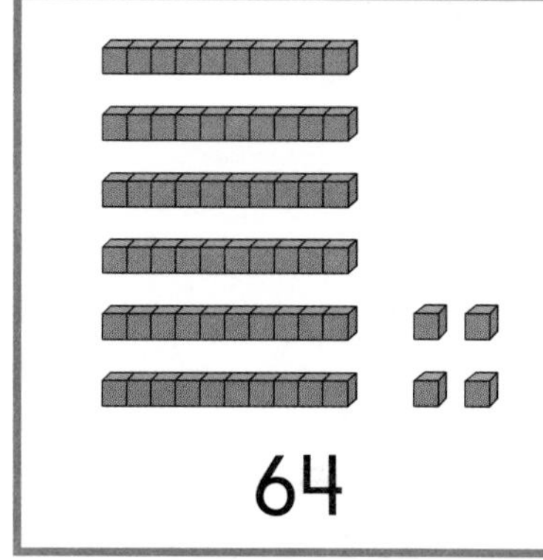

46 < 64

64 > 46

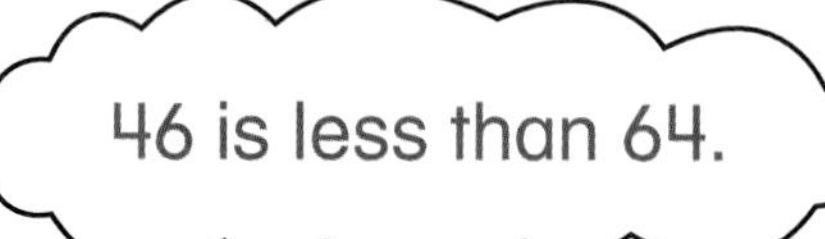

64 is greater than 46.

Ernesto gathered more pine cones than acorns.

Compare. Write > for *is greater than*.
Write < for *is less than*.
Write = for *is equal to*.

Use models to help.

1. 37 (<) 39 58 ◯ 43 80 ◯ 77

2. 25 ◯ 5 63 ◯ 63 39 ◯ 40

3. 66 ◯ 63 12 ◯ 21 58 ◯ 58

How would you compare 4 tens 6 ones and 46 ones?
How would you compare 14, 41, and 44?
Which number is greatest? Which is least?

Practice!

Compare.
Write > or <.

<
is less than

1 9 (>) 2 0 ◯ 3 12 ◯ 18

 42 ◯ 45 90 ◯ 97 71 ◯ 68

 27 ◯ 20 6 ◯ 13 54 ◯ 49

 15 ◯ 25 79 ◯ 69 55 ◯ 71

 87 ◯ 86 24 ◯ 34 98 ◯ 89

 46 ◯ 51 8 ◯ 18 34 ◯ 43

Mixed Review Test Preparation

17	13	16	18	11	14
− 8	− 5	− 7	− 9	− 4	− 8

8 Write the subtraction fact. ______________

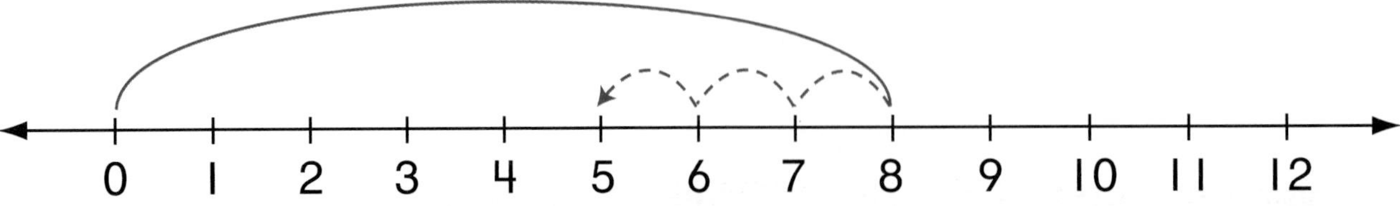

We used the symbols > and < to compare numbers to 100. Have your child tell you which number is greater: 22 or 12.

Name ______________________

The Greater Number Wins

You and your partner need cards for 1 to 100.

- Each player gets 50 cards.
- Turn over your top card. The player with the greater number takes both cards.
- Place winning pairs in your box below. Continue until the last card is played.

Winner: the player with more cards

Play again.

This time, the player with the lesser number takes both cards.

Winner: the player with more cards

Color even numbers orange.

Color odd numbers black.

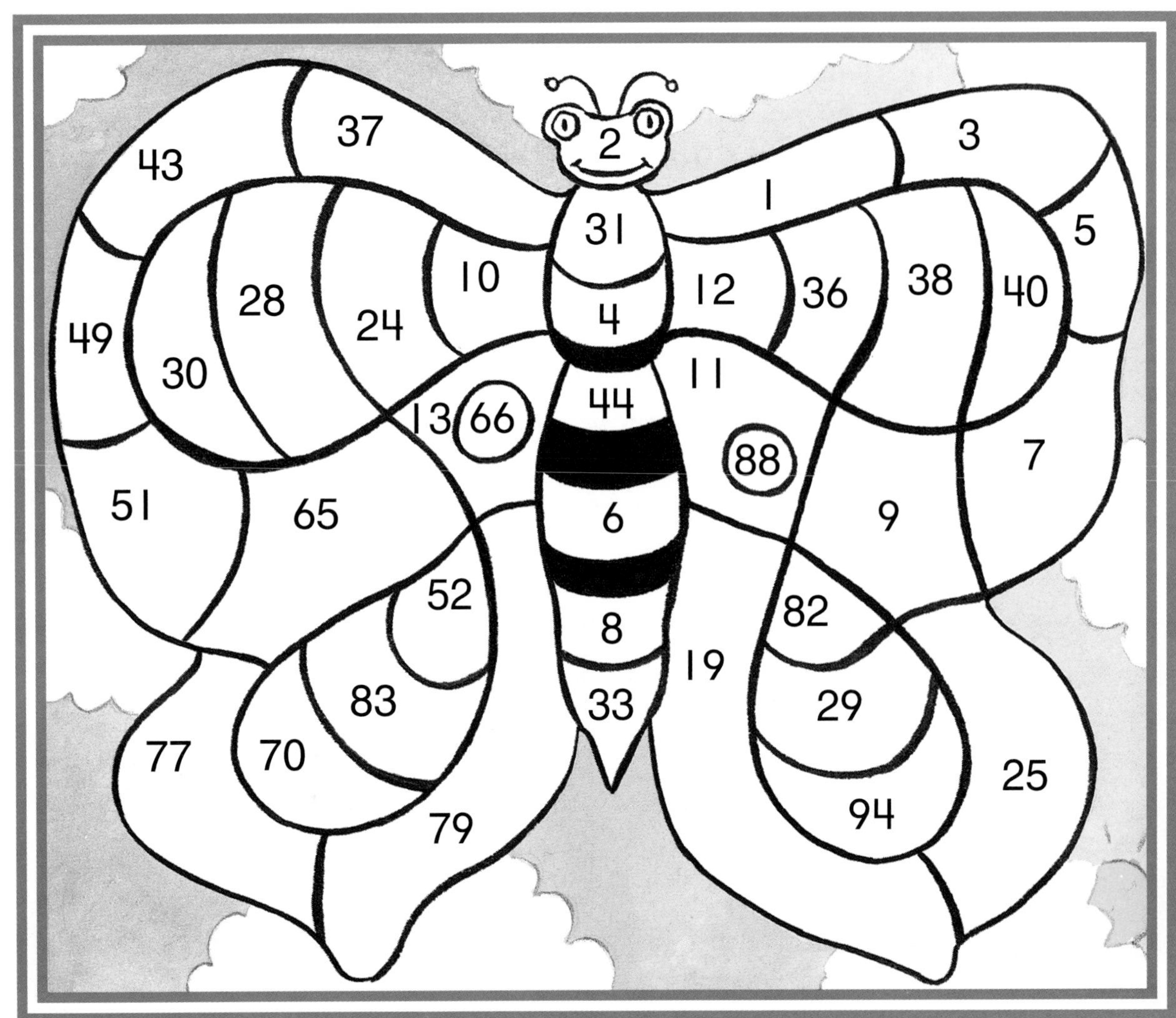

Compare. Write > for *is greater than*.
Write < for *is less than*.

2 83 ◯ 79   38 ◯ 41   60 ◯ 65

3 92 ◯ 99   18 ◯ 8   74 ◯ 82

4 27 ◯ 28   10 ◯ 11   43 ◯ 34

5 16 ◯ 17   22 ◯ 12   74 ◯ 75

6 4 ◯ 44   65 ◯ 55   81 ◯ 80

Name

Use Logical Reasoning

Which one is the centipede?
The number of its legs has 2 ones.
The tens digit is an odd number between 1 and 4.

Plan Can you add or subtract to find the answer? No

What is a 2-digit number with 2 ones?

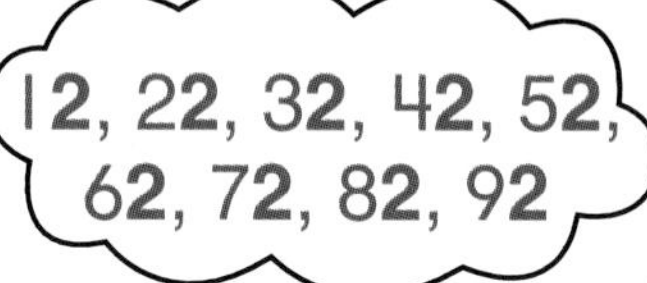

12, 22, 32, 42, 52, 62, 72, 82, 92

Which numbers have a tens digit between 1 and 4? 22, 32

Which tens digit is odd?

Look Back The centipede is the one with 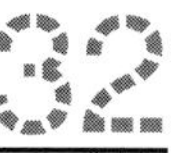 32 legs.

Solve.

1. Which one is the millipede?
The number of its legs has 6 in the tens digit. ______________________

The ones digit is just before 7. ____

The millipede is the one with ____ legs.

2. Which one is the sow bug?
The number of its legs is between 16 and 20. ______________________

The ones digit is even. ____

The sow bug is the one with ____ legs.

Practice!

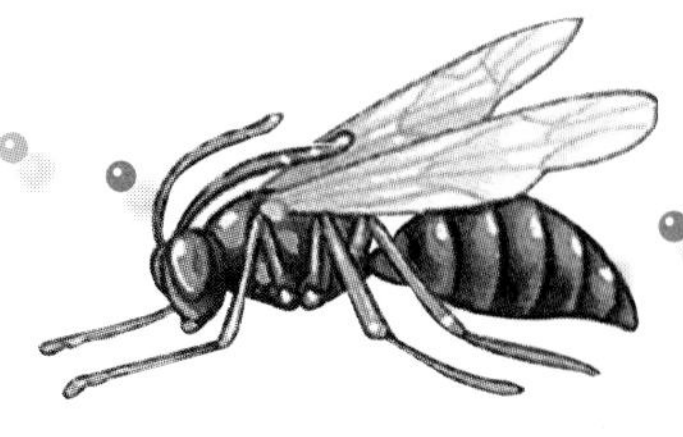

Solve.

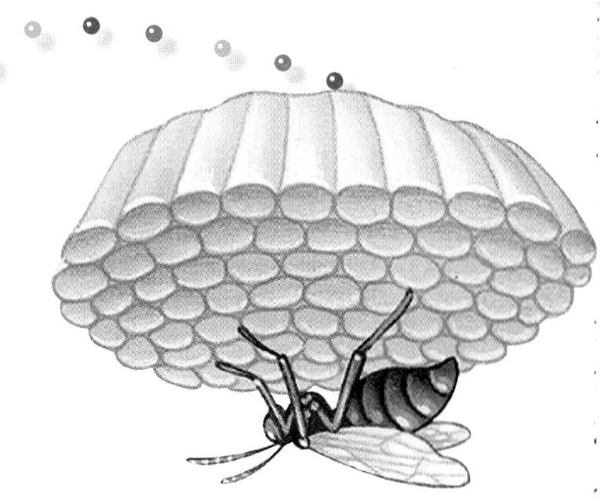

1. How many eggs are in the nest?
   The number of eggs is greater than 70.
   The number is less than 80.
   The tens and ones digits are the same.

   ____ eggs

---

2. How many caterpillars are in the "tent"?
   The number has 5 tens.
   The ones digit is greater than 3.
   The number is less than 55.

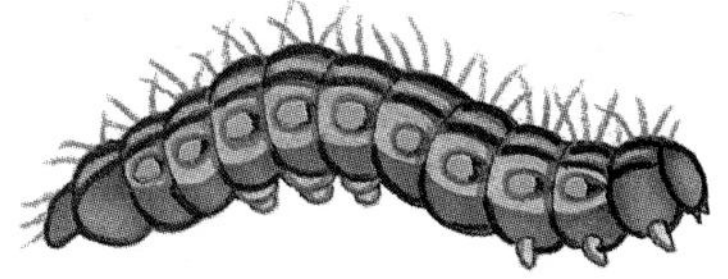
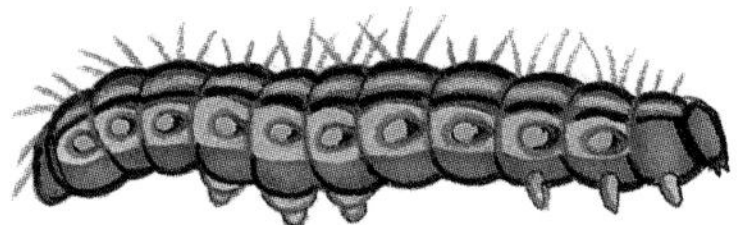

   ____ caterpillars

---

3. How many ants are under the rock?
   The number is between 33 and 46.
   The ones digit is greater than the tens digit.
   There are 4 tens in the number.

   ____ ants

---

4. Write your own problem about critters.
   Give it to a partner to solve.

   ____

   ____

   ____

At Home We used reasoning to solve puzzle problems. Ask your child how to solve the problem he or she wrote.

Name

Working Together

You will need a ▣, a ▣, and a ▣.

Find out which bird your class likes best.

Listen to the names of the birds.

1. Give your teacher the cube whose color is the same as the bird you like best.
2. Count. Write the total number of votes for each bird.

Cardinal

Goldfinch

Blue Jay

3. Use the totals to complete the **bar graph**. Color one space to show each vote.

Glossary

bar graph

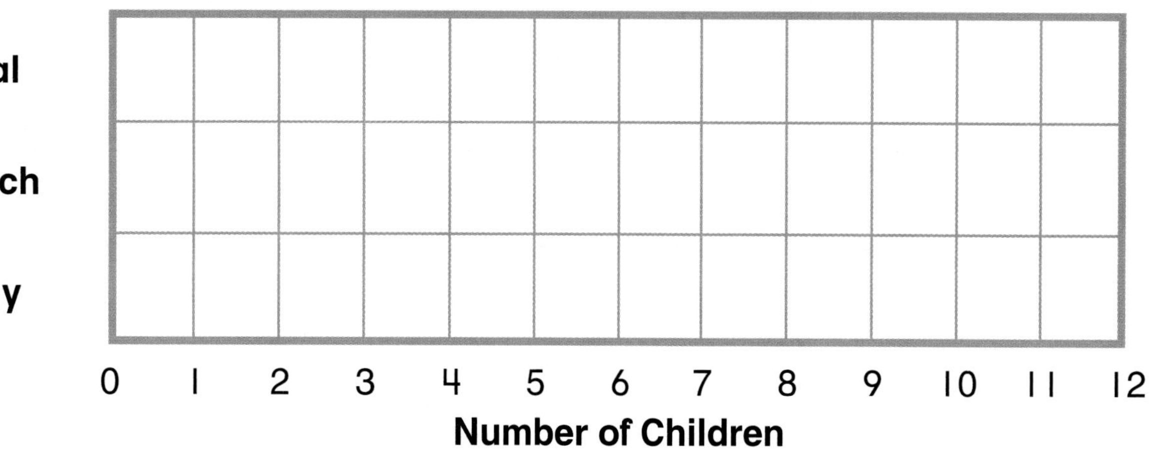

OUR FAVORITE BIRD

Cardinal												
Goldfinch												
Blue Jay												

0 1 2 3 4 5 6 7 8 9 10 11 12

Number of Children

Practice!

Mira counted how many times she saw robins at her feeder.
Here are the totals for each season.

Robins seen	
winter:	1
spring:	12
summer:	10
fall:	4

1. Use the totals to complete the bar graph.

ROBINS SEEN AT MIRA'S FEEDER

Winter
Spring
Summer
Fall

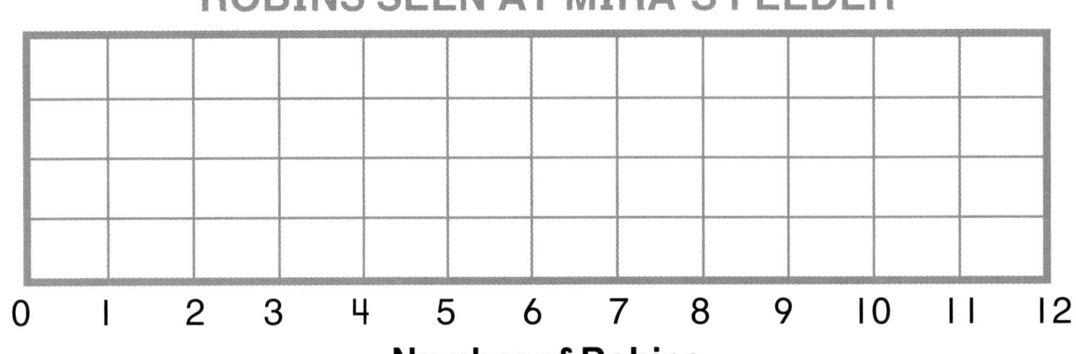

Number of Robins

Use the graph to answer these questions.

2. When were the most robins seen? ____________________

3. When were the fewest robins seen? ____________________

4. How many more robins were seen in summer than in fall? ____

5. How many robins were seen altogether? ____

Graph

Use your lists from *The Icky Bug Counting Book.* Choose three kinds of bugs. Make a bar graph about them.

Write a question about your graph. Have a partner answer it.

At Home: Ask your child to explain how to tell how many robins were seen in the spring.

Name

Working Together

Which insect does your class like most? Survey your class to find out.

Glossary
tally mark (|)
pictograph

1. Record each vote with a **tally mark** (|).

Firefly	Bee

Butterfly	Grasshopper	Other

2. Use your data to make a **pictograph**.
Draw one ☺ for each vote.

OUR FAVORITE INSECT	
Firefly	
Bee	
Butterfly	
Grasshopper	
Other	

Each ☺ stands for 1 vote.

Why is it important to line up the pictures in a pictograph?

Practice!

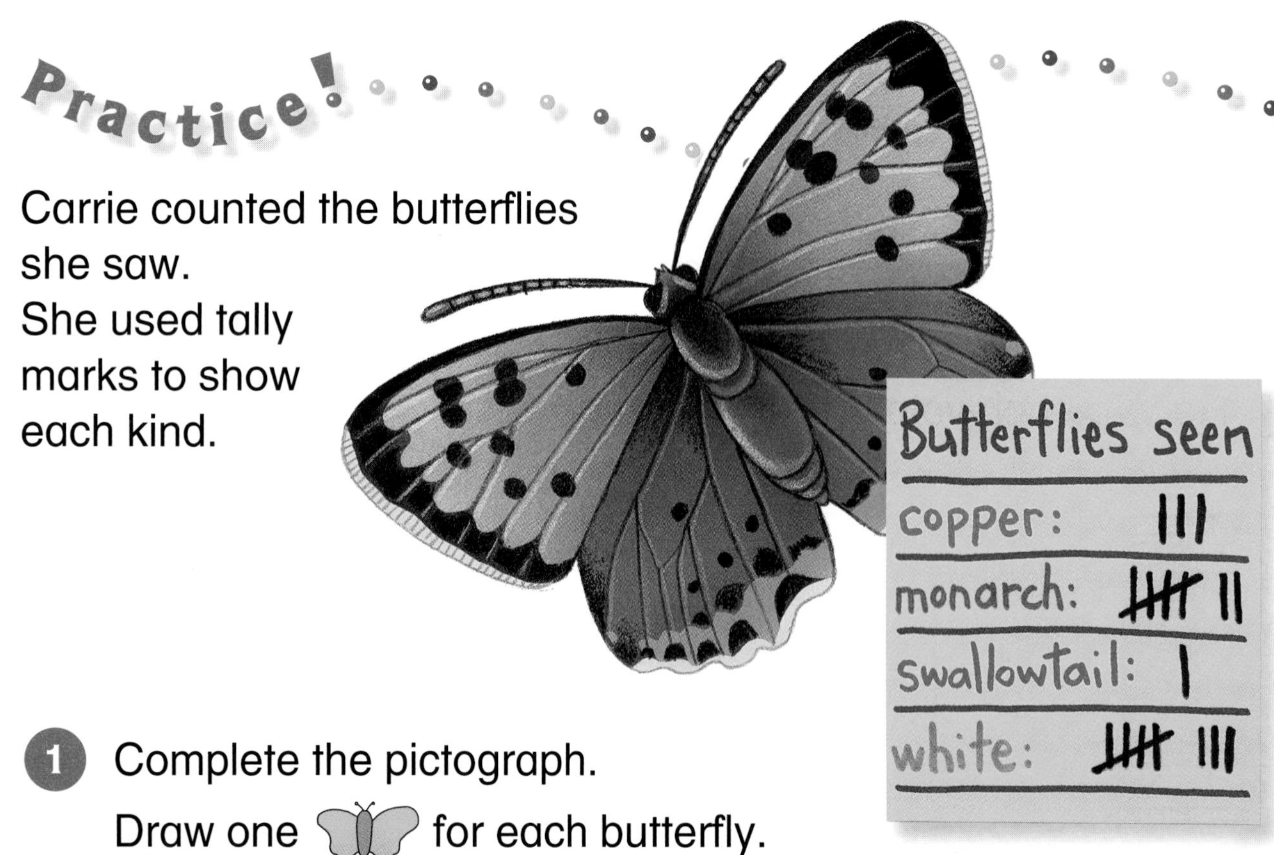

Carrie counted the butterflies she saw. She used tally marks to show each kind.

1. Complete the pictograph. Draw one butterfly for each butterfly.

BUTTERFLIES CARRIE SAW	
Copper	(3 drawn)
Monarch	(7 drawn)
Swallowtail	(1 drawn)
White	(8 drawn)

Each butterfly stands for 1 butterfly.

Use the graph to answer these questions.

2. Which butterfly did Carrie see most? While
3. How many monarchs did she see? 7
4. How many more whites than coppers did she see? 5
5. What was the fewest number of butterflies seen? 1

At Home: Your child took a survey and put the data on a graph. Have your child explain the graph on page 119.

Name ______________________

Use Pictographs

Ely's school sold flower bulbs to raise money. Help Ely make a graph to show the sales.

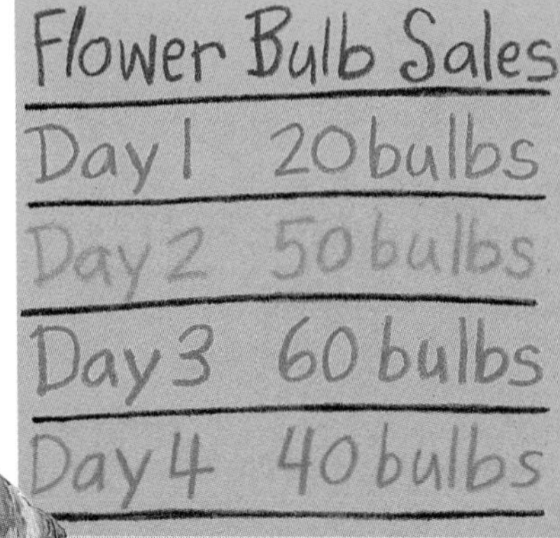

Flower Bulb Sales
Day 1 20 bulbs
Day 2 50 bulbs
Day 3 60 bulbs
Day 4 40 bulbs

How could you show so many bulbs on a graph?

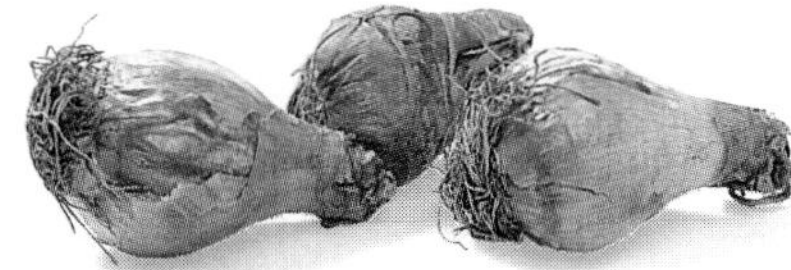

Glossary
key

1. Decide how many bulbs you will show for each picture in the **key**. Complete the pictograph.

FLOWER BULB SALES	
Day 1	
Day 2	
Day 3	
Day 4	

Each stands for ____ flower bulbs.

2. Complete the key to tell how many bulbs each picture means.

3. How did you show 40 bulbs?

____

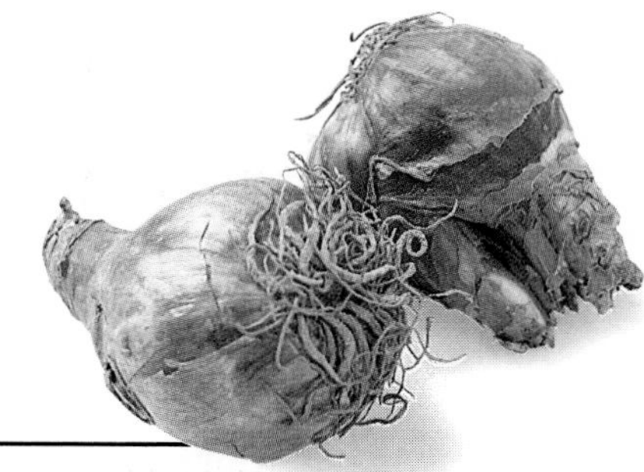

4. *Algebra* **PATTERNS** How did you use patterns as you drew pictures for 40 bulbs?

____

Practice!

Here are the kinds of flower bulbs that were sold.

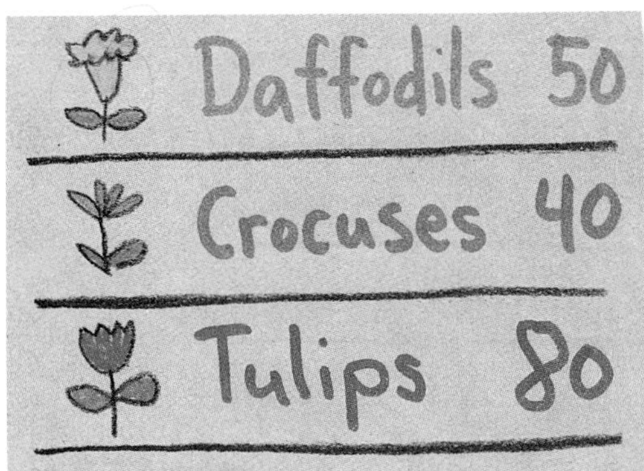

1. Decide on a title for the graph. Complete the pictograph.

______________________	
Daffodils	500

Each  stands for 10 bulbs.

2. How many bulbs does each picture stand for? ____ bulbs

3. How many pictures would you draw to stand for 80 tulips? 8

4. How many more tulips than crocuses were sold? 4

Write about how to make a pictograph.

At Home Your child learned about using a key on a graph. Ask your child to explain the key for the pictograph on this page.

Name

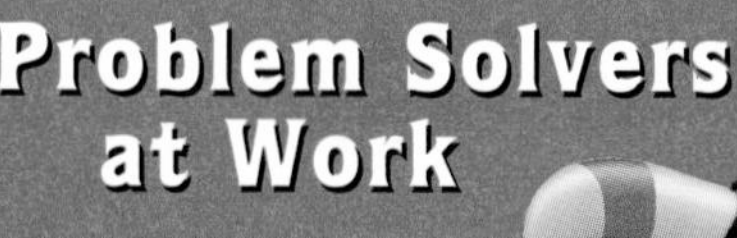

Read
Plan
Solve
Look Back

Use a Graph

Children at the Pleasant Valley School planted trees for Arbor Day.

The pictograph shows what they planted.

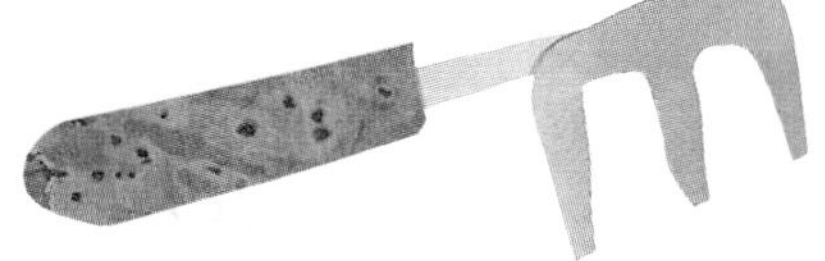

TREES PLANTED FOR ARBOR DAY	
Locust	🌳🌳🌳🌳
Oak	🌳🌳🌳🌳🌳🌳🌳🌳🌳
Maple	🌳🌳🌳🌳🌳🌳
Pine	🌳🌳🌳

Each  stands for 1 tree.

Solve.

1. How many more oak trees than locust trees were planted? 5

2. How many maple trees and pine trees were planted altogether? 9

3. 

Graph Use your list of bugs. Choose three kinds. Make a pictograph to show them.

Practice!

This pictograph shows how many children planted trees on Arbor Day.

CHILDREN WHO PLANTED TREES	
Grade 1	🧍 🧍
Grade 2	🧍 🧍 🧍 🧍
Grade 3	🧍 🧍 🧍

Each 🧍 stands for 5 children.

Solve.

1. How many more grade 2 children planted trees than grade 1 children? 10 children

2. What if 20 grade 4 children helped plant trees. Would there be more grade 4 children or grade 2 children? eqaal

Write and Share

Michael wrote this problem.

How many children planted trees in grades 1, 2, and 3?

Michael Hughes
Snowden School
Memphis, Tennessee

3. Solve Michael's problem. 45
What strategy did you use?
Skip5

4. Write a problem using information from the graph. Have a partner solve it.

Use your own paper.

At Home We used a graph to solve problems. Talk with your child about how to solve the problem that he or she wrote.

Name ____________________

Chapter Review

Language and Mathematics

Choose the correct word to complete the sentence.

even
digit
odd
before

1. The ______ 2 means 20 in the number 23.
2. 2, 4, and 6 are ______ numbers.

Concepts and Skills

Write the number.

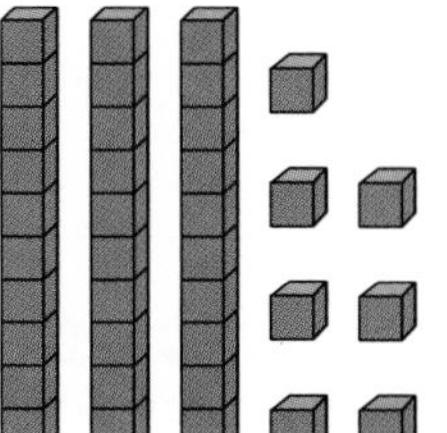

______ tens ______ ones

4. 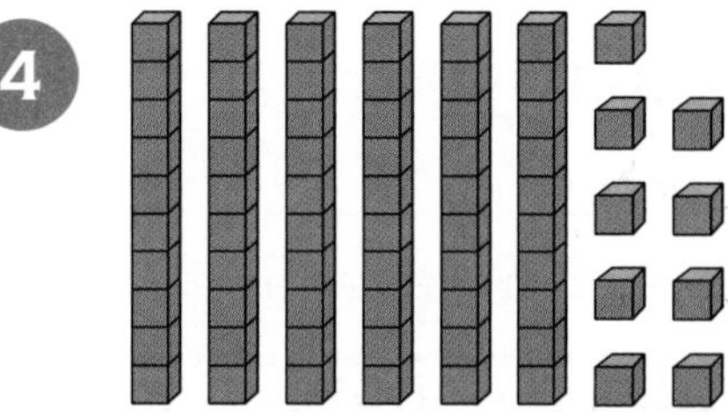

______ tens ______ ones

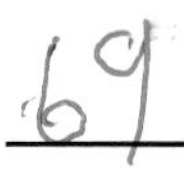

5. eighty ______

Write the number just before, between, or just after.

 , 96  59, ______  19, ______, 21

Skip-count. Write the numbers.

9. 60, 65, 70, , 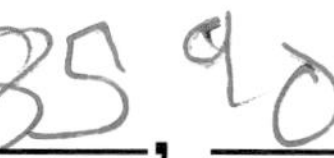, ______, ______, ______, ______

Write *odd* or *even* for each number.

10. 12 ______
11. 7 
12. 21 

Compare. Write > for *is greater than*.
Write < for *is less than*.

13. 78 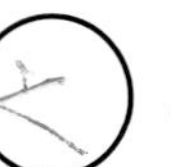 81
14. 39 ◯ 29
15. 58  85

Problem Solving

16 How many acorns are there?
The number is odd.
The tens digit is 2.
The ones digit is less than 3.

21

17 How many seeds are there?
The ones digit is 5.
The tens digit is between 3 and 6.
The number is greater than 45.

55

Use the graph to answer these questions.

SEEDS IN FRUIT	
Cherry	
Lemon	
Melon	

Each stands for 1 seed.

18 How many seeds are in the lemon? ____

19 How many seeds would be in 10 cherries? ____

20 Which fruit has the most seeds? ____________

What Do You Think?

What do you like most about graphing?
☑ Check one.

☐ Bar graphs ☐ Pictographs ☐ Tally marks

Why? ______________________________

Is 59 greater than or less than 63?
Draw or write to explain.

Name Gagan F.B 6-26-07

Chapter Test

Write the number.

1 

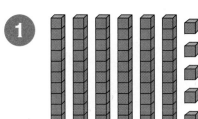

65

Write the missing number.

2 54, 55, 56

Skip-count. Write the numbers.

3 26, 28, 30, 32, 34, 36, 38, 40, 42

Write *odd* or *even* for the number.

4 18 even

5 23 odd

Compare. Write < for *is less than*.
Write > for *is greater than*.

6 56 < 72

7 45 > 41

Use the graph to answer these questions.

8 Are there more elm trees or maple trees?

maple trees

9 How many trees are there in all?

10 trees

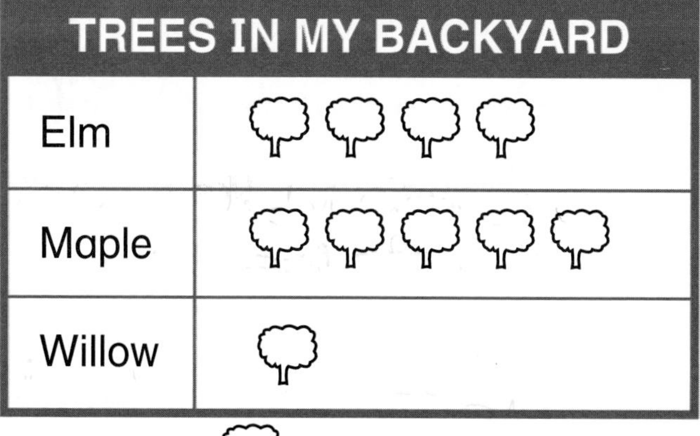

Each [tree] stands for 1 tree.

Solve.

10 How many bugs are there? The number is even. The tens digit is 3. The ones digit is between 0 and 4. How many bugs?

34 bugs

Performance Assessment

What Did You Learn?

Work with a partner.

- Put some ▭ and ▫ in a bag.

- Pick some ▭ and ▫ from the bag.
- Color to show what you picked.
  Write the number.

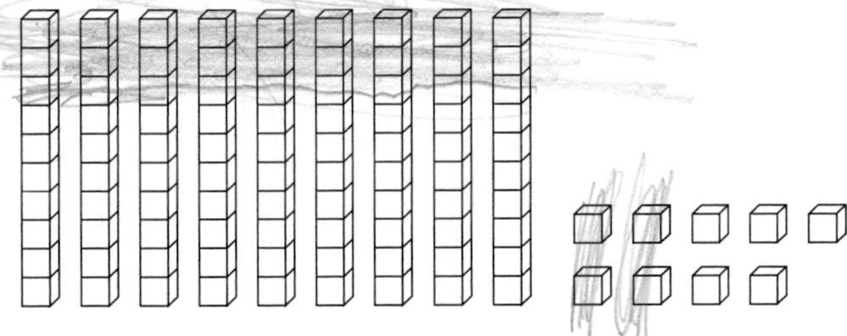

34

- Color to show what your partner picked.
  Write the number.

104

- Compare the numbers that you and your partner picked. Write about comparing numbers.

34 < 104.

You may want to put this page in your portfolio.

Math Connection
Patterns and Functions

Name

Cubes and Numbers

a Algebra **PATTERNS** Continue the pattern. Use ▢. Then write the pattern with numbers.

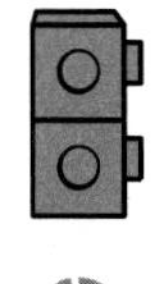

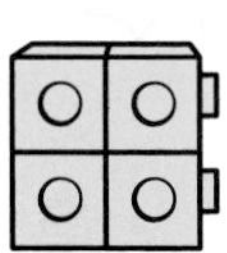
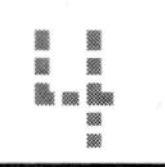

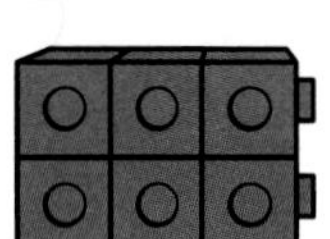

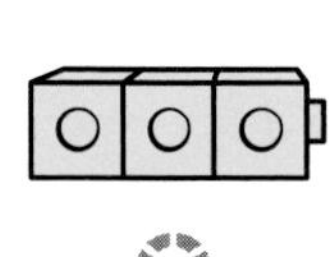
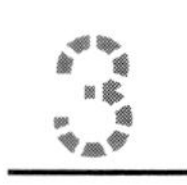

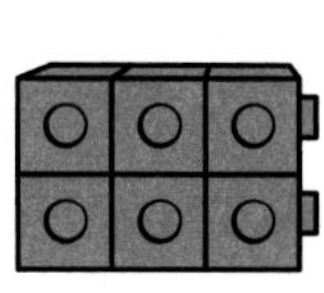

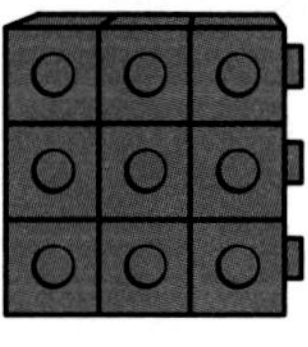

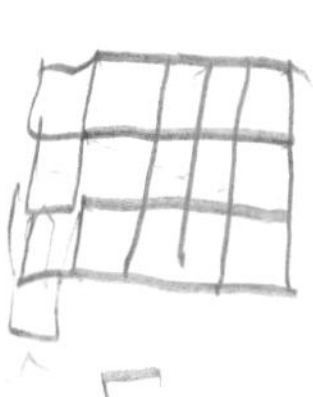

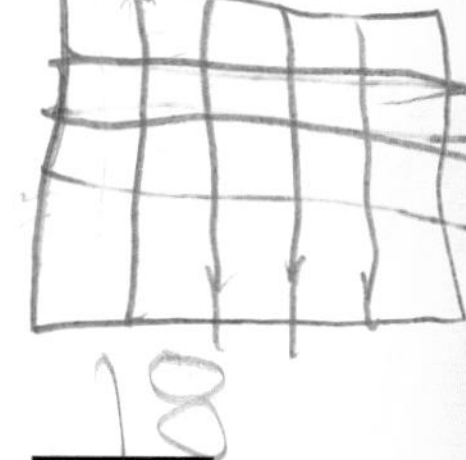

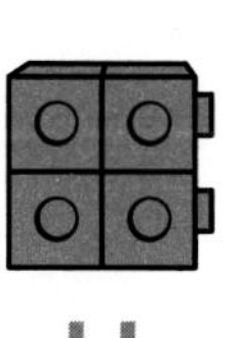
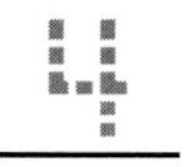

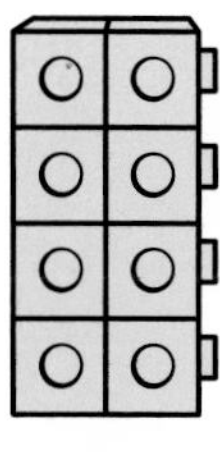

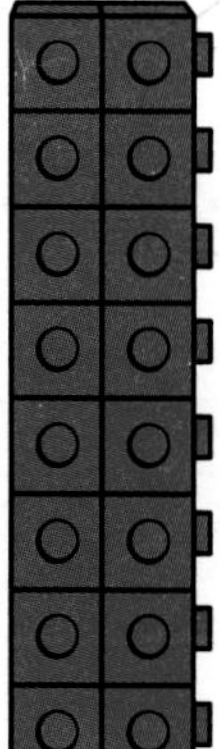

____ ____

How is the last pattern different from the others?

Estimation

This is what it looks like to find 50 bugs under a leaf!

How many bugs are under each leaf?
Choose your estimate.
Then count and write the total.

50 bugs

1

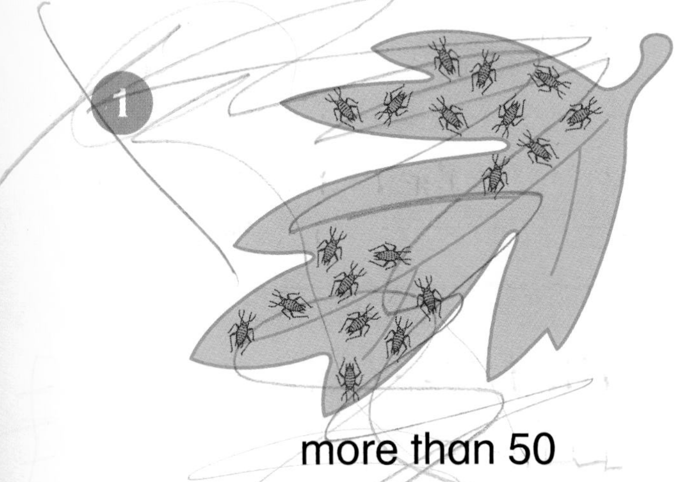

more than 50

less than 50

Total: ____________

2

more than 50

less than 50

Total: 65

3

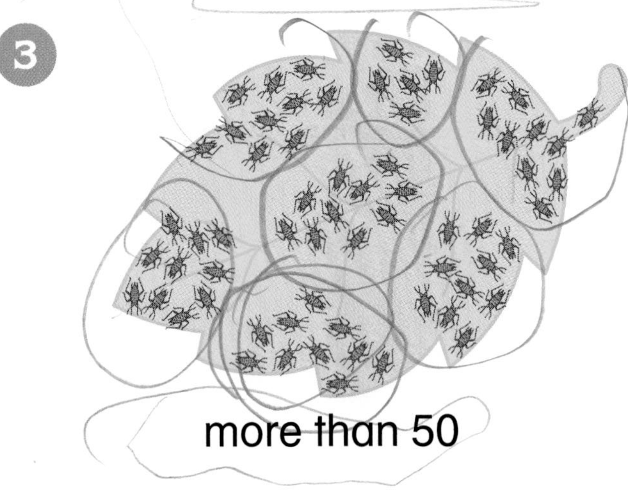

more than 50

less than 50

Total: 70

4

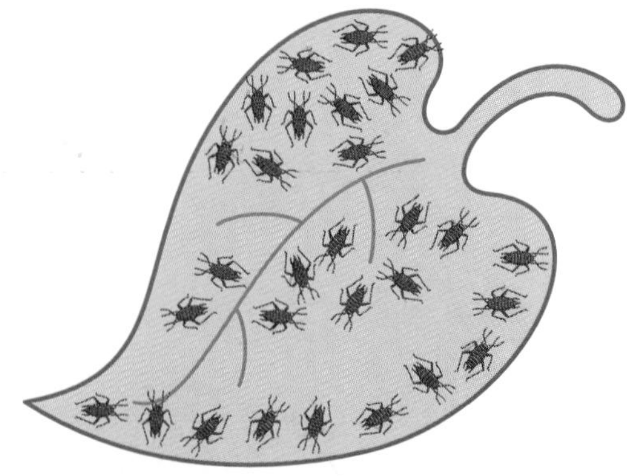

more than 50

less than 50

Total: 32

Name

Cumulative Review

Read each question and choose the best answer.

1

$$\begin{array}{r} 9 \\ +\ 5 \\ \hline \end{array}$$

- ○ 4
- ○ 13
- ○ 14
- ○ 15

2 Find the number that means 9 tens 6 ones.

- ○ 68
- ○ 80
- ○ 81
- ○ 96

3 Find the group that shows even numbers.

○	1	3	5	7
○	2	4	6	8
○	4	5	6	8
○	10	12	14	15

4

$$\begin{array}{r} 13 \\ -\ 6 \\ \hline \end{array}$$

- ○ 19
- ○ 8
- ○ 7
- ○ 5

5 What is the missing number in the number pattern?

10, 15, 20, ☐

- ○ 25
- ○ 15
- ○ 10
- ○ 5

6 What is the missing number in the number pattern?

☐, 50, 51

- ○ 52
- ○ 48
- ○ 49
- ○ 32

TEST PREPARATION

7 There were 15 birds flying. 9 landed. How many are still flying?

- ⬭ 15
- ⬭ 9
- ⬭ 7
- ⬭ 6

8 The number is odd. The tens digit is between 3 and 5. What is the number?

- ⬭ 24
- ⬭ 31
- ⬭ 45
- ⬭ 46

9 The graph shows our favorite drinks.

How many people like milk and juice?

- ⬭ 4
- ⬭ 6
- ⬭ 9
- ⬭ 10

10 Bob has 8 big bugs and 6 small bugs. Which shows how many bugs Bob has in all?

- ⬭ $8 - 6 = 2$
- ⬭ $8 + 6 = 14$
- ⬭ $8 - 8 = 0$
- ⬭ $6 - 6 = 0$

11 Ani saw 5 birds and 3 flies. Which did she see more of?

- ⬭ birds
- ⬭ flies
- ⬭ bugs
- ⬭ frogs

12 The graph shows how many bugs were found.

Bugs Found	
Ants	🐞🐞🐞🐞🐞🐞🐞🐞
Bees	🐞🐞🐞🐞

Each 🐞 stands for 1 bug.

How many more ants than bees were found?

- ⬭ 2
- ⬭ 4
- ⬭ 6
- ⬭ 8

Chapter 3 Wrap-Up

Name ____________________

Estimate, Count, Graph!

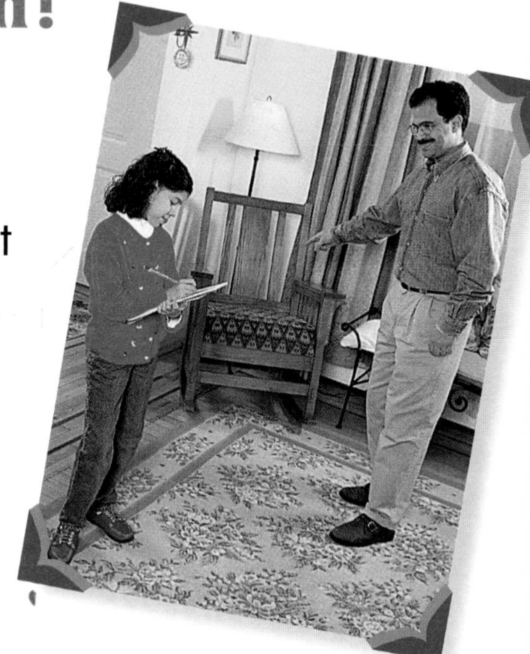

DIRECTIONS Ask your child to estimate the number of each of the pictured objects in your home. Then count and record how many of each. Compare. Talk about the estimates and the counts.

Estimate: 12 **windows**	**Estimate:** 8 **doors**	**Estimate:** 9 **chairs**
Count: 10 **windows**	**Count:** 16 **doors**	**Count:** 9 **chairs**

Show the counts on the graph.
Color the boxes.

OUR HOME COUNT

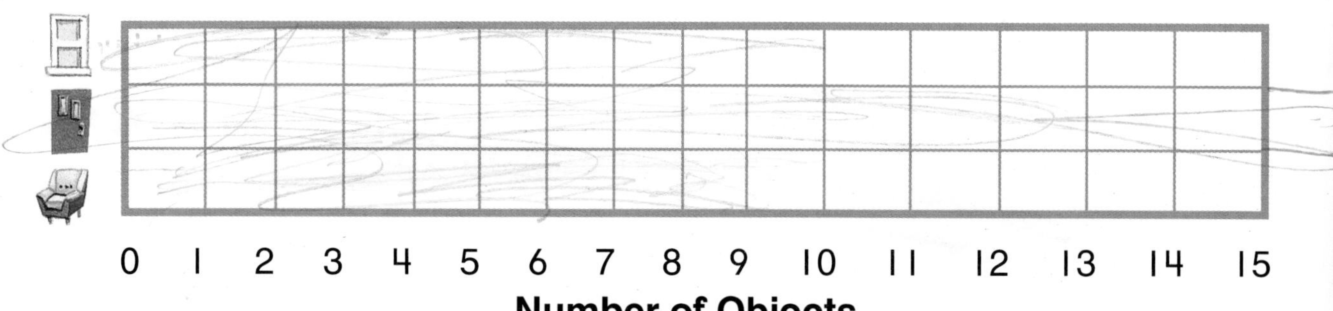

Your child has been learning about numbers to 100 and graphing. This activity will reinforce these skills and also develop estimating skills. You may extend the activity by asking questions about information shown in the graph.

Dear Family,

I am beginning a new chapter in mathematics. During the next few weeks I will be learning about coins and bills and their value.

I will also be talking about saving and spending money.

Learning About Saving and Spending

Let's talk about things we can save for. We can make a list of different things.

My Math Words

I am going to use these math words in this chapter.

Please help me make word cards so I can practice the math words in this chapter. I can use the cards to learn about coins and their value.

- dime
- nickel
- penny
- quarter
- half dollar
- guess and test
- dollar
- change
- most likely
- less likely

Your child,

____

Signature

Money

Theme: Saving and Spending

CHAPTER 4

Steps in a Process After you listen to *A Chair for My Mother,* write a sentence that tells why the people in the story saved coins.

Listen to the story.

How did Mama get a new chair? What did she do first? What did she do next?

Name

What Do You Know?

Count the money.

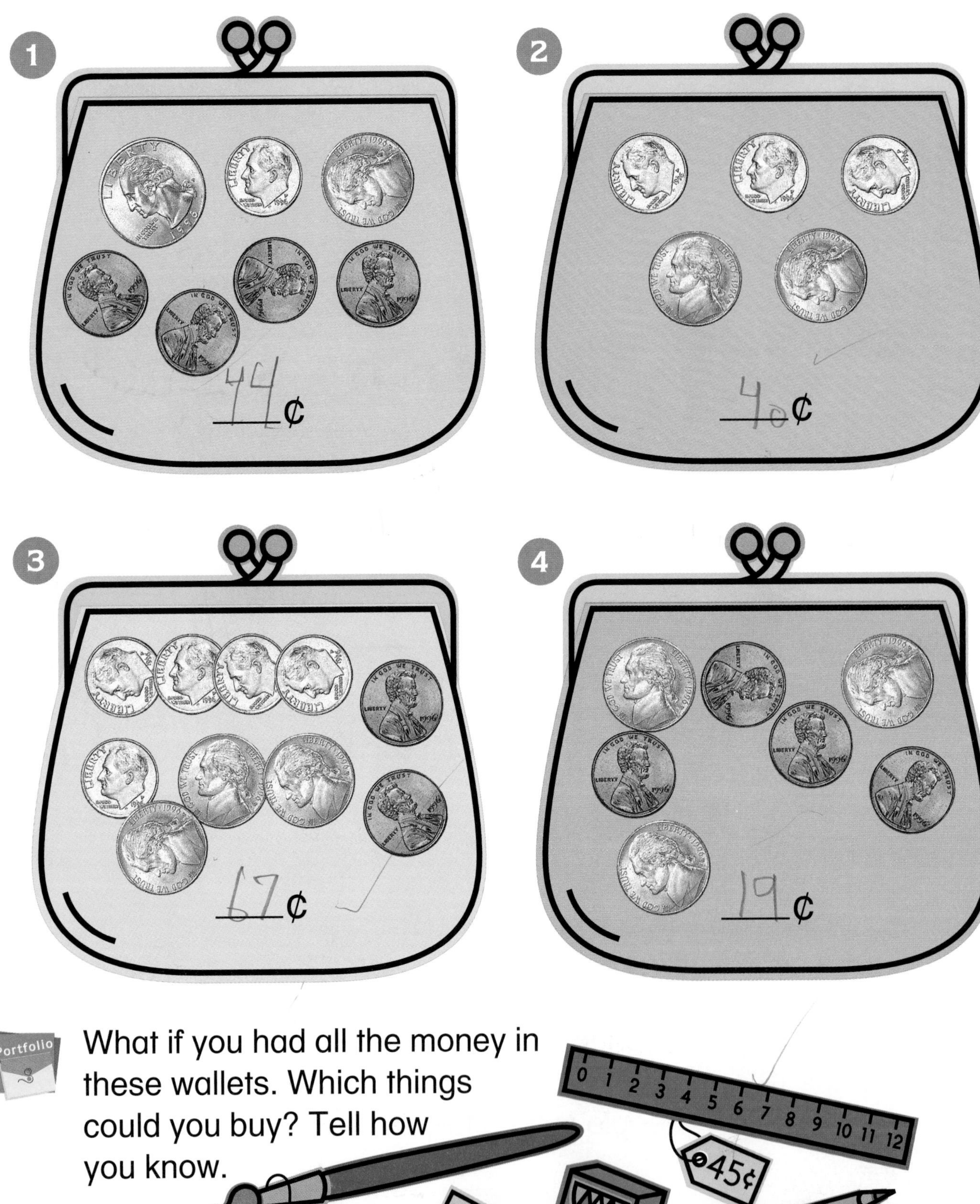

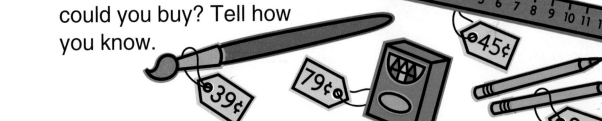

Portfolio

What if you had all the money in these wallets. Which things could you buy? Tell how you know.

45¢
79¢
39¢
24¢

Name

Pennies, Nickels, Dimes

Count the money.

dime	nickel	penny	
10¢	5¢	1¢	16¢
10¢	15¢	16¢	

Glossary
dime
nickel
penny

Working Together

You and your partner need 10 pennies, 10 nickels, and 5 dimes.

Count dimes by tens.
Count nickels by fives.

Take turns.

- Pick up a handful of coins.
- Write how many of each coin.
- Your partner writes how much money.
- Return the coins to the pile.

1. 1 dimes 2 nickels 3 pennies 23¢
2. 2 dimes 1 nickels 0 pennies 25¢
3. 3 dimes 4 nickels 1 pennies 51¢
4. 4 dimes 1 nickels 3 pennies 48¢

Talk Tell your partner how you count coins.

Practice!

Count. Write how much money.

40¢ 45¢ 50¢ 55¢ 56¢ 57¢ 58¢

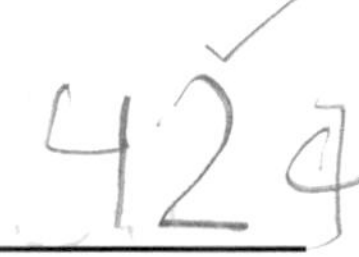

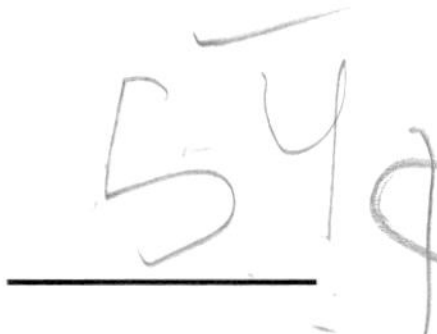

Cultural Connection

Moroccan Coins

In Morocco coins are called dirham and centimes.
100 centimes = 1 dirham
Count. Write how many dirham.

____ centimes ____ centimes ____ dirham

We are learning to count money. Ask your child to count the sets of coins on this page.

Name ______________________

Explore Activity

Quarters

 or 

quarter
25¢

Glossary
quarter

Working Together

You and your partner need a ,
, and 20 .

Take turns.

- Toss the cube.
- Put that much money on your money sorter.
- Trade coins when you can.

Play until someone can trade for a quarter.

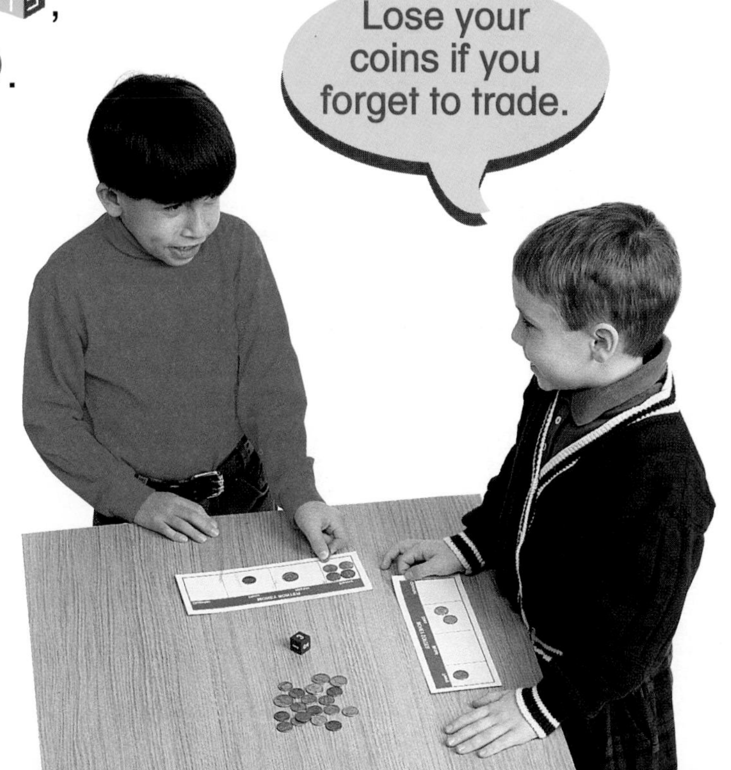

MONEY SORTER			
Quarter	**Dime**	**Nickel**	**Penny**

How many different ways can you show 25¢?
Make a list like this.

MAKE 25¢

Quarter	Dime	Nickel	Penny
1			
	2		5
	1	3	

Practice!

Remember to count on from 25.

Count. Write how much money.

1.     

25¢ 35¢ 40¢ 45¢

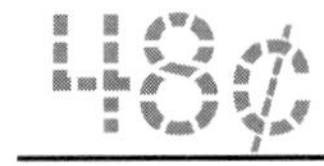

2.     ______

3.    ______

4.     ______

Mixed Review Test Preparation

5. Complete the fact family.

$$\begin{array}{r} 6 \\ +\ 4 \\ \hline \end{array} \quad \begin{array}{r} 4 \\ +\ 6 \\ \hline \end{array} \quad \begin{array}{r} 10 \\ -\ 4 \\ \hline \end{array} \quad \begin{array}{r} 10 \\ -\ 6 \\ \hline \end{array}$$

Skip-count. Write the numbers.

6. 65, 70, 75, ______, ______, ______, ______, ______

7. 27, 37, 47, ______, ______, ______, ______, ______

We counted sets of coins. Have your child tell the total amount for 1 quarter, 2 dimes, and 5 pennies.

Name ______________________

Count Quarters

How much did Rita save?
Count by twenty-fives to find out.

75¢

Rita saved 75¢.

Count. Write how much money.

3

There are 2 coins in your pocket. What is the most you could have? What is the least?

Practice!

Count. Write how much money.

1

97¢

2
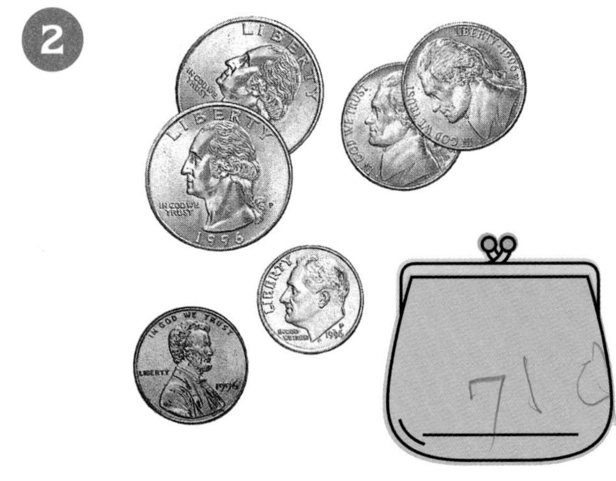
71¢

3

82¢

4

90¢

More to Explore Money

A **half dollar** is worth 50¢.
Count. Write how much money.

Glossary
half dollar

50¢ 75¢ 85¢ 90¢ ______

______

At Home: We counted sets of coins. Have your child count a group of 2 quarters, 2 dimes, and 4 pennies.

Name

Use Guess and Test

Problem-Solving Strategy

Read
Plan
Solve
Look Back

Read Melody spent 15¢ at the pet store. Which two things did she buy?

Plan What plan could you use to find the answer?

You can use a **guess-and-test** strategy.

Solve Guess that she bought a ball and a brush.

7¢ + 9¢ = 16¢

Try the ball and the bone.

7 + 8 = 15

Glossary
guess and test

Look Back What is the answer to the problem? 15

Solve. You may use , 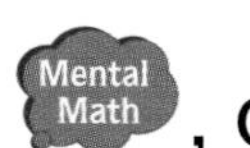, or 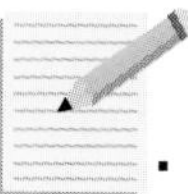.

1. Andy spent 9¢.
   Which two things did he buy?
   A Mouse, Dog Bicuit

2. Chris spent 17¢.
   Which two things did she buy?
   Bone, Brush

Practice!

Solve. You may use 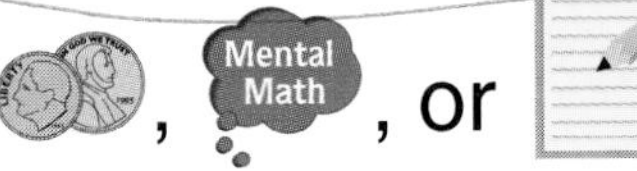, or .

1. Barry has 12¢ to spend.
   Which two things can he buy?
   Book, car

2. Find two other things Barry can buy.
   Pencil, Doll

3. Juan spent 11¢.
   Which two things did he buy?
   Boat, Book

Steps in a Process

Use the pictures at the top of the page.

Tawana has 15¢ to spend.
Which 3 things can she buy?

Tell how you use Read, Plan, Solve, Check.

Boat, car, Cards

At Home: We used a guess-and-test strategy to solve problems. Ask your child to explain how to solve problem 1 above.

Name

Midchapter Review

Count. Write how much money.

Do your best!

1   25¢

2   5¢

3   10¢

4   37¢

5   53¢

6   ______

7  ______

Solve.

8 Roberto spent 13¢.
Which things did he buy?
Jumprope, BuBBles

9 Fran spent 16¢.
Which things did she buy?
whistle jump rope

10 How did you solve problem 9? 

______

Explain how you would count 2 quarters, 3 dimes, 1 nickel, and 8 pennies.

Extra Practice

Game!

Save for a Rainy Day

You and your partners need a and a .

You each need 1 , 3 , 4 ,
and 20 .

Take turns.

- Put all of your coins in this pocket.
- Roll the cube. Spin the spinner.
- Move the amount rolled on the cube to the *Store* to spend money. Move to the *Bank* to save money.
- Play until one player has no money left in the pocket.

Play again.

Name ______________________

Three-Jar Savings

Listen to *A Chair for My Mother.*

What would you buy with the money in the jar?

Working Together

You and your partner need (quarter), (dime), and (nickel).

Act it out. What if you get 30¢ allowance each week?

- Let Jar 1 be for money to spend on little things, like snacks.
- Let Jar 2 be for money you save for bigger things, like toys.
- Let Jar 3 be for money you save for really big things, like a vacation.
- Write how much of the 30¢ you would put in each jar each week.

____¢ 

____¢ 

____¢ 

Decision Making

1. How much would be in each jar after 4 weeks? Decide how to find out. You can use

, , or a .

Jar 1: ____¢ **Jar 2:** ____¢ **Jar 3:** ____¢

2. Decide on a toy you want. Make up its cost. ________________

3. Which jar would have enough money in it first to buy the toy? Why? ________________

____

Write a report.

4. Tell what you learned about saving money.

5. Tell how you found the amount in each jar after 4 weeks.

More to Investigate

PREDICT How long will it take you to save for the toy in problem 2?

EXPLORE What other ways are there to save money?

FIND Find out how to start a savings account at a bank.

Name ____________________

Dollars

1 dollar
100¢ or $1.00

Glossary
dollar

Working Together

You and your partner need coins, a [dollar bill], and a [spinner].

Take turns.

- Spin the spinner.
- Take one of that coin. Put it on your wallet workspace.
- Trade coins when you can.
- Continue until one partner has exactly enough to trade for a one-dollar bill.

What if you have 8 coins and your partner has 5 coins. Who has more money? Explain.

Practice!

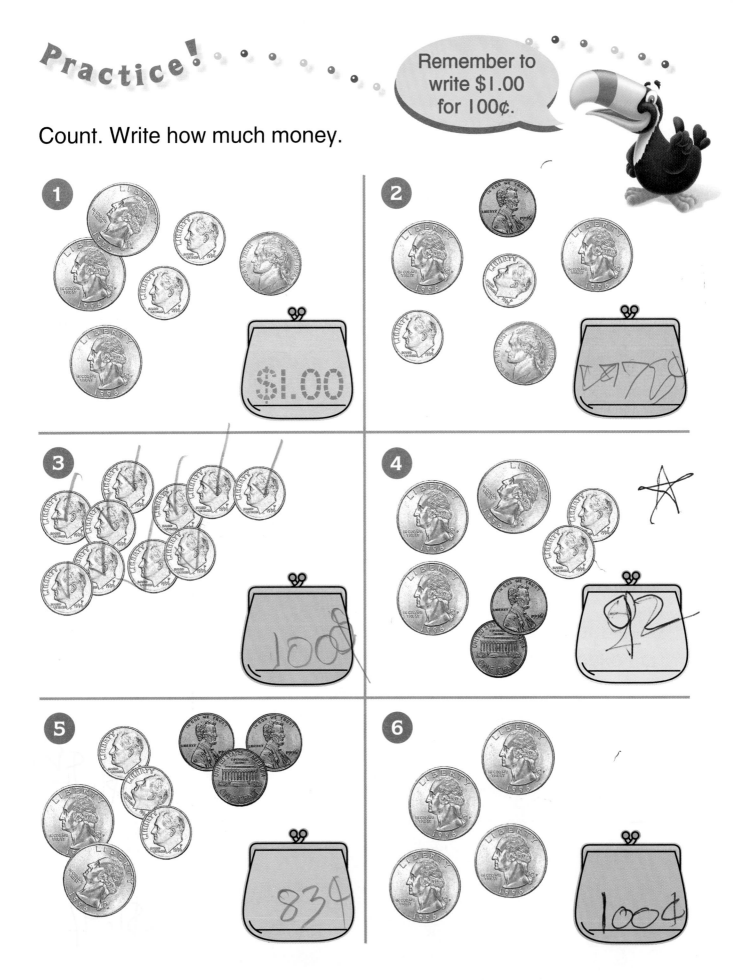

Remember to write $1.00 for 100¢.

Count. Write how much money.

1. $1.00

2.

3.

4.

5.

6.

How many different ways can you make $1.00 using all of the same coin? Draw or write to show how.

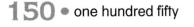

Today we made $1.00 with coins. Have your child place more coins in each purse so that every problem shows $1.00 in coins.

Name

Dollars and Cents

How much did the children earn washing cars?

First count the dollars. Then count the cents.

$1.00

$1.25

$1.35

$1.35

Count. Write how much money.

1

$1.00, $2.00, $3.00

$3.05

$3.10

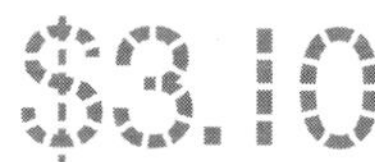
$3.10

2

25¢

50¢

75¢

$1.00

$1.10

$1.15

3

Critical Thinking

Why do you think people use dollar bills?

Count. Write how much money.

2

____

3

____

Mixed Review Test Preparation

4

9	7	18	5	15	10
+ 5	+ 9	− 9	+ 5	− 8	− 6

Compare. Write > for *is greater than.*
Write < for *is less than.*

 42  36   20  24   69 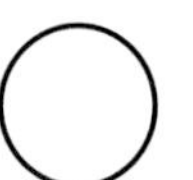 70

At Home

We learned to count dollars and cents. Have your child tell the amount of money shown by 3 dollars, 2 quarters, and 4 nickels.

Name ______________________

Working Together

You and your partner need 6 quarters, 6 dimes, 8 nickels, and 10 pennies.

Take turns.

- Scoop up some coins.
- Your partner counts and writes how much money.
- Do you have enough money to buy the object? Choose *yes* or *no*.
- Return the coins to the pile.

	How much money?	Want to buy.	Enough money?
1	______	$1.60	yes no
2	______	98¢	yes no
3	______	$1.15	yes no
4	______	Crayola CRAYONS $1.50	yes no

When can you buy an item?

Practice!

Count. Is there enough money?
Choose *yes* or *no*.

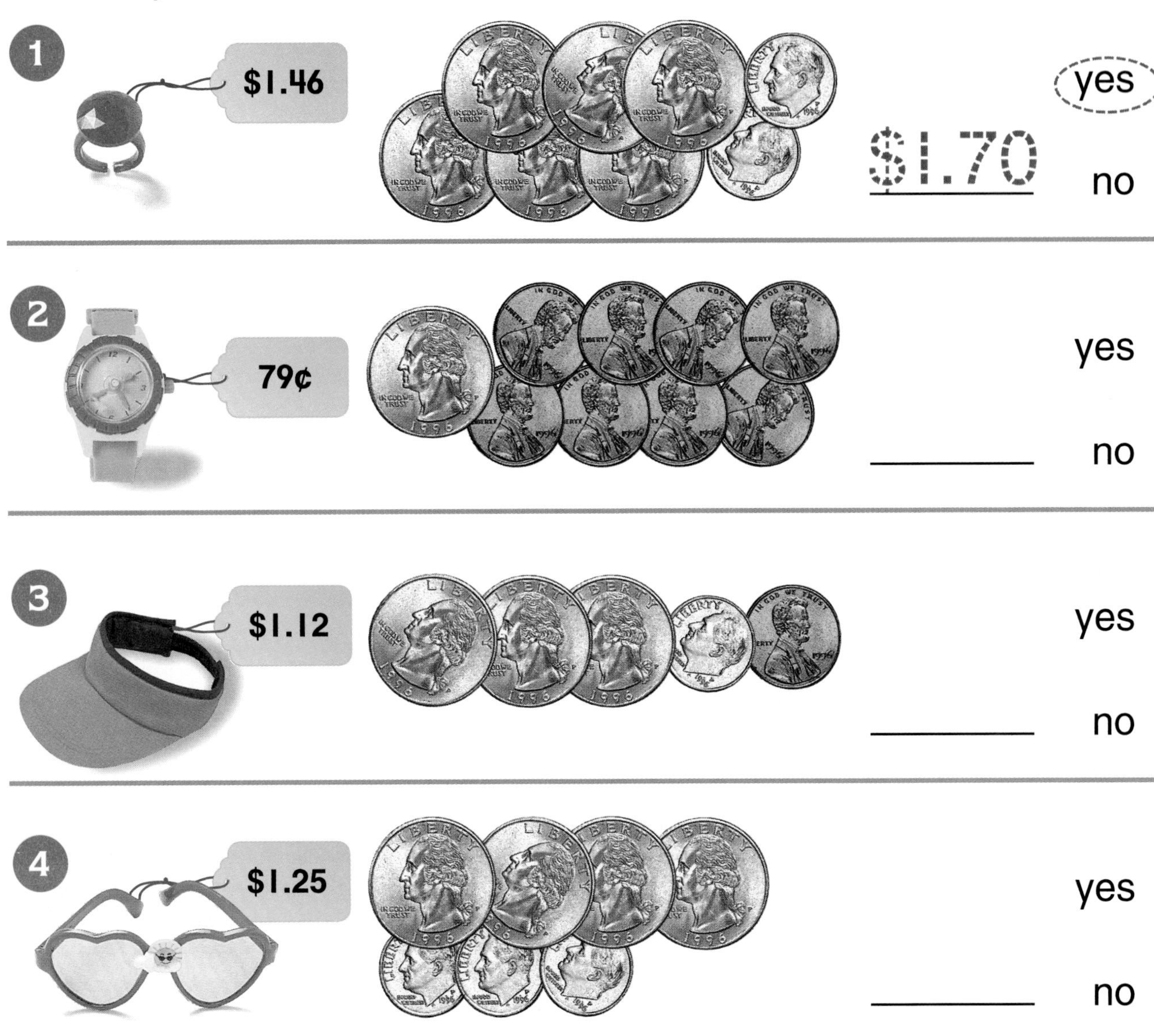

More to Explore — Estimation

Choose the estimate you think is best.

Joe has 2 quarters, 30 pennies.
He has

more than $1.00.

less than $1.00.

Inez has 8 dimes, 7 nickels.
She has

more than $1.00.

less than $1.00.

At Home Ask your child if 4 quarters, 1 dime, and 1 penny is enough to buy the object in problem 3.

Name

Money in the Bank

You and your partner each need 2 dollars in coins and a [counter].

- Put your [counter] on *Start.*
- Take turns. Flip a penny.
- Tails—you move 2 spaces. Heads—you move 1 space. Follow the directions in the space.
- Play until you both reach *Finish.*
- The player with more money in the bank wins.

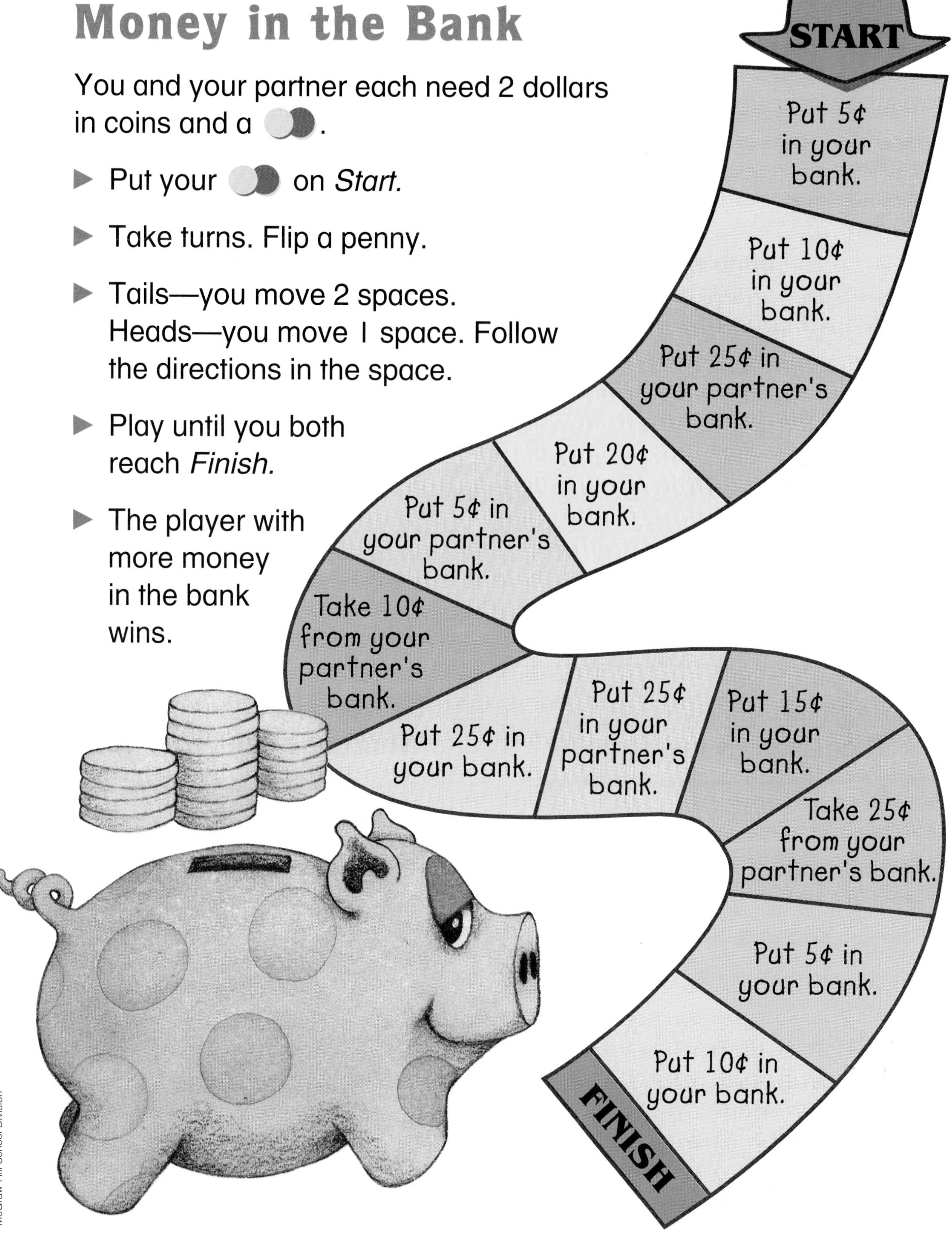
START
Put 5¢ in your bank.
Put 10¢ in your bank.
Put 25¢ in your partner's bank.
Put 20¢ in your bank.
Put 5¢ in your partner's bank.
Take 10¢ from your partner's bank.
Put 25¢ in your bank.
Put 25¢ in your partner's bank.
Put 15¢ in your bank.
Take 25¢ from your partner's bank.
Put 5¢ in your bank.
Put 10¢ in your bank.
FINISH

Count. Write how much money.

1 

______

2 

______

Solve. Use the picture.

3 Chuck has 17¢.
Can he buy a pad and a pencil?

______

4 Sue spent 15¢.
Which things did she buy?

______

5 Cara has $1.45.
Can she buy the game?

______

What could she buy?

______

6 Bill has $1.00.
What can he buy?

______

______

______

Cultural Note

Rice, beads, shells, and stones have all been used as money at different times in history.

Name ____________________

Make Change

Diwa bought a pin at the museum gift shop. He gave the clerk $1.00. What should the change be?

Why should Diwa get **change**?

Glossary
change

To find the change, start with the cost.
Then count up to the amount given.

Cost of Pin					Gave the clerk:
78¢	79¢	80¢	90¢	$1.00	$1.00

Then count the coins.

Diwa should get 22¢ change.

Use coins to find the change.
Show how you count up.

1. Jasper bought a shell.
   He gave the clerk 50¢. 44¢ ____________________ ______ change

2. Terry bought a toy.
   She gave the clerk $1.00. ____________________ ______ change

You give the clerk 3 quarters, 1 dime, and 1 nickel for a toy. Is 2¢ the correct change? Explain.

Practice!

Use coins to count up to make change.

1. Rosa bought a ball for 42¢. She gave the clerk 50¢. What was her change? ____ change

2. What if the ball Rosa bought was on sale for 32¢. How much change would she get? ____ change

How did you solve problem 2?

Write and Share

Ahmed wrote this problem.
Robert bought a turtle for 97¢.
He gave the clerk $1.00.
What was his change?

Ahmed Kamal
Mandarin Oaks School
Jacksonville, Florida

3. Solve Ahmed's problem. ____________________

4. READING ARITHMETIC WRITING **Steps in a Process** Write a problem about buying an item and getting change. Have a partner solve it.

Write the steps you will use to solve your partner's problem.

____

____

____

At Home: Ask your child to tell you how to solve the problem he or she wrote.

Name

Chapter Review

Language and Mathematics

Choose the correct word to complete the sentence.

1. You can trade 10 pennies for a ________.

2. You can trade 25 pennies for a ________.

dime
nickel
half dollar
quarter

Concepts and Skills

Match.

3.    

penny　　dime　　quarter　　nickel

Count. Write how much money.

4. 

____

5. 

____

Is there enough money? Choose *yes* or *no.*

6. 

yes

no

Problem Solving

Solve. Which two items did they buy?

7 Mallory spent 17¢.

____

____

8 Tyrone spent 13¢.

____

____

Write the amount of change.

9 Miguel bought milk.
He gave the clerk 40¢.

______ change

10 Faith bought juice.
She gave the clerk $1.00.

______ change

What Do You Think?

Which is the easiest way to count a lot of coins?

☑ Check one.

☐ Count them one at a time.

☐ Group the same coins and count.

☐ Use a calculator.

Why? ____

Draw a group of coins. Draw or write to explain how to find the amount you have.

Name ______________________

Chapter Test

Draw lines to match.

dime penny quarter

2

1¢ 5¢ 10¢ 25¢

Count. Write how much money.

3

______

4

______

5

______

6

______

Is there enough money? Choose *yes* or *no*.

7

yes

no

8

yes

no

Solve. Which two items did they buy?

Erin spent 14¢.

____

Abdul spent 10¢.

____

Performance Assessment

What Did You Learn?

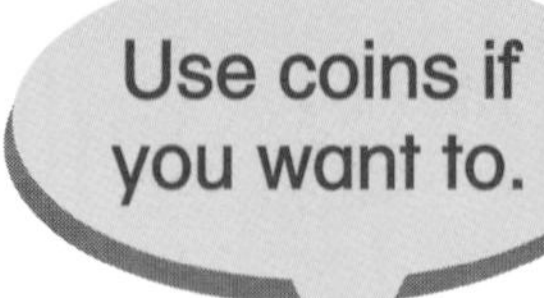

Complete the chart.
Show different numbers of coins to make $1.00.

		quarter	dime	nickel	penny
1	Use 4 coins.				
2	Use 6 coins.				
3	Use 7 coins.				
4	Use 10 coins.				
5	Use 12 coins.				
6	Use 24 coins.				

You may want to put this page in your portfolio.

Math Connection

Probability

Name

Coin Toss

If you toss a penny, is it **more likely** or **less likely** to land heads up or tails up?

Glossary

more likely
less likely

Try it with a partner.
Toss a penny 10 times. For each toss, make a tally mark (|) to show heads or tails.

1

		Totals
Heads		
Tails		

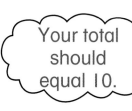

Your total should equal 10.

If you toss 20 times, will the penny land more on one side than the other?

____

Try it. Show your results with tally marks.

2

		Totals
Heads		
Tails		

Write what you think is likely to happen if you toss the penny 100 times.

Show the Same Amount

How do you find different ways to show the same amount of money?

You can use a computer to help you.

1. Count. Write how much money. ______

At the Computer

Dollar	Quarter	Dime	Nickel	Penny
	1	12	1	

2. How many different ways can you show the amount in the picture? Make a list like this.

3. What happens if you keep trading up until you cannot trade anymore?

____

4. Show a money amount. Have a partner show it another way.

Home Connection

Chapter 4 Wrap-Up

Name ______________________________

Buy It!

MATERIALS coins, dollar bills, paper for price tags

DIRECTIONS Work with your child to make price tags for several food items in your home. Keep prices under $5.00.

Give your child coins and bills to "buy" the items. Have your child show you the exact amount needed to buy each item.

Play "store" with your child. Switch roles and have your child tell you if you have shown the correct amount.

Dear Family,

I am starting a new chapter in mathematics. I will be learning about time, from a minute to a year.

I will also be talking about making apple pies and the ingredients that are used.

Learning About Pies

Let's talk about different kinds of pies that people like. We can make a list.

My Math Words

I am going to use these math words in this chapter.

Please help me make word cards for the math words. I can use these word cards when I practice telling time.

- minute
- second
- hour
- half hour
- quarter hour
- a quarter after
- half past
- a quarter to
- work backward
- calendar
- ordinal numbers

Your child,

Signature

Telling Time

Theme: Apple Pie Time

CHAPTER 5

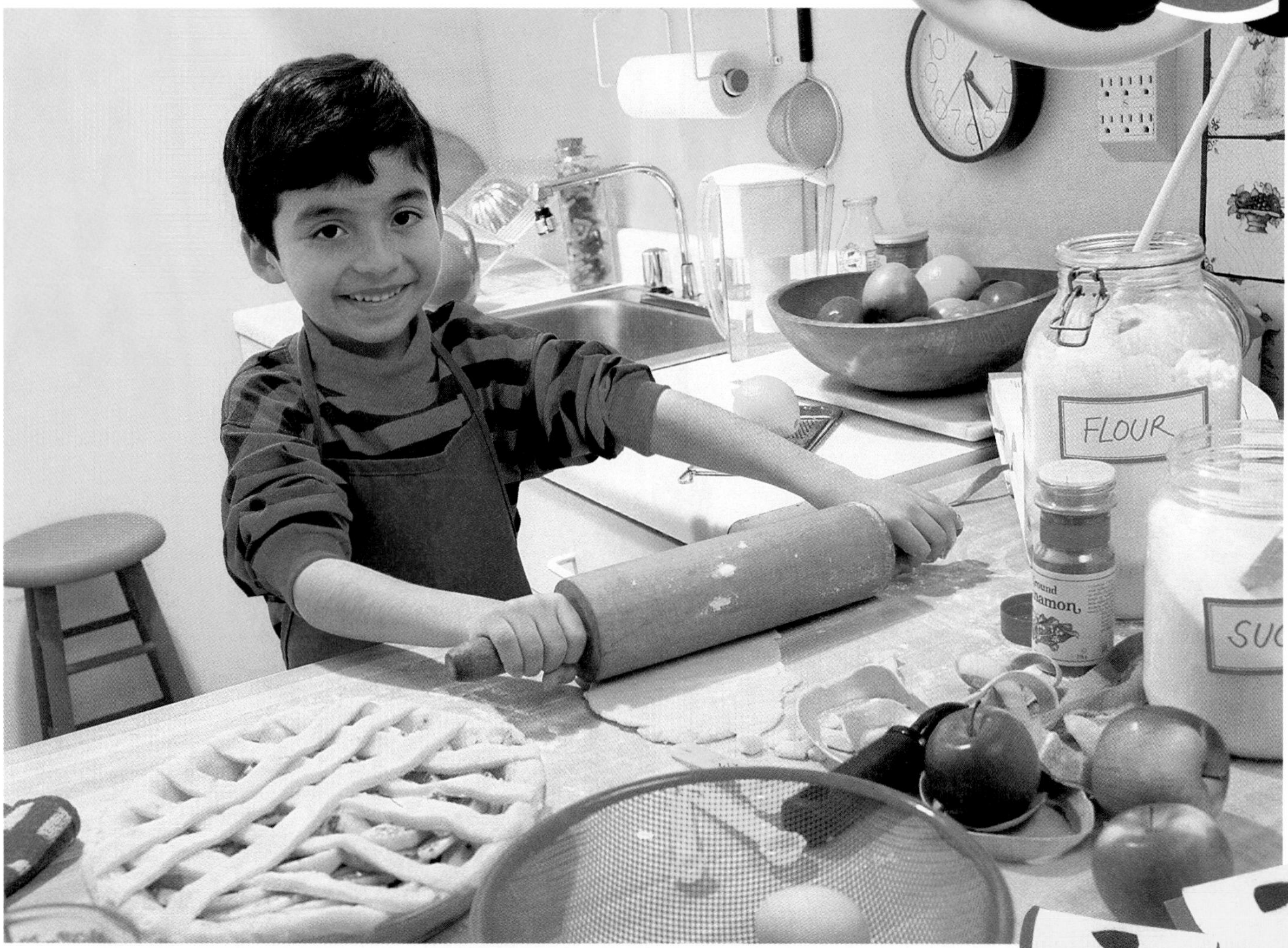

Write How-To Directions Some stories tell how to make things.

Listen to the story *How to Make an Apple Pie and see the world.* Then make a list of ingredients for the pie.

Tell how to make an apple pie. Use all the ingredients from your list.

Name

What Do You Know?

1. Write the number for each hour on the clock.

2. What time is shown? ____________

Portfolio Write a morning time. Draw or write about something you do at this time. Write the time you finish.

Name ______________________

Explore Activity
Time

Working Together

You and your partner need a ⏱ or class clock.

Take turns.

- Estimate how many times you can do the activity in 1 **minute**.
- Your partner says "Go!" and watches the clock.
- Record the actual number of times.

ACTIVITY	ESTIMATE	ACTUAL
Write your whole name.	____ times	____ times
Say the ABCs.	____ times	____ times
Hop on 1 foot.	____ times	____ times
Say a rhyme.	____ times	____ times
Count by ones to 100.	____ times	____ times
Snap your fingers.	____ times	____ times

Describe activities that take about a second to do once.

Glossary
minute
seconds

Practice!

Ring things that take less than 1 minute to do.

1. Read a book.

2. Brush teeth.

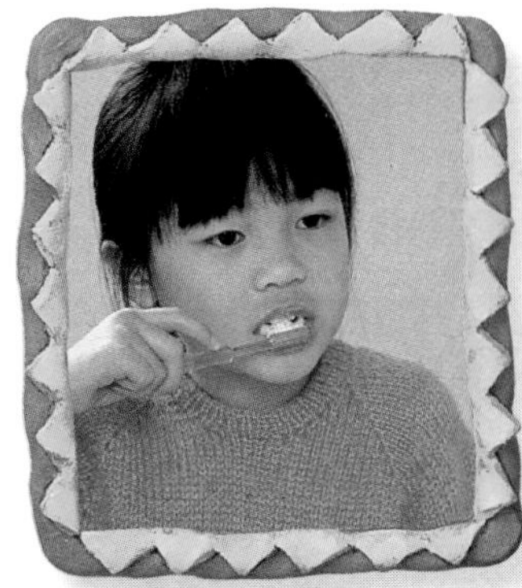

3. Eat a cookie.

4. Sleep at night.

5. Count to 10.

6. Play tag.

Talk: Talk about your answers with a partner.

Mixed Review — Test Preparation

Compare. Use > or <.

7. 33 ◯ 45   86 ◯ 59   31 ◯ 30

Algebra **PATTERNS** How many pieces of pie? Skip-count by fives.

8. 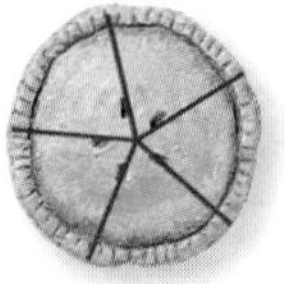 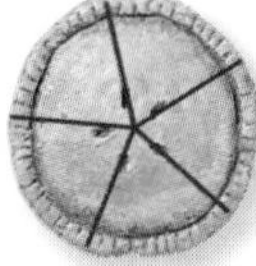 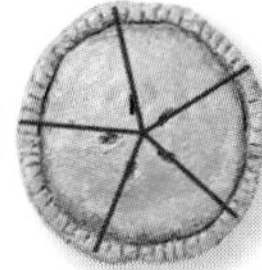  

_____ pieces

At Home: We explored how many times we could do an activity in 1 minute. Ask your child to answer exercise 2 above.

Name

Hour and Half Hour

Talk How does each kind of clock show the time?

Glossary
hour
half hour

Write the time.

Why can you also say *half past seven* for 7:30?

Practice!

Draw the missing minute hand to show the same time.

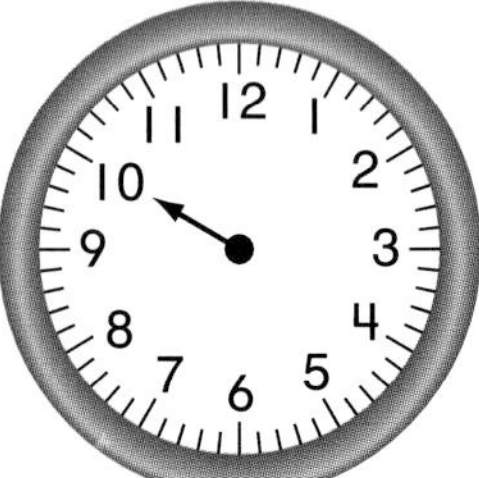

5

7

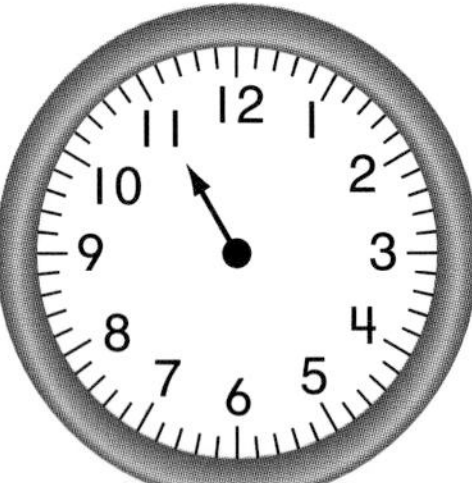

Solve.

9 The apple pie will bake for one hour. At what time will it be done?

____

Draw clock hands to show 3:30. Why does the minute hand point to 6?

Ask your child to tell you the time at various points in the evening.

Name 

Quarter Hour

Glossary
quarter hour
a quarter after
half past
a quarter to

2 o'clock

A **quarter hour** is 15 minutes.

15 minutes after 2
a quarter after 2

30 minutes after 2
half past 2

45 minutes after 2
a quarter to 3

Show the same time.
Draw the missing minute hand.

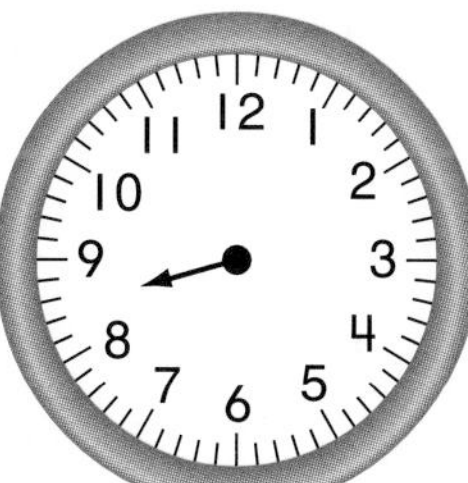

What is the difference between *a quarter after* and *a quarter to*?

Practice!

Write the time.
Write the time 15 minutes later.

1  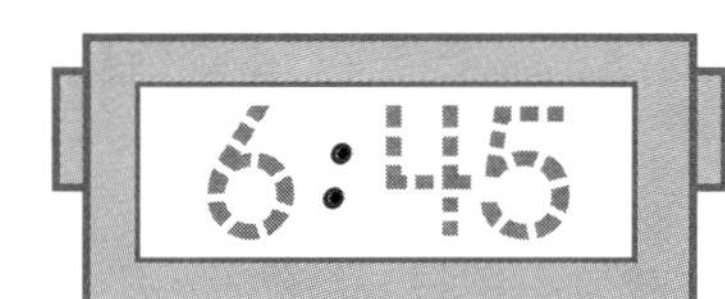

15 minutes later

7:00

2  

15 minutes later

___:___

3  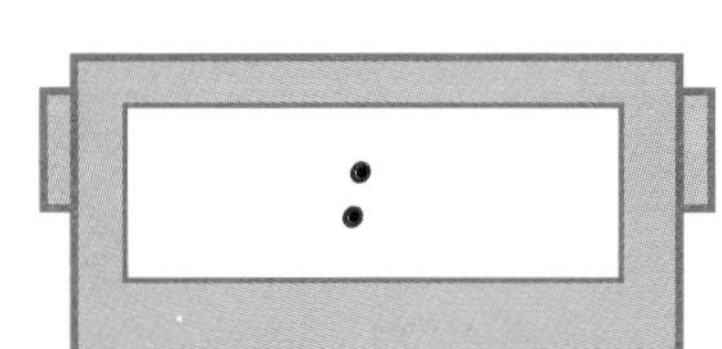

15 minutes later

___:___

4  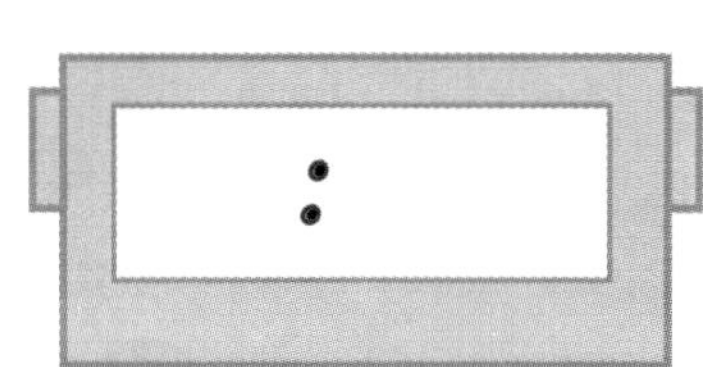

15 minutes later

___:___

More to Explore Patterns

PATTERNS Find the pattern. Complete the train schedule.

Leave:	2:30	2:45	3:00	:	:	:
Arrive:	4:00	4:15	:	4:45	:	:

At Home: Have your child count from 6:00 to 6:45 in 5-minute intervals.

Name

Working Together

You and your partner need a [number cube] and a [clock].

Take turns.

- Start with 11 o'clock.
- Roll the number cube.
- Write that many minutes later.
- Draw the new time on the clock.

Could you get a time later than 12:00 on your first roll? Explain.

Turn 1

____ minutes later

Turn 2

____ minutes later

Turn 3

____ minutes later

Turn 4

____ minutes later

Turn 5

____ minutes later

Turn 6

____ minutes later

What is the latest time that you could get? What is the earliest time? Explain.

Practice!

Write the time.

10:05

___:___

___:___

___:___

2

___:___

___:___

___:___

___:___

Cultural Connection

Maya Monuments

Long ago the Maya people carved monuments to record important dates.

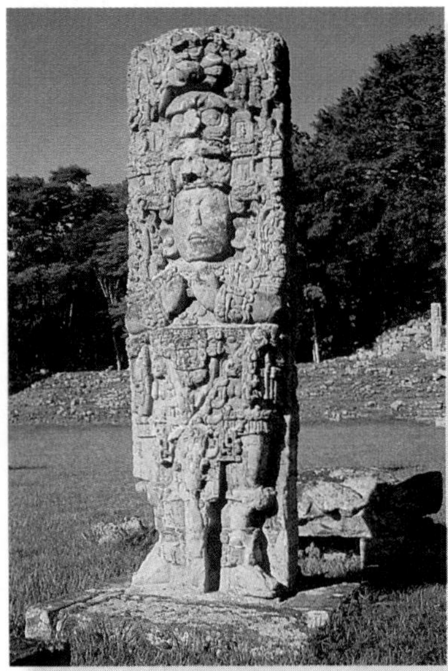

Look at these Maya symbols for numbers.

•	••	•••	••••	—
one	two	three	four	five
• —	•• —	••• —	•••• —	=
six	seven	eight	nine	ten

Write the Maya symbol.

7 ____ 10 ____

Design a Maya monument.

We learned to tell time to 5-minute intervals.
Ask your child to tell you the time when it is 7:20.

Name

More Minutes

To tell the time, count by fives to 8:20.

Count by fives. Then count on by ones to 8:23.

5 10 15 20

8:20

20 minutes after 8

5 10 15 20 21 22 23

8:23

23 minutes after 8

Write the time.

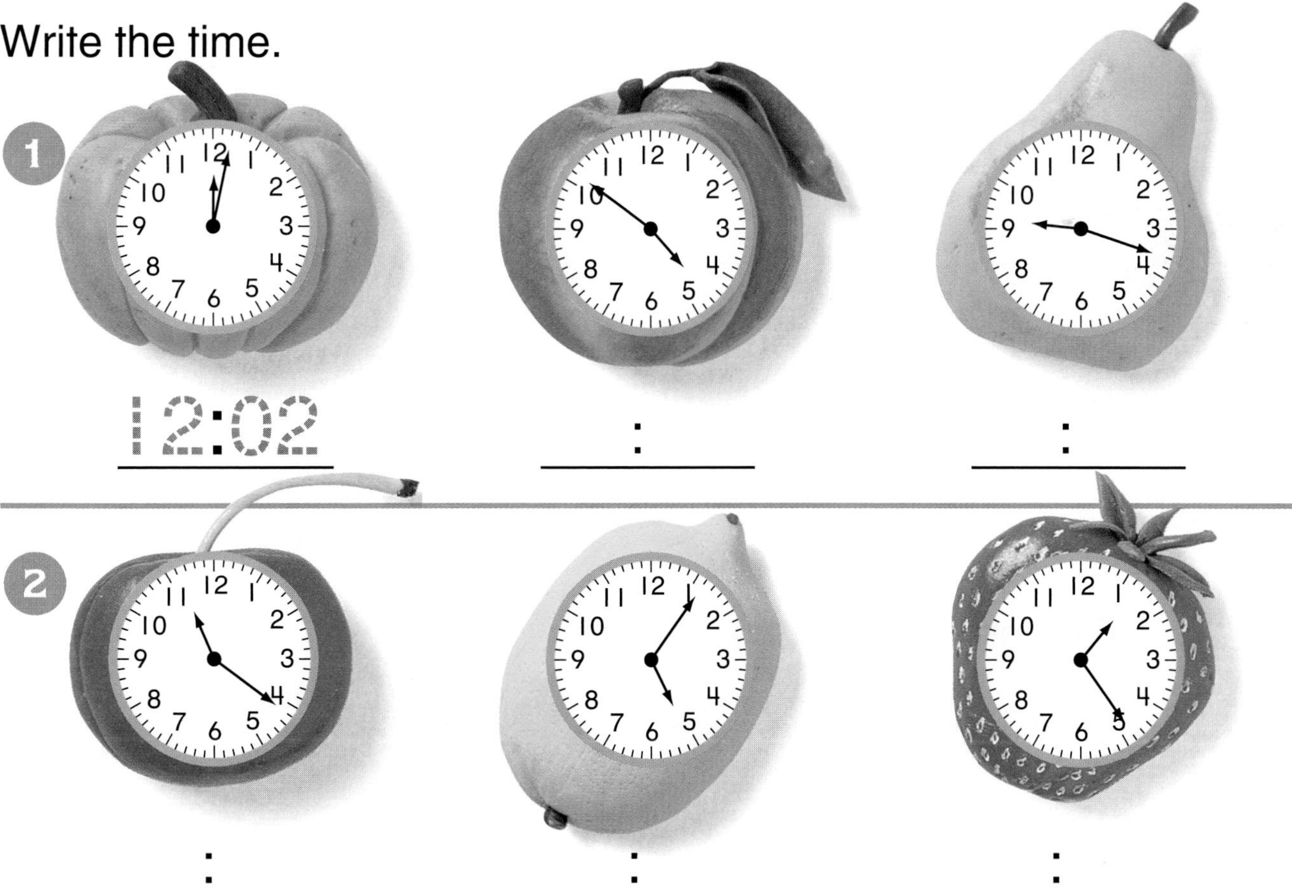

The time is 11:59. How would you write the time for 1 minute later?

Practice!

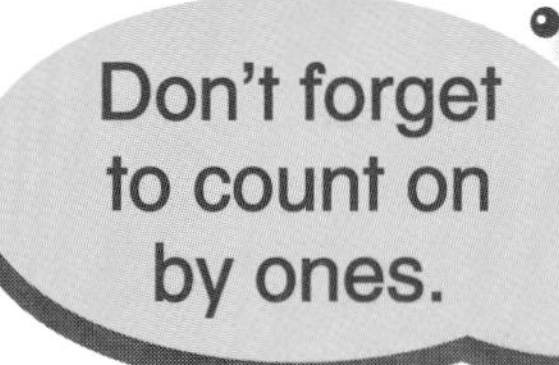

Write the time.

1  

4 minutes later 

2  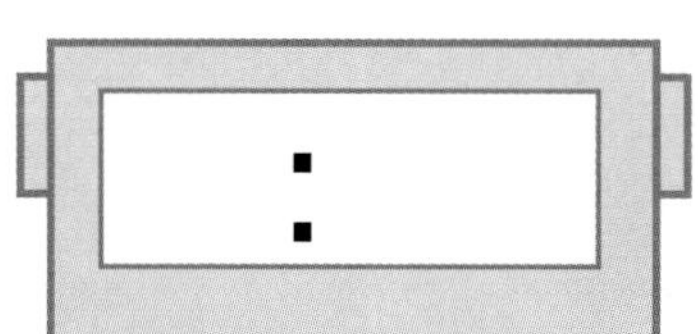

2 minutes later 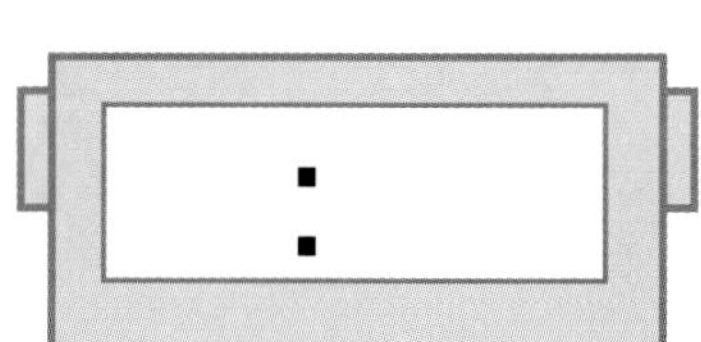

3  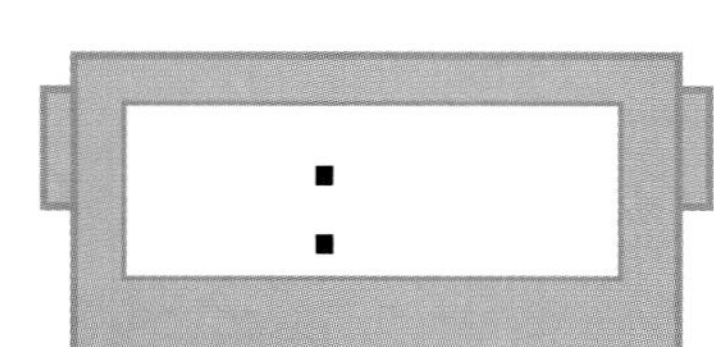

3 minutes later 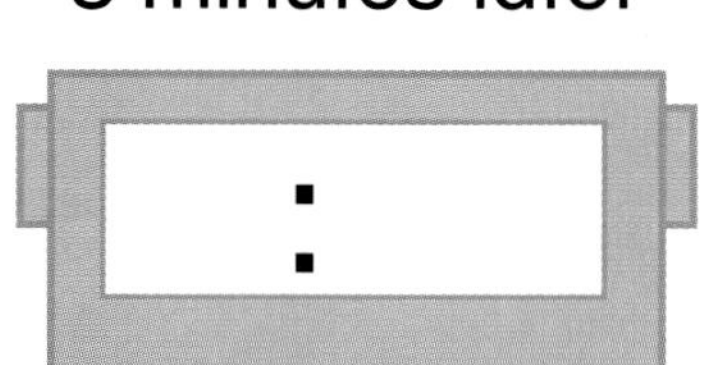

Mixed Review Test Preparation

Write the number that comes between.

4 61 _____ 63   44 _____ 46   89 _____ 91

Count. Write how much money.

5   _____

6   _____

At Home: We learned to tell time to the minute. Ask your child to explain exercise 3 to you.

Name ______________________

Time to Shop

The clocks show the time that Josie got to each store.

- ▶ Write the time.
- ▶ Draw a line to connect the clocks in order.

Write the time.

4:45

___:___

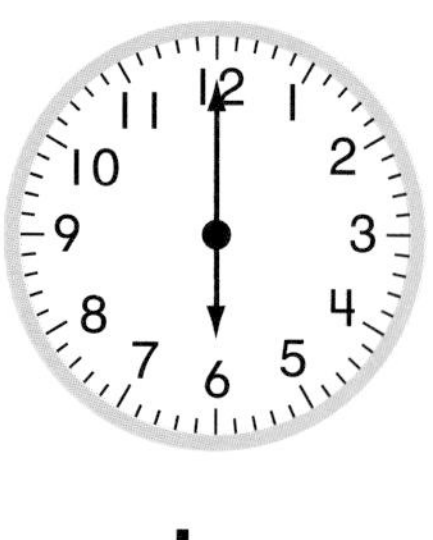

___:___

___:___

Write the time. Write the later time.

3:00

15 minutes later

3:15

3

___:___

10 minutes later

___:___

4

___:___

30 minutes later

___:___

5

___:___

5 minutes later

___:___

Write How-To Directions

Tell how to find a book about apples in the library. Show the directions in order.

Trade directions with a partner. Find a book.

Write a report about how the directions helped. Tell how you used numbers.

Name ________________________________

Midchapter Review

Do your best!

Write the time.

1 

____ : ____

2 

____ : ____

3 

____ : ____

4 

____ : ____

5 

____ : ____

6 

____ : ____

Show the same time. Draw the missing minute hand.

7 

8 

Write the time.

9 

____ : ____

15 minutes later

____ : ____

10 

____ : ____

3 minutes later

____ : ____

Journal How do you find 5 minutes later than 3:21?

Extra Practice

Game!

Watch the Time

Cultural Note
Some things are called "as American as apple pie."

You and your partner need 14 counters.

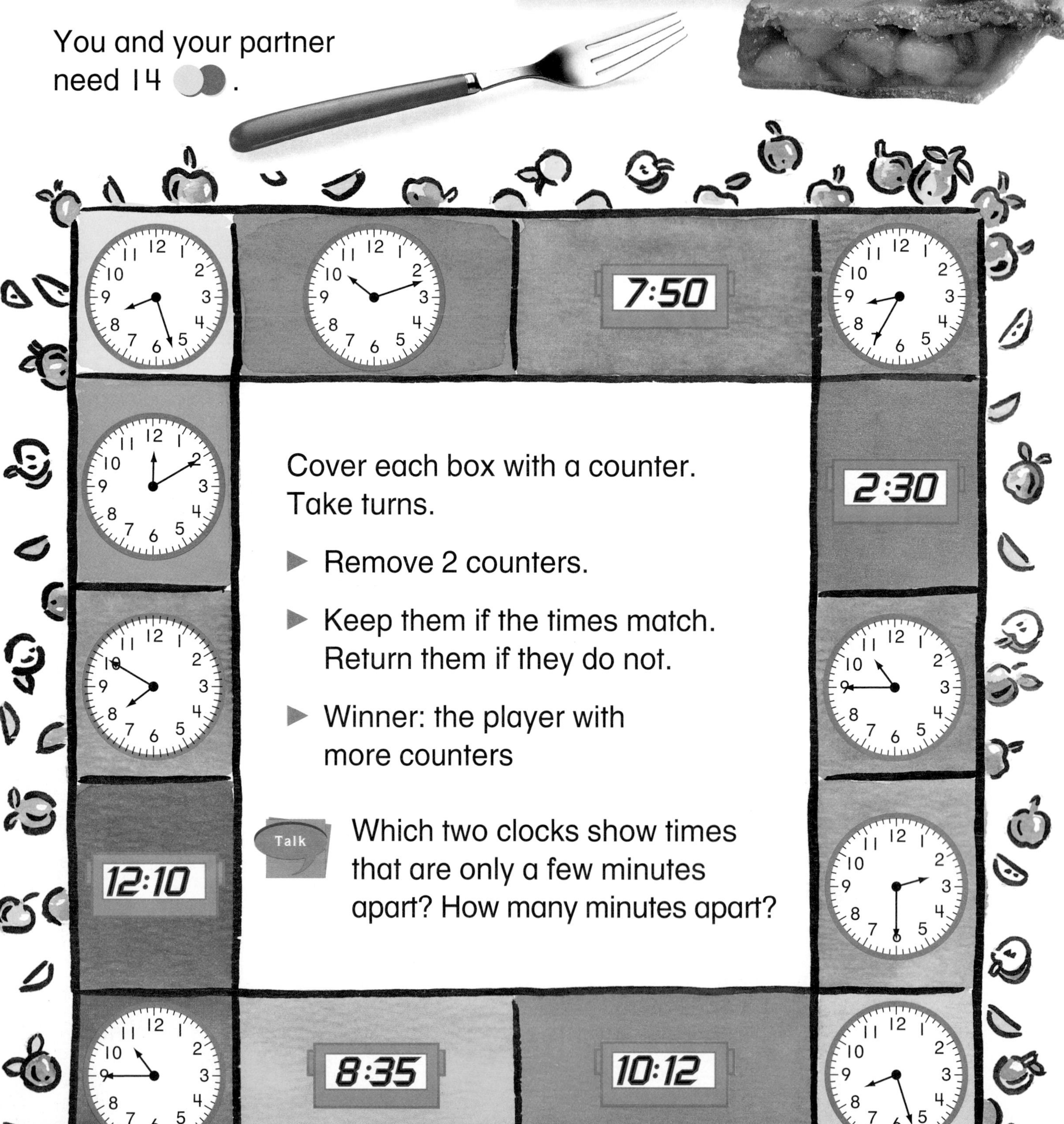

Cover each box with a counter. Take turns.

- Remove 2 counters.
- Keep them if the times match. Return them if they do not.
- Winner: the player with more counters

Talk: Which two clocks show times that are only a few minutes apart? How many minutes apart?

Real-Life Investigation

Applying Time

Name ________________________________

Make a Schedule

A schedule helps people look at information quickly.

What are some different kinds of schedules that people use?

Working Together

Work with a partner. Make up a schedule for a school day.

- Write the day.
- Write the time you would do each activity.
- Write the name of the activity.

Day of the week ____________________	
Time	**Activity**

Decision Making

How do you think a teacher would change your schedule?

Write a report.

1. Tell how you decided what to put on your schedule.
2. Describe how your schedule compares to your teacher's schedule.

Day of the week Monday

Time	Activity
9:30	Math
10:00	Recess
11:00	Reading
12:00	Lunch
1:00	Gym

More to Investigate

PREDICT What if you made a schedule for a Saturday. How might it be the same? How might it be different?

EXPLORE Make a Saturday schedule.

FIND Compare the schedules. Describe how the schedules are alike and different.

Name ______________________

Work Backward

Problem-Solving Strategy

Read | Plan | Solve | Look Back

Read The bake sale starts at 12:00. The bakers need to arrive 2 hours before it starts. At what time should the bakers arrive?

Plan You can **work backward** to solve the problem.

Solve Start with 12 o'clock. Count back 2 hours.

11 o'clock, 10 o'clock

The bakers should arrive at 10 o'clock.

Look Back Does your answer make sense? Explain.

Glossary
work backward

Solve.

1. Miguel took his cupcakes out of the oven at 3:30. They took 1 hour to bake. When did he put them in the oven? ____:____

2. Sunny left the bake sale at 2:00. She was there for 2 hours. When did she arrive? ____:____

Talk Tell a partner how you solved problems 1 and 2.

Practice!

Solve.

1. Tanya finished baking raisin squares at 9:00. It took 3 hours altogether. At what time did Tanya start?

2. It took Aaron 2 hours to peel apples for his pies. He finished at 3:00. When did he begin?

3. The class made pies until 3:00. Paula helped for the last 4 hours. When did she start helping?

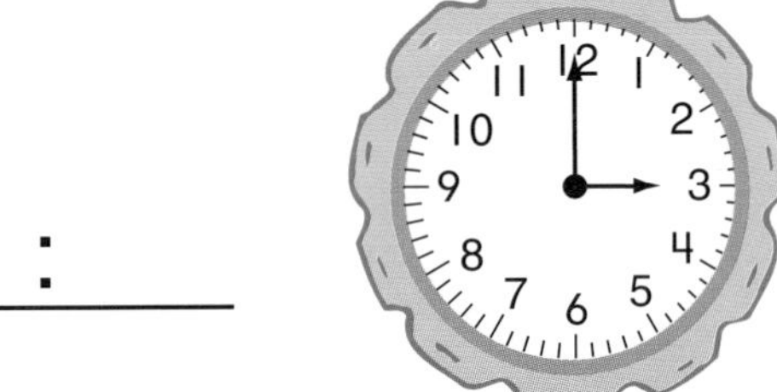

4. Taro wants his cookies to be ready by 10:30. It will take 2 hours in all. At what time should he start?

___ : ___

5. Write your own problem. Have a partner solve it.

____

____

____

____

At Home We counted backward to solve problems. Ask your child to tell you what time it was 2 hours ago.

Name ____________________

Use a Calendar

January

Sun	Mon	Tues	Wed	Thurs	Fri	Sat
				1	2	3
4	5	6	7	8	9	10
11	12	13	14	15	16	17
18	19	20	21	22	23	24
25	26	27	28	29	30	31

February

Sun	Mon	Tues	Wed	Thurs	Fri	Sat
1	2	3	4	5	6	7
8	9	10	11	12	13	14
15	16	17	18	19	20	21
22	23	24	25	26	27	28

March

Sun	Mon	Tues	Wed	Thurs	Fri	Sat
1	2	3	4	5	6	7
8	9	10	11	12	13	14
15	16	17	18	19	20	21
22	23	24	25	26	27	28
29	30	31				

April

Sun	Mon	Tues	Wed	Thurs	Fri	Sat
			1	2	3	4
5	6	7	8	9	10	11
12	13	14	15	16	17	18
19	20	21	22	23	24	25
26	27	28	29	30		

May

Sun	Mon	Tues	Wed	Thurs	Fri	Sat
					1	2
3	4	5	6	7	8	9
10	11	12	13	14	15	16
17	18	19	20	21	22	23
24/31	25	26	27	28	29	30

June

Sun	Mon	Tues	Wed	Thurs	Fri	Sat
	1	2	3	4	5	6
7	8	9	10	11	12	13
14	15	16	17	18	19	20
21	22	23	24	25	26	27
28	29	30				

July

Sun	Mon	Tues	Wed	Thurs	Fri	Sat
			1	2	3	4
5	6	7	8	9	10	11
12	13	14	15	16	17	18
19	20	21	22	23	24	25
26	27	28	29	30	31	

August

Sun	Mon	Tues	Wed	Thurs	Fri	Sat
						1
2	3	4	5	6	7	8
9	10	11	12	13	14	15
16	17	18	19	20	21	22
23/30	24/31	25	26	27	28	29

September

Sun	Mon	Tues	Wed	Thurs	Fri	Sat
		1	2	3	4	5
6	7	8	9	10	11	12
13	14	15	16	17	18	19
20	21	22	23	24	25	26
27	28	29	30			

October

Sun	Mon	Tues	Wed	Thurs	Fri	Sat
				1	2	3
4	5	6	7	8	9	10
11	12	13	14	15	16	17
18	19	20	21	22	23	24
25	26	27	28	29	30	31

November

Sun	Mon	Tues	Wed	Thurs	Fri	Sat
1	2	3	4	5	6	7
8	9	10	11	12	13	14
15	16	17	18	19	20	21
22	23	24	25	26	27	28
29	30					

December

Sun	Mon	Tues	Wed	Thurs	Fri	Sat
		1	2	3	4	5
6	7	8	9	10	11	12
13	14	15	16	17	18	19
20	21	22	23	24	25	26
27	28	29	30	31		

Use the **calendar**.

1. How many days in each month?

   July 31 May ____ March ____ June ____

2. On what day of the week is the date?

   August 15 ____________ June 1 ____________

   January 18 ____________

What is the same about April and July? What is different?

Glossary

calendar

Practice!

Complete the calendar.
Then solve.

JANUARY						
Sunday	Monday	Tuesday	Wednesday	Thursday	Friday	Saturday
				1	2	3
4	5	6	7	8	9	10
11	12	13	14			

1. January has ____ days.

2. January has ____ Fridays.

3. The play is on January 13. The class will practice on the Friday before. What is the date of the practice? ________

4. The drama club meets every Thursday. How many times will they meet in January? ____

5. Yuri's birthday is one week after January 21. When is his birthday? ________

6. On which day of the week does January begin? ________

At Home: Ask your child to find your birthday on the calendar and to tell on what day of the week it falls.

Name ______________________________

Ordinal Numbers

You can use **ordinal numbers** to tell about the days and the weeks in a month.

Glossary
ordinal numbers

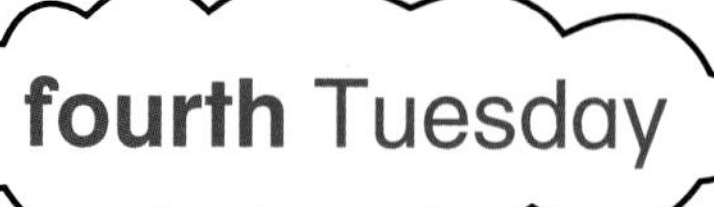

May **twenty-first**

third week

Janell will visit the doctor the fifth Friday in May.

That date is May 29.

MAY

Sun	Mon	Tues	Wed	Thurs	Fri	Sat
					1	2
3	4	5	6	7	8	9
10	11	12	13	14	15	16
17	18	19	20	21	22	23
24/31	25	26	27	28	29	30

1. On what date does the second week in May begin? ______________

2. What is the date of the third Tuesday? ______________

3. What is the sixth day of the week? ______________

4. What day of the week is the thirty-first of May? ______________

5. What date is the fourth Tuesday in May? ______________

6. What date is the first Monday in May? ______________

Why are the twenty-fourth and the thirty-first of May shown in the same box?

Practice!

Ring the date.

1. first Thursday (blue)
   third Tuesday (red)
2. nineteenth of February (green)
   twenty-third of February (yellow)
3. second Monday (orange)
   fourth Wednesday (purple)

FEBRUARY

Sun	Mon	Tues	Wed	Thurs	Fri	Sat
1	2	3	4	5	6	7
8	9	10	11	12	13	14
15	16	17	18	19	20	21
22	23	24	25	26	27	28

More to Explore Logical Reasoning

Draw lines to show order.

Slice the apples.
Watch out for seeds.

1st

Bake the pie until it is done.

2nd

Buy apples and flour and other good things.

3rd

Put the apples in a nice crust.

Have your child tell you on which day of the week the fifteenth of this month falls.

Name ____________________

Use a Schedule

The Saturday TV shows before 12:00 noon are A.M.

The Saturday TV shows after 12:00 noon are P.M.

SATURDAY TV							
Channel	10:00 A.M.	10:30 A.M.	11:00 A.M.	11:30 A.M.	12:00 noon	12:30 P.M.	1:00 P.M.
48	French for Kids	Wild Animals	Learn Japanese		English Is Easy	Chinese Cooking	Spanish Cartoons
53	Gym-nastics	Fly a Kite		Science Fun	Basketball Tips	Sing-Along	Make It Yourself

How many choices do you have at 12:00 noon?

To find out, look across the chart to 12:00 noon. Then read the show titles under 12:00 noon.

English Is Easy
Basketball Tips

There are 2 choices.

Solve.

1. How long is the TV show *Learn Japanese*? ____________________

2. Can you watch *Wild Animals* and *Fly a Kite*? Explain.

____

3. **Write How-To Directions** Yoko wants to watch *Science Fun.* Tami wants to watch *English Is Easy.* Can they each watch their shows? Write directions to help a partner find out.

Use your own paper.

Why do people use schedules?

Practice!

Channel	11:30 A.M.	12:00 noon	12:30 P.M.	1:00 P.M.
1	Cartoons	Figure Skating		Computer Whiz
9	Superkid	TV Weekly	Sea World	

Solve.

1. Which shows are 1 hour long? ______

2. Can you watch *Computer Whiz* and *Sea World*? Explain. ______

Write and Share

Jessica wrote this problem.

Tina wants to watch "Figure Skating." Jessica wants to watch "Computer Whiz." Can they each watch their program? Explain.

Jessica Boullosa
O'Rourke School
Mobile, Alabama

3. Solve Jessica's problem. Explain your answer. ______

______

4. Write a problem using information from the schedule. Have a partner solve it and explain the answer.

How did your partner explain his or her answer? ______

______

At Home: Have your child use the schedule above and tell you which shows are on at 12:00 noon.

Name

Chapter Review

Language and Mathematics

Choose the correct word to complete the sentence.

hour half hour quarter hour minute

1. A ______________ is 30 minutes.
2. 15 minutes is a ______________.

Concepts and Skills

Write the time.

___:___ ___:___ ___:___

Write the time.
Write the time 5 minutes later.

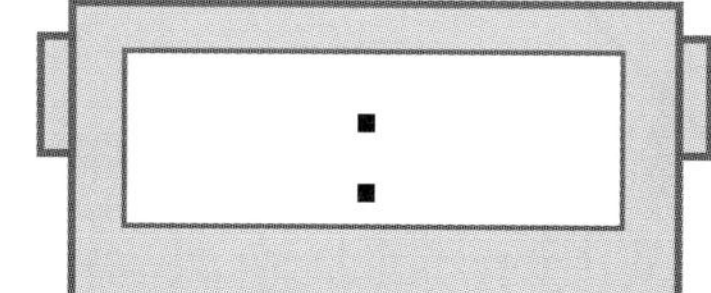
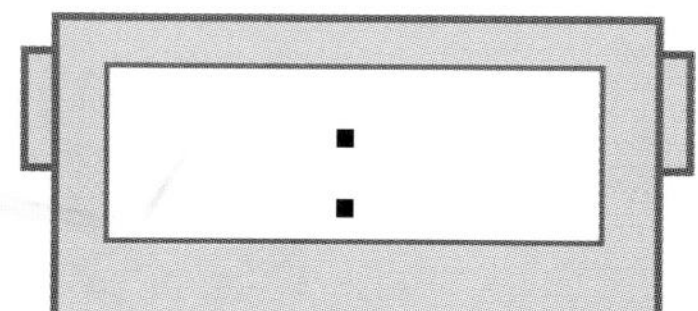

Problem Solving

Solve.

Louie got to the train station at 11:00. It took him 1 hour to get to the station.
At what time did he leave? ___:___

Use the calendar to solve.

8. How many days in April?

30 days

9. What day of the week is the twenty-ninth of April?

Wed

10. What date is the fifth Wednesday in April?

29

APRIL						
Sun	Mon	Tues	Wed	Thurs	Fri	Sat
			1	2	3	4
5	6	7	8	9	10	11
12	13	14	15	16	17	18
19	20	21	22	23	24	25
26	27	28	29	30		

What Do You Think?

Which one do you use most often?
✔ Check one.

DECEMBER						
Sun	Mon	Tues	Wed	Thurs	Fri	Sat
			1	2	3	4
5	6	7	8	9	10	11
12	13	14	15	16	17	18
19	20	21	22	23	24	25
26	27	28	29	30	31	

Why? ______________________

Write the time. 5:40
Explain how you can use counting to find the time.

Name

Chapter Test

Write the time.

2 

3 

Write the time and the time 5 minutes later.

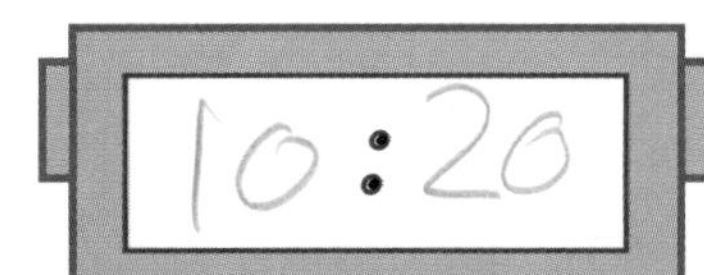

Use the calendar to solve problems 5 to 8.

JULY						
Sun	Mon	Tues	Wed	Thurs	Fri	Sat
			1	2	3	4
5	6	7	8	9	10	11
12	13	14	15	16	17	18
19	20	21	22	23	24	25
26	27	28	29	30	31	

5. On what day of the week is the Fourth of July? 

6. What date is the fourth Sunday in July? 

7. On which day of the week is the twenty-second of July? ______

8. How many Fridays are there in July? ______

9. Percy rides the bus for 1 hour to get to school. He gets to school at 8:00. What time does he leave? ______

10. Luke got to his sister's house at 2:30. It took him 2 hours to get there. What time did he leave? ______

Performance Assessment

What Did You Learn?

Complete the train schedule.

Then add two more stops to the schedule. Show the times for each.

TRAIN SCHEDULE		
Train Leaves	**Train Arrives**	**How Long Does It Take?**
Ashville 9:30	Dover 9:45	15 min
Dover 9:55	Liberty 10:20	25 minutes
Liberty 10:30	Suntown 11:01	31 min
Suntown 11:10	Blue Valley 12:00	50 min
____	____	____
____	____	____

You may want to put this page in your portfolio.

Math Connection

Patterns

Name ______________________________

Calendar Detective

Algebra **PATTERNS** You can find number patterns on a calendar.

AUGUST						
Sun	Mon	Tues	Wed	Thurs	Fri	Sat
						1
2	3	4	5	6	7	8
9	10	11	12	13	14	15
16	17	18	19	20	21	22
23/30	24/31	25	26	27	28	29

Look for number patterns on the calendar. You may want to use a calculator to help.

1. Ring some numbers that go  (right arrow).
2. Ring some numbers that go (down arrow).
3. Ring some numbers that go (down-left arrow).
4. Ring some numbers that go  (down-right arrow).

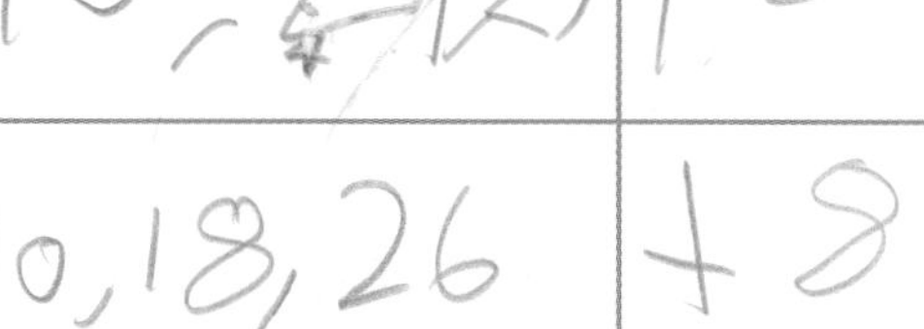

Write the numbers	Name the pattern
2, 3, 4, 5	+1
6, 13, 20	+7
15, 21, 27	+6
10, 18, 26	+8

Technology Connection
Computer

Make a Schedule

In what ways can a schedule change?

You can use a computer spreadsheet to help you make and change a schedule quickly.

PARTY SCHEDULE			
Activity	**Start Time**	**How Long It Takes**	**End Time**
Welcome guests	12:30	10 minutes	12:40
Musical chairs	12:40	20 minutes	
Sing songs		10 minutes	
Play games		20 minutes	
Eat cake		10 minutes	
Open presents		10 minutes	
Give out party favors		5 minutes	
Say goodbye		5 minutes	

At the Computer

1. Complete the spreadsheet.
   When will the party be over? ______

2. Change the start of the party to 1:00.
   What happens to the schedule? ____________

   ____

3. Change the length of time for playing games to 40 minutes.
   What happens to the schedule? ____________

   ____

Home Connection

Chapter 5 Wrap-Up

Name

Picture Clock

MATERIALS paper, crayons, scissors, clasp

DIRECTIONS Make a clock. Draw a picture for each activity you do. Tell about the activity. Show the time you do it.

As you and your child do this activity, it will help him or her develop a sense about the sequence of events that occur during the day.

Dear Family,

I am beginning an exciting new chapter in mathematics. I will be learning more about mental math and how to use what I know to add and subtract bigger numbers. Some of my work will look like this:

40 + 40 36 + 20 80 – 40 56 – 20

I will also be talking about games I play.

Learning About Games

Let's talk about games we like to play. We can make a list.

My Math Words

I am going to use these math words in this chapter.

Please help me make word cards for the math words. I can use these word cards when I explore adding and subtracting 2-digit numbers.

mental math
count on
count back

Your child,

Signature

Exploring 2-Digit Addition and Subtraction

Theme: Fun and Games

CHAPTER 6

READING ARITHMETIC WRITING

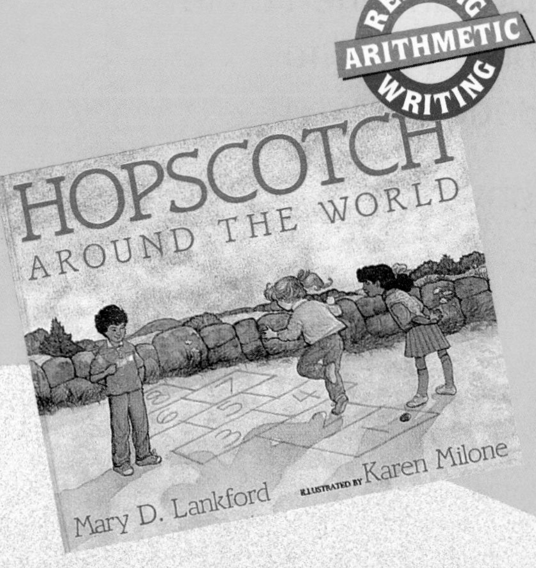

HOPSCOTCH
AROUND THE WORLD
Mary D. Lankford
ILLUSTRATED BY Karen Milone

Sequence of Events When you play games you need to follow the rules in order.

Listen to the stories from *Hopscotch Around the World.*

How do you play hopscotch? Tell the rules in order.

Name ____________________

What Do You Know?

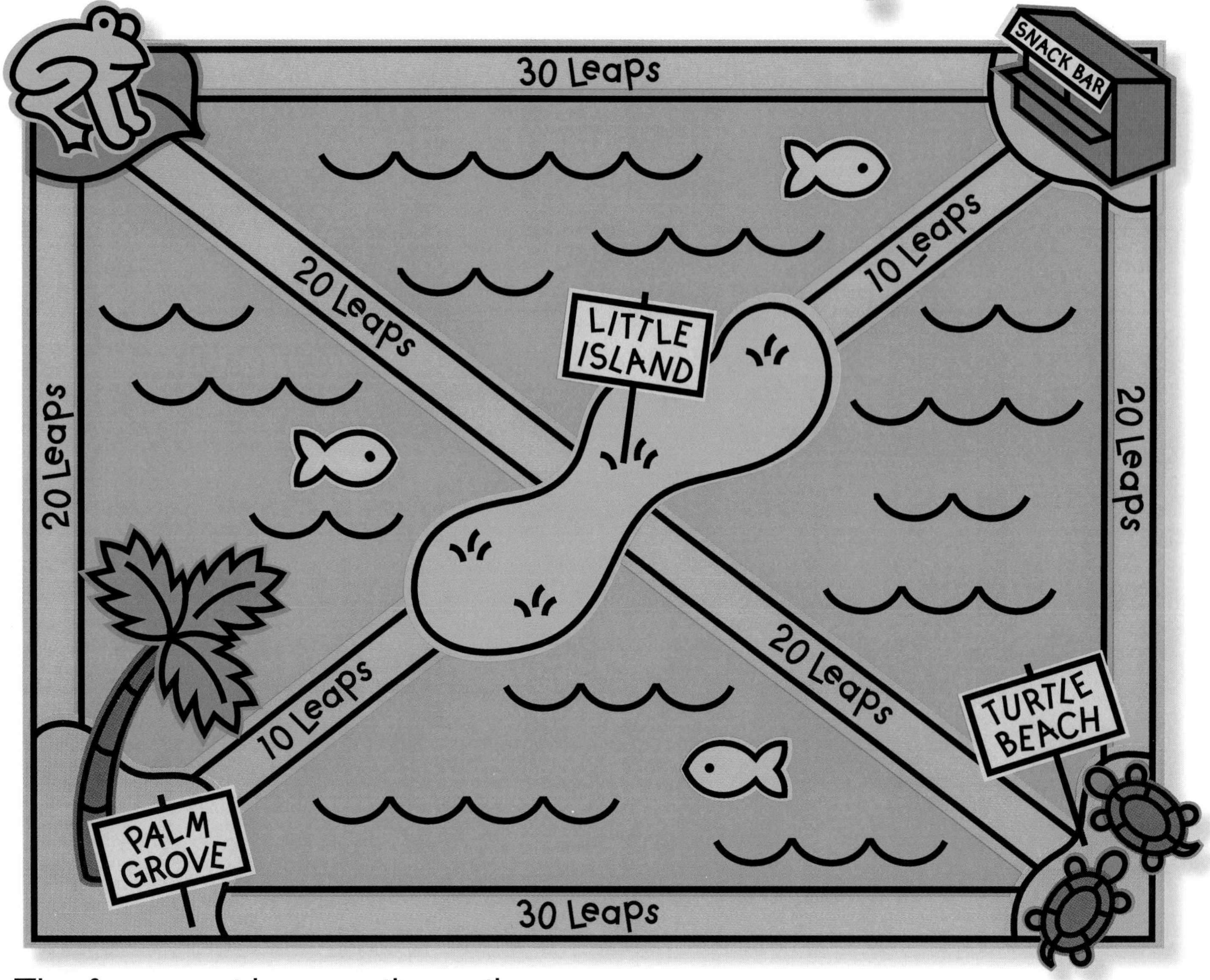

The frog must leap on the paths.
Find the total number of frog leaps.
Use mental math.

1. Find the shortest way for Frog to get from his pad to Turtle Beach.

   How many leaps? ________

2. Frog wants to stop at the Snack Bar and then Little Island on his way to Turtle Beach.

   How many leaps? ________

Write a problem about frog leaps. Explain how to solve it.

Name ______________________________

Explore Activity

Mental Math

Working Together

You and your partner need a [spinner].

Take turns.

- Choose a starting number. Write it in the first arrow.
- Spin. Write the + or – sign and the number.
- Your partner makes up a problem with the numbers.
- You solve the problem and write the total.

Start with 62 points. Lose 3 points. How many points are left?

	Starting Number	Spin + or –	Total Points
1			
2			
3			
4			
5			
6			

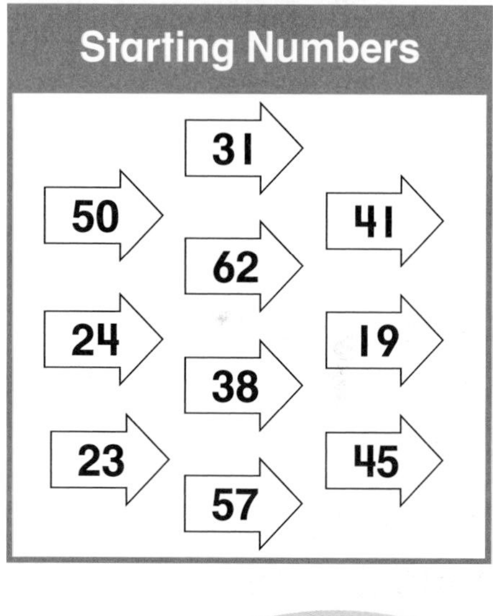

Starting Numbers
31
50
41
62
24
19
38
23
45
57

Use a starting number only once.

Practice!

Find the total number of points.

	Starting Number	+ or –	Total Points
1	28	– 2	26
2	31	+ 3	___
3	49	+ 1	___
4	64	– 1	___

	Starting Number	+ or –	Total Points
5	20	– 2	___
6	45	+ 2	___
7	56	+ 3	___
8	32	– 3	___

Tell a partner how you found the total points.

Mixed Review Test Preparation

Write the time.

9  ___ : ___ 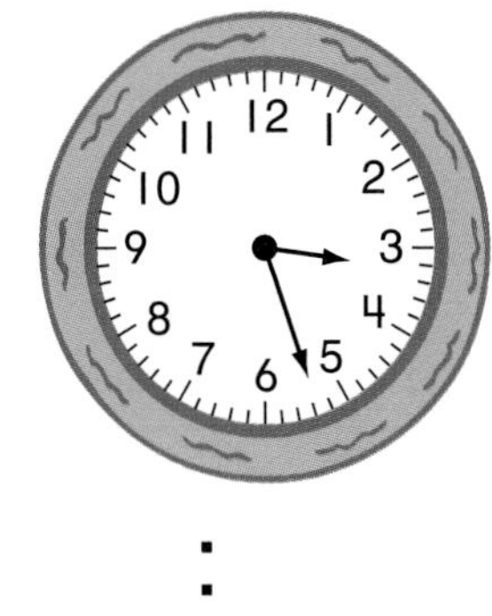 ___ : ___  ___ : ___

Count on to complete.

10 22, 32, 42, 52, ___, ___, ___, ___

11 9, 19, 29, ___, ___, ___, ___, ___

We counted on and counted back to add and subtract 1, 2, and 3. Ask your child how to add 52 + 3.

Name ______________________

More Mental Math

You know
1 + 1 = 2,
so you know
10 + 10 = 20.
You know
3 – 1 = 2,
so you know
30 – 10 = 20.

You can use **mental math** to solve these problems.

1. There are 4 red counters and 4 blue counters.
   How many counters in all? 8 counters

   What if there were 40 red counters
   and 40 blue counters.
   How many counters in all? 80 counters

2. There are 8 balloons.
   2 of the balloons are green.
   The rest of them are pink.
   How many balloons are pink? ____ balloons

   What if there were 80 balloons
   and 20 were green.
   How many balloons would be pink? ____ balloons

3. There are 2 big balls and 3 small balls.
   How many balls in all? ____ balls

   What if there were 20 big balls
   and 30 small balls.
   How many balls in all? ____ balls

How is 40 + 40 different from 4 + 4?
How is 80 – 20 different from 8 – 2?

Glossary
mental math

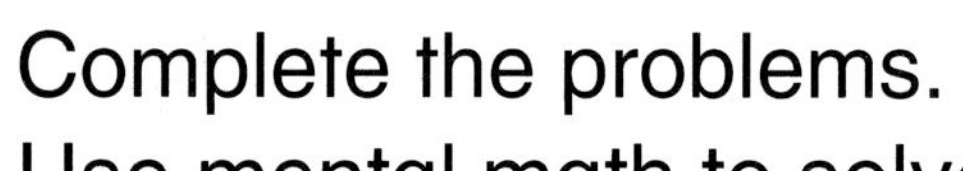

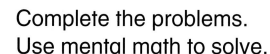

Practice!

Complete the problems.
Use mental math to solve.

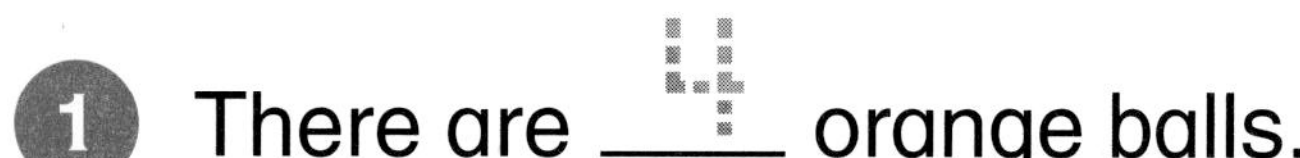

1 There are 4 orange balls.

There are 2 green balls.

How many balls in all? ____ balls

What if there are 40 orange balls

and 20 green balls?

How many balls in all? ____ balls

2 There are ____ kites.

____ kites fly away.

How many kites are left? ____ kites

What if there are ____ kites

and ____ fly away?

How many kites are left? ____ kites

Add or subtract.

3 $6 - 2 =$ ____ $1 + 4 =$ ____ $8 - 3 =$ ____

$60 - 20 =$ ____ $10 + 40 =$ ____ $80 - 30 =$ ____

4 $3 + 4 =$ ____ $5 + 4 =$ ____ $7 - 7 =$ ____

$30 + 40 =$ ____ $50 + 40 =$ ____ $70 - 70 =$ ____

At Home: We are learning how to use facts to solve problems with tens. Have your child explain problem 2 above.

Name

Explore Activity

Count On by Tens

Glossary

count on

Find how many of each toy the store has.

Working Together

You and your partner need 6 counters.

Take turns.

- Put a counter on one of the boxes below.
- Write the number in the addition sentence.
- **Count on** by tens to find the total.
- Your partner checks your work.

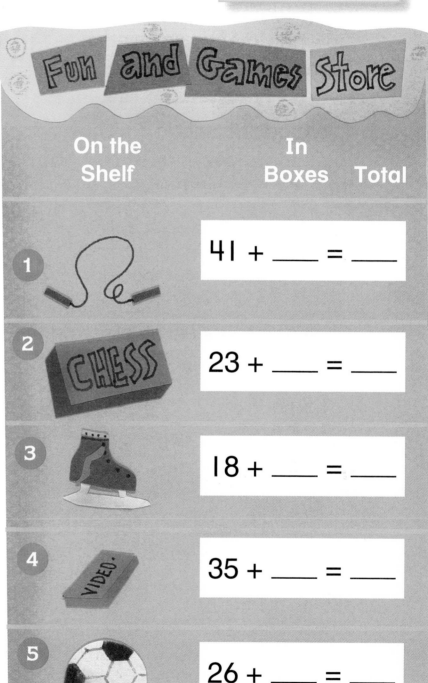

Fun and Games Store

	On the Shelf	In Boxes	Total
1	41 +	___ =	___
2	23 +	___ =	___
3	18 +	___ =	___
4	35 +	___ =	___
5	26 +	___ =	___
6	34 +	___ =	___

What is the greatest total you could get? Explain.

You can count on by tens: 46, 56, 66.

Solve.

1. Mr. Tong had 46 games to sell. He got a box with 20 more games. Now how many games does he have to sell?

66 games

---

2. There are 32 dolls in a store window. Another window has 10 more dolls than the first window. How many dolls are in the second window? ____ dolls

---

3. Mr. Tong placed 25 toy cars on one shelf. He placed 30 cars on another shelf. How many cars did he place on the two shelves? ____ cars

Add.

4. $43 + 10 =$ ____
5. $27 + 30 =$ ____
6. $65 + 20 =$ ____
7. $72 + 10 =$ ____
8. $10 + 17 =$ ____
9. $39 + 30 =$ ____
10. $54 + 20 =$ ____
11. $83 + 10 =$ ____
12. $76 + 20 =$ ____
13. $30 + 44 =$ ____
14. $51 + 30 =$ ____
15. $62 + 10 =$ ____

At Home: We counted on 10, 20, or 30 to add. Ask your child to tell you how to solve problems 1 to 3 above.

Name ______________________

Count Back by Tens

Working Together

You and your partner need a 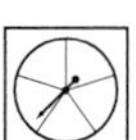 and 2 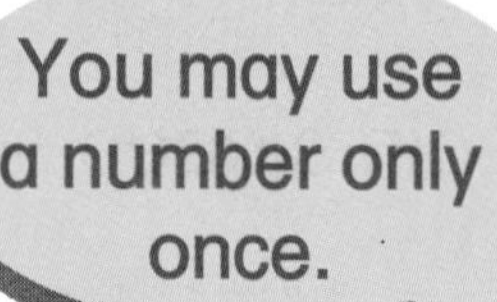.

Take turns.

- Put a counter on the wheel.
- Write the number to start a subtraction sentence.
- Your partner spins to get tens and writes the number in the sentence.
- **Count back** by tens to find the difference.

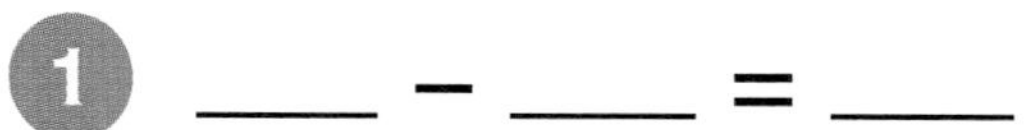

1. ____ – ____ = ____
2. ____ – ____ = ____
3. ____ – ____ = ____
4. ____ – ____ = ____
5. ____ – ____ = ____
6. ____ – ____ = ____
7. ____ – ____ = ____
8. ____ – ____ = ____
9. ____ – ____ = ____
10. ____ – ____ = ____

What is the least difference you could get? Explain.

You can count back by tens: 65, 55, 45.

Solve.

1. Alana scored 65 points.
   Then she lost 20 points.
   How many points does she have now?

2. To win a game takes 77 points.
   Ryan has 30 points.
   How many more points does he need? ____ points

3. Ella has 29 points.
   Her brother has 20 points.
   How many more points does Ella have? ____ points

Subtract.

4. 88 – 30 = ____
5. 37 – 30 = ____
6. 45 – 20 = ____
7. 61 – 20 = ____
8. 58 – 10 = ____
9. 82 – 10 = ____
10. 72 – 20 = ____
11. 56 – 20 = ____
12. 97 – 30 = ____
13. 75 – 30 = ____
14. 64 – 10 = ____
15. 99 – 10 = ____

Write about how you use mental math to solve some problems.

At Home: We counted back 10, 20, or 30 to subtract. Ask your child to tell you how to solve problems 1 to 3 above.

Name ______________________

Use Mental Math

There were 67 people at the game.
Then 30 more people came.
How many people are at the game now?

Which mental math strategy would you use to solve this problem?

There are 97 people at the game.

Cultural Note
Boys and girls in 81 countries around the world play on Little League teams.

Solve.

1. There are 75 children who play ball.
   This week 20 of them did not play.
   How many children played ball this week? _____ children

2. The home team made 30 points.
   Then they made 40 more points.
   How many points did they make in all? _____ points

3. The class had 83 tickets to sell.
   They have 30 tickets left.
   How many tickets did they sell? _____ tickets

   The class sold the tickets for $1 each.
   How much money did they make? _____

Practice!

Solve.

1. There are 36 bags of popcorn.
There are 20 bags of chips.
How many more bags of popcorn are there than bags of chips? 16 bags

2. The children sold 38 hot dogs.
Then they sold 3 more.
How many hot dogs did they sell? ____ hot dogs

3. The children made 24 cookies to sell.
Someone ate 2 cookies.
How many cookies do they have to sell? ____ cookies

4.  Choose a pair of numbers.
Write a problem.
Have a partner solve it.

48	2

25	20

30	62

____

____

____

More to Explore — Number Sense

54 people are going to the game.
Each bus holds 30 people.
How many buses are needed?

____ buses

The school has 34 helmets.
Each team needs 10 helmets.
How many teams can use the helmets at one time?

____ teams

Ask your child to tell you about problem 4 above. Try to solve it.

Name ____________________

Extra Practice
Game!

Addition/Subtraction Race

You and your partner need a [number cube], a [calculator], and 2 [counters].

Take turns.

- Put your counter on *Start.*
- Roll a number cube.
  Move that many spaces.
- Tell the sum or difference.
  Check your answer with a calculator.
- If correct, stay in the space.
  If wrong, move back one space.
- The winner is the first player to reach *End.*

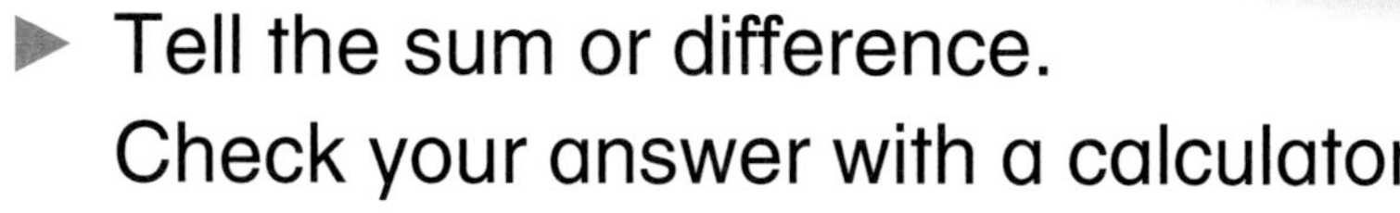

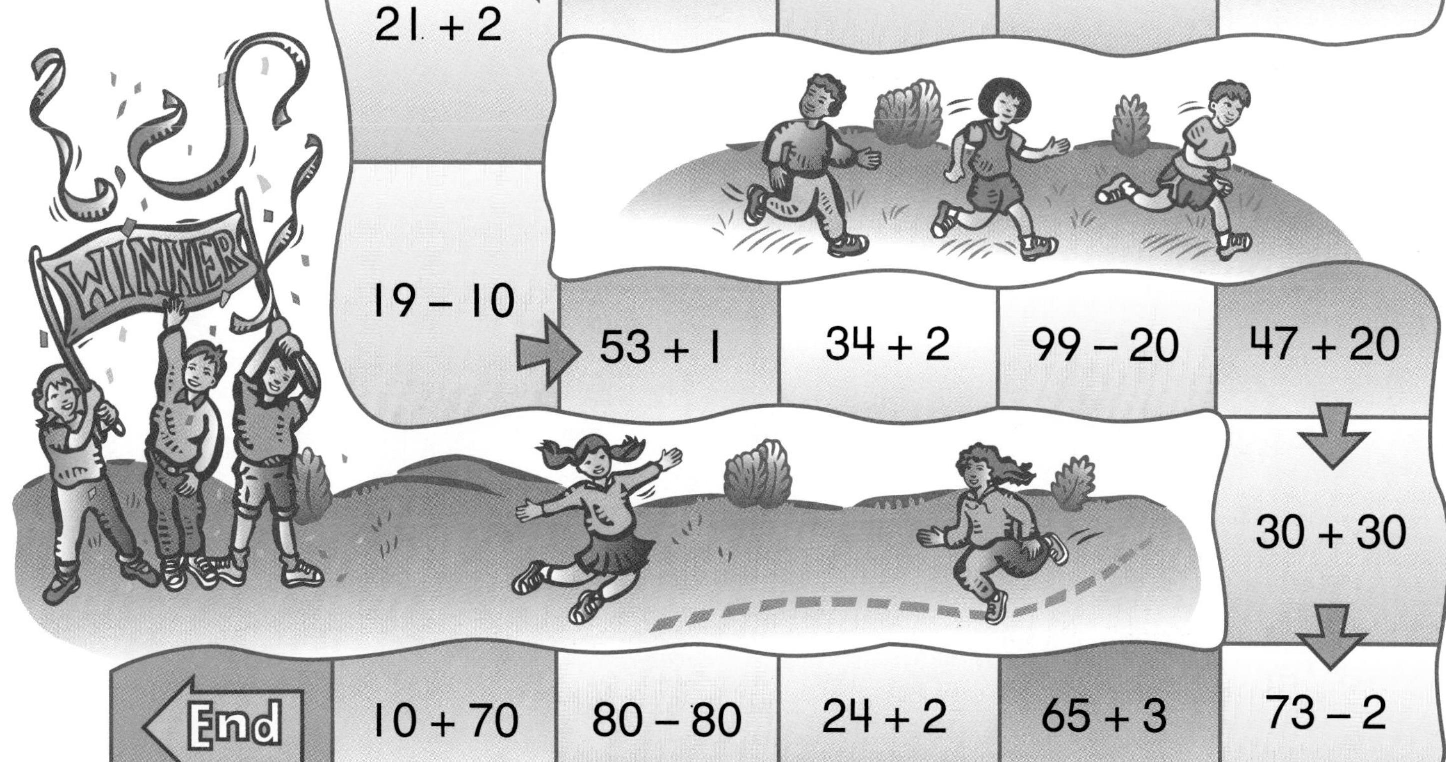

Add or subtract.

1	14 + 3 = 17	20 + 40 = ____	38 − 10 = ____
2	80 − 1 = ____	95 − 3 = ____	47 + 20 = ____
3	63 + 1 = ____	18 + 30 = ____	73 − 20 = ____
4	30 + 26 = ____	52 − 30 = ____	81 + 2 = ____
5	24 − 2 = ____	10 + 68 = ____	45 − 10 = ____
6	70 − 20 = ____	96 − 30 = ____	25 + 20 = ____
7	87 + 3 = ____	30 + 2 = ____	72 − 30 = ____

Mixed Review Test Preparation

Compare. Write $>$ for is greater than.
Write $<$ for is less than.

8	26 ◯ 15	31 ◯ 42	56 ◯ 51
9	96 ◯ 82	75 ◯ 89	45 ◯ 37
10	7 ◯ 19	22 ◯ 32	61 ◯ 51

11

____

12

____

Name ______________________

Problem-Solving Strategy

Solve 2-Step Problems

Read
Plan
Solve
Look Back

Dana put 25 stars on her notebook.
Her cat licked off 10 of the stars.
Then Dana put 3 new stars on the book.
How many stars are on Dana's notebook now?

Plan

What strategies can you use?
Do you need more than one?

Solve

Step 1

25 stars
10 licked off
How many left?

____ stars

Step 2

____ stars left
3 more stars
Now how many stars?

____ stars

How did you do Step 1? ______________________

____

How did you do Step 2? ______________________

____

Look Back

Does your answer make sense? Why?

____

____

Practice!

Solve. Show how you found your answer.

1. Kim made 39 cards.
   She sent out 10 cards yesterday.
   Today she sent out 20 cards.
   How many cards does Kim have left? ____ cards

   Step 1: ______________ Step 2: ______________

2. Mary put 27 flowers on a shirt.
   10 flowers fell off in the wash.
   3 flowers fell off when she wore the shirt.
   How many flowers are still on the shirt? ____ flowers

   Step 1: ______________ Step 2: ______________

3. Joel had 31 points.
   He scored 20 more points.
   Then he lost 3 points.
   How many points does Joel have now? ____ points

   Step 1: ______________ Step 2: ______________

Sequence of Events

You can work here.

Mario scored 16 points in a game.
Kareem scored 10 points, then he lost 2 points.
Mario scored 3 more points, then he lost 5 points.
Now the game is over. Who won? __________

Show how you found the winner.

We solved two-step problems. Ask your child how to solve problem 3 above.

Name ___

Midchapter Review

Add or subtract.

1. 26 + 3 = ___
2. 65 − 2 = ___
3. 50 − 30 = ___
4. 30 + 30 = ___
5. 17 + 30 = ___
6. 58 − 20 = ___
7. 46 + 20 = ___
8. 96 − 10 = ___

Solve.

9. Simon had 51 cards.
He gave 20 of them to his brother.
How many cards does Simon have now? ___ cards

Solve. Show how you found your answer.

10. Lucie put 68 beads on a string.
Then she put 3 more beads on the string.
The string broke and 20 beads fell off.
How many are on the string now? ___ beads

Step 1: ___ Step 2: ___

Write about how you use mental math to subtract 74 − 30.

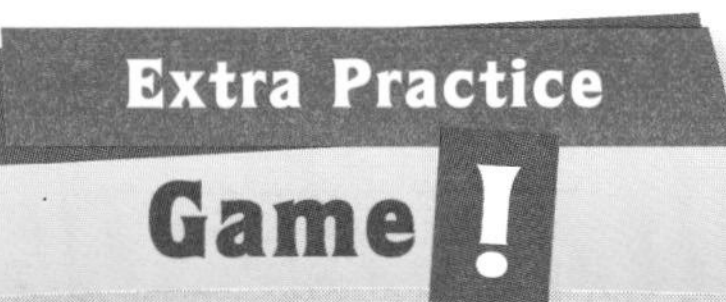

Color by Number

You and your partner need a [spinner], [counter],
[red crayon], and [yellow crayon].

Choose red or yellow.

Take turns.

- Drop the counter on the board. This number is your starting number.
- Spin to get another number.
- Add or subtract. Your partner checks.
- If correct, color the space with your color. If wrong, color the space with your partner's color.

The player with more spaces colored wins.

35	36	63	70	42
75	45	47	39	68
72	52	66	59	72

Red score: ____ Yellow score: ____

Real-Life Investigation
Applying Mental Math

Name ______________________

Play Lu-Lu!

> **Cultural Note**
> Lu-Lu is a Hawaiian game. The word *lu-lu* means "to shake."

Working Together

You and your partners need a , 4 cardboard circles, and a cup.

- Take turns. Each player gets two tosses a turn.
- Shake the four circles in a cup and toss them. Count the dots.
- If all four pieces land faceup, toss them all again.
- If some pieces land facedown, toss only the facedown pieces on your second toss.
- Use mental math to add the points to your score. Use the calculator to check.
- The winner is the first player to score 100 points.

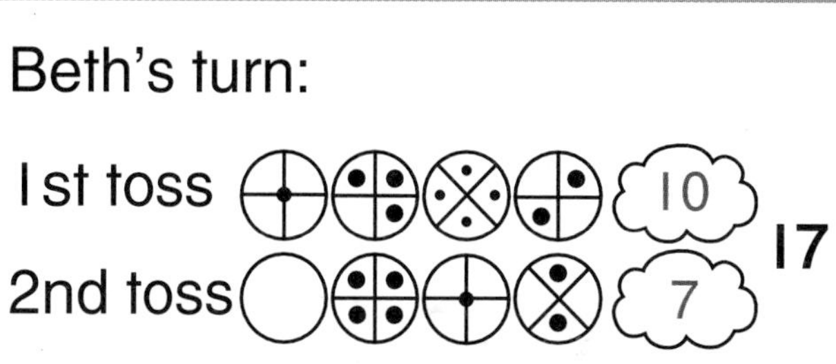

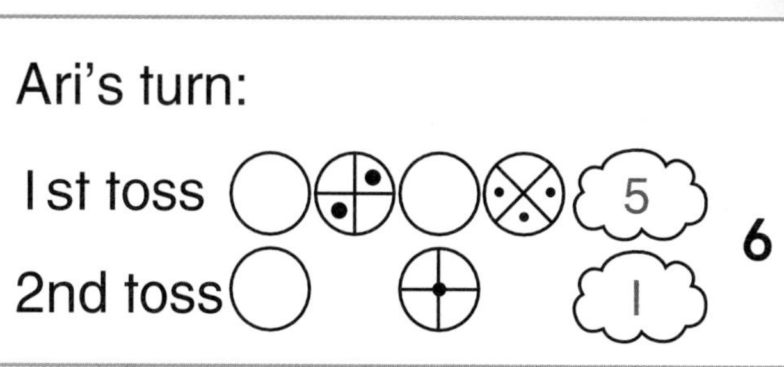

SCORE CARD

Beth	Ari
10	12
+17	+ 6
27	18

Decision Making

1. What if you have 48 points and you score 15 more points?
   What strategy would you use to add? ______________________

   ____

2. Make up new rules for the game.
   Then try it.
   How does the game work now? ______________________

   ____

Write a report.

3. Tell how you added the scores for each round.

4. Tell how you changed the game.

More to Investigate

PREDICT What kind of game could you make up that uses mental math to subtract?

EXPLORE Work with your group. Make up a subtraction game. Write the rules. Play the game.

FIND How is your game like the Lu-Lu game? How is it different? Trade games with another group and play.

Name ______________________

Addition Strategies

There are 45 big marbles.
There are 23 small marbles.
How many marbles in all?

45 + 23 = ?

Here are some mental math strategies you can use.

40 + 20 = 60
60 + 5 = 65
65 + 3 = 68

There are 68 marbles in all.

What are some other strategies you could use?

Working Together

Use mental math to solve.
Share your strategies with your partners.

1. Didi has 32 marbles.
   Carl has 18 marbles.
   How many do they have altogether? ____ marbles

2. José has 21 marbles.
   He buys 54 more.
   Now how many marbles does he have? ____ marbles

Practice!

Solve. Use mental math.

1. Lara's game has 32 number cards.
   It has 26 letter cards.
   How many cards are in the game? ____ cards

---

2. Sari has 19 colored pencils.
   Ben has 33 colored pencils.
   How many pencils do they have altogether? ____ pencils

3. Explain how you solved problem 2. ________________________________

   ____

Add. Use mental math.

4. 21 + 18 = ____   17 + 30 = ____   46 + 44 = ____

5. 79 + 13 = ____   21 + 75 = ____   8 + 57= ____

More to Explore Number Sense

Cam used 3 packs of cards for a game.
There were 30 cards in each pack.
How many cards did she use?

____ cards

Jonah used 4 bags of counters for a game.
There were 20 counters in each bag.
How many counters did he use?

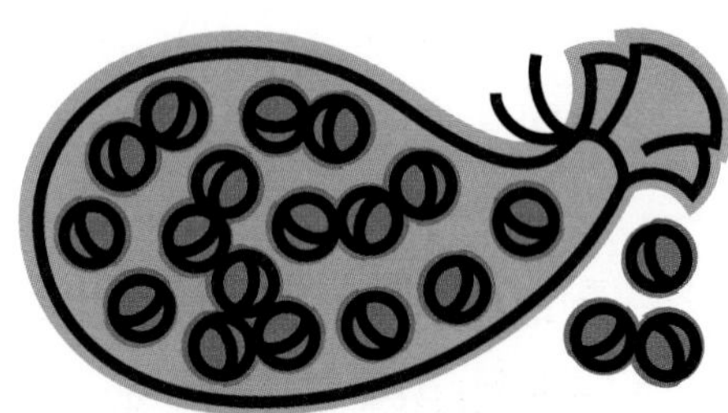

____ counters

At Home: We solved addition problems by using mental math strategies. Have your child explain how to solve problem 1.

Name ____________________

Explore Activity

Subtraction Strategies

There are 62 puzzle pieces.
13 pieces are from one puzzle.
How many pieces are from another puzzle?

62 − 13 = __?__

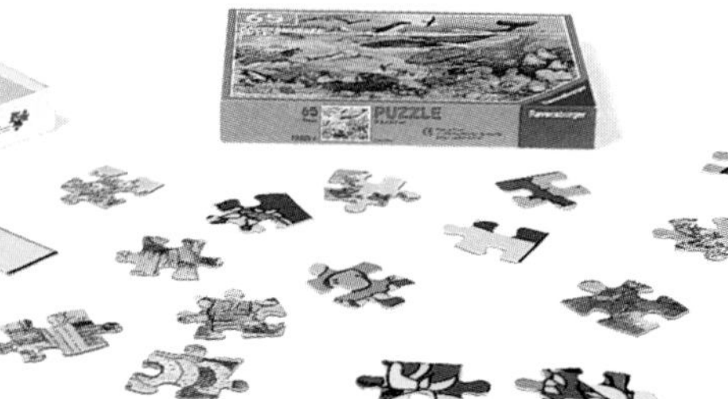

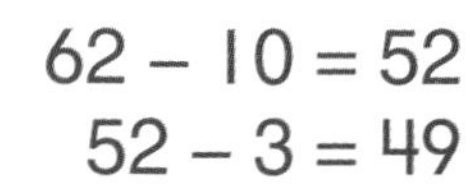

62 − 10 = 52
Count back
51, 50, 49.

There are __49__ pieces from another puzzle.

What are some other strategies you could use?

Working Together

Use mental math to solve.
Share your strategies with your partners.

1. Jo had a puzzle with 59 pieces.
   She lost 12 pieces.
   How many pieces does she have now? ____ pieces

2. Adam built a house with 78 blocks.
   He built a wall with 34 blocks.
   How many more blocks did he use for the house? ____ blocks

Practice!

Solve. Use mental math.

1. Jeanne has 27 dolls. She has 16 dresses for the dolls. How many more dolls than dresses does she have? ____ dolls

2. Lou had \$46. He spent \$42. How much money does Lou have now? ____

---

3. 68 – 34 = ____   46 – 13 = ____   35 – 2 = ____

4. 31 – 20 = ____   24 – 5 = ____   46 – 26 = ____

Cultural Connection

English Darts

Darts is an old English game played around the world. In the outside ring, points are doubled. In the inside ring, points are tripled.

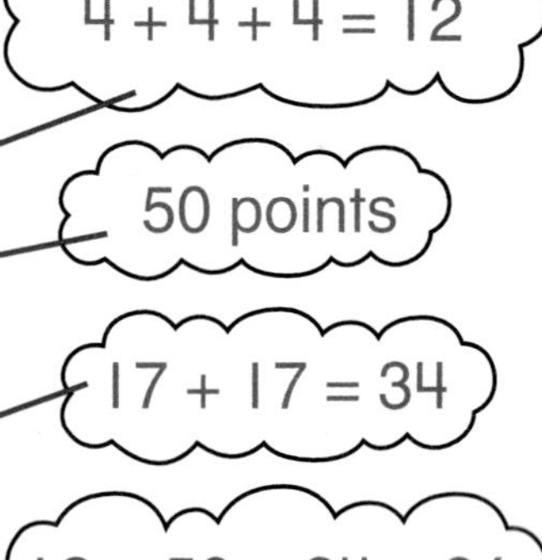

Find the scores.
Then check with a calculator.

____

____

____

At Home: Have your child explain how to solve problem 1 above.

Name

Solve Multistep Problems

Mrs. Festa put 20 bows and 5 flowers on her new hat. The wind blew off 3 bows and 2 flowers. How many things are left on Mrs. Festa's hat?

What will you need to do to find the answer?

It helps to write each step.

Step 1: $20 + 5 = \underline{25}$

Step 2: $3 + 2 = \underline{5}$

Step 3: $25 - 5 = \underline{20}$

There are  20 things on Mrs. Festa's hat.

Solve. Show your work.

1. Isabel had 35 flowers. She bought 10 more. Then she gave away 3 of them. She just got 20 more flowers. How many flowers does Isabel have now?

____ flowers

2.  **Sequence of Events** Write a story about Isabel and her flowers. Tell four things that happen. Use the numbers and words from the list.

30 6 9 5
first
next
then
last
gave away

Practice!

Solve. Show your work.

1. Flo put 34 buttons and 26 bows on her hat. The wind blew off 3 buttons and 1 bow. How many things are left? ____ things

2. What if the wind blew off 13 buttons and 11 bows. How many things are left? ____ things

Write and Share

STUDENT TO STUDENT

Deric wrote this problem.

Deric Hughes
Emma School
Asheville, North Carolina

I went to the store and got 30 grapes for my hat. Then I went to the plant store and got 10 roses. My mom gave me 10 buttons for my hat. My sister ate 20 grapes. My dad wanted 6 roses. How many things are still on my hat?

3. Show how to solve Deric's problem.

Write

4. Write a word problem that uses addition and subtraction. Have a partner solve it.

Use your own paper.

At Home: We solved problems with several steps. Ask about the problem your child wrote.

Name

Chapter Review

Language and Mathematics

Choose the correct word to complete the sentence.

1. You can ____________ to subtract 30 – 20.
2. You can ____________ by tens to add.

mental math
count on
count back

Concepts and Skills

Use mental math to add or subtract.

3. 40 + 30 = ____
4. 37 + 30 = ____
5. 86 – 30 = ____
6. 51 – 20 = ____
7. 68 + 3 = ____
8. 41 + 2 = ____
9. 16 – 3 = ____
10. 20 + 60 = ____
11. 50 – 20 = ____
12. 39 – 2 = ____
13. 22 + 38 = ____
14. 90 – 10 = ____
15. 87 – 45 = ____
16. 35 + 53 = ____

Solve.

17. Brad made 25 pictures.
Then he made 30 more.
How many pictures did he
make in all? ____ pictures

Problem Solving

Solve. Show how you found your answer.

18. Chim had 45 baseball cards.
He got 3 more.
Then he gave 10 cards to Pete.
How many cards does Chim have now? ____ cards

____

19. Sherry had 38 points. She lost 2 points.
Then Sherry got 30 more points.
How many points does Sherry have now? ____ points

____

20. Mr. Delano put 10 birdhouses and
15 bird feeders in a tree.
The wind blew down 2 birdhouses
and 2 bird feeders.
How many things are still in the tree? ____ things

____

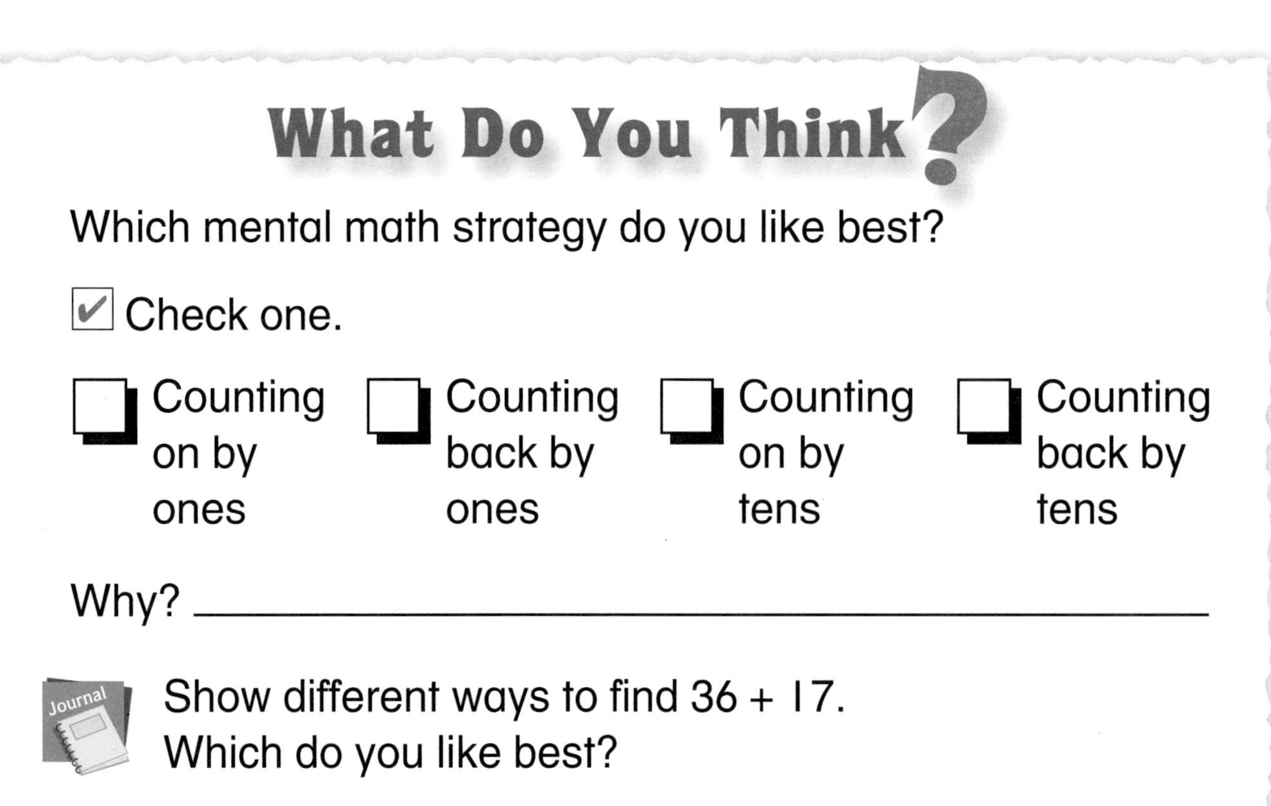

What Do You Think?

Which mental math strategy do you like best?

☑ Check one.

- ☐ Counting on by ones
- ☐ Counting back by ones
- ☐ Counting on by tens
- ☐ Counting back by tens

Why? ____

Journal: Show different ways to find 36 + 17.
Which do you like best?

Name ______________________________

Chapter Test

Use mental math to add or subtract.

1. $85 - 3 =$ ____
2. $51 + 3 =$ ____
3. $60 - 30 =$ ____
4. $38 + 10 =$ ____
5. $43 + 34 =$ ____
6. $52 - 12 =$ ____
7. $67 + 3 =$ ____
8. $96 - 23 =$ ____

Solve.

9. Ian made 56 cards.
He used 30 cards.
How many cards does
Ian have left? ____ cards

Solve. Show how you found your answer.

10. Tina had 58 points in a game.
Then she lost 3 points.
On her next turn, she made
10 more points. How many
points does Tina have now? ____ points

____

____

____

Performance Assessment

What Did You Learn?

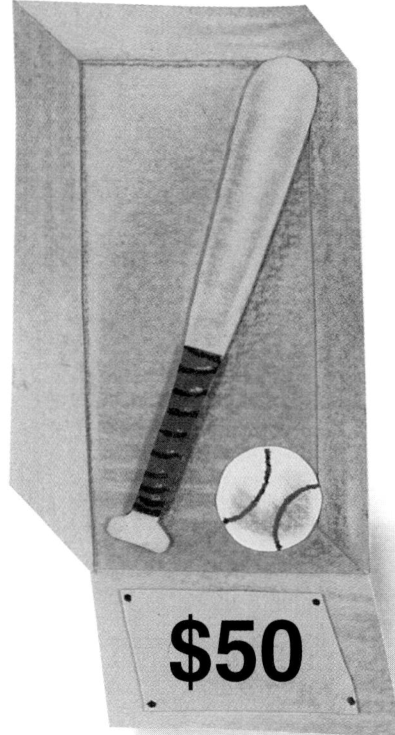

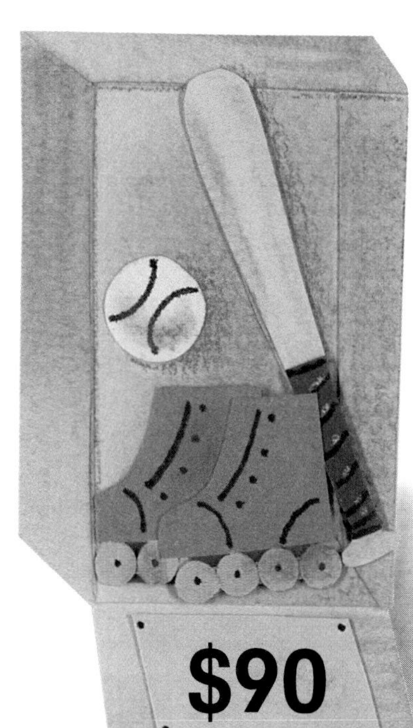

Find out what each item costs.

1. The [skates] cost ______.
2. The [ball] costs ______.
3. The [bat] costs ______.
4. Explain how you find the costs.

____

____

____

You may want to put this page in your portfolio.

Math Connection

Calculator

Name ______________________________

Sums and Differences

Predict what your calculator will show.

Enter [+] [3].
What number will you get
after you press [=] [=] [=] [=]? ______

Try it. What number is in the display? ______

Predict these sums.
Then press the keys to check.

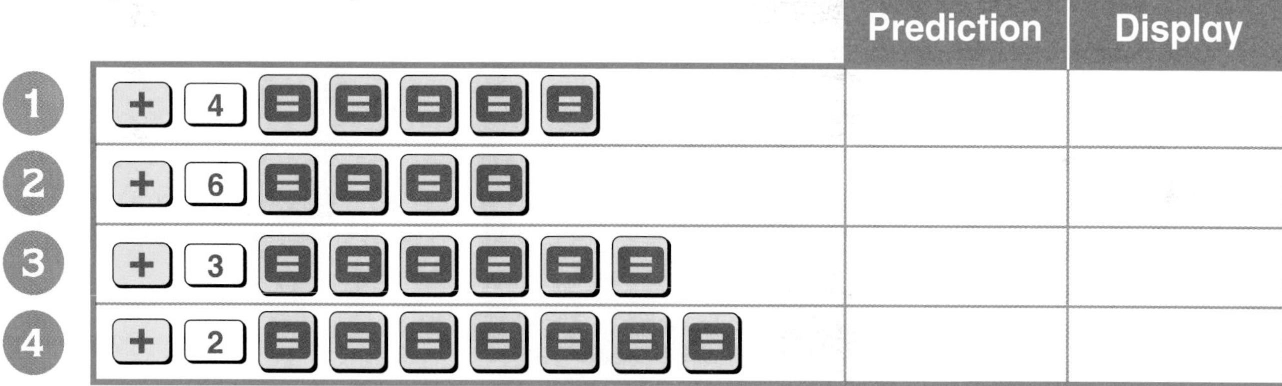

	Keys	Prediction	Display
1	[+] [4] [=] [=] [=] [=] [=]		
2	[+] [6] [=] [=] [=] [=]		
3	[+] [3] [=] [=] [=] [=] [=] [=]		
4	[+] [2] [=] [=] [=] [=] [=] [=] [=]		

Predict these differences.
Then press the keys to check.

	Keys	Prediction	Display
5	[4] [0] [−] [2] [=] [=]		
6	[3] [0] [−] [3] [=] [=] [=]		
7	[2] [8] [−] [2] [=] [=] [=] [=]		
8	[5] [7] [−] [1] [=] [=] [=] [=] [=]		

Curriculum Connection

Language Arts

Jump-Rope Rhymes

Listen to this poem.

Rope Rhyme

Get set, ready now, jump right in
Bounce and kick and giggle and spin
Listen to the rope when it hits the ground
Listen to the clappedy-slappedy sound
Jump right up when it tells you to
Come back down, whatever you do
Count to a hundred, count by ten
Start to count all over again
That's what jumping is all about
Get set, ready now
jump
right
out!

—Eloise Greenfield

Write your own jump-rope rhyme.
It can be long or short, but use some numbers.

Get a jump rope and some friends.
Try out your rhyme.

Name

Cumulative Review

Read each question and choose the best answer.

1. 48 + 20 = ___

- 28
- 50
- 68
- 78

2. Find the number that means 7 tens 8 ones.

- 57
- 68
- 78
- 94

3. What is the time on the clock?

- 2:00
- 2:15
- 2:30
- 3:30

4. 74 – 30 = ___

- 34
- 44
- 71
- 77

5. What is the missing number in the pattern?

40, 45, 50, ☐

- 50
- 55
- 60
- 65

6. How much money does Lisa have?

- 36¢
- 45¢
- 46¢
- 61¢

TEST PREPARATION

7 Rosa has 15 tapes. Mark has 8 tapes. Which number sentence could you use to find out how many more tapes Rosa has than Mark?

- ⬭ 15 + 8 = ____
- ⬭ 15 − 8 = ____
- ⬭ 8 − 8 = ____
- ⬭ 8 − 0 = ____

8 Wes has 3 dimes. Max gave him 2 nickels. How much money does Wes have now?

- ⬭ 5¢
- ⬭ 30¢
- ⬭ 32¢
- ⬭ 40¢

9 The park had 47 trees. The club planted 10 more. Then 3 trees died. Which number shows how many trees the park has now?

- ⬭ 37
- ⬭ 44
- ⬭ 54
- ⬭ 60

10 Sara has 55 crayons. She gives away 20. Which number sentence could you use to find how many crayons Sara has left?

- ⬭ 55 + 20 = ____
- ⬭ 55 − 10 = ____
- ⬭ 20 − 20 = ____
- ⬭ 55 − 20 = ____

11 Kim had 25 tickets. She bought 20 more. How many does she have now?

- ⬭ 55
- ⬭ 45
- ⬭ 20
- ⬭ 5

12 The graph shows how many eggs were laid.

Number of Eggs Laid

Day 1	⬭⬭⬭⬭⬭⬭
Day 2	⬭⬭⬭⬭⬭
Day 3	⬭⬭⬭⬭⬭⬭⬭

Each ⬭ stands for 1 egg.

How many eggs were laid in all on Day 1 and Day 2?

- ⬭ 5
- ⬭ 6
- ⬭ 10
- ⬭ 11

TEST PREPARATION

Home Connection

Chapter 6 Wrap-Up

Name ______________________________

Number Card Game

PLAYERS 2 or more

MATERIALS 10 index cards, pencil

DIRECTIONS Write a 2-digit number on each card. Spread cards facedown on a table. Take turns. Pick two cards. Use mental math to add. If your answer is correct, keep the cards. The person with the most cards at the end of the game is the winner.

As you play this game with your child, have your child discuss what strategies he or she used to find the answer.

Dear Family,

I am beginning a new chapter in mathematics. During the next few weeks I will be learning to add 2-digit numbers such as:

$$\begin{array}{r} 38 \\ +\ 19 \\ \hline \end{array} \qquad \begin{array}{r} 57 \\ +\ 25 \\ \hline \end{array}$$

I will also be talking about how math is used at fairs.

Learning About Fairs

Let's talk about different kinds of fairs and carnivals. We can make a list of things to buy or win at fairs.

My Math Words

I am going to use these math words in this chapter.

Please help me make word cards for the math words. I can use these word cards when I practice adding 2-digit numbers.

ones
tens
regroup
2-digit numbers
estimate

Your child,

____
Signature

Adding 2-Digit Numbers

Theme: Fun at the Fair

CHAPTER 7

Write an Advertisement After you listen to the story, make a list of words about the county fair.

Listen to the story *Sam Johnson and the Blue Ribbon Quilt.*

How would you advertise the county fair? Use the words from your list.

Name

What Do You Know?

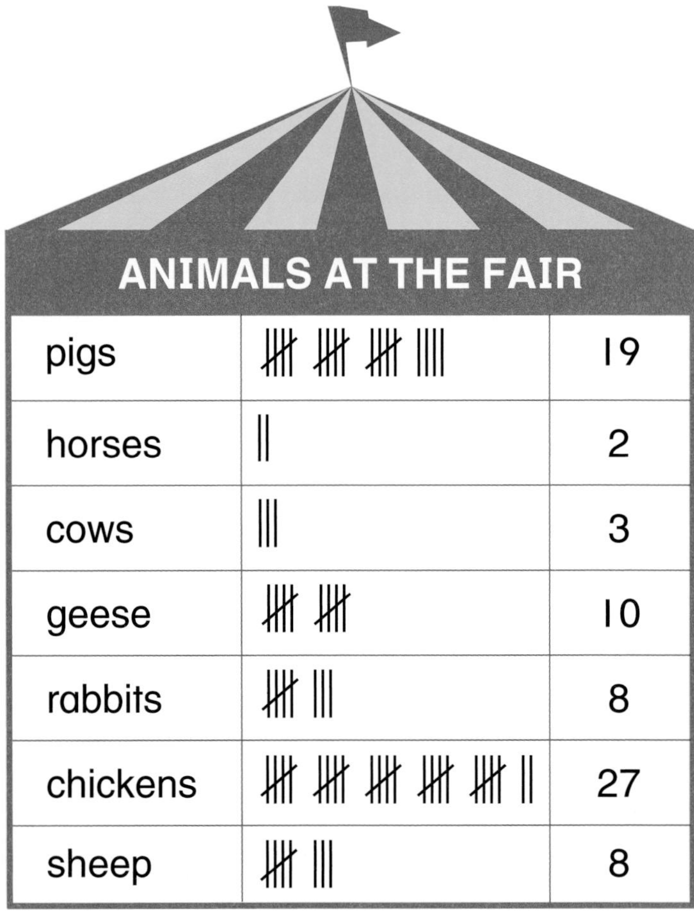

ANIMALS AT THE FAIR		
pigs	𝍸 𝍸 𝍸 ||||	19
horses	||	2
cows	|||	3
geese	𝍸 𝍸	10
rabbits	𝍸 |||	8
chickens	𝍸 𝍸 𝍸 𝍸 𝍸 ||	27
sheep	𝍸 |||	8

Jane counted the animals she saw at the fair.
Use the table. Find the total.

1. How many cows and sheep? ____
2. How many pigs and horses? ____
3. How many of the animals that Jane saw have feathers? ____

Use the table.
Write pairs of numbers that are easy to add.
Do as many as you can.
Explain an interesting strategy that you used to add.

Name

Regrouping

Working Together

You and your partner need 2 [tens] and 20 [ones].

- You show some **ones.**
- Your partner shows some ones.
- Make **tens** and ones. **Regroup** when you can.

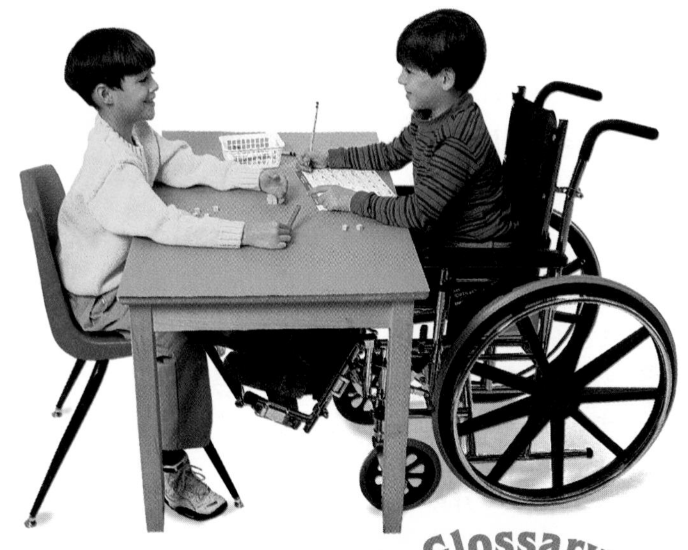

Glossary

ones
tens
regroup

	How many ones?	Can you regroup?		How many tens and ones?
1	12 ones	(yes)	no	1 ten 2 ones
2	____ ones	yes	no	____ ten ____ ones
3	____ ones	yes	no	____ ten ____ ones
4	____ ones	yes	no	____ ten ____ ones
5	____ ones	yes	no	____ ten ____ ones
6	____ ones	yes	no	____ ten ____ ones
7	____ ones	yes	no	____ ten ____ ones

When can't you regroup?

Practice!

Use [ten rod] and [unit cube]. Show the ones.
Regroup when you can.
Complete the chart.

		Can you regroup?		How many tens and ones?
1	16 ones	(yes)	no	1 ten 6 ones
2	9 ones	yes	no	____ ten ____ ones
3	13 ones	yes	no	____ ten ____ ones
4	10 ones	yes	no	____ ten ____ ones
5	5 ones	yes	no	____ ten ____ ones
6	19 ones	yes	no	____ ten ____ ones

Mixed Review Test Preparation

Complete.

7 

____ : ____

8 

____¢

9 

____¢

10 ____, ____, 65, 70, 75, ____, ____, ____

At Home: We regrouped when we had more than 10 ones. Ask your child how to regroup 15 ones.

Name ______________________

More Regrouping

You need 5 [tens] and 20 [ones].

Show the numbers 16 and 8.

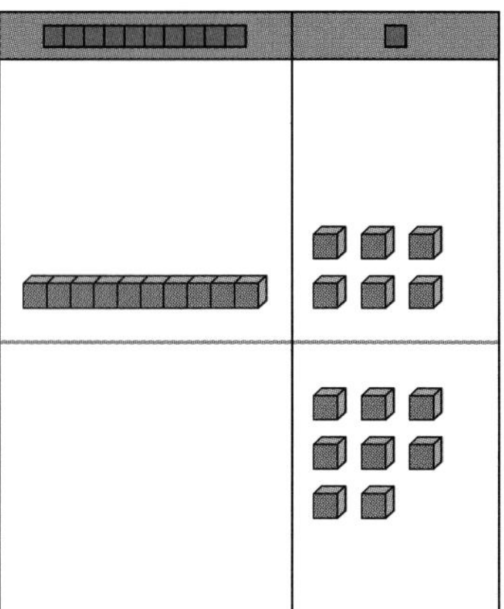

Regroup when you can.

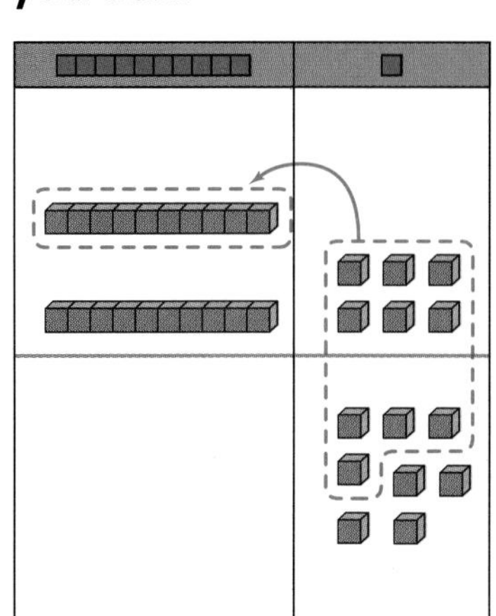

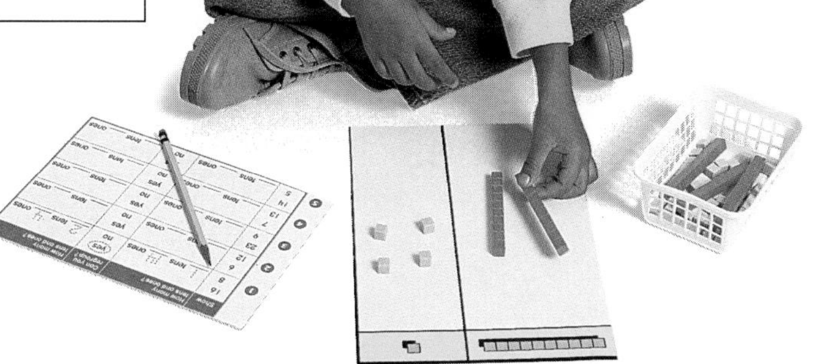

	Show	How many tens and ones?	Can you regroup?	How many tens and ones?
1	16 8	1 tens 14 ones	(yes) no	2 tens 4 ones
	6 12	____ tens ____ ones	yes no	____ tens ____ ones
	23 9	____ tens ____ ones	yes no	____ tens ____ ones
	7 13	____ tens ____ ones	yes no	____ tens ____ ones
	14 5	____ tens ____ ones	yes no	____ tens ____ ones

PATTERNS Tell a partner about a pattern you found.

Use [tens rod] and [ones cube].

Show the tens and ones.
Regroup when you can.
Write the number.

1. I ten 18 ones

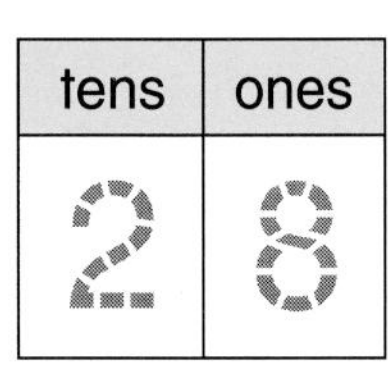

tens	ones
2	8

2. 2 tens 7 ones

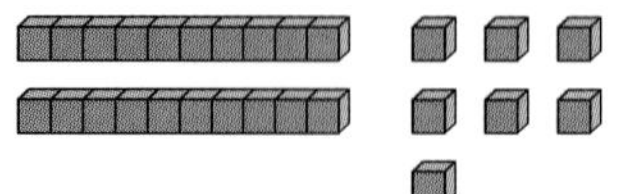

tens	ones
2	7

3. I ten 16 ones

tens	ones

4. 3 tens 10 ones

tens	ones

5. 15 ones

tens	ones

6. I ten 6 ones

tens	ones

7. 2 tens 14 ones

tens	ones

8. 19 ones

tens	ones

9. 4 tens 3 ones

tens	ones

10. I ten 10 ones

tens	ones

How do you know when to regroup?

At Home: We regrouped greater numbers. Have your child explain exercise 10.

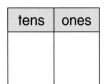

Name ____________________

Add 2-Digit Numbers

Glossary

2-digit numbers

You need 9 [tens] and 20 [ones].

You can use models to add **2-digit numbers**.

$$\begin{array}{r} 39 \\ +\ 15 \\ \hline 54 \end{array}$$

Show the numbers.

Regroup ones when you can.

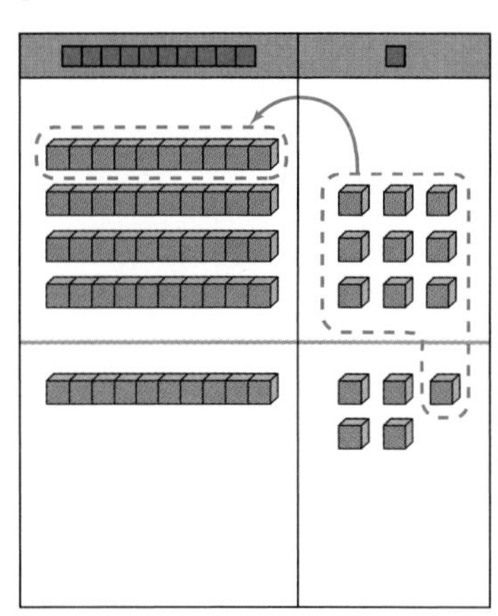

Count to find the sum.

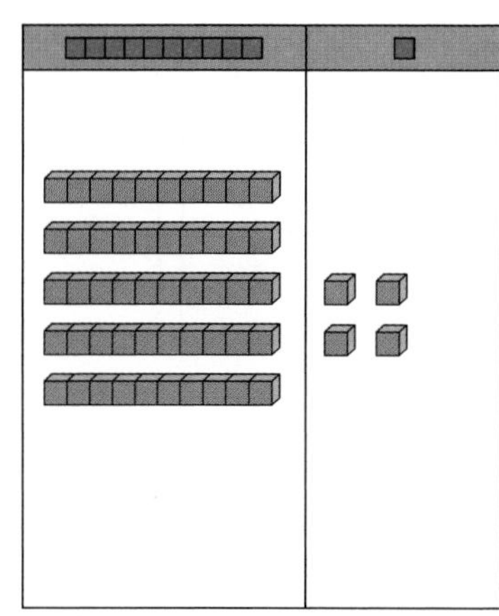

You can add without tens and ones models.

Add the ones.

	tens	ones
	□	
	3	9
+	1	5

14 ones

Regroup when you can.

	tens	ones
	1	
	3	9
+	1	5
		4

1 ten 4 ones

Add all the tens.

	tens	ones
	1	
	3	9
+	1	5
	5	4

5 tens

Add. Use tens and ones models to help.

1

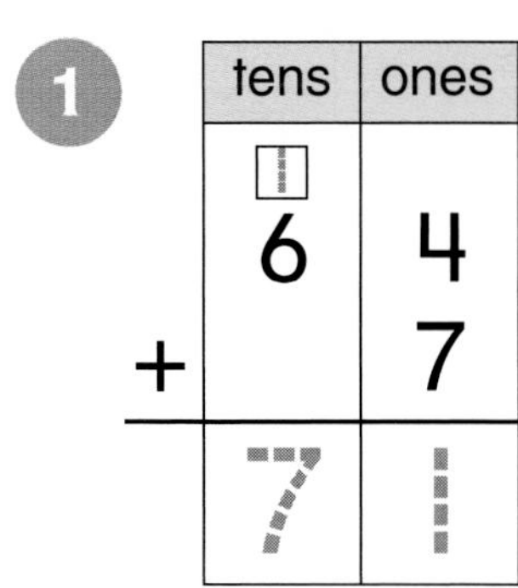

	tens	ones
	1	
	6	4
+		7
	7	1

	tens	ones
	□	
	4	1
+	2	3

	tens	ones
	□	
	3	6
+	4	6

	tens	ones
	□	
	2	8
+	3	5

Practice!

Add. Use tens and ones models to help.

1

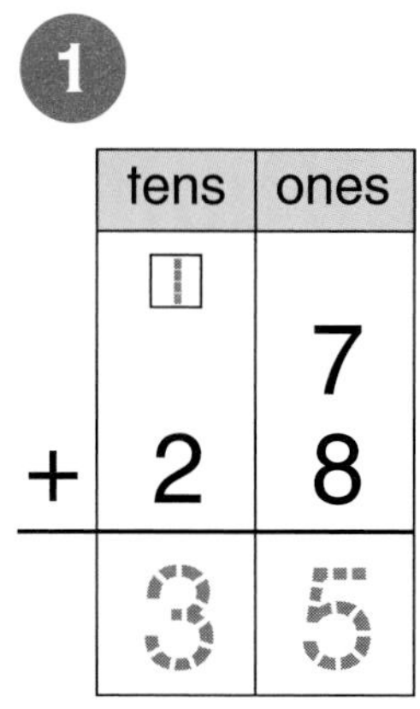

tens	ones
	7
+ 2	8
3	5

2

tens	ones
3	3
+ 2	8

tens	ones
1	2
+	9

tens	ones
6	4
+ 1	6

tens	ones
1	4
+ 5	3

3

tens	ones
2	7
+ 1	8

tens	ones
4	6
+ 4	7

tens	ones
4	5
+ 1	6

tens	ones
	8
+ 2	5

4

tens	ones
3	5
+ 2	4

tens	ones
	6
+ 2	1

tens	ones
4	1
+ 2	9

tens	ones
3	8
+ 1	9

At Home: We began adding with 2-digit numbers today. Ask your child to tell you about adding 7 + 28.

Name

More Adding 2-Digit Numbers

Use the table.
How many dolls did
Sam and Tama sell?

DOLLS SOLD	
Sam	23 dolls
Tama	25 dolls

Write the numbers.	Add the ones. Do you need to regroup?	Add the tens.
23 + 25	□ 23 + 25 = 8 (8 ones)	□ 23 + 25 = 48 (4 tens)

They sold 48 dolls in all.

Add. Did you regroup?

1. □ 36 + 16 = 52 yes / no □ 45 + 22 yes / no □ 17 + 41 yes / no

2. □ 58 + 34 yes / no □ 23 + 8 yes / no □ 63 + 16 yes / no

Do you need to show tens and ones to tell if you need to regroup? How do you know?

Practice!

Add. Use tens and ones models to help.

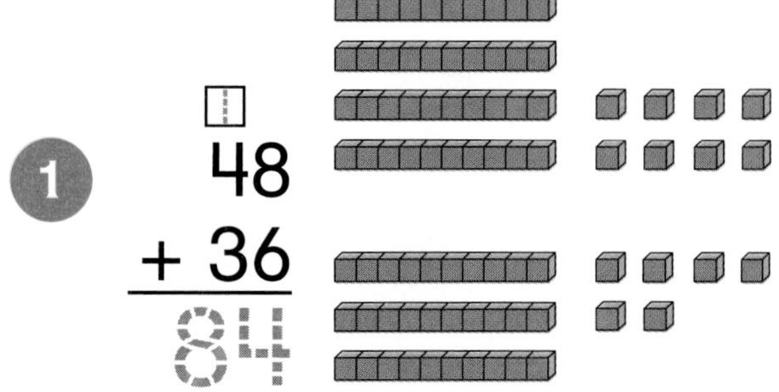

1

☐
48
+ 36
84

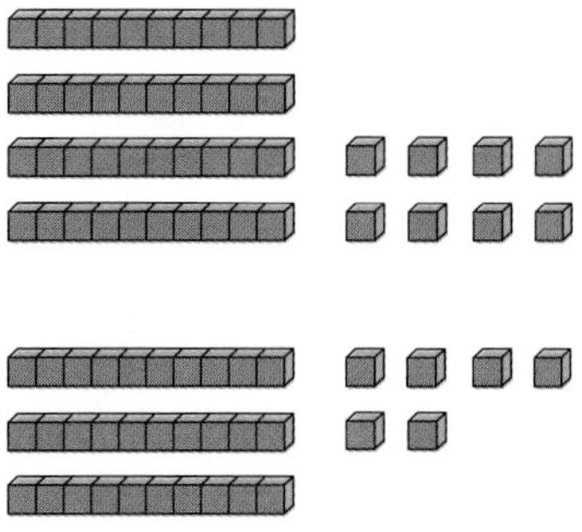

2

☐
22
+ 37
59

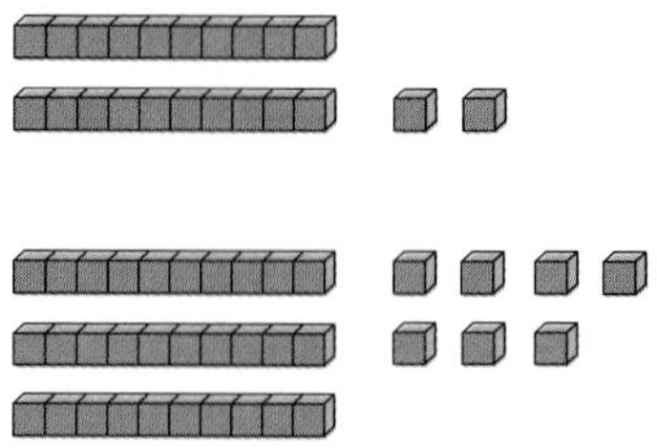

3

☐	☐	☐	☐	☐	☐
25	32	43	29	54	45
+ 46	+ 26	+ 45	+ 13	+ 19	+ 34

4

☐	☐	☐	☐	☐	☐
33	14	27	42	58	22
+ 28	+ 16	+ 6	+ 24	+ 17	+ 43

5

☐	☐	☐	☐	☐	☐
65	13	37	7	35	52
+ 27	+ 44	+ 33	+ 66	+ 28	+ 26

More to Explore

Algebra Sense

You can use a calculator.

Algebra

Find the missing numbers.

36 + ☐ = 61   23 + ☐ = 39

56 + ☐ = 93   64 + ☐ = 92

☐ + 45 = 52   ☐ + 58 = 84

At Home

We continue to add with 2-digit numbers. Ask your child to explain how to add 35 + 28 and 52 + 26.

Name ______________________

Add to Solve Problems

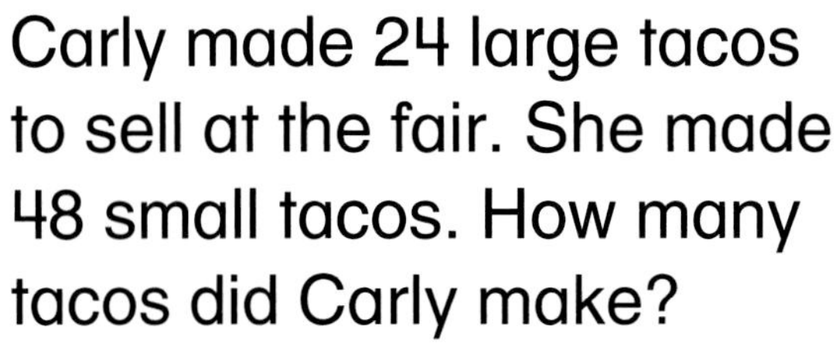

Carly made 24 large tacos to sell at the fair. She made 48 small tacos. How many tacos did Carly make?

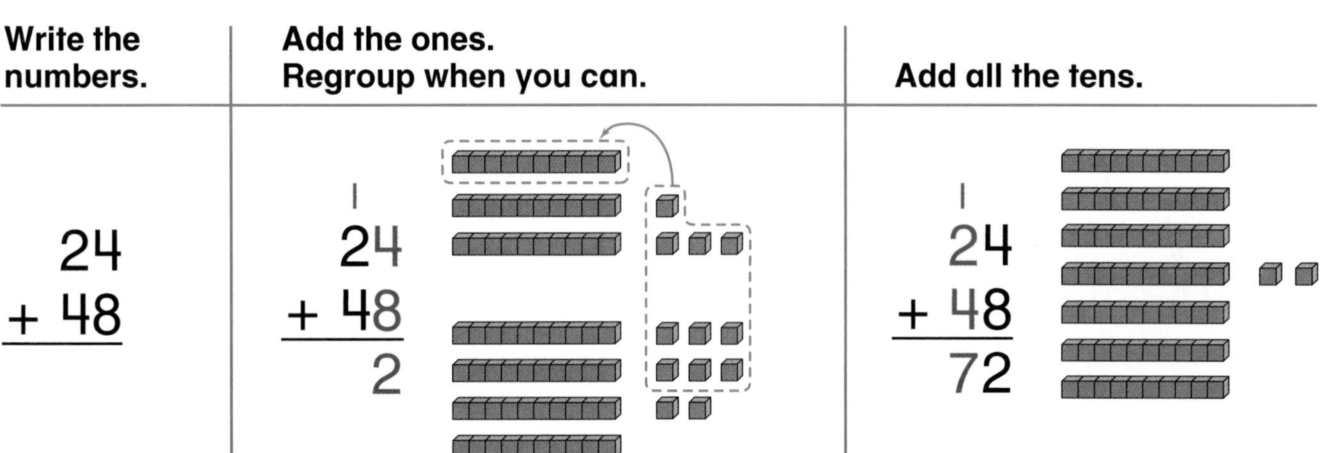

Write the numbers.	Add the ones. Regroup when you can.	Add all the tens.
$\begin{array}{r} 24 \\ +\ 48 \\ \hline \end{array}$	$\begin{array}{r} 1 \\ 24 \\ +\ 48 \\ \hline 2 \end{array}$	$\begin{array}{r} 1 \\ 24 \\ +\ 48 \\ \hline 72 \end{array}$

Carly made 72 tacos.

Solve.

Workspace

1. Mr. Lewis bought 13 small tacos. He bought 8 large tacos. How many tacos did he buy? ____

2. Carly sold 46 tacos in the morning. She sold 24 tacos in the afternoon. How many tacos did she sell? ____

Did Carly sell all the tacos she made? How do you know?

Practice!

	Workspace
1 The judges tasted 29 apple cakes. They tasted 35 nut cakes. How many cakes did the judges taste? 64	1 29 + 35 64
2 Jamie's club won 11 yellow ribbons and 8 blue ribbons. How many more yellow ribbons did the club win? ____	
3 Lee used 17 ride tickets. Tito used 14 ride tickets. How many tickets did the boys use? ____	
4 Anna watched the sheep contest. There were 38 black and 10 white sheep. How many more black sheep did Anna see? ____	

Mixed Review Test Preparation

PATTERNS Complete.

5 $5 - 2 =$ ____ $4 + 5 =$ ____ $3 + 3 =$ ____

$50 - 20 =$ ____ $40 + 50 =$ ____ $30 + 30 =$ ____

6 Compare. Write > or <.

42 ◯ 22 61 ◯ 83 56 ◯ 47

We used addition to solve problems. Read problem 4 but use the numbers 26 and 19. Have your child find the answer.

Name

Use Estimation

Problem-Solving Strategy

Read | Plan | Solve | Look Back

Read Tom played two games.
He scored a total of about 80 points.
Which two scores are his?

Plan **Estimate** to find about 80 points.

Glossary
estimate

Solve Try 22 and 43 points.

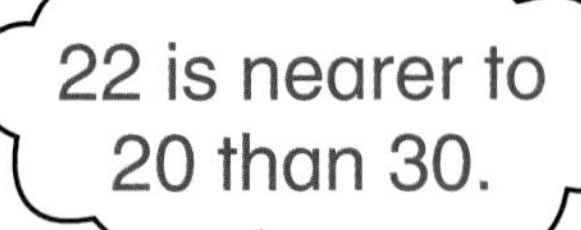

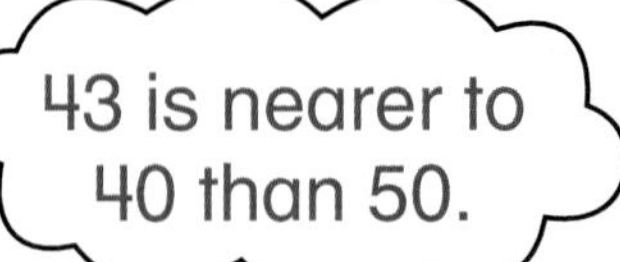

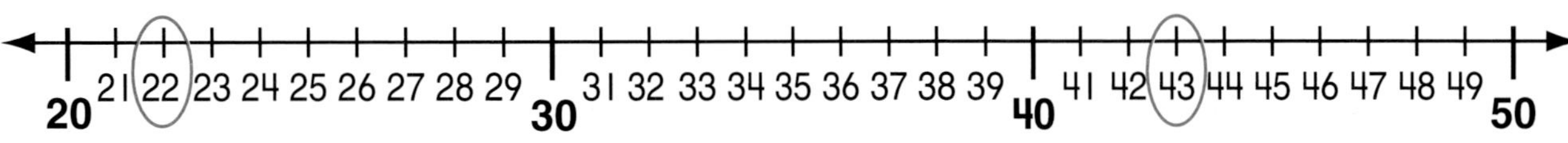

20 + 40 = 60

Now try 38 and 43 points.

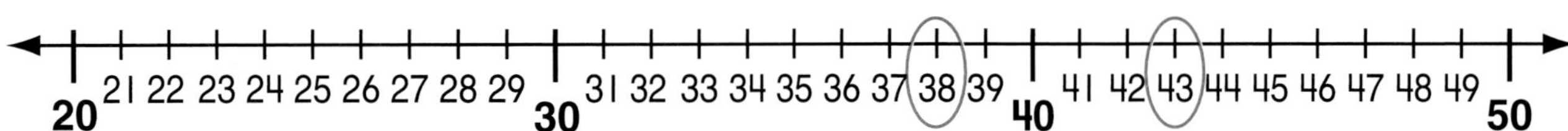

40 + 40 = 80

Tom's scores are 38 and 43.

Look Back Do the scores of 38 and 43 make sense? ________

Would scores of 48 and 22 make sense for a total of about 60 points? Explain.

Practice!

Solve. Use estimation.

1. Joey played two games of ring toss.
He scored a total of about 60 points.
Which two scores are his? __________

2. Joyce sold tickets for two rides.
She sold about 80 tickets.
Which two groups of tickets did she sell? __________

3. Tim played two games of ball toss.
He scored a total of about 50 points.
Which two scores are his? __________

4. Tiffany tried to ring the bell.
She took two swings with the hammer.
She scored a total of about 70 points.
Which two scores are Tiffany's? __________

37 21

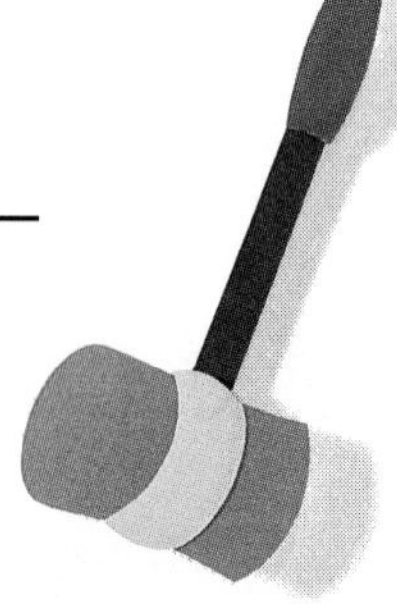

At Home: We estimated to solve problems. Ask your child to explain how to solve problem 4.

Name

Midchapter Review

Add. Use tens and ones models if you want to.

1

	tens	ones
	□	
	1	9
+	5	4

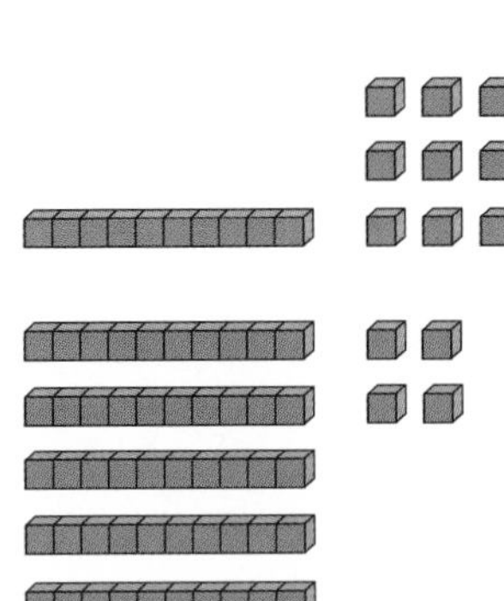

2

	tens	ones
	□	
	5	1
+	3	6

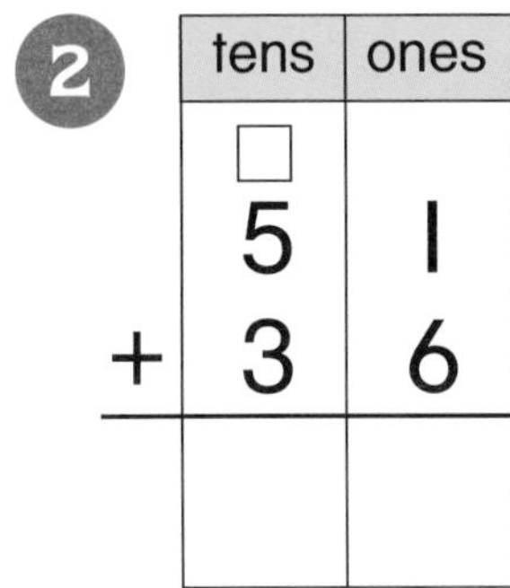

3

	tens	ones
	□	
	1	5
+		6

4 $\begin{array}{r} 42 \\ +\ 36 \\ \hline \end{array}$

5 $\begin{array}{r} 53 \\ +\ 29 \\ \hline \end{array}$

6 $\begin{array}{r} 24 \\ +\ 45 \\ \hline \end{array}$

7 $\begin{array}{r} 47 \\ +\ 27 \\ \hline \end{array}$

8 $\begin{array}{r} 16 \\ +\ 66 \\ \hline \end{array}$

Estimate to solve.

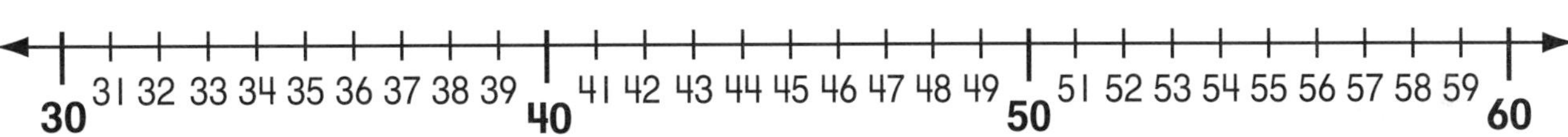

9 Rita sold about 70 tickets for the school fair. Which two groups of tickets did she sell? ______

52

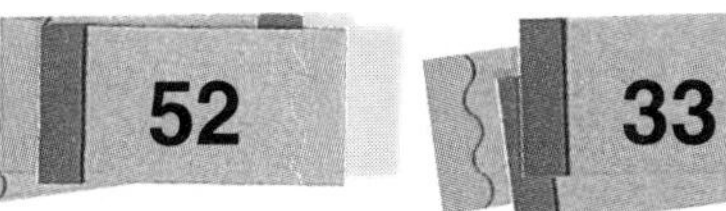

10 How did you estimate to solve problem 9?

____

____

Journal

How is estimating the sum of 33 and 38 different from adding 33 and 38?

Extra Practice

Game !

Get to the Fair!

You and your partner need 2 , 9 , 20 , and a .

Take turns.

- Put your game marker on *Start.* Show 25 with tens and ones models.
- Spin for another number and show that many tens and ones.
- Combine the tens and ones.
- Move ahead one space if you regroup the ones. Stay in the space if you cannot regroup.
- For each turn, show the number in the space and the number you spin.

Name

Patch Patterns

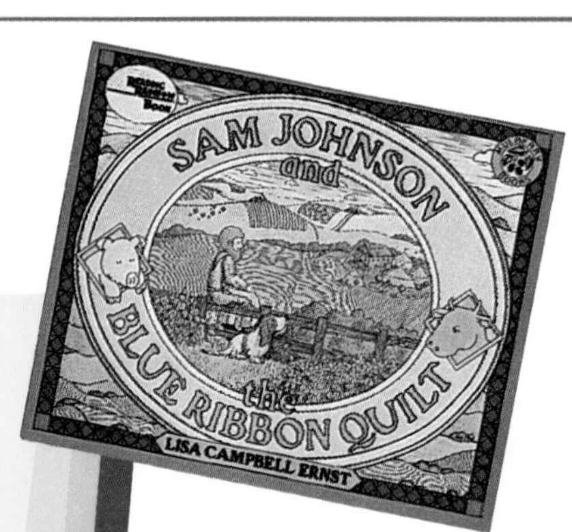

Listen to *Sam Johnson and the Blue Ribbon Quilt.*

A patch pattern can be a square like this. Squares are sewn together to make a patchwork quilt.

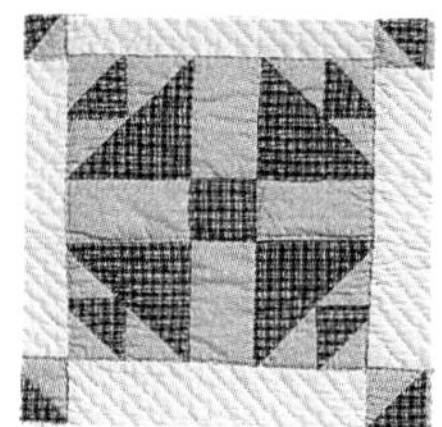

Cultural Note

This is an Amish quilt called *Double Wedding Ring.*

Working Together

You and your partner will make patchwork squares.

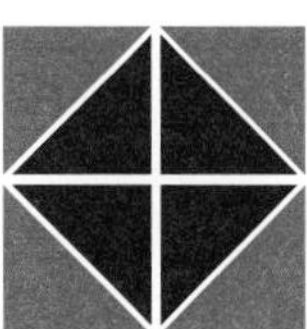

You each need crayons and 8 paper ◺ in two different colors.

- Use 8 ◺ to make a patchwork square.
- Draw your patch pattern and color it.
- Make 3 more patch patterns. Make all the patterns different. Draw and color them.

Decision Making

Use the price list.

1. What is the total cost of this patch pattern? _____

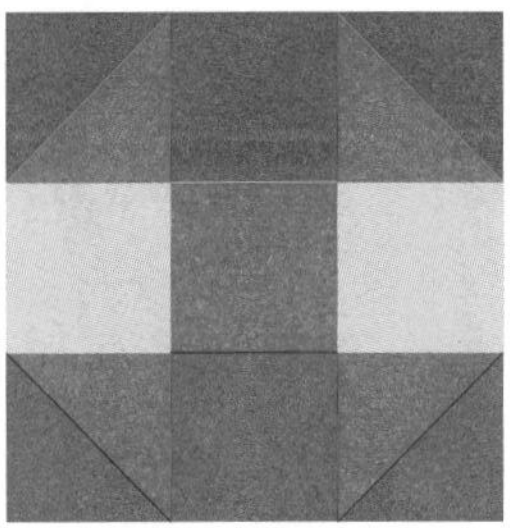

PRICE LIST	
Shape	**Cost**
red ■	12¢
yellow ■	9¢
green ■	8¢
red ◣	6¢
green ◣	4¢

2. Choose one of your patchwork squares. Decide on a price for each color shape. What is the total cost of your square? _____

Write a report.

3. Tell how you decided on a price for each color shape.

4. Tell how you found the total cost of your patchwork square.

More to Investigate

Tape or glue your patchwork pattern to a square piece of paper.

PREDICT What if you make a class quilt. Will the squares make a rectangle?

EXPLORE Try it. Make sure there are no holes in the rectangle.

FIND Find the total cost of the class quilt.

Name ______________________________

Check Addition

Jim's group made 18 posters to advertise the fair. Paul's group made 16 posters. How many posters did they make in all?

Jim added this way to find out.	Paul added this way to find out.
$\begin{array}{r} \overset{1}{1}8 \\ +\ 16 \\ \hline 34 \end{array}$	$\begin{array}{r} \overset{1}{1}6 \\ +\ 18 \\ \hline 34 \end{array}$

Why did they get the same answer?

You can check addition by adding the numbers in a different order.

Add. Check your work.

1	$\begin{array}{r} 23 \\ +\ 19 \\ \hline \end{array}$	$\begin{array}{r} 71 \\ +\ 4 \\ \hline \end{array}$	$\begin{array}{r} 37 \\ +\ 18 \\ \hline \end{array}$	$\begin{array}{r} 52 \\ +\ 29 \\ \hline \end{array}$	$\begin{array}{r} 63 \\ +\ 8 \\ \hline \end{array}$	$\begin{array}{r} 9 \\ +\ 19 \\ \hline \end{array}$
2	$\begin{array}{r} 81 \\ +\ 6 \\ \hline \end{array}$	$\begin{array}{r} 28 \\ +\ 62 \\ \hline \end{array}$	$\begin{array}{r} 14 \\ +\ 48 \\ \hline \end{array}$	$\begin{array}{r} 25 \\ +\ 14 \\ \hline \end{array}$	$\begin{array}{r} 46 \\ +\ 15 \\ \hline \end{array}$	$\begin{array}{r} 52 \\ +\ 7 \\ \hline \end{array}$
3	$\begin{array}{r} 47 \\ +\ 45 \\ \hline \end{array}$	$\begin{array}{r} 45 \\ +\ 43 \\ \hline \end{array}$	$\begin{array}{r} 24 \\ +\ 27 \\ \hline \end{array}$	$\begin{array}{r} 7 \\ +\ 36 \\ \hline \end{array}$	$\begin{array}{r} 55 \\ +\ 5 \\ \hline \end{array}$	$\begin{array}{r} 37 \\ +\ 19 \\ \hline \end{array}$

Practice!

Add. Check your work.

1	75 + 17 = 92	5 + 26	46 + 50	12 + 17	19 + 7	37 + 32
2	42 + 23	18 + 19	3 + 52	33 + 27	19 + 43	45 + 16
3	39 + 5	56 + 17	27 + 27	7 + 41	16 + 8	68 + 22

Write an Advertisement

You can use words and numbers to make the fair sound exciting.

Make a poster for the fair. Use numbers and words from the list.

28	50	32
49	16	7

booths
games
rides
shows
contests
quilts

Write a report.

- Write about what the poster advertises.
- Tell how many games and rides in all.
- Tell how many booths and games there are.

We learned to check addition. Ask your child how he or she checks addition.

Name

Score 10

You and your partner need 2 counters.

Take turns.

- Drop two counters on the squares.
- Write the addition and find the sum.
- Your partner checks your work.
- Score 10 points for each correct sum.

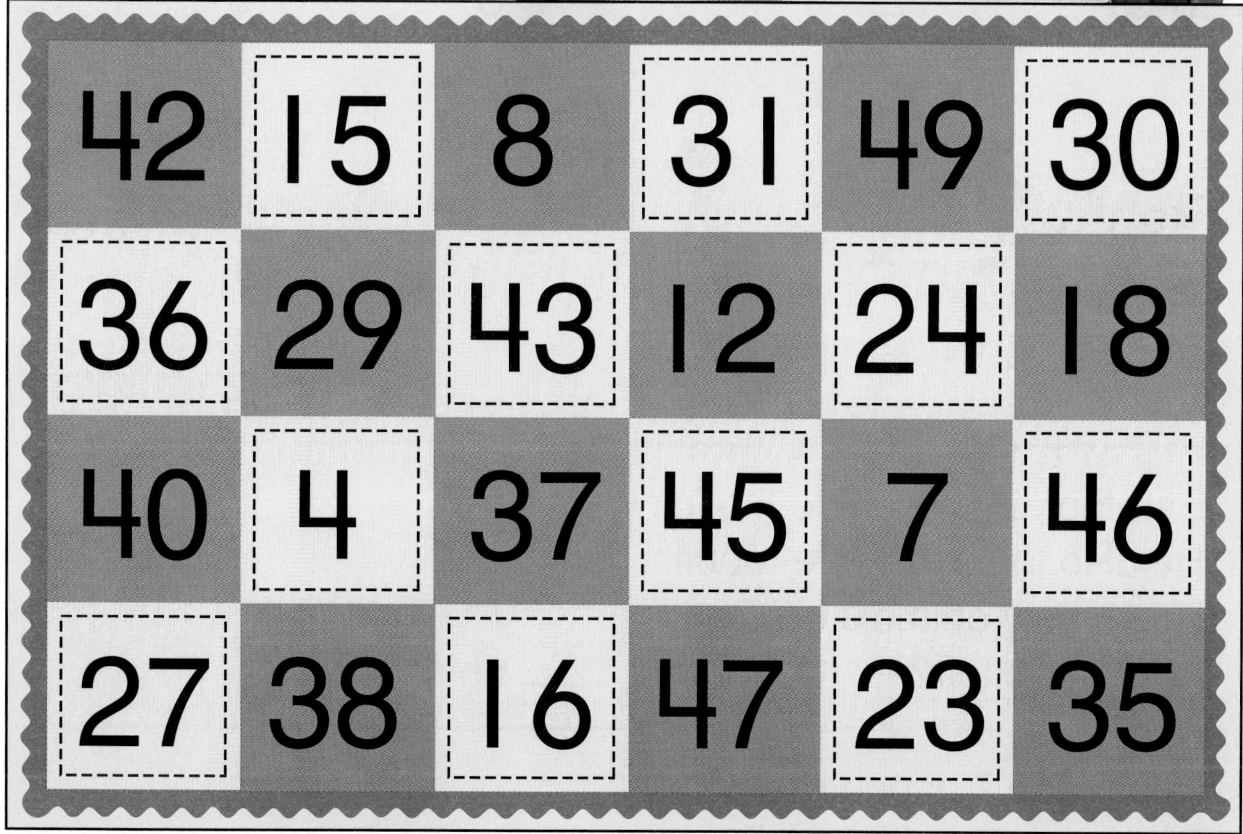

42	15	8	31	49	30
36	29	43	12	24	18
40	4	37	45	7	46
27	38	16	47	23	35

Color to show your score.

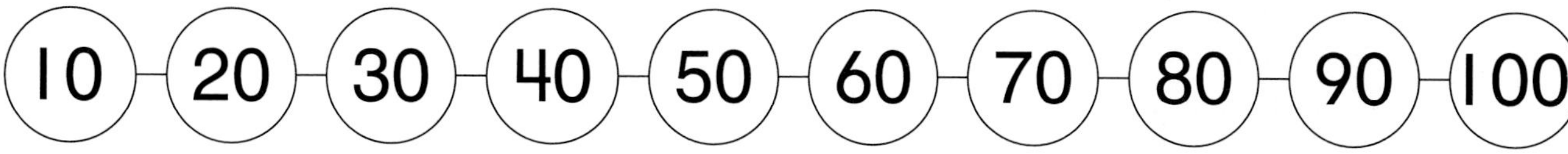

Add.

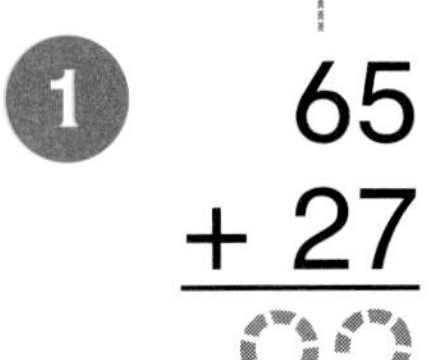

1	65 + 27 92	51 + 8	47 + 34	35 + 24	6 + 14	75 + 5
2	23 + 56	6 + 9	42 + 23	53 + 24	8 + 5	31 + 36
3	19 + 13	52 + 39	7 + 7	27 + 26	79 + 18	3 + 85
4	8 + 37	45 + 12	63 + 17	7 + 8	59 + 26	21 + 48

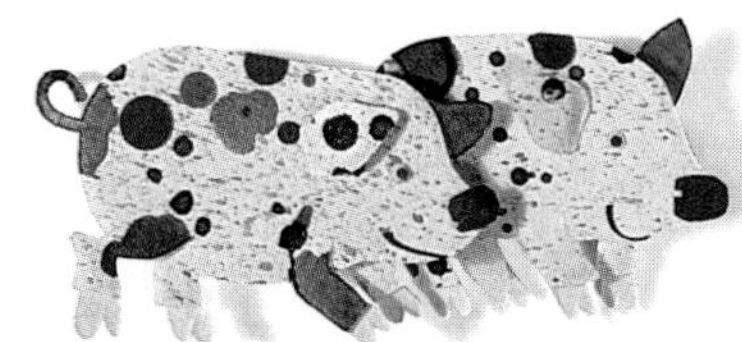

Solve.

Workspace

5 Ben took 24 piglets to the fair. He also took 18 white rabbits. How many animals did Ben take to the fair? ____ animals

6 Rita made 7 puppets to sell. She made 9 dolls to sell. How many more dolls than puppets did Rita make? ____ dolls

Name ______________________

Explore Activity

Add Money

Put price tags like these on things in your classroom.

Working Together

Take turns choosing two things to order. Fill out an order form. You and your partners find the total with coins, calculator, and paper and pencil.

Compare totals. Write the total on the order form.

Order Form	
Item	**Price**

Order Form	
Item	**Price**

Order Form	
Item	**Price**

How is adding money like adding numbers?

Practice!

Remember to write a ¢.

SCHOOL FAIR SNACK TENT

yogurt	juice	peanuts	popcorn	milk	taco
48¢	34¢	35¢	47¢	25¢	59¢

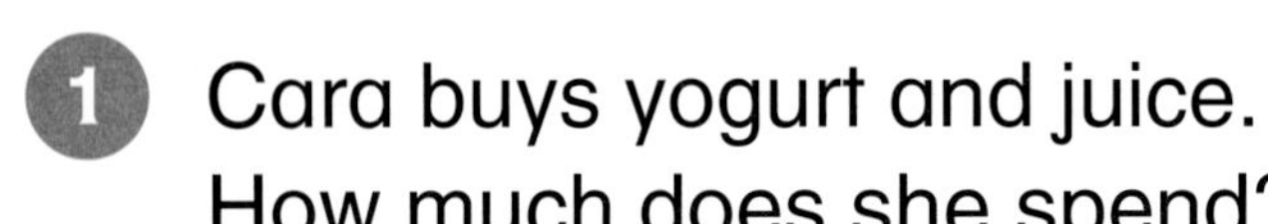

Workspace

1. Cara buys yogurt and juice. How much does she spend? 82¢
2. Eric buys juice and peanuts. How much does he spend? ______
3. Kim buys peanuts and milk. How much more are the peanuts? ______
4. Jon wants to buy milk and a taco. Is 75¢ enough money? ______

More to Explore Algebra Sense

PATTERNS Complete. Then make up another pattern.

$$\begin{array}{r} 8 \\ +\ 7 \\ \hline 15 \end{array} \qquad \begin{array}{r} 8 \\ +\ 17 \\ \hline \end{array} \qquad \begin{array}{r} 8 \\ +\ 27 \\ \hline \end{array} \qquad \begin{array}{r} 8 \\ +\ 37 \\ \hline \end{array} \qquad \begin{array}{r} 8 \\ +\ 47 \\ \hline \end{array}$$

At Home: Ask your child to show you how to add 25¢ and 59¢. He or she may use pennies and dimes.

Name ______________________

More Adding Money

Roger bought three toys at the crafts fair.
You can add to find how much he spent.

Add the ones. Regroup when you can.	Add all the tens.
$\begin{array}{r} ^{1}\\ 16¢ \\ 23¢ \\ +\ 34¢ \\ \hline 3 \end{array}$ Look for a 10.	$\begin{array}{r} ^{1}\\ 16¢ \\ 23¢ \\ +\ 34¢ \\ \hline 73¢ \end{array}$ Think of doubles.

How much did Roger spend? 73¢

Add.

1.
$\begin{array}{r} 42¢ \\ 13¢ \\ +\ 28¢ \\ \hline \end{array}$
$\begin{array}{r} 32¢ \\ 21¢ \\ +\ 15¢ \\ \hline \end{array}$
$\begin{array}{r} 20¢ \\ 2¢ \\ +\ 29¢ \\ \hline \end{array}$
$\begin{array}{r} 13¢ \\ 16¢ \\ +\ 33¢ \\ \hline \end{array}$
$\begin{array}{r} 3¢ \\ 64¢ \\ +\ 12¢ \\ \hline \end{array}$

2.
$\begin{array}{r} 28¢ \\ +\ 54¢ \\ \hline \end{array}$
$\begin{array}{r} 24¢ \\ +\ 1¢ \\ \hline \end{array}$
$\begin{array}{r} 44¢ \\ +\ 21¢ \\ \hline \end{array}$
$\begin{array}{r} 27¢ \\ +\ 19¢ \\ \hline \end{array}$
$\begin{array}{r} 9¢ \\ +\ 22¢ \\ \hline \end{array}$

What strategies did you use to add?

Practice!

Add.

1	16¢ + 25¢ 41¢	60¢ + 22¢	42¢ + 19¢	8¢ + 41¢	16¢ + 24¢
2	13¢ + 42¢	24¢ + 18¢	29¢ + 31¢	18¢ + 33¢	15¢ + 8¢
3	7¢ 22¢ + 11¢	55¢ 16¢ + 14¢	19¢ 20¢ + 22¢	35¢ 3¢ + 29¢	14¢ 13¢ + 24¢

Cultural Connection

Indian Addition

In ancient India, Bhaskara invented this method of adding.

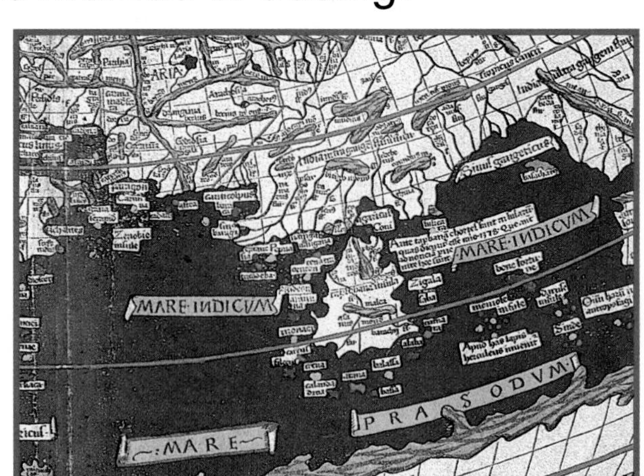

$2 + 5 + 23 + 48$

sum of ones	2	5	3	8	18
sum of tens			2	4	+ 6
					78

Add these numbers.
Use the same method.

$6 + 8 + 34 + 51$

sum of ones ____ ____ ____ ____

sum of tens ____ ____ + ____

At Home: Ask your child to show you how to add three numbers.

Name

Choose the Method

Problem Solvers at Work

Read
Plan
Solve
Look Back

Lulu sells her crafts at the market. The chart shows what she sold.

SALES	
Item	**Number Sold**
jar	32
small bowl	47
large bowl	24
giant bowl	10
mug	38

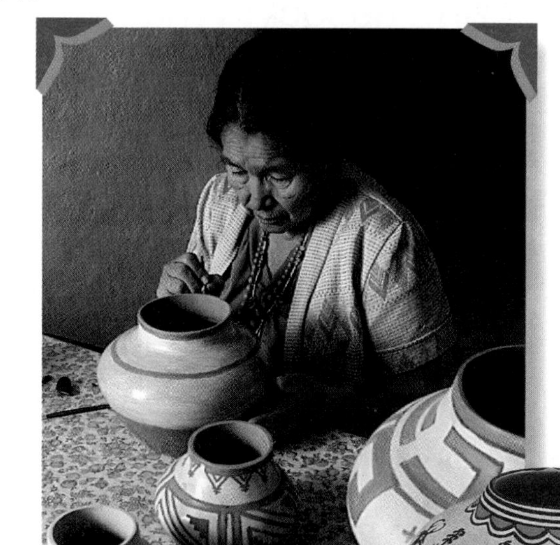

Solve. Choose the best method for you.

1. How many bowls did Lulu sell? ____

How did you solve the problem?

____

2. How many jars and mugs did Lulu sell? ____

____

3. Which two things did Lulu sell the least of?

____

4. 

Write an Advertisement
Help Lulu sell these two things. Use words and numbers to make people want to buy.

Practice!

1. What if Lulu sold 18 jars and 16 mugs on Tuesday. What would be the total number sold? ____

2. What if she sold 10 more jars and 10 more mugs on Wednesday. What would be the total for both days? ____

Talk Did you use different methods for problems 1 and 2? Explain.

Write and Share

STUDENT TO STUDENT

Turrelle wrote this problem.
How many large bowls, small bowls, and jars did Lulu sell in all?

Turrelle Sims
Snowden School
Memphis, Tennessee

3. Solve Turrelle's problem. ____

What method did you choose? ________________

____

4. Write Write a problem using information from the chart. Have a partner solve it.

Use your own paper.

What method did your partner use? ________________

What method would you use? ________________

At Home Ask your child to tell you how to solve the problem he or she wrote.

Name ______________________

Chapter Review

Language and Mathematics

Choose the correct word to complete the sentence.

- ten
- ones
- regroup
- estimate

1. You have to __________ when you add 36 + 18.

2. You can regroup 10 __________ as 1 __________.

Concepts and Skills

Add. Did you regroup? Mark *yes* or *no.*

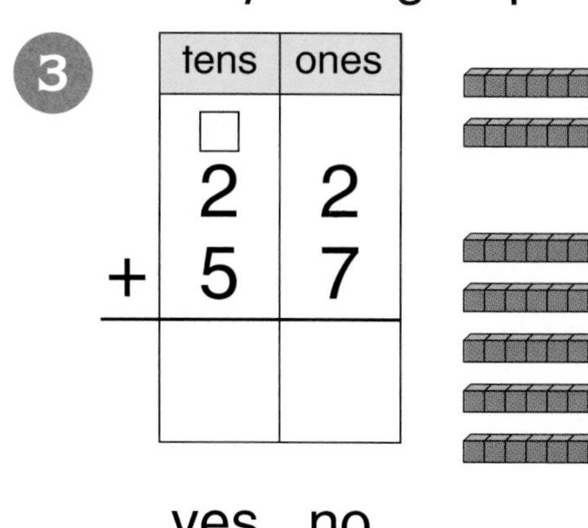

3.

	tens	ones
	□	
	2	2
+	5	7

yes no

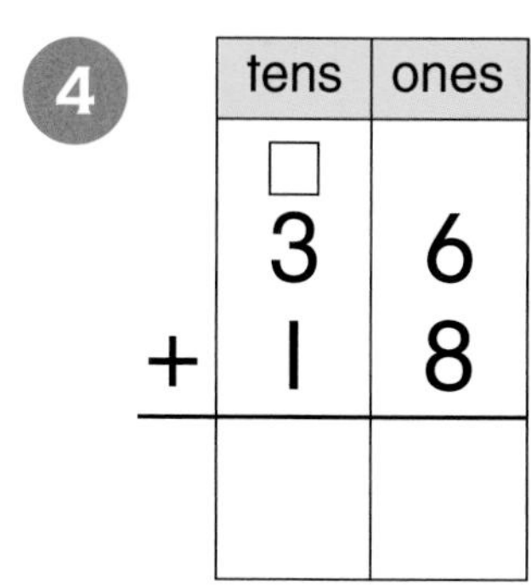

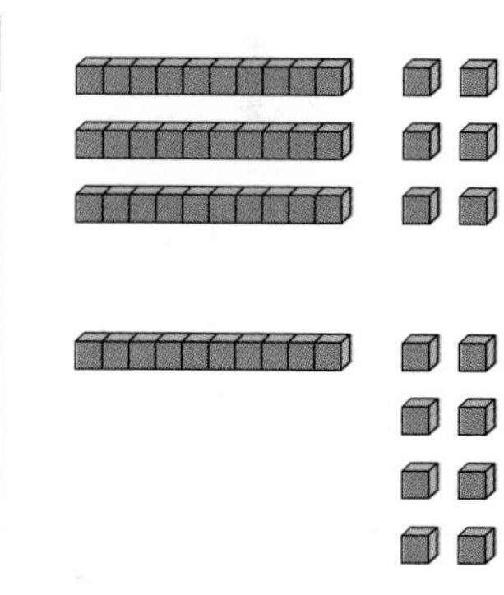

4.

	tens	ones
	□	
	3	6
+	1	8

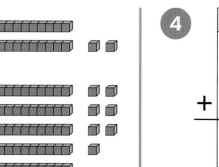

yes no

Add.

5. 59 + 13

6. 84 + 6

7. 8 + 34

8. 56 + 33

9. 74 + 14

10. 72 + 26

11. 69¢ + 8¢

12. 27¢ + 38¢

13. 34 + 25

14. 17 + 16

15. 43 + 4

16. 28¢ + 18¢

Problem Solving

Estimate to solve.

30 31 32 33 34 35 36 37 38 39 40 41 42 43 44 45 46 47 48 49 50 51 52 53 54 55 56 57 58 59 60

17 Liz bowled two games. She scored a total of about 90. Which two scores are hers?

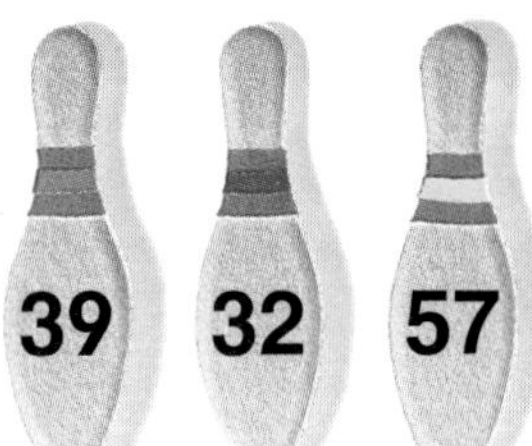

____

18 Sam collects sports cards. He has a total of about 80 cards. Which two groups of cards are Sam's?

____

19 On Monday 52 chicks hatched. On Tuesday 19 more hatched. How many chicks hatched in all?

____ chicks

20 Sara used 27 pounds of feed in May. In June she used 38 pounds. How many pounds of feed did she use?

____ pounds

What Do You Think?

Which is the quickest way to add 15 and 45?

☑ Check one.

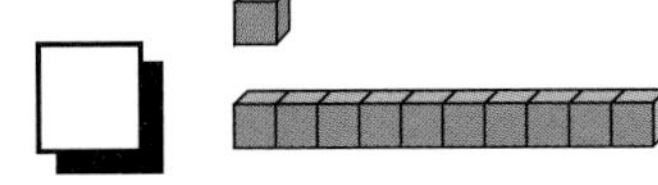

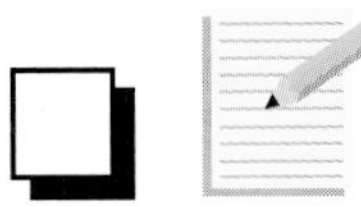

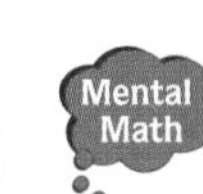

Why? ____________________

Write these exercises in your journal. Find the sums. Explain which is easier to add.

$$\begin{array}{r} 18 \\ +\ 25 \\ \hline \end{array} \qquad \begin{array}{r} 79 \\ +\ 10 \\ \hline \end{array}$$

Name

Chapter Test

Add.

1.

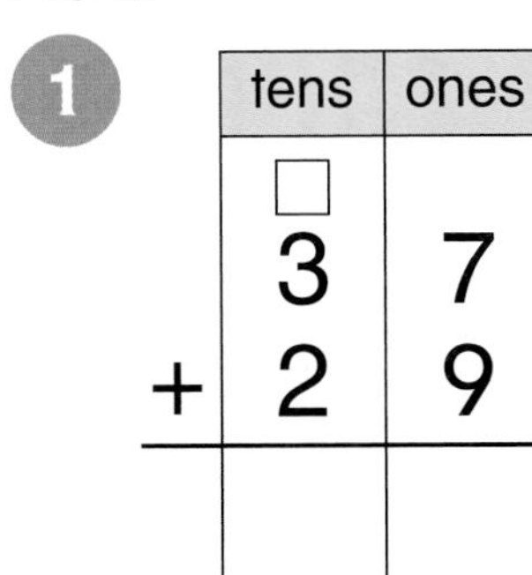

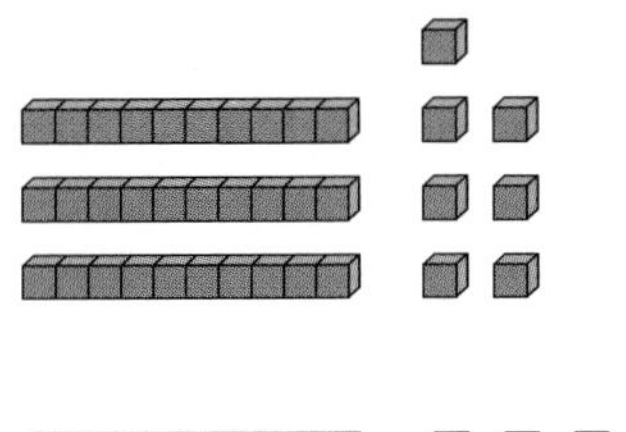

2. 53 + 37

3. 31 + 18

4. 75 + 9

5. 24 + 18

6. 8¢ + 73¢

7. 13¢ + 84¢

Solve.

8. José made 26 small cakes.
He made 38 large cakes.
How many cakes did José make? _____ cakes

Estimate to solve.

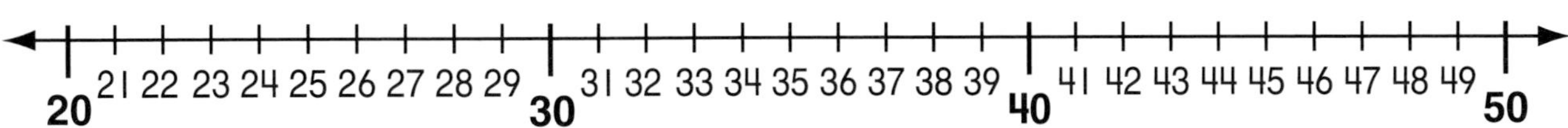

9. Tina sold tickets at the fair.
She sold about 40 tickets.
Which two groups of tickets did she sell? __________

10. Kim plays two games at the fair.
He scores a total of about 30 points.
Which two game scores are Kim's? __________

Performance Assessment

What Did You Learn?

What is ■ ? ____

How do you know? ______________________________

____

____

____

What is ■ ? ____

How do you know? ______________________________

____

____

____

You may want to put this page in your portfolio.

7
2
1
5
6

Name

Addition Tables

Algebra Look at the numbers. What patterns do you see?

6
16
26
36

Add 2. What patterns do you see?

	+ 2
6	
16	
26	
36	

Complete each table.

	+ 6
32	
42	
52	
62	

	+ 8
24	
34	
44	
54	

	+15
5	
15	
25	
35	

	+ 29
3	
13	
23	
	62

Make your own table. Your partner tells you what sums to write. Talk about the patterns.

Show a
number pattern
in this column.

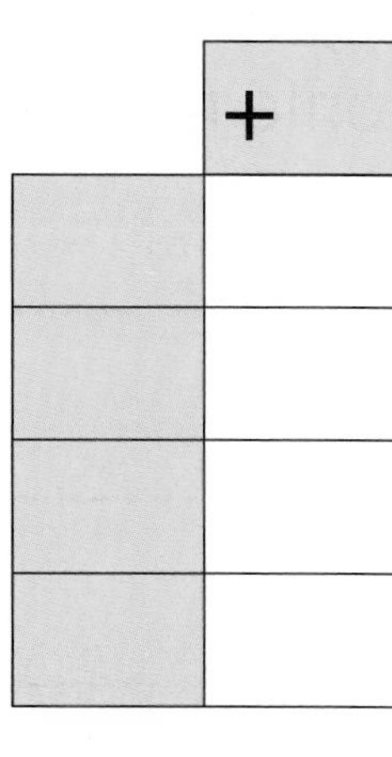

	+

Write a number
to add here.

Technology Connection

Computer

Make a Bar Graph

What is your favorite ride at the fair? This computer spreadsheet shows what some people chose.

FAVORITE RIDES				
Rides	**Children**	**Teachers**	**Parents**	**Total**
Ferris Wheel	35	2	27	
Roller Coaster	13	1	25	
Carousel	26	1	44	

At the Computer

1. Complete the spreadsheet.

   How many people chose the Ferris wheel?

   _____ people

2. Use the data in the spreadsheet to make a bar graph.

   What does the bar graph tell you about people's favorite rides?

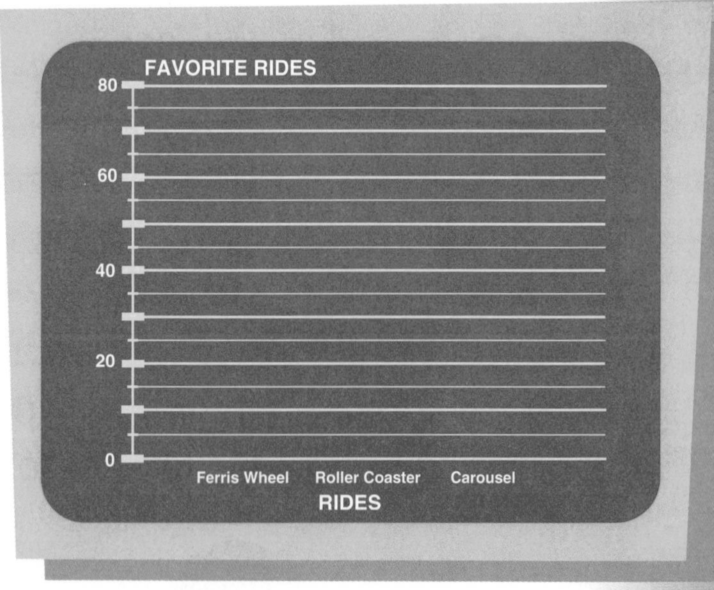

____

____

____

Home Connection

Chapter 7 Wrap-Up

Name ______________________________

Game of the Century!

PLAYERS 2 or more

MATERIALS pencil and paper

DIRECTIONS The first player writes any number between 1 and 5 on a sheet of paper. Then each player in turn adds another number between 1 and 15 and writes the sum.

The winner is the player who adds to get a sum of exactly 100.

As the sum reaches 70, players must plan ahead to increase their chance of being able to be the last player able to add to get exactly 100.

Dear Family,

I am beginning a new chapter in mathematics. During the next few weeks I will be learning to subtract 2-digit numbers such as:

$$\begin{array}{r} 47 \\ -\ 29 \\ \hline \end{array} \quad \text{and} \quad \begin{array}{r} 30 \\ -\ 12 \\ \hline \end{array}$$

I will also be talking about animals that migrate from one place to another.

Learning About Animals That Migrate

Let's talk about different kinds of animals that migrate. We can make a list of different animals.

My Math Words

I am going to use these math words in this chapter.

Please help me make word cards for the math words. I can use these word cards when I practice subtracting 2-digit numbers.

regroup
tens
ones
make a list
table
extra information

Your child,

Signature

Subtracting 2-Digit Numbers

Theme: Animals on the Move

READING ARITHMETIC WRITING

the Great Monarch Butterfly Chase

by R.W.N. Prior

illustrated by Beth Glick

Summarize Listen to the story *the Great Monarch Butterfly Chase.* What did you find out about monarch butterflies?

Tell about other animals that migrate.

Name

What Do You Know?

There are 18 cards in each set of animal cards.

Find the number of cards you need to complete each set.

ANIMALS-ON-THE-GO COLLECTION		
Set of Cards	**Cards You Have**	**Cards You Need**
Insects	17	
Birds	10	
Fish	9	
Mammals	5	
Reptiles/Amphibians	3	

Tell how you found the number of cards needed to complete each set. What strategies did you use? Explain.

Name

Working Together

You and your partner need 5 [tens] and 20 [ones].

Take turns.

- You show **tens** and **ones**.
- Your partner **regroups** if needed. Then your partner takes away ones.
- Write how many tens and ones are left.

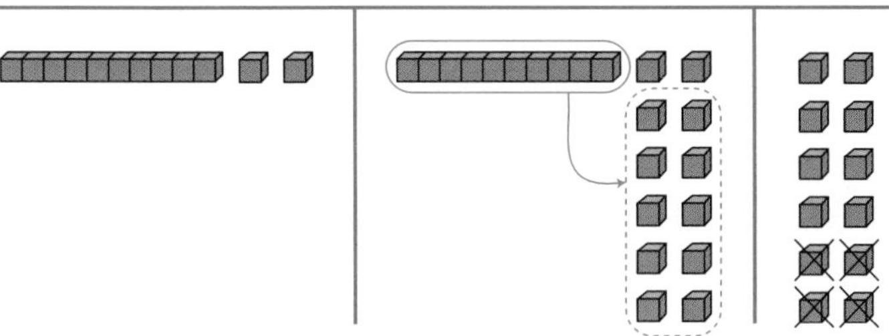

Glossary
regroup
tens
ones

	Show.	Take away.	Did you regroup?	How many tens and ones are left?
1	I ten 2 ones	4 ones	yes no	0 tens 8 ones
2	I ten 8 ones	6 ones	yes no	___ tens ___ ones
3	I ten 3 ones	8 ones	yes no	___ tens ___ ones
4	I ten 6 ones	9 ones	yes no	___ tens ___ ones
5	I ten 5 ones	I one	yes no	___ tens ___ ones

When don't you need to regroup?

Practice!

Regroup when you need to.

Use [ten rod] and [one cube].
Complete the chart.

	Show.	Take away.	Did you regroup?	How many tens and ones are left?
1	2 tens 6 ones	8 ones	(yes) no	1 tens 8 ones
2	1 ten 6 ones	5 ones	yes no	___ tens ___ ones
3	4 tens 3 ones	7 ones	yes no	___ tens ___ ones
4	1 ten 4 ones	6 ones	yes no	___ tens ___ ones
5	3 tens 9 ones	8 ones	yes no	___ tens ___ ones

Mixed Review Test Preparation

Write the number.

6 [3 tens, 9 ones] ___

7 [4 tens, 7 ones] ___

Count back to complete.

8 90, 80, 70, ___, ___, ___, ___, ___

9 85, 75, 65, 55, ___, ___, ___, ___

10 77, 67, 57, ___, ___, ___, ___, ___

At Home

We explored regrouping for subtraction. Ask your child how to regroup 1 ten 4 ones.

Name ______________________________

Explore Activity

More Regrouping

Working Together

You and your partner need 5 [tens] and 20 [ones].
Take turns.

- Your partner shows tens and ones.
- You regroup if needed. Take away tens and ones.
- Write the number that is left.

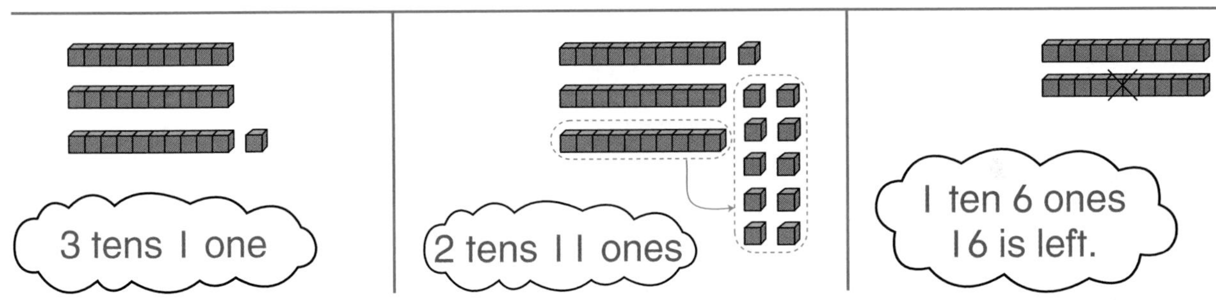

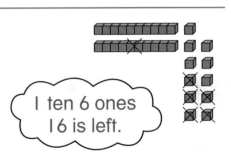

	Show.	Take away.	Did you regroup?	Number left.
1	31	15	(yes) no	16
2	26	19	yes no	____
3	55	21	yes no	____
4	41	6	yes no	____
5	37	12	yes no	____
6	28	9	yes no	____

Regroup when you need to.

Use [tens block] and [ones cube].
Complete the chart.

	Show.	Take away.	Did you regroup?	Number left.
1	45	26	(yes) no	19
2	29	13	yes no	
3	31	24	yes no	
4	25	6	yes no	
5	56	30	yes no	
6	50	16	yes no	
7	28	7	yes no	
8	47	38	yes no	
9	16	11	yes no	
10	20	19	yes no	

At Home: We regrouped with greater numbers. Ask your child to explain exercise 10 above.

Name ____________________

Subtract 2-Digit Numbers

You need 9 [tens] and 20 [ones].

You can use tens and ones models to subtract.

43
− 15
28

Show 43.

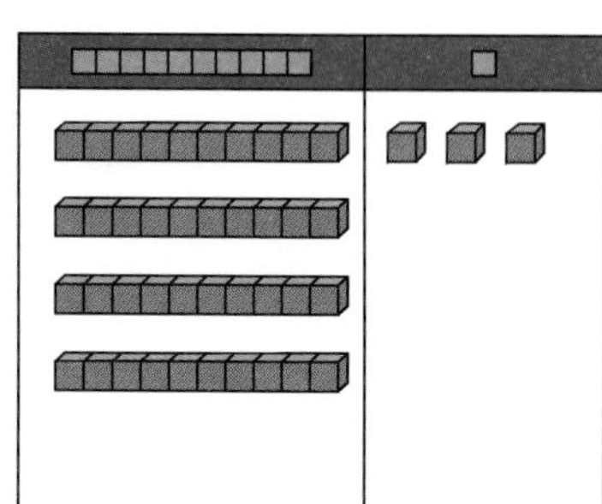

Look at the ones. Regroup 1 ten as 10 ones if you need to.

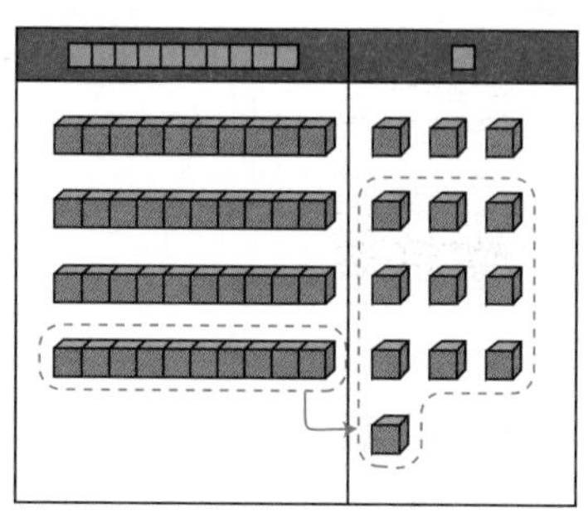

Take away ones. Take away tens.

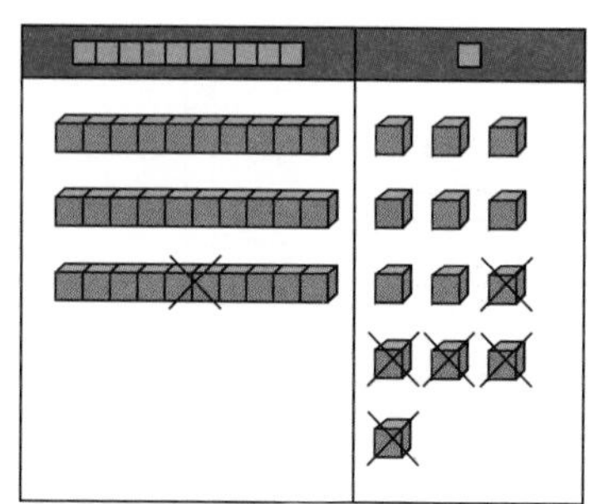

You can subtract without tens and ones models.

Look at the ones.

	tens	ones
	☐	☐
	4	3
−	1	5

3 ones are not enough.

Regroup if you need to.

	tens	ones
	3	13
	~~4~~	~~3~~
−	1	5

3 tens 13 ones

Subtract the ones.

	tens	ones
	3	13
	~~4~~	~~3~~
−	1	5
		8

8 ones are left.

Subtract the tens.

	tens	ones
	3	13
	~~4~~	~~3~~
−	1	5
	2	8

2 tens are left.

Subtract. Use tens and ones models to help.

1

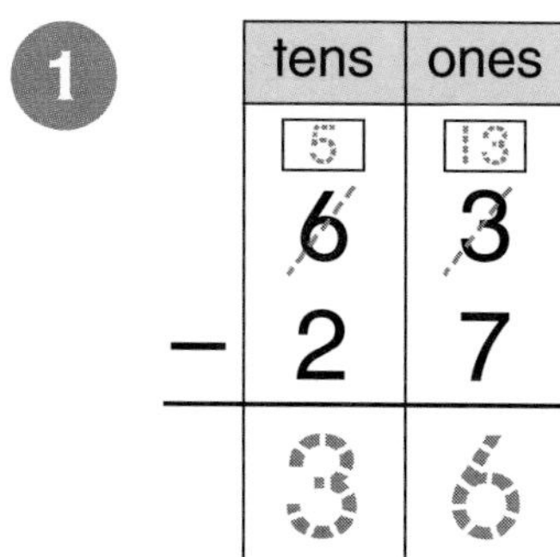

	tens	ones
	5	13
	~~6~~	~~3~~
−	2	7
	3	6

	tens	ones
	☐	☐
	3	8
−		9

	tens	ones
	☐	☐
	8	6
−	4	2

	tens	ones
	☐	☐
	2	1
−	1	8

Do you get the same answer with and without tens and ones models? Explain.

Practice!

Subtract. Use tens and ones models to help.

1

	tens	ones
	4	11
	~~5~~	~~1~~
−	2	9
	2	2

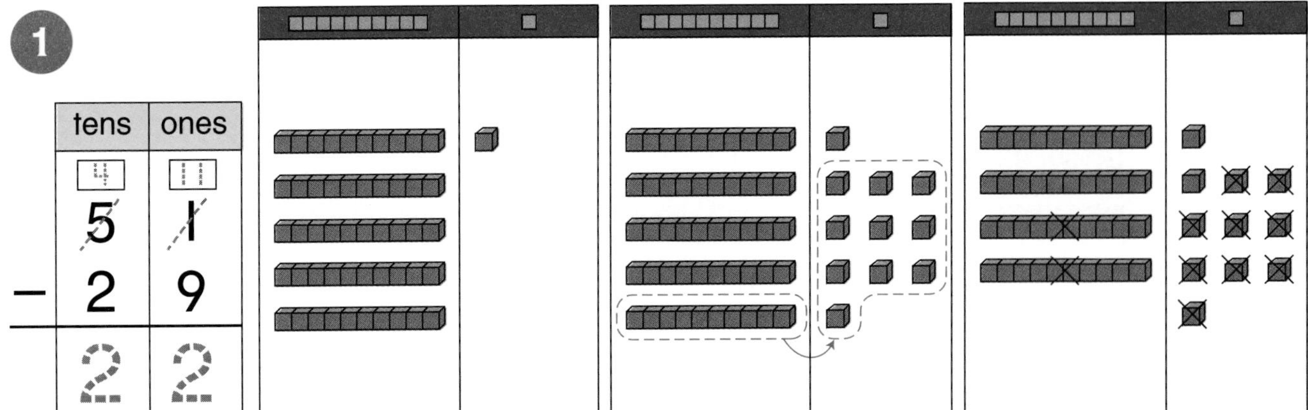

2

	tens	ones
	3	6
−	1	9

	tens	ones
	4	2
−		7

	tens	ones
	9	1
−	4	3

	tens	ones
	3	8
−	2	2

3

	tens	ones
	4	5
−	2	5

	tens	ones
	2	4
−	1	5

	tens	ones
	5	9
−	3	1

	tens	ones
	7	3
−	3	4

4

	tens	ones
	2	7
−		6

	tens	ones
	6	2
−	1	5

	tens	ones
	8	0
−	4	6

	tens	ones
	5	4
−	1	8

Journal

Write a subtraction rule that tells you when you need to regroup.

At Home

We subtracted with and without tens and ones models. Ask your child to explain how to subtract 54 − 18.

Name ____________

More Subtracting Numbers

Use the **table**.
How many more swallowtails are there than painted lady butterflies?

BUTTERFLY WATCH	
Swallowtail	26
Painted lady	14

Swallowtail

Painted Lady

Glossary
table

Write the numbers.	Regroup if you need to. Subtract the ones.	Subtract the tens.
26 − 14	26 − 14 = 2 (2 ones)	26 − 14 = 12 (1 ten)

There are 12 more swallowtails.

Subtract. Did you regroup?

1. 34 − 25 = 9 (yes) no   98 − 40 yes no   60 − 31 yes no

2. 36 − 23 yes no   57 − 9 yes no   82 − 27 yes no

Practice!

Subtract. Use tens and ones models if you want to.

1

5 14
64
− 38
26

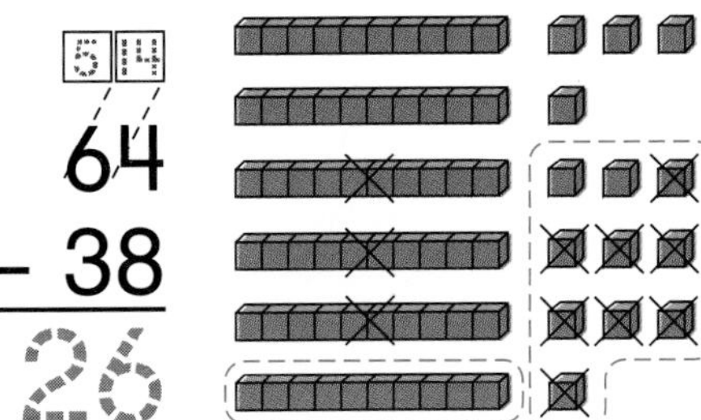

2

57
− 43
14

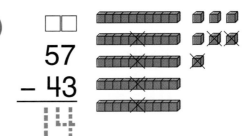

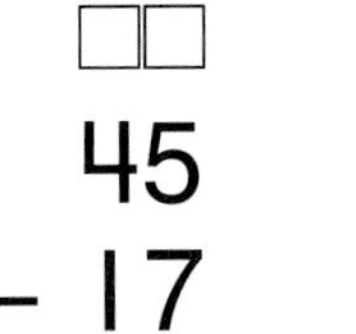

3 45 − 17   68 − 33   20 − 4   31 − 21   96 − 59   59 − 51

4 82 − 8   29 − 15   34 − 29   73 − 37   86 − 40   41 − 16

5 48 − 5   94 − 65   83 − 46   50 − 30   37 − 12   75 − 29

Solve.

Workspace

6 How many more zebra butterflies than monarchs are there?

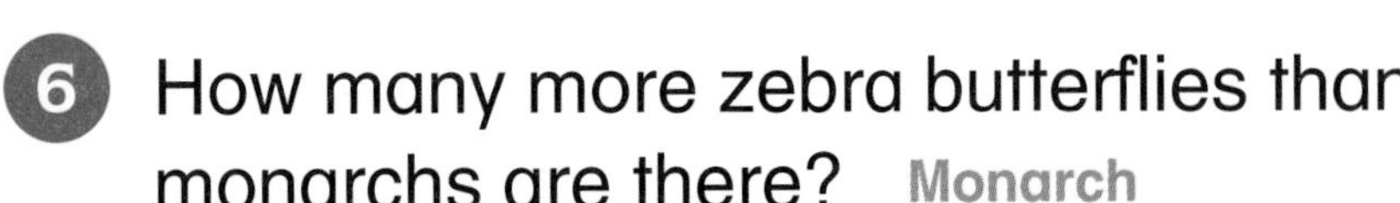

BUTTERFLY WATCH	
Monarch	18
Zebra	30

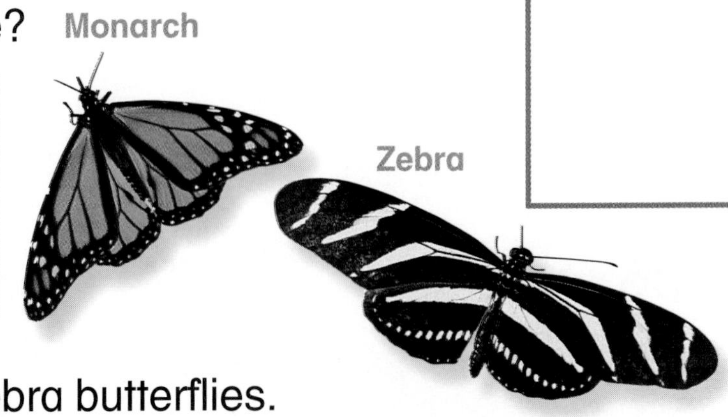

Monarch

Zebra

There are _____ more zebra butterflies.

At Home: We continue to subtract 2-digit numbers. Ask your child to explain how to subtract 37 − 12 and 75 − 29.

Name

Subtract to Solve Problems

A bird spreads its wings to fly.
This measure is called *wingspan.*

Osprey
54 inches

Wood Duck
28 inches

Prairie Falcon
40 inches

Bald Eagle
80 inches

How much larger is the wingspan of the falcon than the wingspan of the duck?

Regroup if you need to. Subtract the ones.	**Subtract the tens.**
3 10 ~~40~~ − 28 2 2 ones	3 10 ~~40~~ − 28 12 1 ten

The wingspan of the falcon is 12 inches larger.

Solve.

1. How much larger is the wingspan of the osprey than of the duck?

   ____ inches

2. How much larger is the wingspan of the eagle than of the osprey?

   ____ inches

Why do you subtract to compare?

Practice!

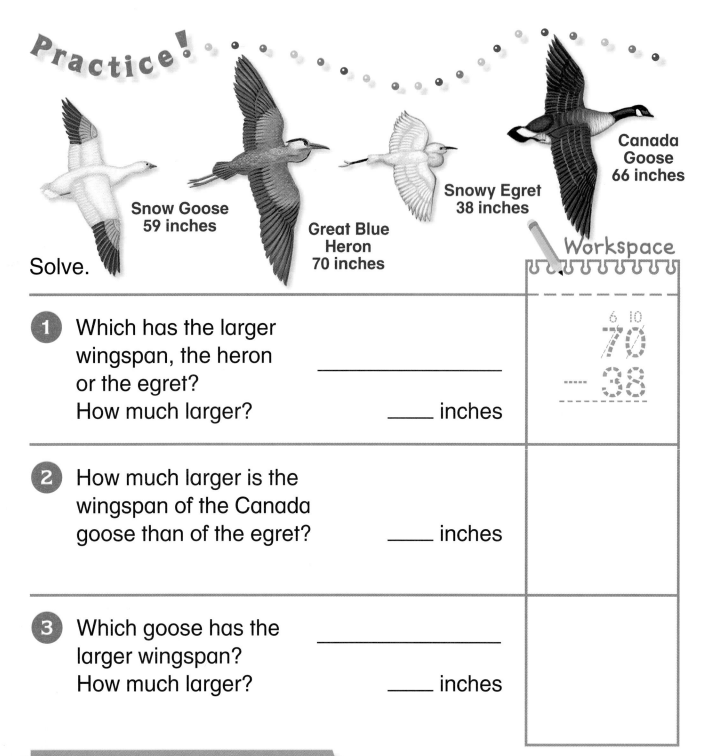

Snow Goose
59 inches

Great Blue
Heron
70 inches

Snowy Egret
38 inches

Canada
Goose
66 inches

Solve.

Workspace

1. Which has the larger wingspan, the heron or the egret? ________________
   How much larger? ____ inches

   $$\begin{array}{r} \overset{6\ 10}{\cancel{7}\cancel{0}} \\ -\ 38 \\ \hline \end{array}$$

2. How much larger is the wingspan of the Canada goose than of the egret? ____ inches

3. Which goose has the larger wingspan? ________________
   How much larger? ____ inches

More to Explore Number Sense

Solve.

Each van can hold 8 people. 56 people will ride in the vans to the birdwatch. How many vans are needed?

____ vans

We used subtraction to solve problems. Have your child explain how to solve problem 3 above.

Name ______________________________

Blackbird, Fly!

You and your partner need a [spinner], 6 [tens], and 20 [ones].

Take turns.

- Each of you starts with 3 [tens]. These are your "blackbirds."
- Each of you spins for the number of "blackbirds" that fly south for the winter.
- Subtract that number. Regroup if you need to.
- Write each new total.
- Play until all of one player's "blackbirds" are gone.

Subtract.

1	7 16 ~~86~~ − 17 69	67 − 46	32 − 28	44 − 39	68 − 47	96 − 47
2	60 − 48	30 − 16	27 − 19	62 − 48	93 − 60	88 − 72
3	23 − 19	44 − 26	51 − 29	88 − 46	72 − 44	63 − 18
4	45 − 23	75 − 68	37 − 29	71 − 18	39 − 21	80 − 65

Summarize

Write two sentences to tell about the story.

Then write a subtraction problem. Use information from the story.

Blackbirds

One day Bob and Marie went for a walk in the park. It was a cool day. They saw blackbirds everywhere!

Bob counted 76 blackbirds in one flock. Marie counted 59 blackbirds in another flock.

Name ______________________

Problem-Solving Strategy

Read | Plan | Solve | Look Back

Make a List

Scientists tag some animals to help keep track of them.

Read Dr. Ross puts tags on butterflies. She uses the numbers 2, 4, and 5 to make 2-digit tag numbers with different digits. How many different tag numbers can Dr. Ross make?

Plan You can **make a list** to organize this information.

Solve The list shows the 6 possible tag numbers.

Start with	Tag Numbers
2	24, 25
4	42, 45
5	52, 54

Look Back Have you answered the question?

Glossary
make a list

Make a list to solve.

1. Dr. Soto tags geese. He uses the numbers 1, 3, and 7 to make 2-digit tag numbers with different digits. How many tag numbers can Dr. Soto make?

Start with	Tag Numbers
1	
3	
7	

____ tag numbers

Practice!

Make a list to show all the 2-digit numbers with different digits.

1. Dr. Johnson tags ducks. She uses the numbers 3, 5, and 9 to make 2-digit tag numbers. What numbers can she make?

35 39

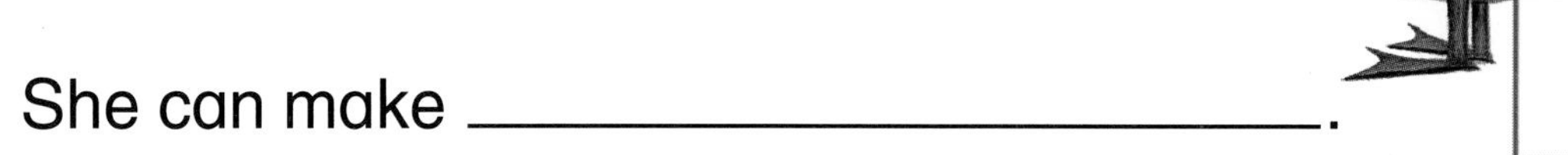

She can make ______________________.

2. A group of scientists has to tag seals. The scientists use the numbers 4, 6, and 8 to make 2-digit tag numbers. What numbers can they make?

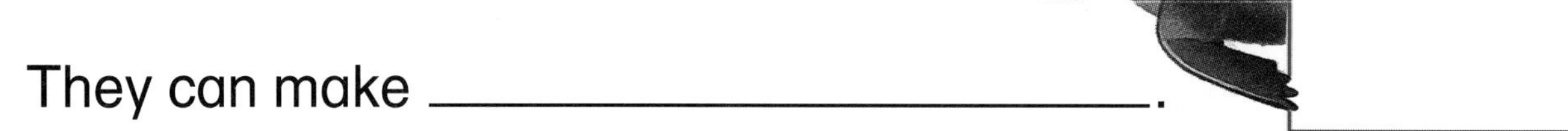

They can make ______________________.

3. Dr. Sanchez made tags for crabs. Then he lost his list. What 2-digit numbers did he make with 3, 4, and 7?

He made ______________________.

4. Two scientists tag geese. The scientists use the numbers 1, 2, 3, and 4 to make 2-digit tag numbers. What numbers can they make?

They can make ______________________

______________________.

How many more 2-digit numbers can you make with 4 numbers than with 3 numbers?

Name

Midchapter Review

Subtract. Use tens and ones models if you want to.

1

	tens	ones
	3	3
−	1	7

2

	tens	ones
	5	2
−	3	0

3

	tens	ones
	2	6
−	1	9

4 $52 - 5$

5 $73 - 48$

6 $41 - 12$

7 $39 - 24$

8 $45 - 36$

Solve.
Make a list to find all the 2-digit numbers with different digits.

9 Dr. Beck made tags for some birds. He used the numbers 5, 7, and 9 to make 2-digit tag numbers. What numbers did he make?

He made ______________________.

10 How did you solve problem 9? ______________________

____

For 2-digit numbers, how is regrouping in subtraction different from regrouping in addition?

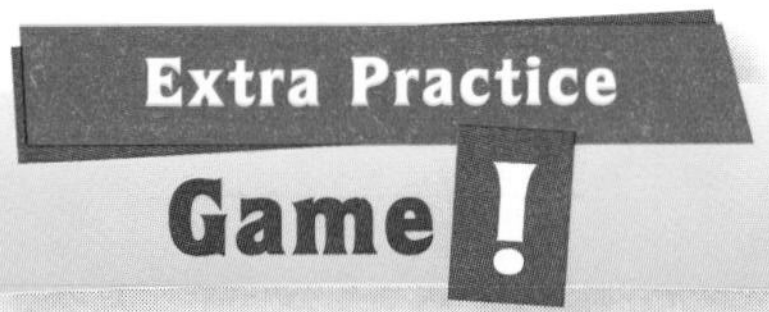

Fly South to Mexico!

Listen to *the Great Monarch Butterfly Chase.*

You and your partner need 2 counters, a calculator, and a spinner.

Take turns. Pretend you are both butterflies on your way to Mexico.

- Put your counter on **Start**.
- Spin the spinner twice. Subtract the lesser number from the greater number.
- Your partner checks your work.
- Move ahead one space if you are correct. If not, go back one space.

The winner is the first player to reach *Mexico.*

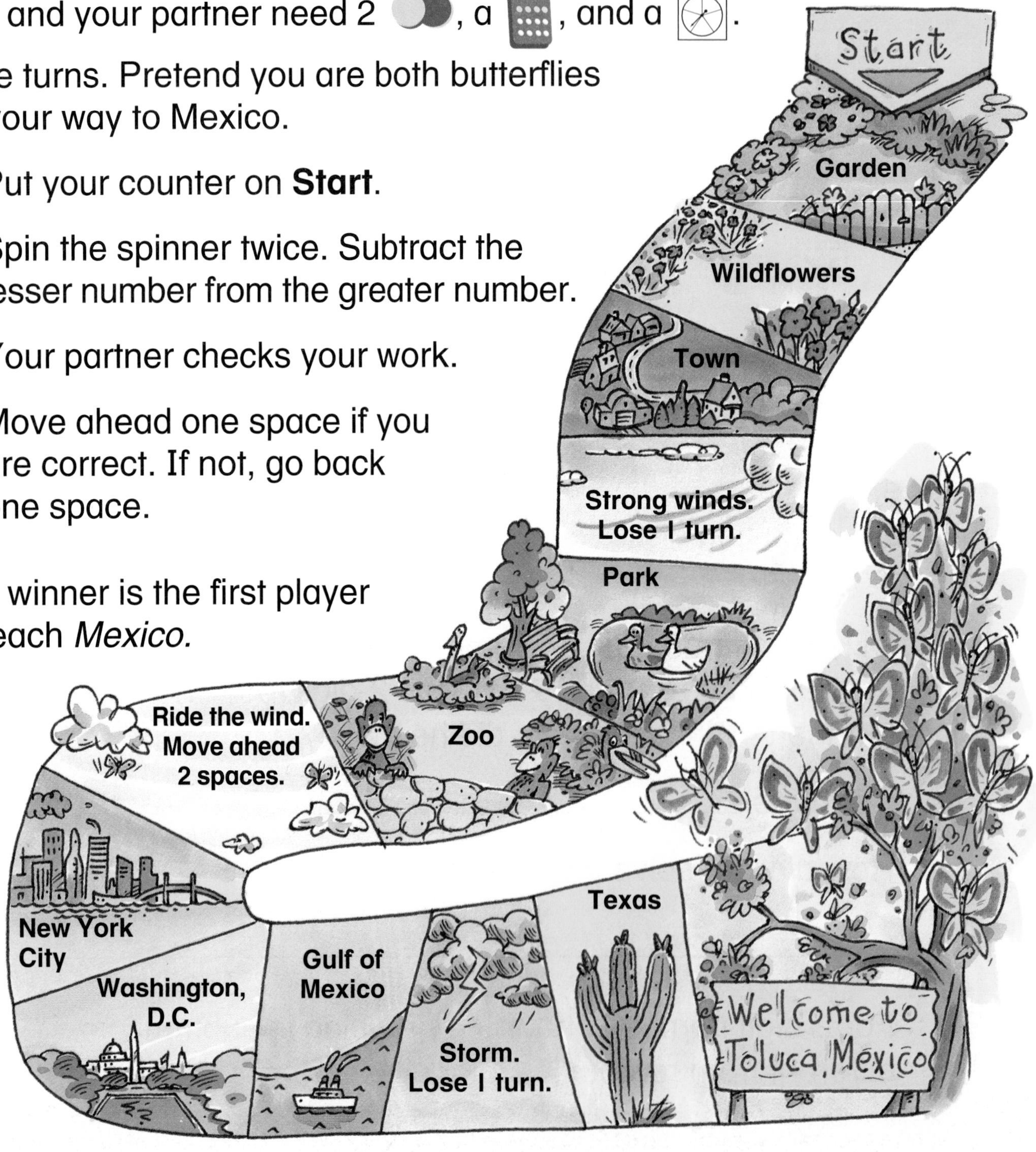

Name

Bird Count

You can learn a lot about birds by watching and counting them.

Tell the class about the kinds of birds that live near you.

Working Together

- Make a feeder like this one.
- Hang the feeder on a tree or on a pole.
- Find out the kinds of birds that visit the feeder before you start to count.
- Each group member decides which kind of bird he or she will count.
- Count the birds for a half hour. Use tally marks to show each bird.
- Find the total for each kind of bird.

Decision Making

1. Decide how to show what your group found. You can make a picture, a graph, or another kind of display.

2. 

How many birds did your group count in all? ___________

3. How many more or fewer birds did you count than each of your group members? ___________

____

4. What do you think you learned about the kind of bird that you counted? ___________

____

Write a report.

5. Tell what your group learned about the numbers and kinds of birds counted.

6. Tell how your group decided to show what they found.

More to Investigate

PREDICT Will the numbers and kinds of birds be different at another time of the day?

EXPLORE Choose a different time of the day. Count and record the new information.

FIND Find the total for each kind of bird. Compare the totals with what you found before.

Name ______________________

Subtract Money

Working Together

Take turns.

- Choose an amount of money and an item to buy.
- You and your partners use dimes, pennies, paper and pencil, and a calculator to find how much money is left. Act it out.
- Compare your differences.
- Write the subtraction.

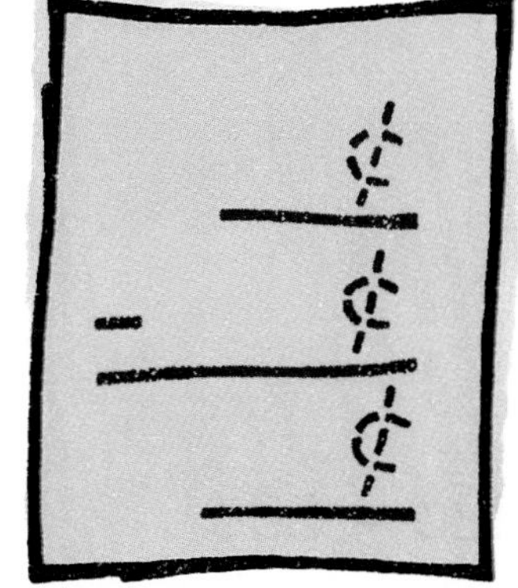

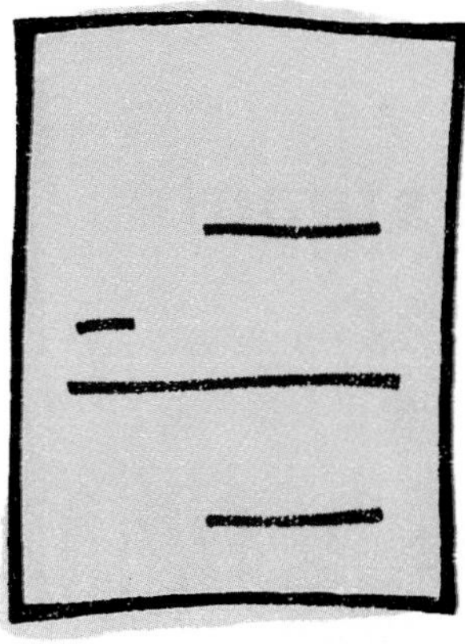

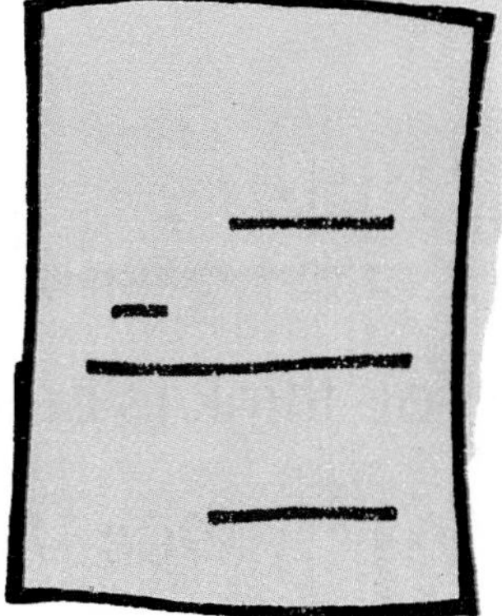

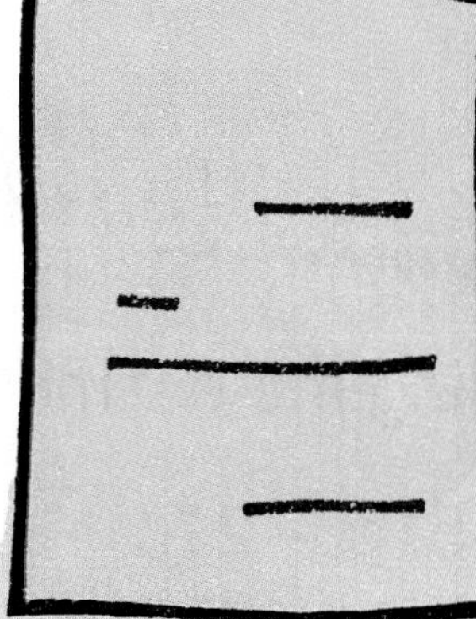

How is subtracting money like subtracting numbers?

Practice!

Solve.

1. You have 30¢. How much more do you need to buy a bird call? 24¢

   Workspace: 54¢ − 30¢ = 24¢

2. You want to buy a pen and a notepad. How much money do you need? ______

3. You have a quarter. How much more do you need to buy a bird book? ______

4. 

Write your own word problem. Have a partner solve it.

   Use your own paper.

More to Explore Estimate

Ring the estimate you think is best.

51¢ − 29¢	90¢ − 31¢	82¢ − 38¢
more than 50¢	more than 50¢	more than 50¢
less than 50¢	less than 50¢	less than 50¢

At Home: We subtracted money amounts. Ask your child to tell you about the problem he or she wrote.

Name ____________________

Catch the Salmon!

Salmon return each year to the same rivers where they were hatched.

You and your partner need a red and orange.
Choose your color crayon.
Take turns.

- ▶ Choose a salmon. Subtract.
- ▶ Your partner checks your work.
- ▶ If correct, color the fish with your crayon. If not correct, color the fish with your partner's crayon.

The winner is the one with more salmon colored.

$\begin{array}{r} 52 \\ -\ 45 \\ \hline \end{array}$

$\begin{array}{r} 50 \\ -\ 31 \\ \hline \end{array}$

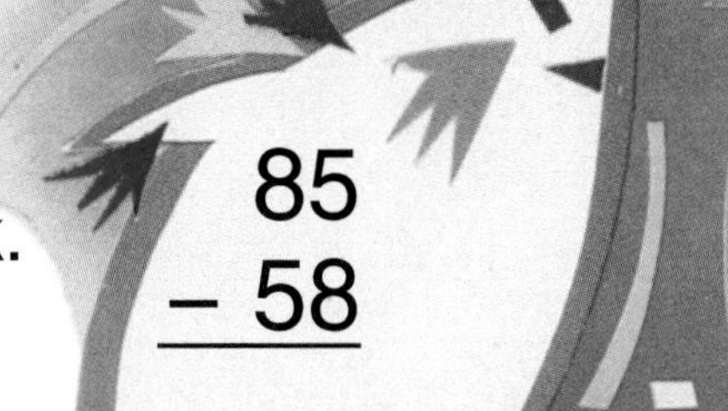

$\begin{array}{r} 85 \\ -\ 58 \\ \hline \end{array}$

$\begin{array}{r} 55 \\ -\ 30 \\ \hline \end{array}$

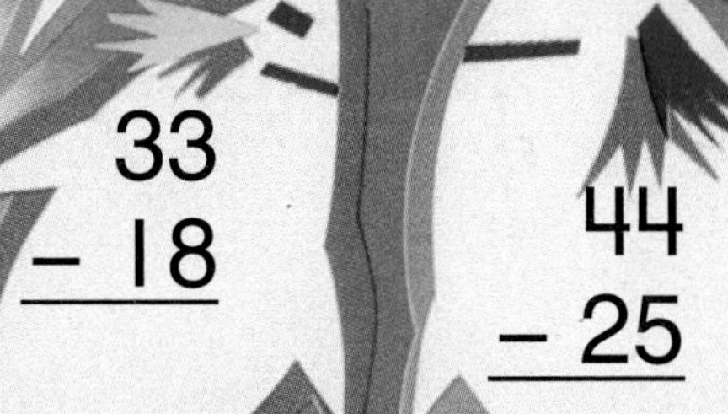

$\begin{array}{r} 33 \\ -\ 18 \\ \hline \end{array}$

$\begin{array}{r} 44 \\ -\ 25 \\ \hline \end{array}$

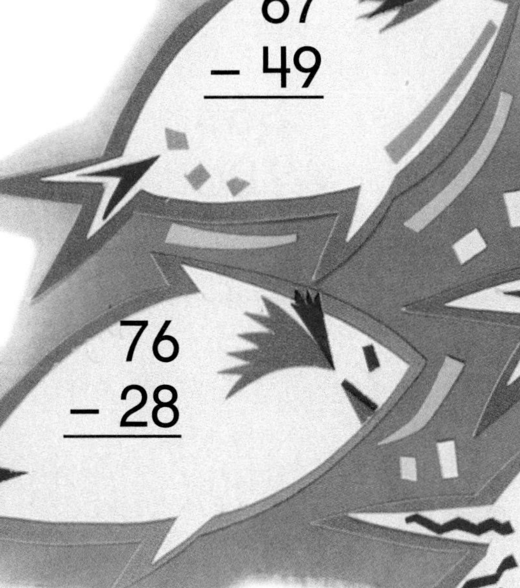

$\begin{array}{r} 67 \\ -\ 49 \\ \hline \end{array}$

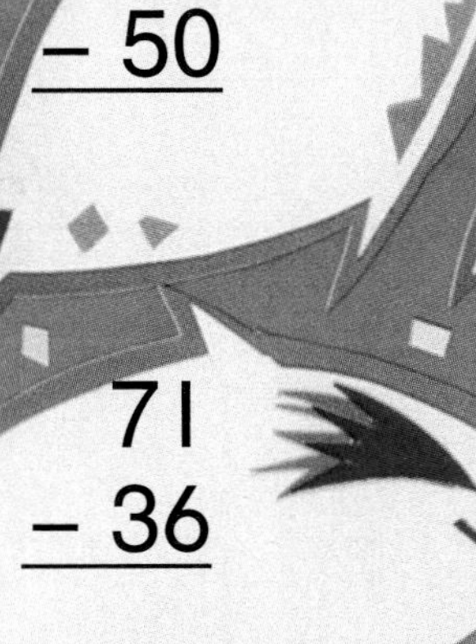

$\begin{array}{r} 99 \\ -\ 50 \\ \hline \end{array}$

$\begin{array}{r} 66 \\ -\ 47 \\ \hline \end{array}$

$\begin{array}{r} 23 \\ -\ 17 \\ \hline \end{array}$

$\begin{array}{r} 76 \\ -\ 28 \\ \hline \end{array}$

$\begin{array}{r} 71 \\ -\ 36 \\ \hline \end{array}$

Subtract.

1.

${\overset{6}{\not7}}{\overset{18}{\not8}}$	44	95	25	53	30
$-\ 49$	$-\ 38$	$-\ 73$	$-\ 7$	$-\ 14$	$-\ 19$
29					

2.

43	17	82	63	74	87
$-\ 15$	$-\ 15$	$-\ 48$	$-\ 36$	$-\ 56$	$-\ 44$

3.

90	55	51
$-\ 37$	$-\ 9$	$-\ 23$

4.

64	96	38
$-\ 45$	$-\ 56$	$-\ 38$

Cultural Note

The main industry for the Haida of Canada is salmon fishing.

Mixed Review Test Preparation

5.

23	46	14¢	27	36¢
$+\ 26$	$+\ 38$	$+\ 27$¢	$+\ 57$	$+\ 10$¢

Count. Write how much money.

6.

______

7.

______

Name

Check Subtraction

Dr. Dell buys field glasses for the whale watch. The glasses cost $43. She gives the clerk $60. The clerk gives her $17 change. Is her change correct?

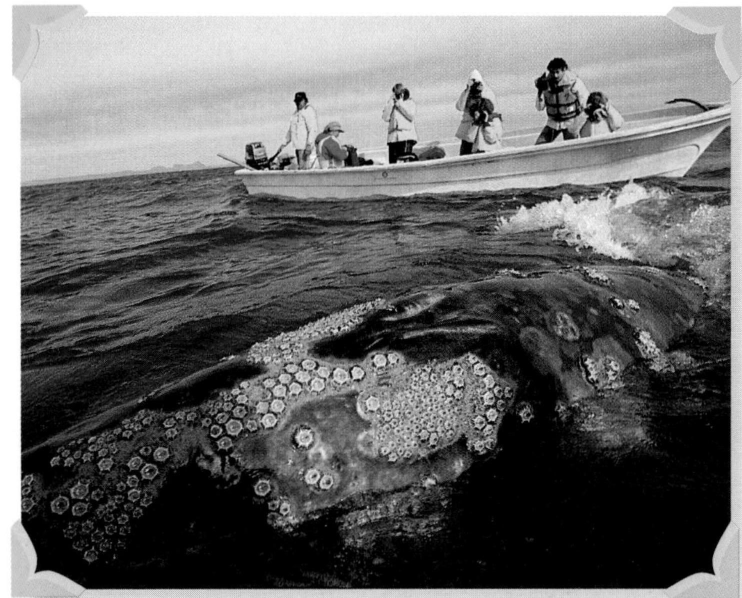

Subtract.

$$\begin{array}{r} \overset{5\,10}{\$\not6\not0} \\ -\ 43 \\ \hline \$17 \end{array}$$

Add to check.

$$\begin{array}{r} \overset{1}{\$17} \\ +\ 43 \\ \hline \$60 \end{array}$$

Talk What do you notice about the numbers?

Dr. Dell's change is correct.

Subtract. Then add to check the difference.

1. $\begin{array}{r} \overset{3\,15}{\not4\not5} \\ -\ 18 \\ \hline 27 \end{array}$ $\begin{array}{r} \overset{1}{27} \\ +\ 18 \\ \hline 45 \end{array}$ $\begin{array}{r} 80¢ \\ -\ 65¢ \\ \hline \end{array}$

2. $\begin{array}{r} 52 \\ -\ 29 \\ \hline \end{array}$ $\begin{array}{r} 75¢ \\ -\ 18¢ \\ \hline \end{array}$

Critical Thinking What does it mean if the sum is not the same as the number you subtract from?

Practice!

Subtract. Then add to check the difference.

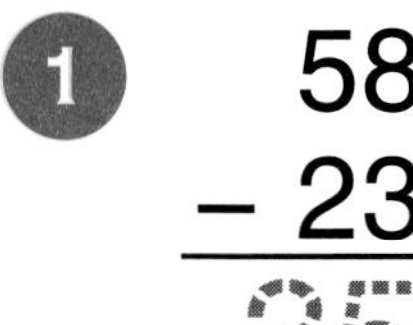

1. $\begin{array}{r} 58 \\ -\ 23 \\ \hline 35 \end{array}$ $\quad \begin{array}{r} 35 \\ +\ 23 \\ \hline \end{array}$ $\quad \begin{array}{r} 71 \\ -\ 22 \\ \hline \end{array}$ $\quad \begin{array}{r} 35¢ \\ -\ \ 7¢ \\ \hline \end{array}$

2. $\begin{array}{r} 81 \\ -\ 43 \\ \hline \end{array}$ $\quad \begin{array}{r} 45 \\ -\ 18 \\ \hline \end{array}$ $\quad \begin{array}{r} 60¢ \\ -\ 44¢ \\ \hline \end{array}$

3. $\begin{array}{r} 55 \\ -\ 32 \\ \hline \end{array}$ $\quad \begin{array}{r} \$76 \\ -\ \ 69 \\ \hline \end{array}$ $\quad \begin{array}{r} 93 \\ -\ 15 \\ \hline \end{array}$

Solve. Then add to check your answer.

4. The team counted 47 sea lions in the morning. They counted 29 in the afternoon. How many more sea lions did they count in the morning? ____ sea lions

5. Jorge counted 18 of the 47 sea lions. How many of the sea lions did Jorge *not* count? ____ sea lions

We added to check subtraction. Ask your child to explain how to check subtraction.

Name ______

Add or Subtract to Solve Problems

There were 56 seals on the rocks.
Then 48 seals jumped in the water.
How many seals are still on the rocks?

How do you decide if you should add or subtract?

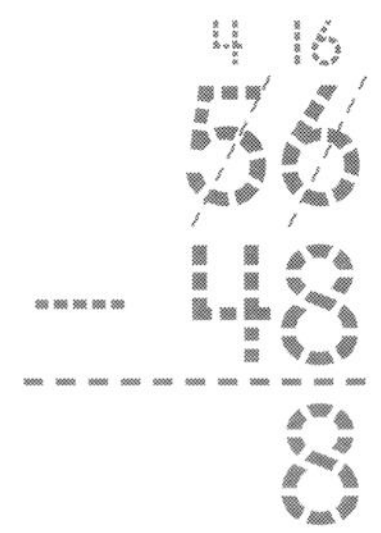

$$\begin{array}{r} \overset{4}{\cancel{5}}\overset{16}{\cancel{6}} \\ -\ 48 \\ \hline 8 \end{array}$$

8 seals are still on the rocks.

Add or subtract to solve.

Workspace

1. Lydia sees 33 seals.
15 of the seals are sleeping.
How many seals are awake? ____ seals

2. 38 seals are born on Monday.
25 seals are born on Tuesday.
How many seals are born? ____ seals

3. Mr. Yoshi spends \$56 for tickets to see the seals and \$14 for film.
How much does he spend in all? ______

When might you decide to use mental math to solve a problem?

Practice!

Add or subtract to solve.

Workspace

1. There are 86 seals on land. There are 42 seals in the water. How many more seals are on land? ________

2. A ticket to the seal show costs $14. How much will it cost to buy 2 tickets? ________

3. Tony has $37 for 3 tickets. Three tickets cost $42. How much more money does he need? ________

4. 
Write
Use the numbers 53 and 29. Write your own word problem. Have a partner solve it.

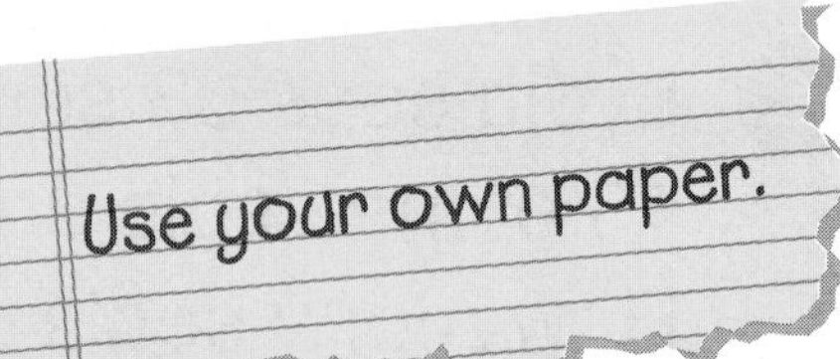
Use your own paper.

Cultural Connection

Guatemala

People in Guatemala like to shop at outdoor markets. The money they use is *quetzales*.

Margarita bought a case of candies at a market. One case costs 20 quetzales.

Margarita gave the seller 50 quetzales.

How much money does Margarita have left? ____ quetzales

At Home: We solved addition and subtraction problems. Ask your child to explain problems 1 to 3 above.

Name

Identify Extra Information

Sea turtles return to land to lay eggs.

1. A green turtle dug a hole
28 inches deep.
It laid 47 eggs in the hole.
The turtle laid 39 eggs in another hole.
How many eggs did it lay in all?

extra information

You can cross out the **extra information**.
Then add to solve the problem.

The turtle laid 86 eggs in all.

$$\begin{array}{r} 47 \\ +\,39 \\ \hline 86 \end{array}$$

Cross out any extra information. Then solve.

Workspace

2. A green turtle is 60 inches long.
A leatherback turtle is 96 inches long.
A hawksbill turtle is 36 inches long.
How much longer is the green
turtle than the hawksbill turtle? ____ inches

3. A snapping turtle lays up to 30 eggs.
It lays eggs 14 inches underground.
A green turtle lays eggs 28 inches
underground.
How much deeper does the
green turtle lay its eggs? ____ inches

4. READING ARITHMETIC WRITING **Summarize** Write a summary that tells about turtles and the eggs they lay. Use numbers in your summary.

Practice!

1. One softshell turtle lays 33 eggs. Another softshell turtle lays 18 eggs. 26 of the eggs hatch. How many eggs were laid altogether?  eggs

   What should the answer be? ____ eggs

2. How could someone get 77 as the answer?

   Write about it. ____

   ____

Write and Share

Rothanna wrote this problem.

A black cat has 2 kittens.
A brown cat has 4 kittens.
The white dog has
5 puppies.
How many kittens are there?

Rothanna Sarath
Shaughnessy School
Lowell, Massachusetts

3. Solve Rothanna's problem. ________

   Use your own paper.

4. Write a problem with extra information. Have a partner solve it.

   What method did your partner use? ________________

Ask your child how to solve the problem he or she wrote.

Name ______________________

Chapter Review

Language and Mathematics

Choose the correct word to complete the sentence.

table
ones
tens
regroup

1. You have to ______________ when you subtract 42 − 28.

2. You can regroup 1 ______________ as 10 ______________.

Concepts and Skills

Subtract. Did you regroup? Mark *yes* or *no*.

3.

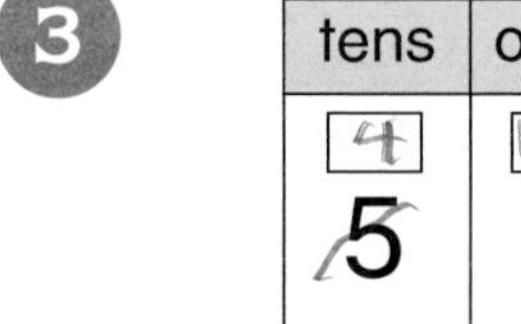

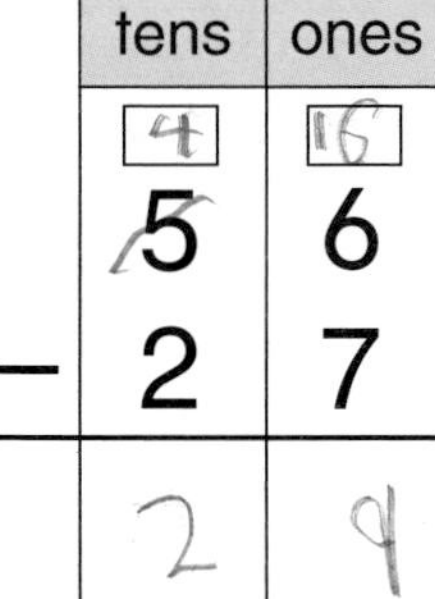

	tens	ones
	5	6
−	2	7

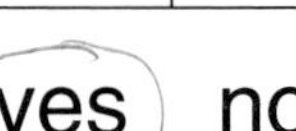

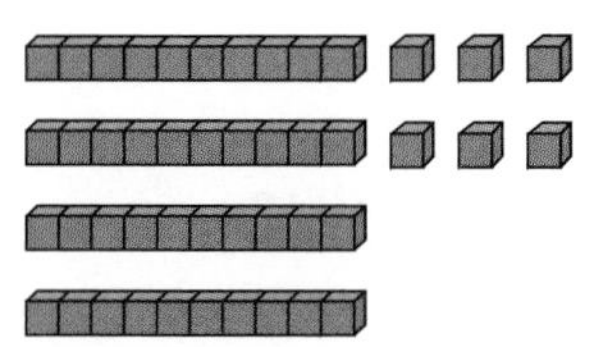

yes no

4.

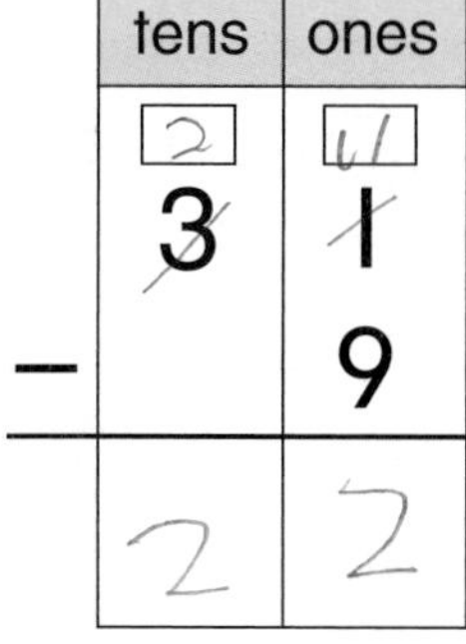

	tens	ones
	3	1
−		9

yes no

Subtract.

5. 48 − 19 = ____

6. 90 − 21 = ____

7. 68 − 63 = ____

8. 53 − 16 = ____

9. 74 − 66 = ____

10. 88¢ − 40¢ = ____

11. 52 − 5 = ____

12. 61 − 37 = ____

13. 77 − 11 = ____

14. 37¢ − 29¢ = ____

15. $84 − 62 = ____

16. 40 − 25 = ____

Problem Solving

Solve.

17. Ann bought a book for 55¢ and a pencil for 36¢. How much did she spend?

____

18. There are 45 ducks on the pond. 23 of them fly away. How many ducks are left?

_____ ducks

19. Gerry made tags. She used the numbers 3, 5, and 9. What 2-digit numbers did she make? Make a list with different digits.

She made ______________________.

Cross out the extra information. Then solve.

20. One turtle laid 21 eggs.
Another turtle laid 34 eggs.
46 eggs hatch.
How many eggs did the two turtles lay? _____ eggs

What Do You Think?

Which is the easiest way to subtract 40 – 15?

☑ Check one.

☐ 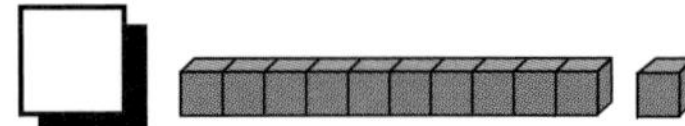 ☐ 

☐ 

☐ 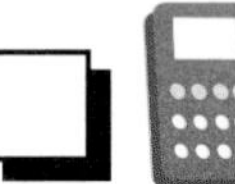

Why? ______________________________

Write 35 – 6. Show the subtraction by drawing models.

Name ______________________________

Chapter Test

Subtract. Did you regroup? Mark *yes* or *no*.

1. 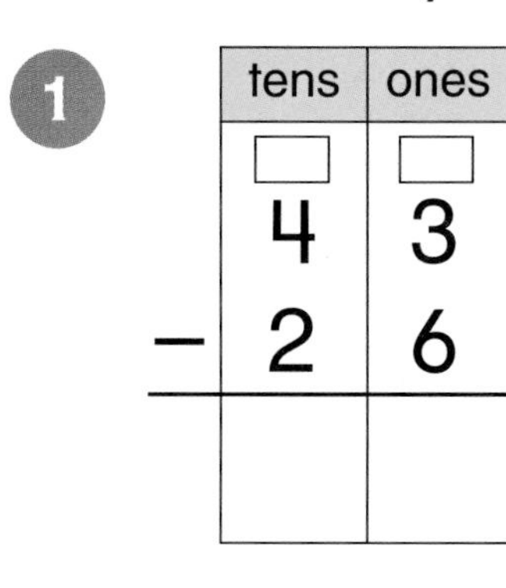

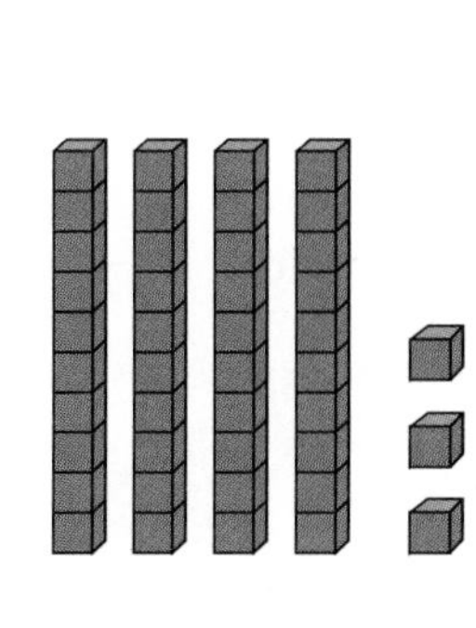

yes no

2. 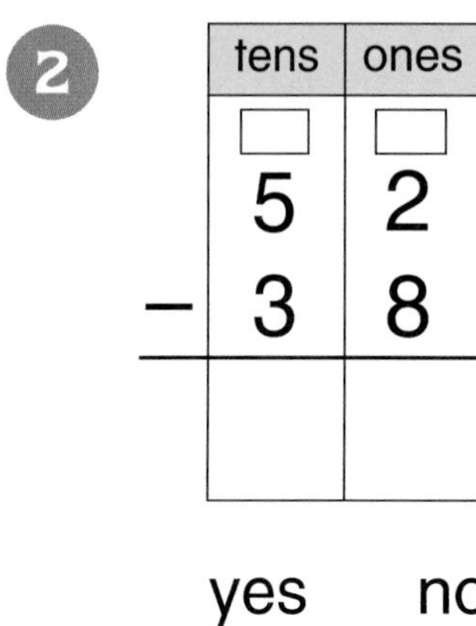

yes no

Subtract.

3. $\begin{array}{r} 91 \\ -\ 23 \\ \hline \end{array}$

4. $\begin{array}{r} 36 \\ -\ 21 \\ \hline \end{array}$

5. $\begin{array}{r} \$72 \\ -\ \ 65 \\ \hline \end{array}$

6. $\begin{array}{r} 25¢ \\ -\ 10¢ \\ \hline \end{array}$

7. $\begin{array}{r} 54 \\ -\ 26 \\ \hline \end{array}$

8. There are 35 seals on the rocks. 15 more seals climb on the rocks. How many seals are there?

_____ seals

9. There are 43 crabs on the beach. 25 crawl away. How many crabs are on the beach now?

_____ crabs

Make a list with different digits to solve.

10. Sarah tags some ducks. She uses the numbers 2, 4, and 8. What 2-digit numbers does she make?

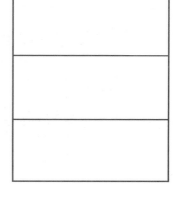

She makes ______________________________.

Performance Assessment

What Did You Learn?

The second-grade class took a survey to find out their favorite bird. Use the clues to tell how the class voted.

FAVORITE BIRDS	
Birds	**Votes**
	8
	24
	14
	38
	27

1. The blue jay was voted the favorite.
2. The crow got 19 votes fewer than the robin.
3. The eagle got 3 votes fewer than the robin.
4. The wren got 10 votes fewer than the eagle.

Explain how you decided where to place each bird in the survey.

You may want to put this page in your portfolio.

Math Connection

Calculator

Name

Missing Number

Take turns.

- Subtract to find the missing number.
  Shh! Do not tell your partner the answer.
- Your partner guesses the missing number and checks it on the calculator.
- Your partner has four guesses.
- After each guess, give your partner a clue such as "Go higher" or "Go lower."
- Then write the missing number.

1. 57 – ☐ = 39
2. 65 – ☐ = 28
3. 24 – ☐ = 18
4. 36 – ☐ = 17
5. 46 – ☐ = 12
6. 70 – ☐ = 54
7. 32 – ☐ = 23
8. 81 – ☐ = 56

How could you use addition to find the missing numbers?

Curriculum Connection

Science

Compare Animal Speeds

Use the table to solve.

1 How much faster is a zebra than an elephant?

____ miles per hour

2 How much faster is an antelope than an elephant?

____ miles per hour

3 Which animal is slower, an elephant or a giraffe? ________

How much slower? ____ miles per hour

ANIMAL SPEEDS	
Animal	**Average Speed (Miles per Hour)**
elephant	25
zebra	39
antelope	61
wildebeest	50
giraffe	28

Write your own subtraction problem about these animals. Then solve it.

Use your own paper.

Home Connection

Chapter 8 Wrap-Up

Name ______________________________

Get to Zero First!

92

PLAYERS 2 or more

MATERIALS pencil and paper

DIRECTIONS The first player writes a starting number between 87 and 93 on a sheet of paper. Then each player in turn chooses a number between 1 and 15 for his or her partner to subtract and write the difference.

The winner is the player who reaches 0 first.

As you play this game, note that as the difference reaches 15, players can plan ahead to increase their chance of being the player to get to 0 first.

Dear Family,

I am beginning a new chapter in mathematics. During the next few weeks I will be learning about geometry and fractions.

I will also be talking about how shapes and patterns are used in art.

Learning About Shapes in Art

Let's talk about different shapes we see in art. We can draw shapes to make pictures.

My Math Words

I am going to use these math words and other math words in this chapter.

Please help me make word cards for the math words. I can use these word cards when I explore geometry and fractions.

cube
sphere
cylinder
cone
rectangular prism
square
circle
triangle
rectangle
halves
fourths
thirds
fraction

Your child,

Signature

Geometry and Fractions

Theme: Shapes in Art

Visualize As you listen to the story *Jamaica Louise James,* try to picture Jamaica Louise's drawings in your head. Tell about the pictures.

Now look at the pictures in the book. How are they like the pictures in your head? What shapes do you see?

Name

What Do You Know?

Look at the shapes.
Choose a way to sort them into two groups.

Write a name for each group inside a circle.

Draw a line from each shape to the group where it belongs.

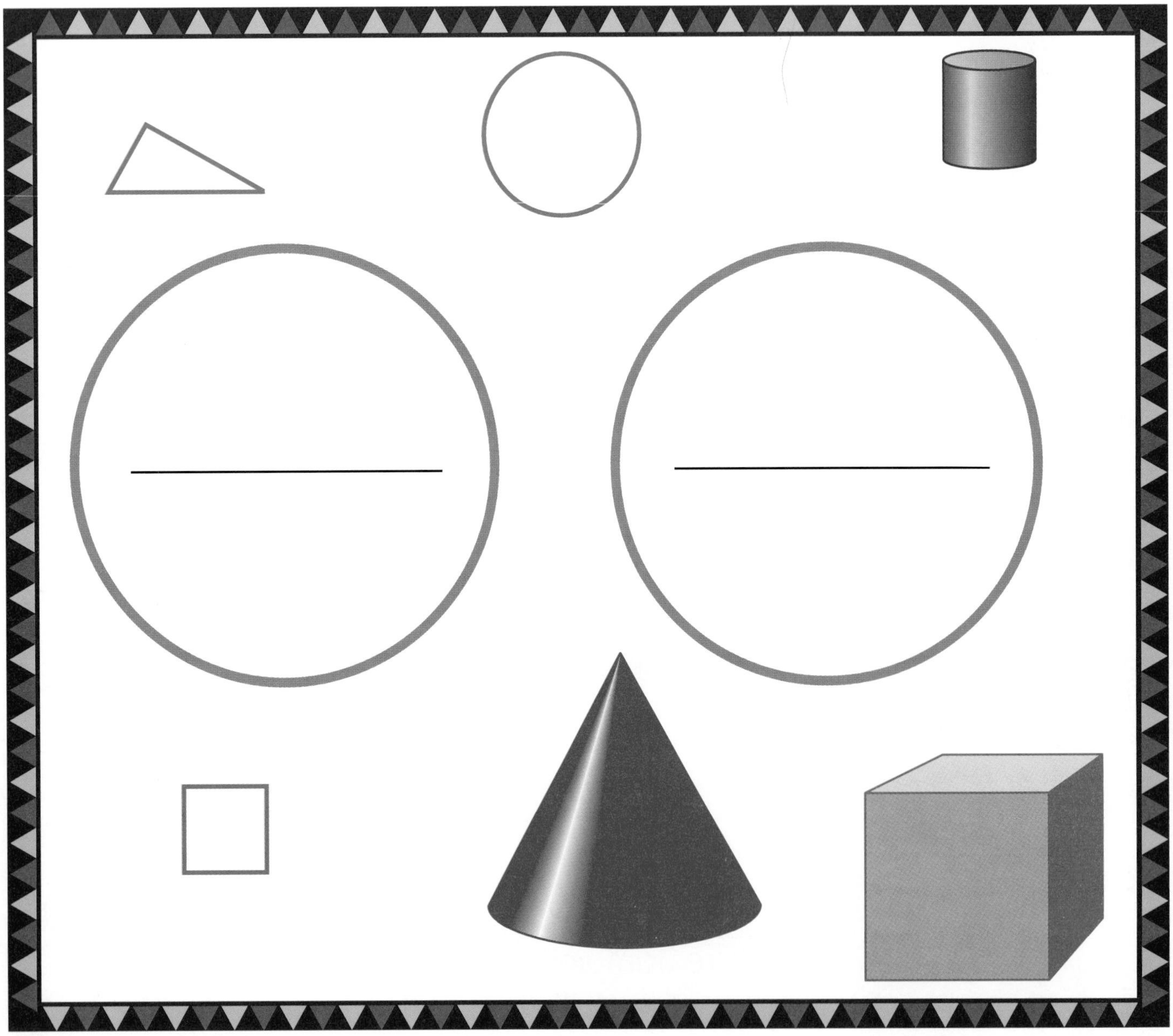

Explain how you sorted.
Then tell about a different way to sort the shapes into two groups.

Name ____________________

Working Together

You and your partner need 40 ▢.

- Use 4 cubes. Build different shapes.
- Your partner builds the same shapes you built.
- Draw the shapes.

How many different shapes did you make? ____________________

- Use 6 cubes. Your partner builds different shapes.
- You build the same shapes your partner built.
- Draw the shapes.

Use your own paper.

Critical Thinking

Can you make more shapes with 4 cubes or with 6 cubes? Why?

Practice!

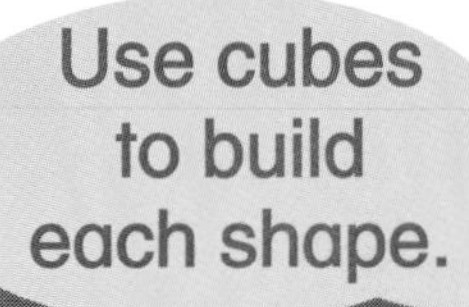

Write the number of cubes in each shape.

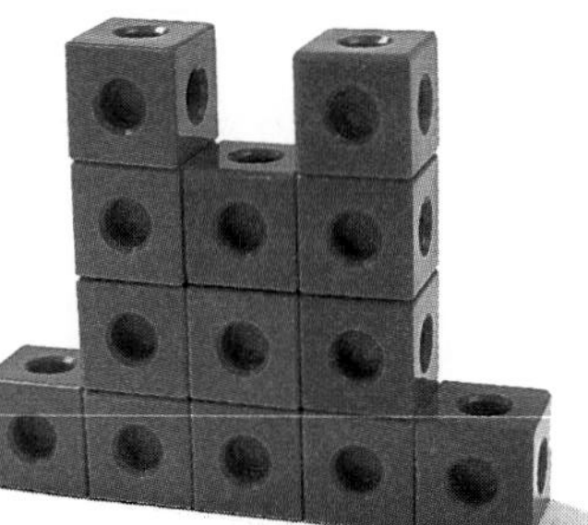

4

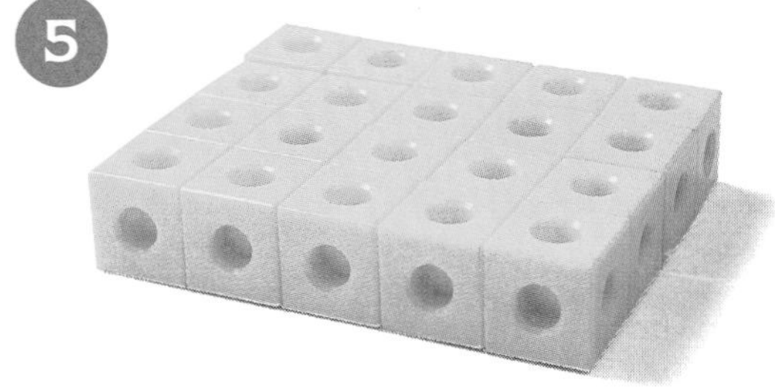

6

More to Explore Spatial Sense

You can look at a shape from different sides.
Each time the shape looks different.

Build your own shape.
Try to draw it from different sides.

Use your own paper.

Ask your child to tell how to find the number of cubes in one of the pictures above.

Name

3-Dimensional Shapes

corner
edge
face
cube
sphere
cylinder
rectangular prism
cone

Glossary

corner
edge
face
cube
sphere
cylinder
cone
rectangular prism

▶ Find classroom objects with these shapes.

▶ Complete the chart.

	object	shape	faces	corners	edges
1		rectangular prism	6	8	12
2					
3					
4					
5					

How are the cube and rectangular prism the same? How are they different?

Find objects with these shapes.
Write or draw a picture of them.

1 sphere

2 rectangular prism

3 cone

4 cylinder

5 cube

Mixed Review Test Preparation

6 $\begin{array}{r} 25 \\ -\ 15 \\ \hline \end{array}$

7 $\begin{array}{r} 93 \\ -\ 58 \\ \hline \end{array}$

8 $\begin{array}{r} 64 \\ -\ 40 \\ \hline \end{array}$

9 $\begin{array}{r} 51 \\ -\ 31 \\ \hline \end{array}$

Write the time.

___:___

___:___

___:___

___:___

At Home: We learned about 3-dimensional shapes. Ask your child to name an object shaped like a sphere.

Name

2-Dimensional Shapes

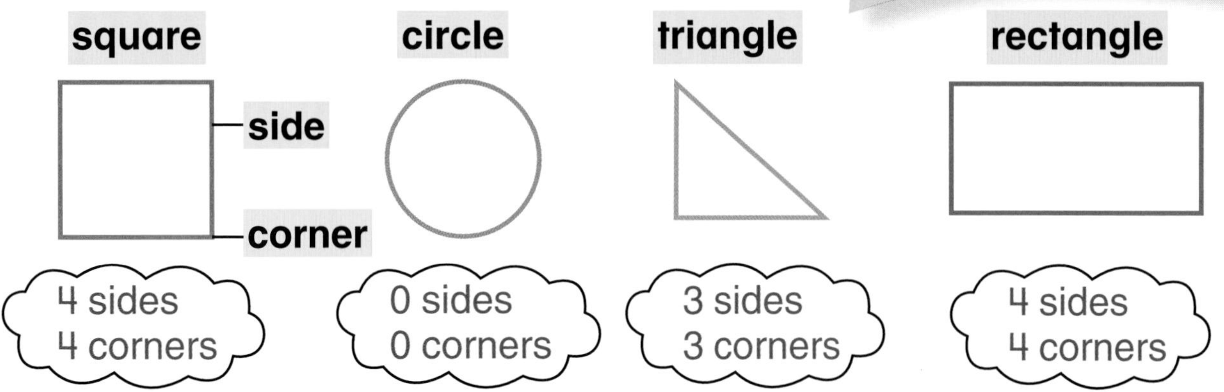

You can make shapes from other shapes.

- Cut out and fold some □, △, and ▭.
- Draw lines to show the folds.
- Write the name of the shapes made by the folds.

Glossary

side
corner
square
circle
triangle
rectangle

1 

triangles ________ ________ ________

2 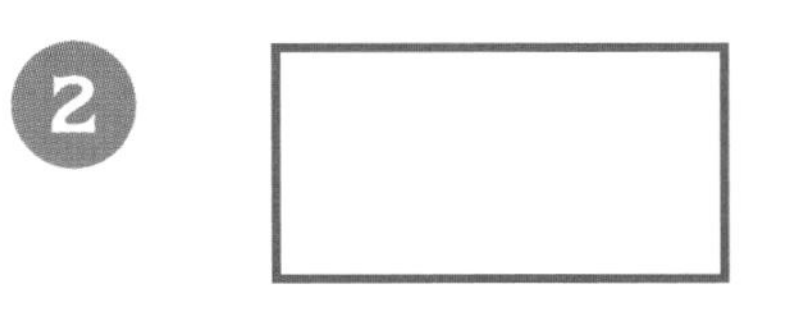

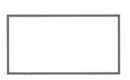

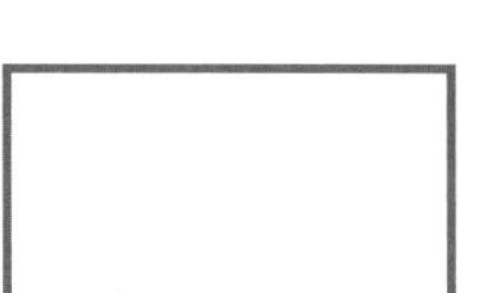

________ ________ ________

3 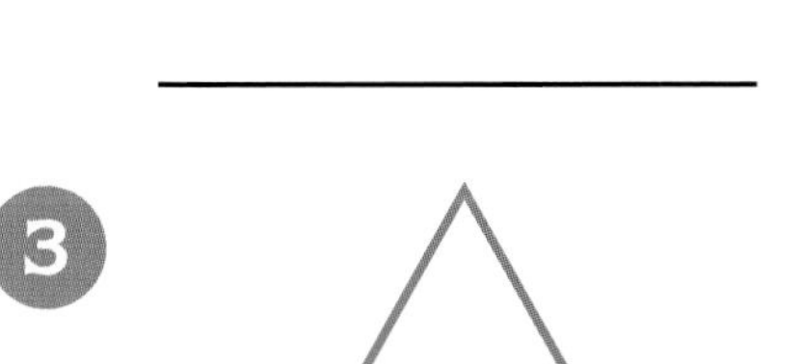

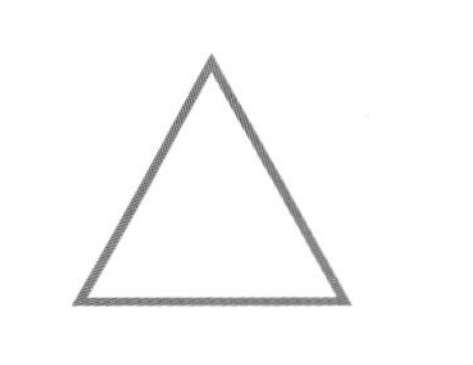

________ ________ ________

Practice!

How many triangles are in these squares?

1 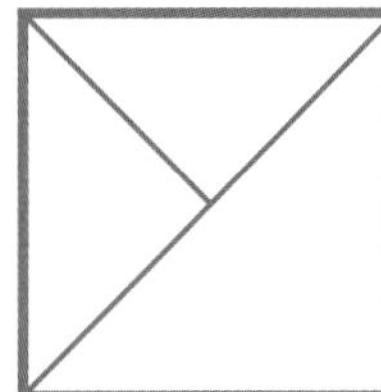 ____

2 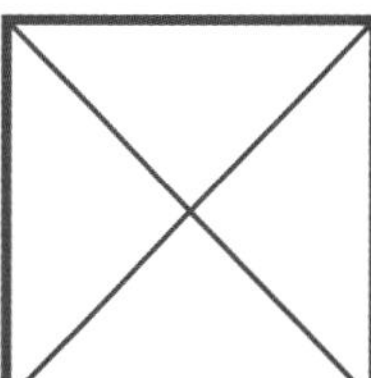 ____

3 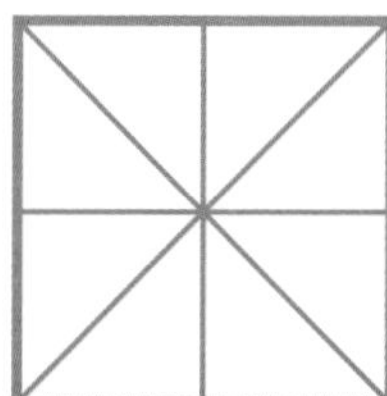 ____

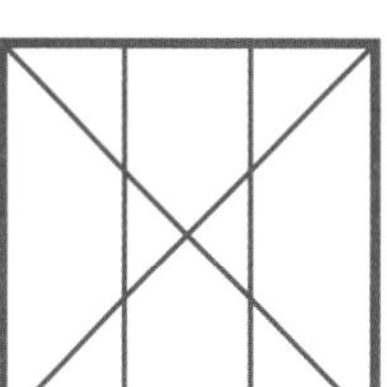

4 How many rectangles are in this square? ____

5 How many triangles? ____

More to Explore Spatial Sense

Here is a large square made up of 4 smaller squares.

Draw the largest possible square you can make on the grid. How many smaller squares is it made of? Color it.

4

At Home: Ask your child to fold a sheet of paper and name the shapes made by the folds.

Name ____________________

Explore Activity

Congruent Shapes

The two shapes in each pair are **congruent**.

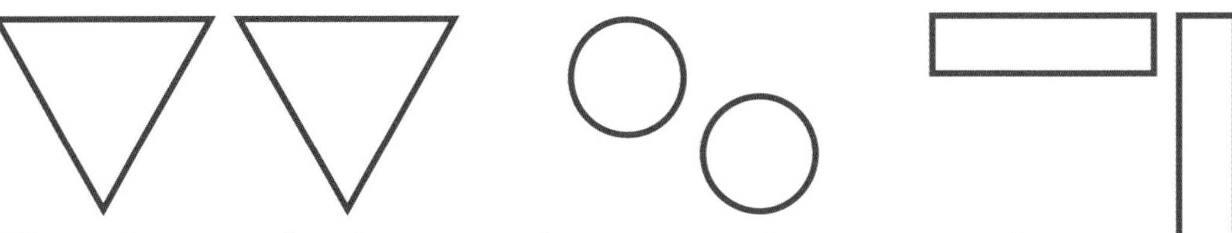

The shapes in these pairs are not congruent.

 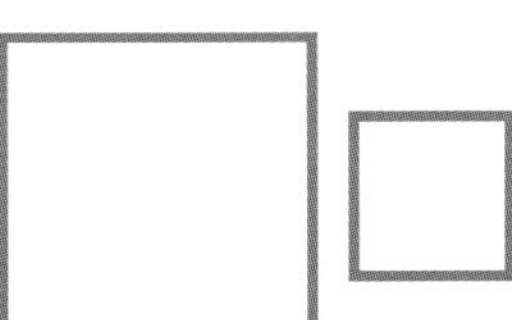 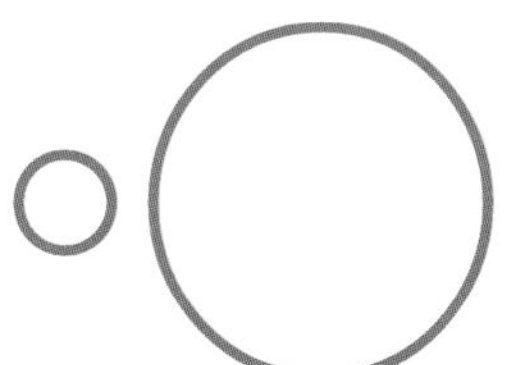

Glossary

congruent

What makes two shapes congruent?

Working Together

You and your partner need scissors, glue, and paper shapes.

- Cut out 4 different shapes.
- Fold each shape to make two shapes that are congruent. Cut on the fold.
- Match a cut-out shape to a congruent shape below. Glue the shape onto the shape it matches.

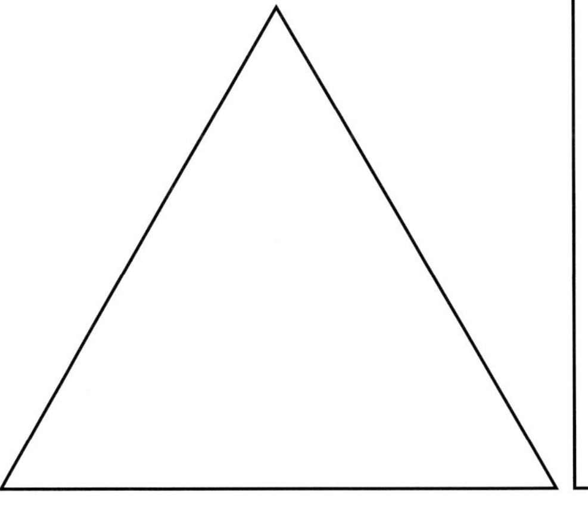  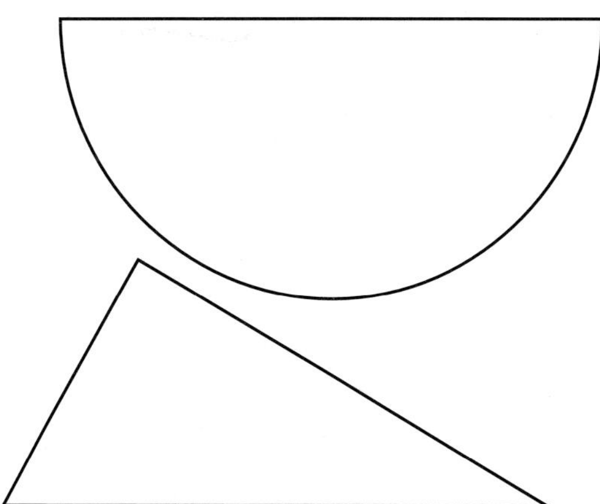

Practice!

Draw a triangle that is congruent.

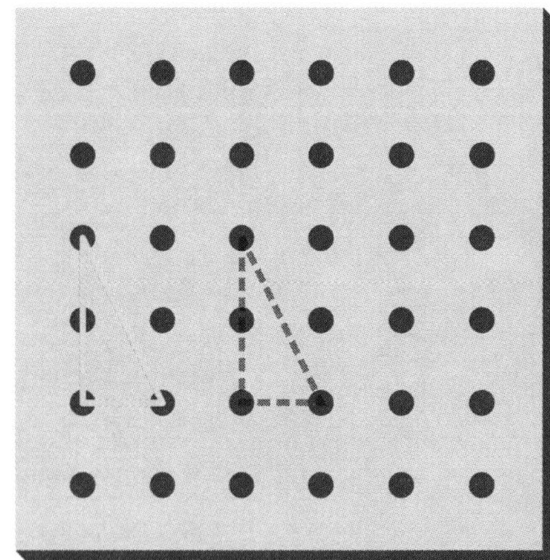

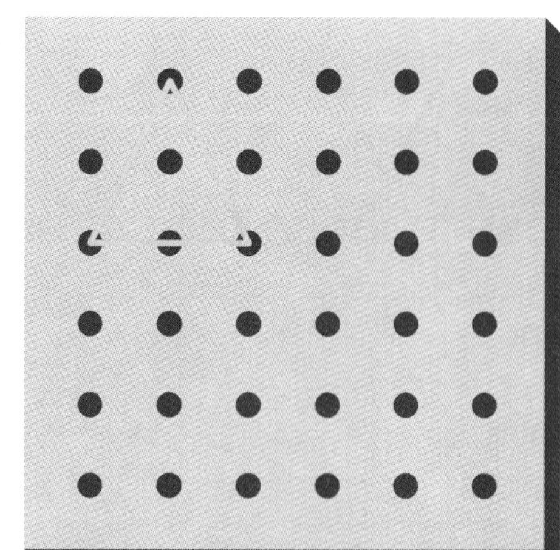

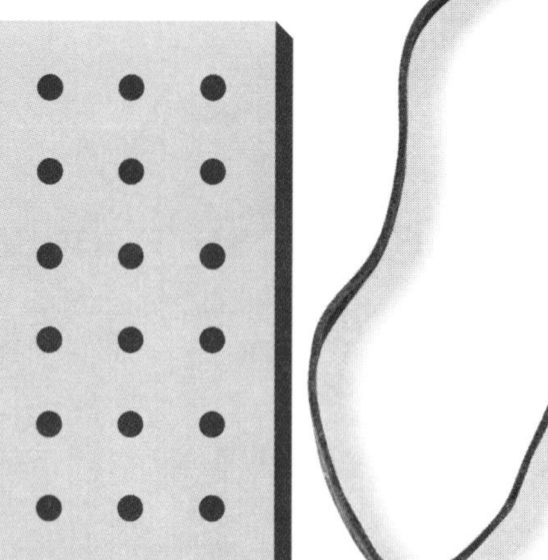

Draw a square that is congruent.

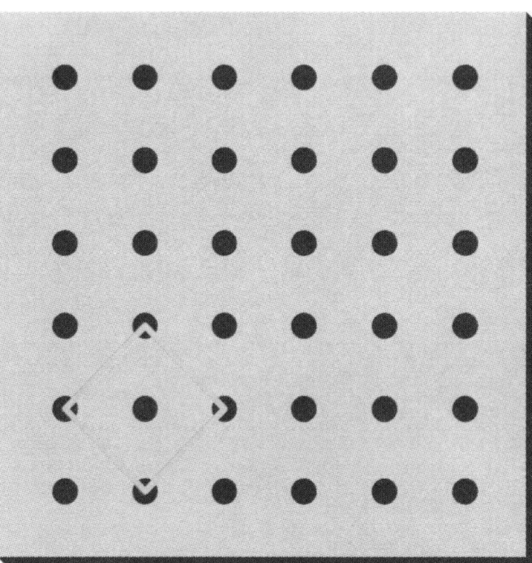

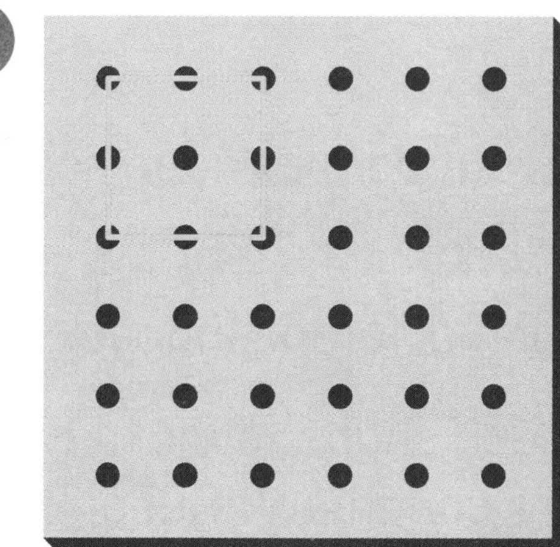

Draw a rectangle that is congruent.

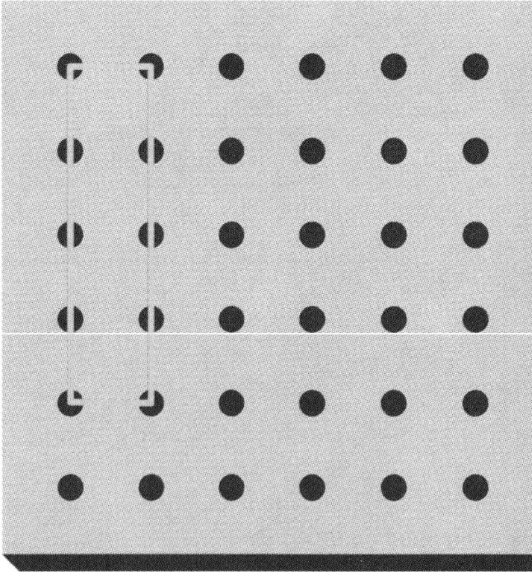

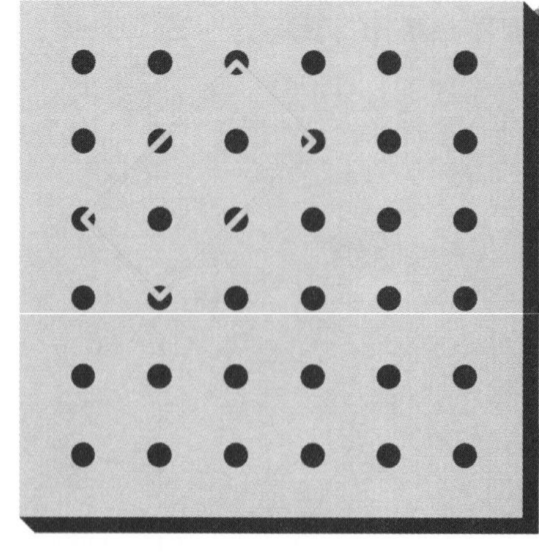

Draw two shapes that are congruent.
Write how you know they are congruent.

We learned about congruent shapes. Ask your child to explain what two congruent shapes are.

Name

Symmetry

These shapes show a **line of symmetry**.

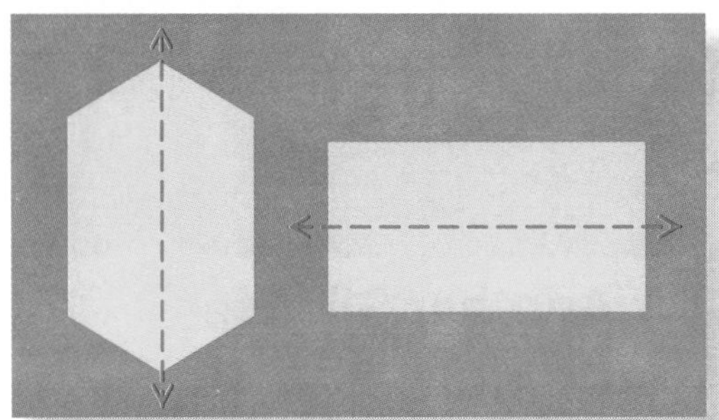

These shapes do not show a line of symmetry.

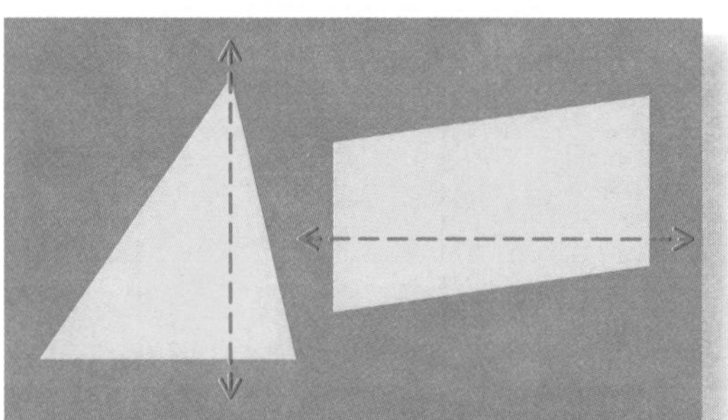

What do you notice about shapes that have a line of symmetry?

Working Together

- Cut out paper shapes.
- Fold each shape to make a line of symmetry.
- Draw the line in the fold.

Glossary

line of symmetry

How do your lines compare with your partner's?

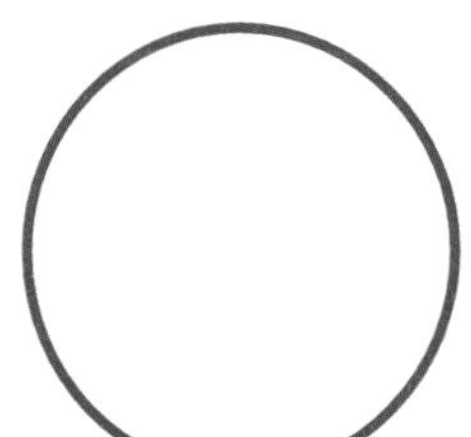

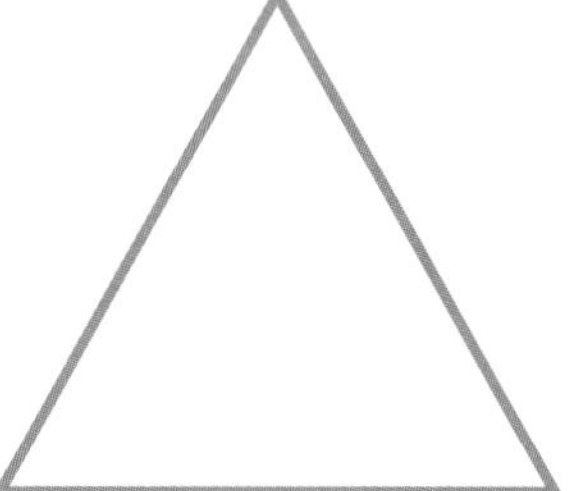

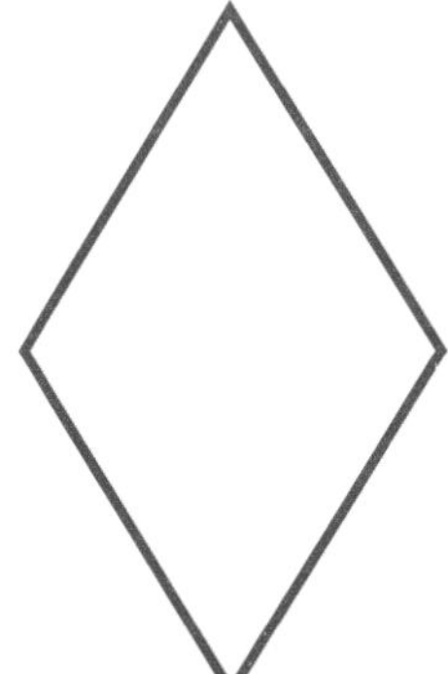

Practice!

Make a shape with a line of symmetry. Draw the matching part.

1 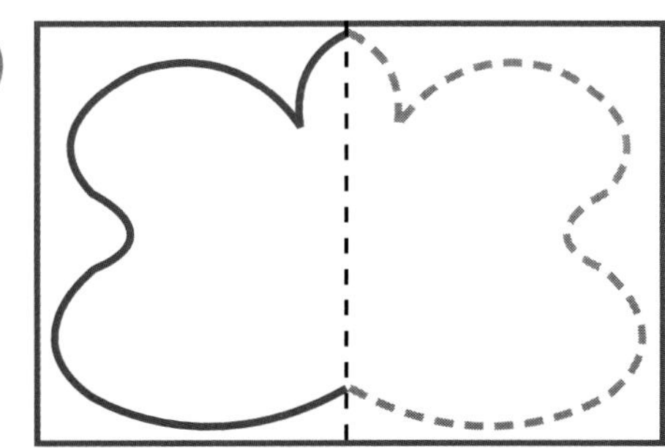

"Another Silence"
by Jimmy Ernst

2 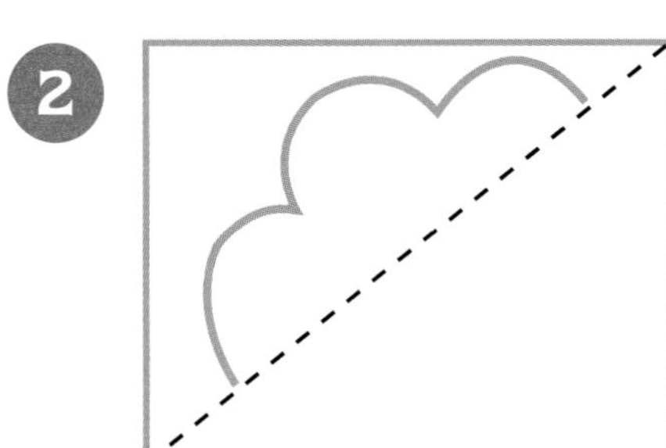 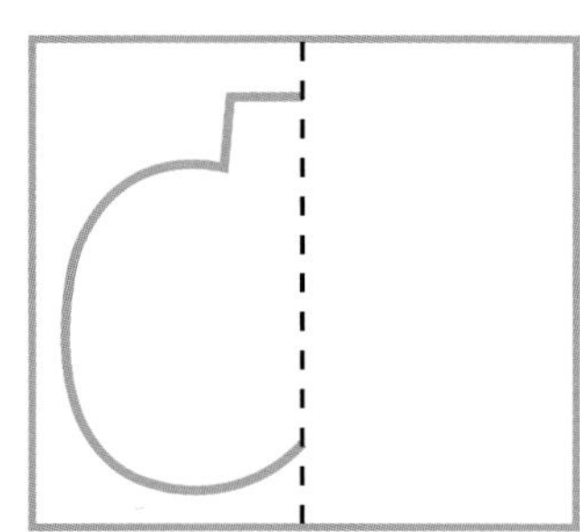 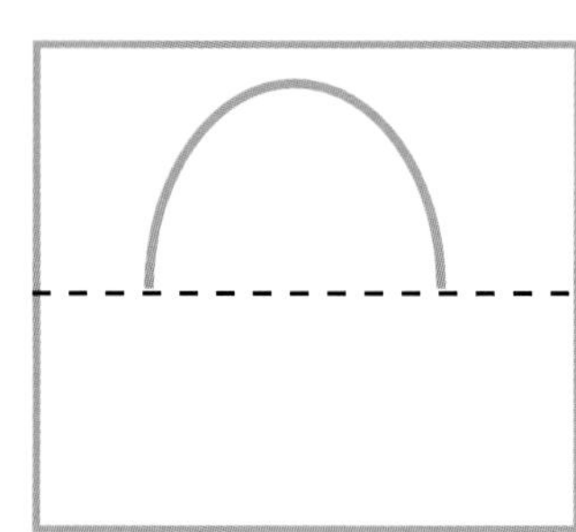

3 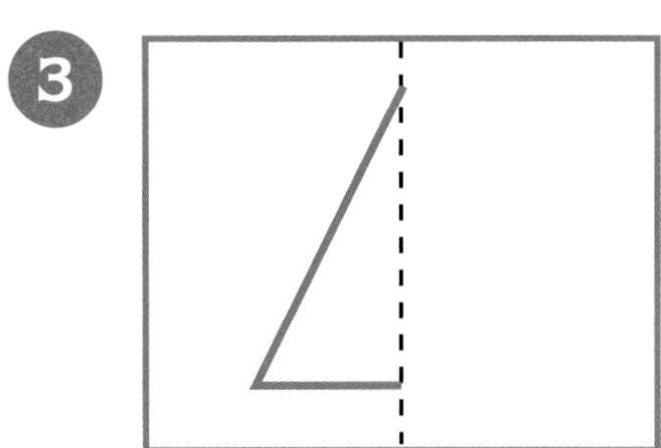 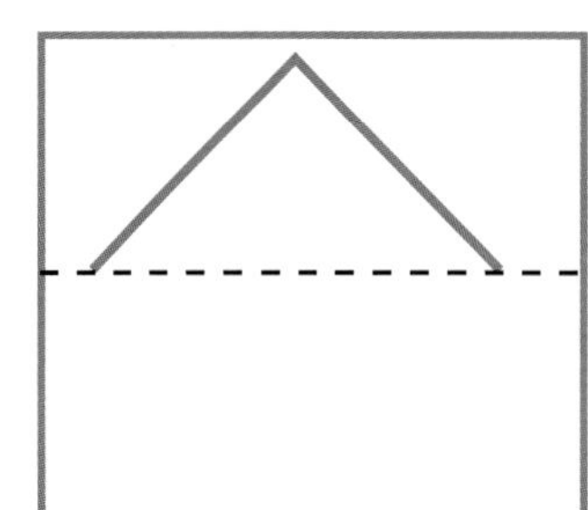 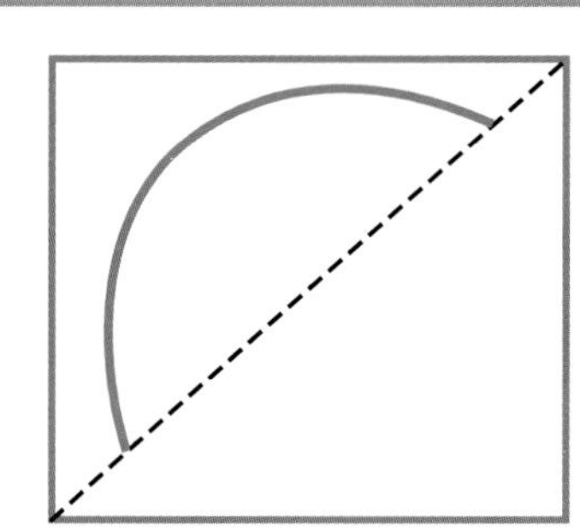

More to Explore Spatial Sense

Color inside the closed figures.

open closed

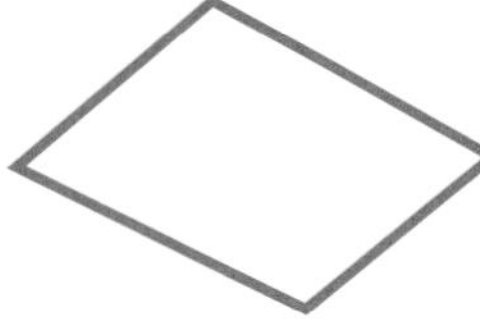

At Home We learned about lines of symmetry. Ask your child to show you how to fold a shape to find a line of symmetry.

Name ______________________________

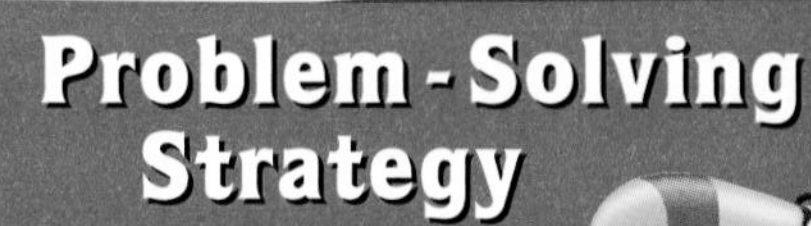

Use a Pattern

Read Plan Solve Look Back

Glossary
use a pattern

Winnie is making a picture with 15 shapes in a pattern. How many triangles does she need?

You can **use a pattern** to solve.

Draw to complete the pattern. Then count the triangles.

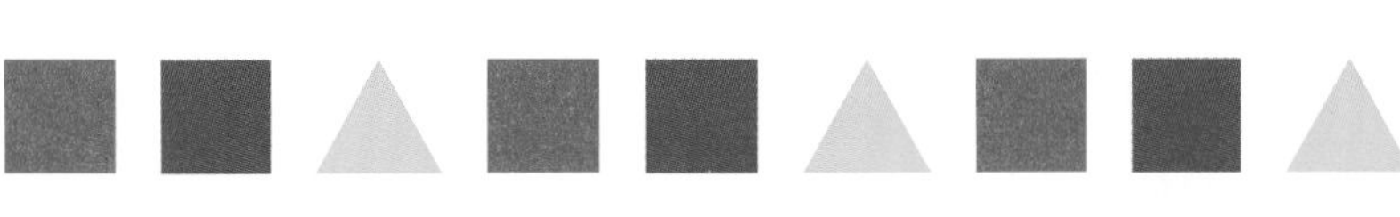

Winnie needs ______________________________.

Look Back

Have you answered the question? Explain.

PATTERNS Use a pattern to solve.

Luke paints pictures of shapes.
He will paint 20 shapes in a row.
How many squares will he paint? ______________

How many circles will he paint? ______________

How are these patterns alike?
How are they different?

Practice!

1. Luke paints patterns on clay pots.
He will paint 17 triangles in a row.
How many triangles will have dots inside? ____________

2. Laura makes a beaded bracelet.
How many red rectangles will she need
to finish this bracelet? ____________

3. George's necklace will have 30 beads.
How many red beads does he use? ____________

How many green beads does he use? ____________

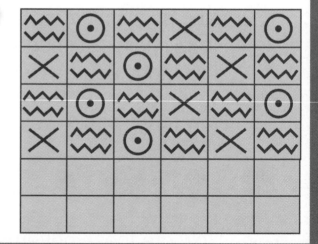

Cultural Connection

The Ashanti of Africa stamp patterns onto cloth. They mix and repeat designs to make patterns.

Draw to complete the pattern. How many of each are in the completed pattern?

 ____ 〰 ____  ____

Ashanti Fabric Patterns

〰	⊙	〰	X	〰	⊙
X	〰	⊙	〰	X	〰
〰	⊙	〰	X	〰	⊙
X	〰	⊙	〰	X	〰

We used a pattern to solve problems. Ask your child to explain how he or she solved problem 2 above.

Name ______________________________

Midchapter Review

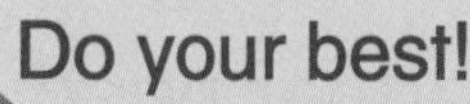

How many faces are on each shape?

 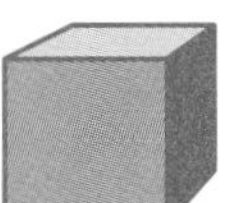 ____

  ____

 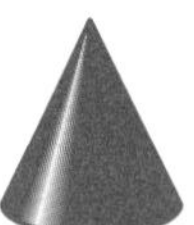 ____

 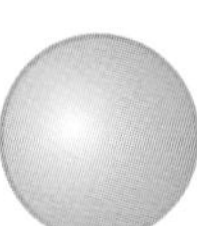 ____

 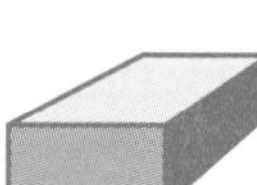 ____

Match.

 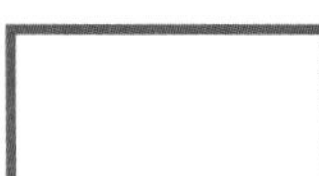   

3 sides 3 corners	4 sides 4 corners	0 sides 0 corners

Color inside the shapes that are congruent.

7 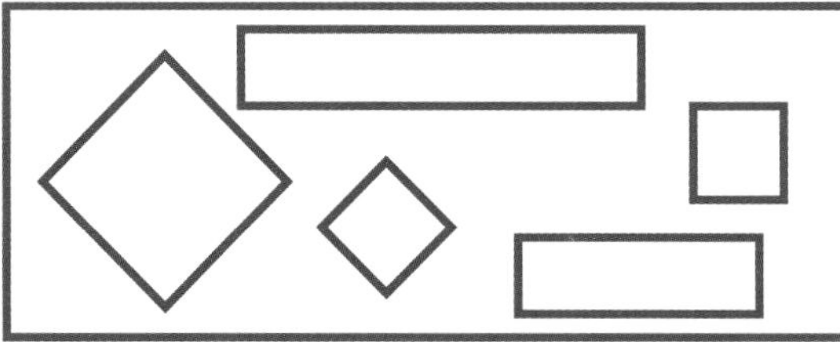

8 

9 How do you know which shapes are congruent? ______________________________

Use a pattern to solve.

10 Rolanda makes a bracelet 18 beads long. How many square beads does she use? ____________________

Draw these shapes in your journal. Explain why they are all triangles.

 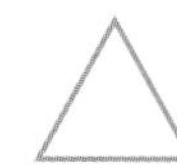 

Tangram Shapes

You and your partner need a .

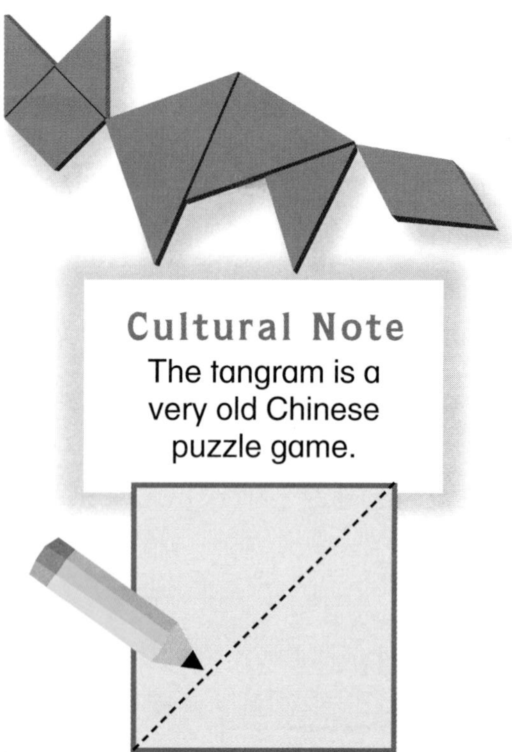

Cultural Note
The tangram is a very old Chinese puzzle game.

Take turns.

- Choose a shape below.
- Use more than one tangram piece to make that shape.
- Draw lines to show the pieces you used.

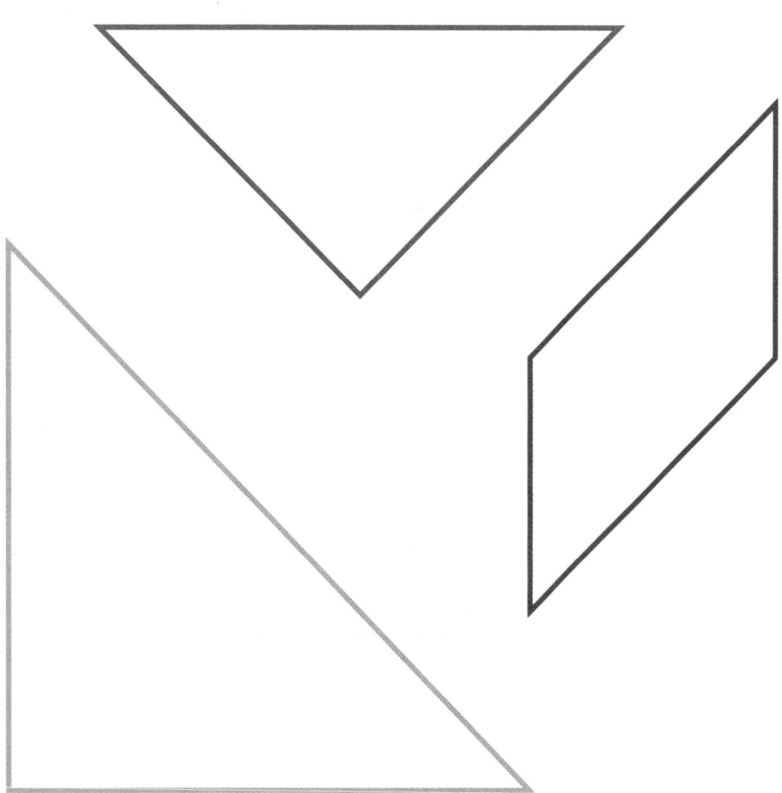

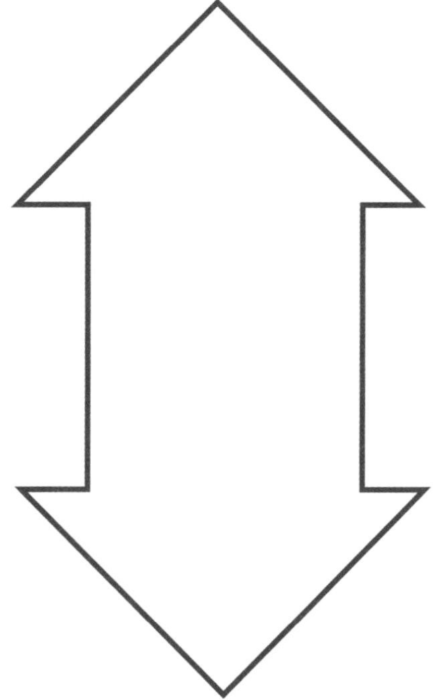

1. How many triangles did you make in the four shapes? ____ triangles

   How many squares did you make in the four shapes? ____ squares

Real-Life Investigation

Applying Geometry

Name

Cover-Up Game

Working Together

You and your partners need ▲, ▰, ⏢, ⬡.

- Take turns. Each player covers part of the shape below with one of the blocks.
- Each color must be used at least once. Each block must touch another on at least one side.
- Continue until the shape is totally covered with pattern blocks.

The winner is the one to place the last block.

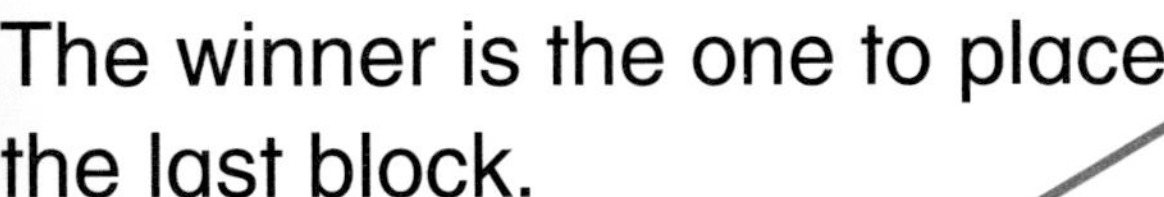

Decision Making

1. Decide on a way to show your covered shape.
2. Compare your shape with those of other groups.

   What was the greatest number of blocks used? ____

   What was the fewest number of blocks used? ____
3. Using the same colors and rules, what would be the most blocks needed to cover the shape? ____________

   Explain how you found your answer.

   ____

Write a report.

4. Write about any strategies you used, or might use, to place the last block.
5. Write about the shapes you used. How are they different? How are they alike?

More to Investigate

PREDICT What if you could change the shape you cover up?

EXPLORE Decide on a shape to cover up. Test your game to see if it works.

Use your own paper.

FIND Trade your cover-up game with another group. Play it.

Name ____________________

Explore Activity

Halves, Fourths, and Thirds

Working Together

You and your partner need scissors and paper shapes.

Take turns.

- Cut out two of the same shape.
- Fold one shape to make 2 **equal parts.** Unfold it. Your partner checks the **halves.** Draw the halves on the matching shape below.
- Fold the shape again to make 4 equal parts. Unfold it. Your partner checks the **fourths.** Draw the fourths below.
- Take the other unfolded shape. Make 3 equal parts. Your partner checks the **thirds.** Draw the thirds below.
- Try again with the other shapes.

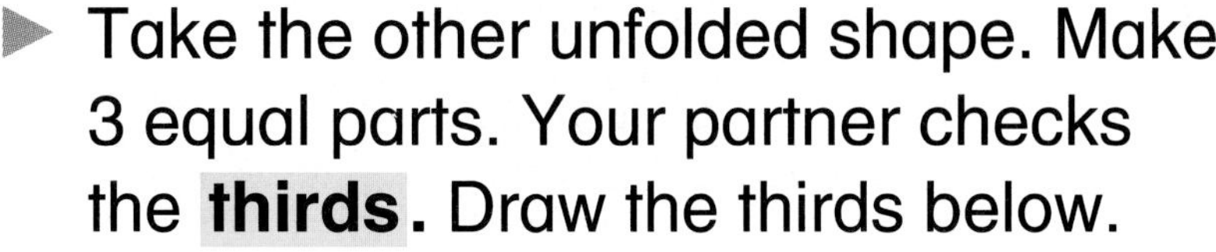

Glossary

equal parts
halves
fourths
thirds

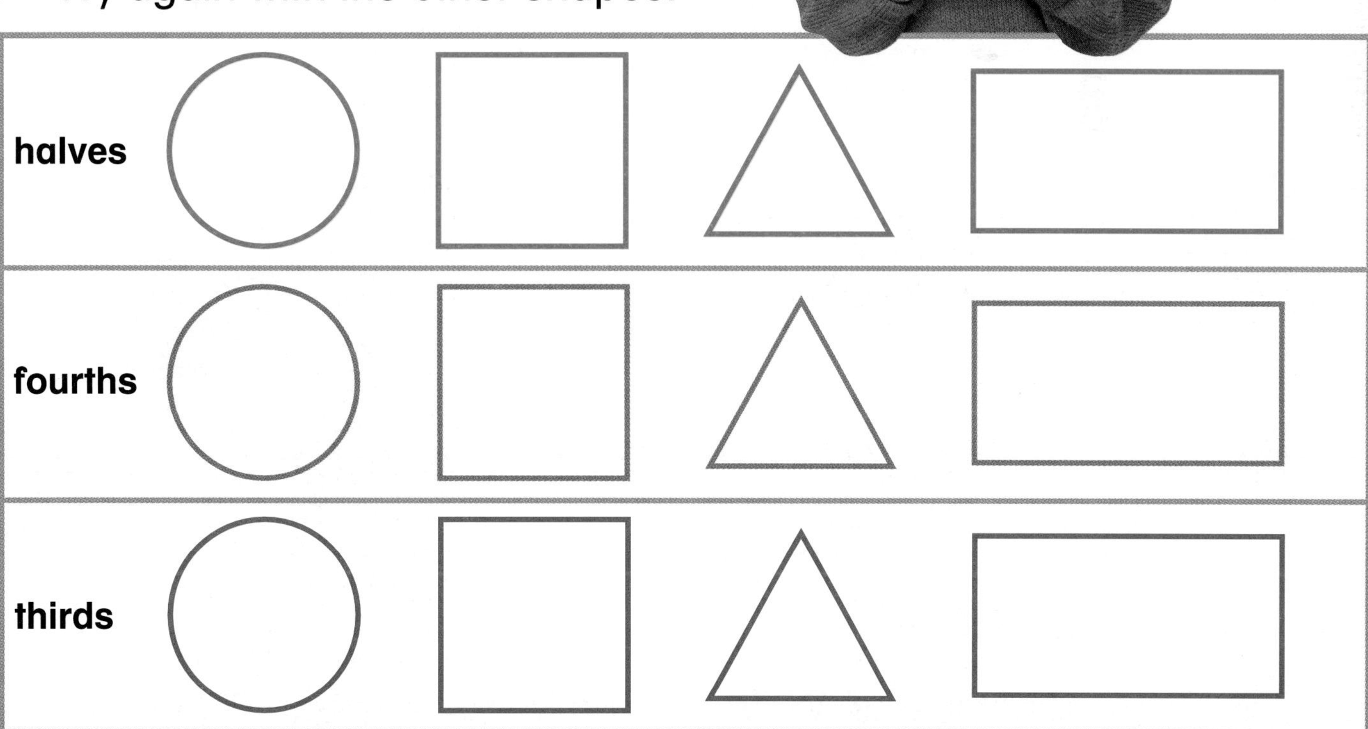

Which shapes were hard to fold into equal parts?

Practice!

Write how many equal parts.

 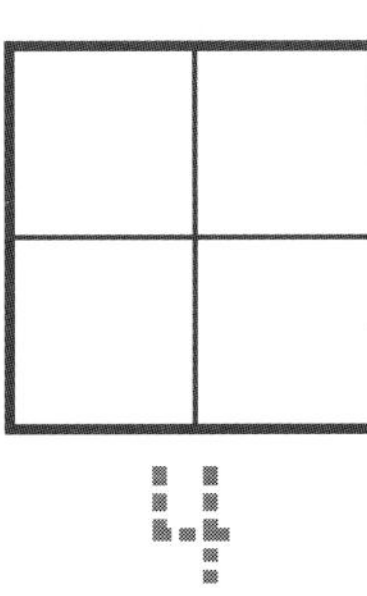 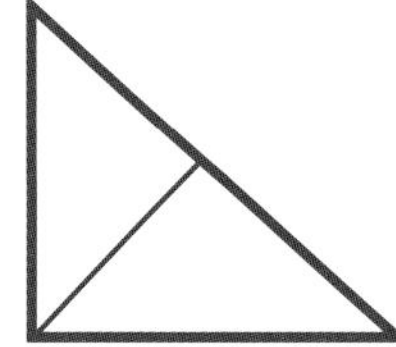 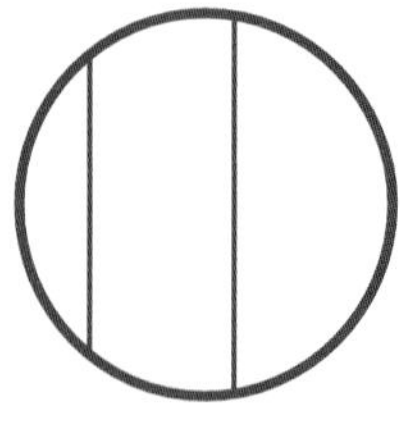

4 ____ ____

2 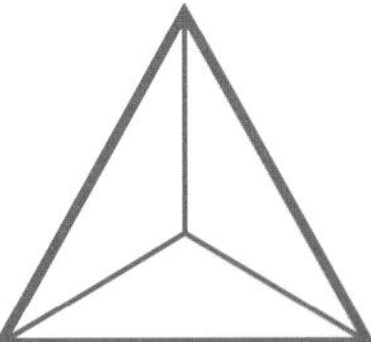 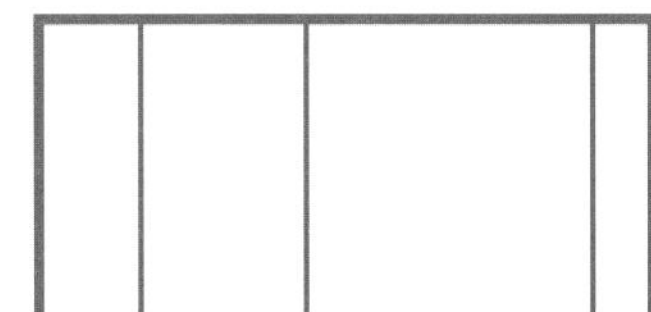 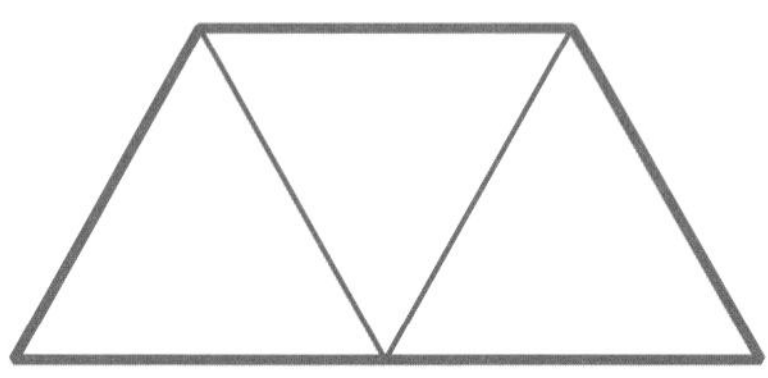

____ ____ ____

3 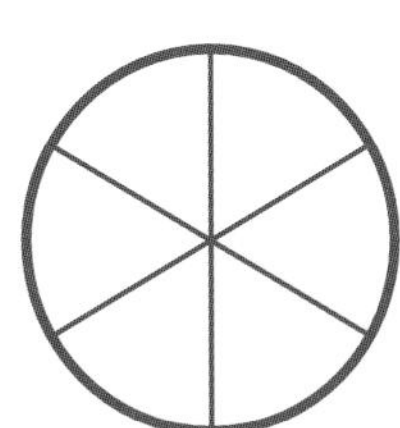 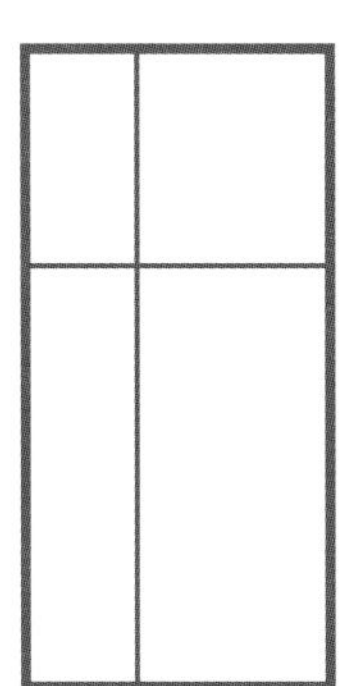 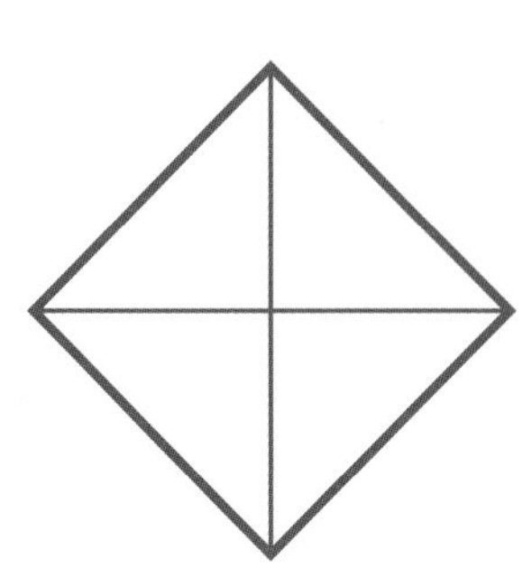

____ ____ ____

Mixed Review Test Preparation

Subtract.

68	97	\$34	51	85¢
− 29	− 44	− 8	− 49	− 37¢

5 Skip-count by tens. Write the numbers.

10, 20, 30, ____, ____, ____, ____, ____, ____, ____

At Home We explored equal parts of shapes. Ask your child to draw squares showing 2, 3, and 4 equal parts.

Name

Fractions

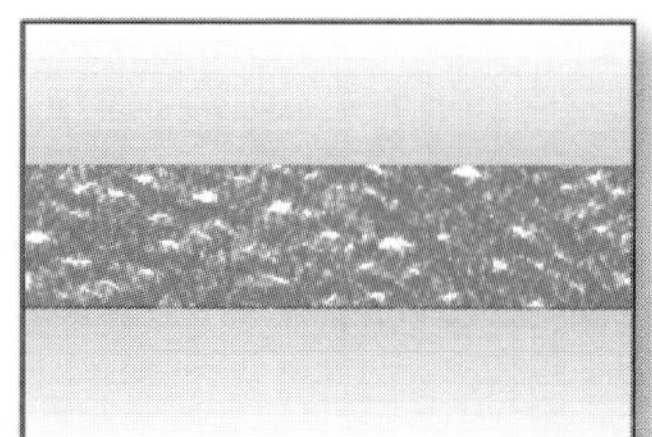

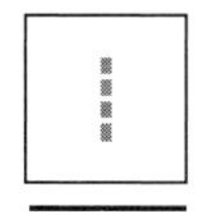

shaded part

equal parts

$\frac{1}{3}$ is a **fraction**.

Working Together

You and your partner need scissors and paper shapes.

Glossary

fraction

- Each of you choose a different shape. Cut out 3 of this same shape.
- Fold the shapes to show halves, thirds, and fourths. Unfold each shape.
- Color one part of each shape. Check each other's work.
- Draw your shapes below.

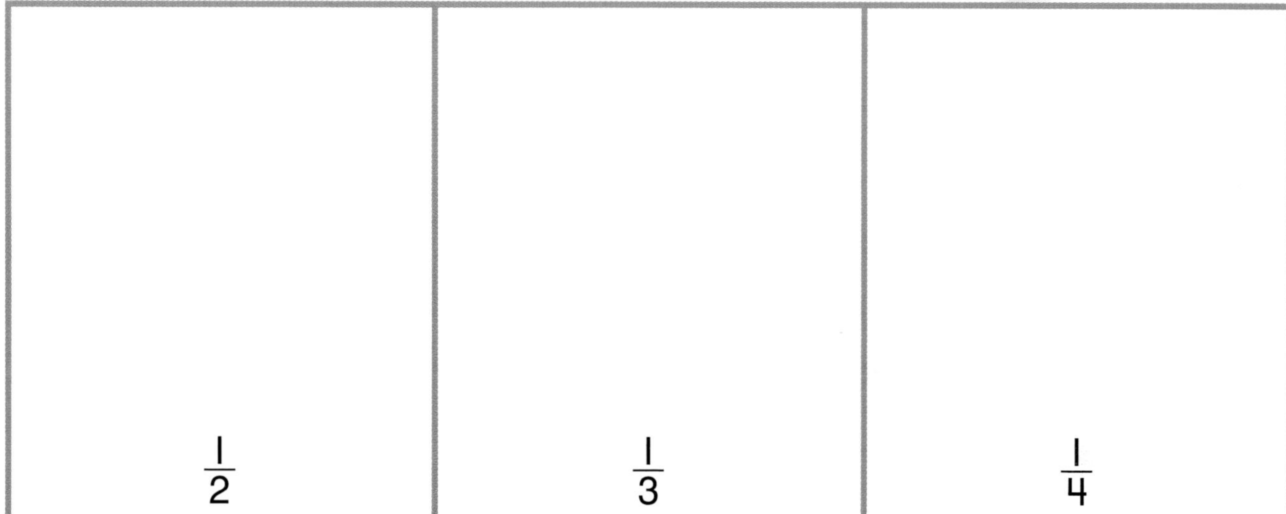

$\frac{1}{2}$	$\frac{1}{3}$	$\frac{1}{4}$

How are the shapes that show $\frac{1}{4}$ the same? How are they different?

Practice!

Write the fraction for the shaded part.

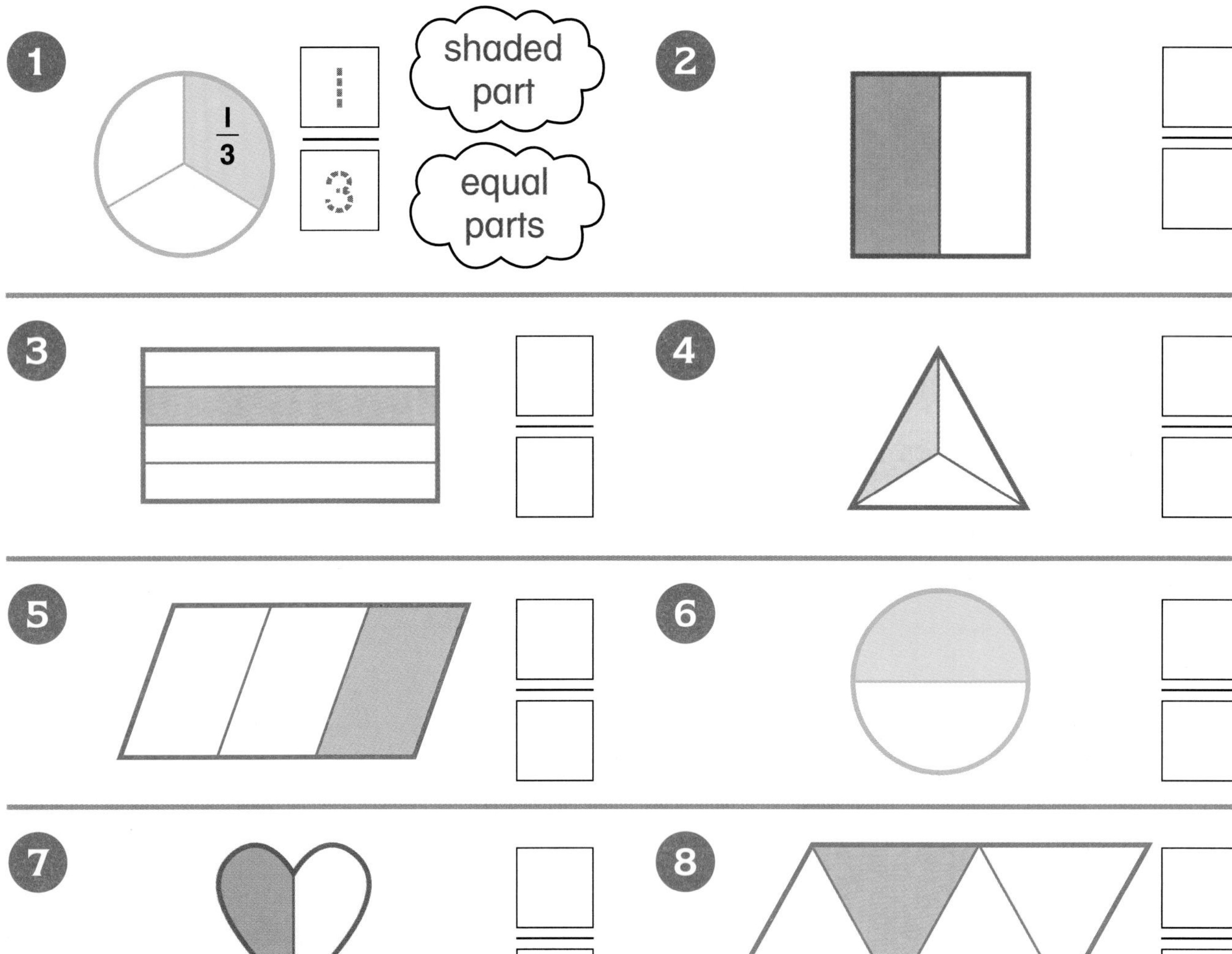

Visualize

Look at the shape. Picture in your head how you can show equal parts. Show equal parts. Then shade 1 part.

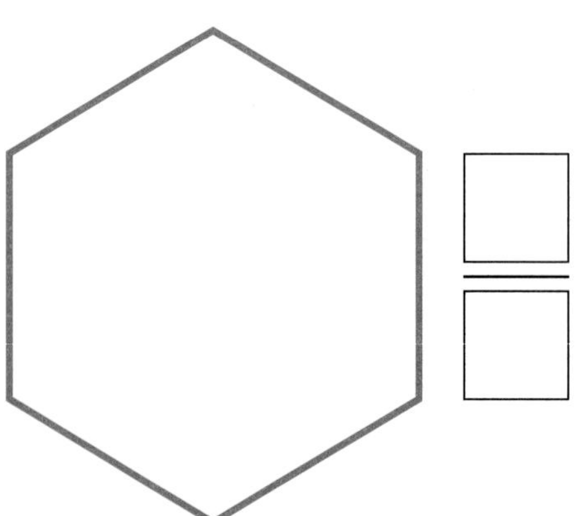

Write the fraction for the shaded part.

What does the fraction mean?

At Home: We looked at $\frac{1}{2}$, $\frac{1}{3}$, and $\frac{1}{4}$ of shapes. Ask your child what fraction is shown by 1 shaded part out of 4 equal parts.

Name ____________________

More Fractions

$\frac{1}{4}$	$\frac{1}{4}$
$\frac{1}{4}$	$\frac{1}{4}$

$\frac{2}{4}$ of the poster board is for Luke.

How much is left?

I get 2 of the 4 equal parts, or 2 fourths.

There are $\frac{4}{4}$ in the whole sheet of board. 2 out of the 4 pieces are for Luke.

$\frac{2}{4}$ of the poster board is left.

Write the fraction for the part that is left.

1. $\frac{1}{2}$ of the wood is for Gary.
   How much is left? 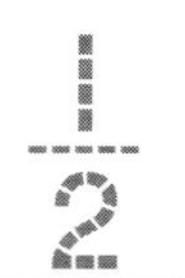

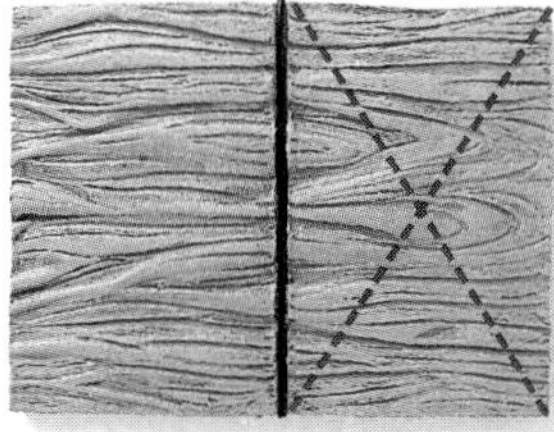

2. $\frac{2}{3}$ of the paint is for Pat.
   How much is left? 

3. $\frac{1}{6}$ of the clay is for Kim.
   How much is left? 

4. $\frac{1}{3}$ of the chalk is for Bud.
   How much is left? 

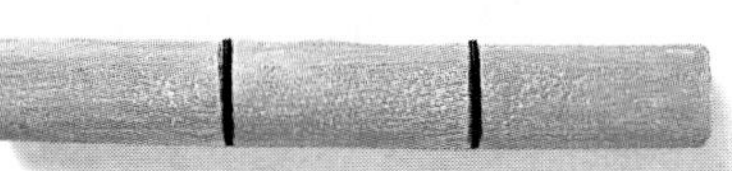

You use $\frac{2}{2}$ of a sheet of paper.
How much is left? Explain.

Write the fraction for the part that is left.

1. $\frac{2}{6}$ of the cake is for Jamal.
How much is left? 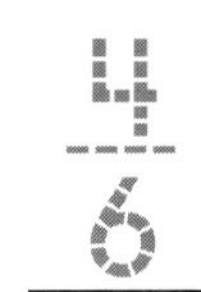 $\frac{4}{6}$

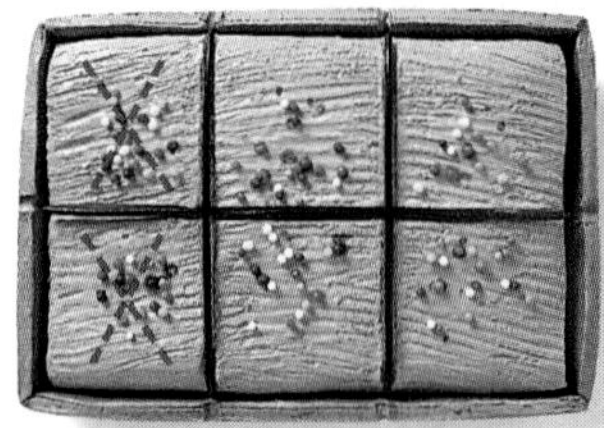

2. $\frac{1}{3}$ of the cheese is for Ana.
How much is left? ____

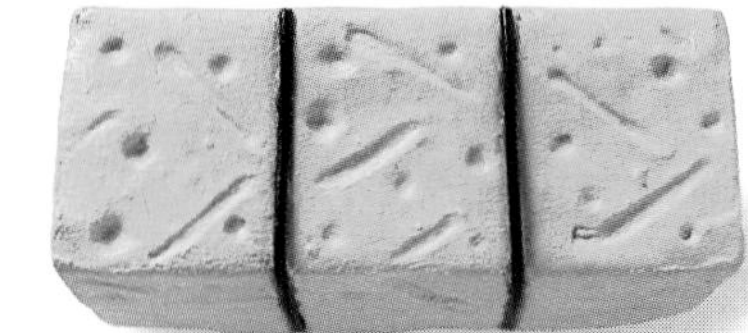

3. $\frac{4}{5}$ of the sandwich is for Pedro.
How much is left? ____

4. $\frac{1}{2}$ of the apple is for David.
How much is left? ____

5. $\frac{1}{4}$ of the bread is for Shawna.
How much is left? ____

6. 

Write a problem about eating pizza. Then solve it.

____

____

At Home We learned more about fractions. Ask your child to tell you the fraction for the whole sandwich in problem 3 above.

Name

Fraction of a Group

3 puppies share 3 cups.
What **fraction of the group** of cups does each puppy get?

Each puppy gets 1 of the 3 cups.
Each puppy gets $\frac{1}{3}$ of the cups.

Still Life with Three Puppies
by Paul Gauguin

Show how two puppies share the pears equally.
Color pears for one puppy red.
Color pears for the other puppy blue.

Glossary
fraction of a group

1. 

Each puppy gets 1 of the 2 pears.

Each puppy gets $\frac{1}{2}$.

2. 

Each puppy gets ____ of the ____ pears.

Each puppy gets ____.

3. 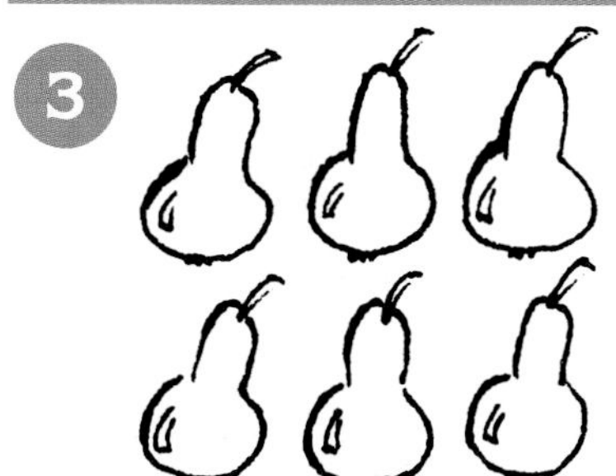

Each puppy gets ____ of the ____ pears.

Each puppy gets ____.

Practice!

Color to show how the children share equally.
Write the fraction that each child gets.

1 3 children share equally

Each child gets 3 of the 9 apples.

Each child gets $\frac{3}{9}$.

2 4 children share equally

Each child gets ____ of the ____ books.

Each child gets ____.

3 3 children share equally

Each child gets ____ of the ____ bananas.

Each child gets ____.

4 4 children share equally

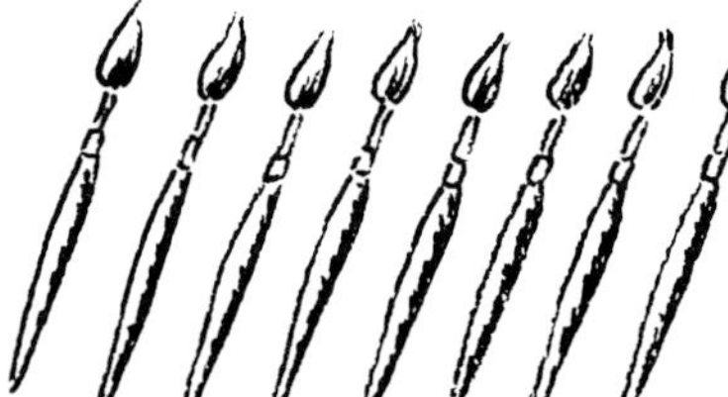

Each child gets ____ of the ____ brushes.

Each child gets ____.

5 2 children share equally

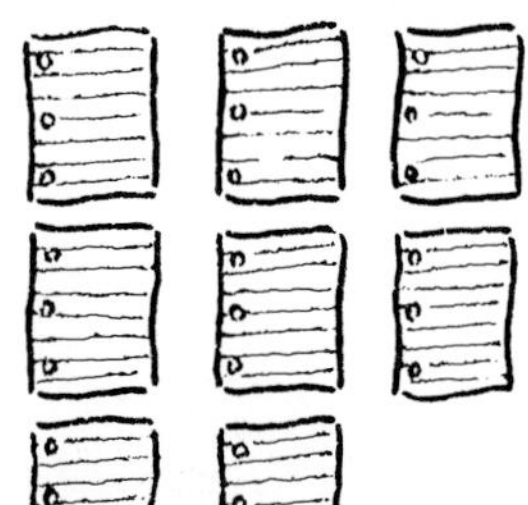

Each child gets ____ of the ____ papers.

Each child gets ____.

We learned about fractions of a group. Ask your child to tell you about these problems.

Name

Draw a Picture

Read
Plan
Solve
Look Back

Rita and 2 friends share a sheet of paper equally.
The paper is cut into 6 pieces.
How many pieces does each person get?

Sometimes you can **draw a picture** to solve.

Draw a rectangle for the paper. Then draw 6 equal parts.

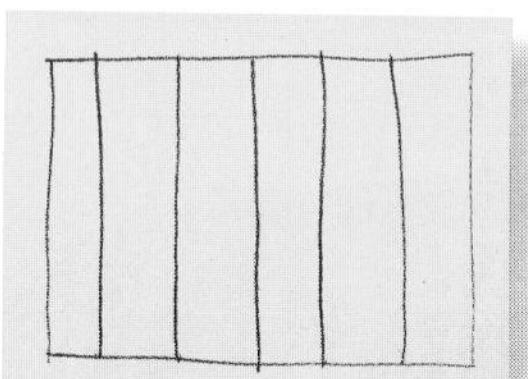

You can color to show how 3 children share the 6 pieces.

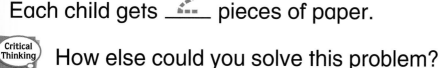

Each child gets 2 pieces of paper.

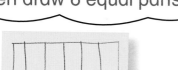

Glossary
draw a picture

How else could you solve this problem?

Draw a picture to solve.

1. Tanya and her sister share a round ball of clay.
The clay is cut into 6 pieces.
How many pieces does each child get? ______

2. Ricky and 4 friends share a box of 10 pencils.
How many pencils does each child get? ______

3. 

Visualize Picture a drawing in your head.

Joe and Nina share 4 jars of paint.
How many jars does each child get? ______ jars

Practice!

Draw a picture to solve.

1. Tony and his friend each want half of a box of 8 markers. How many markers does each child get? ________

2. What if there were 6 markers in the box. How many markers each would Tony and his friend get? ________

Write and Share

Brittany wrote this problem.

Teddy and Sarah had 6 rulers. They had to share them. How many rulers did Sarah and Teddy get?

Brittany Lang
West Lake School
Apex, North Carolina

3. Draw a picture to solve Brittany's problem. ________

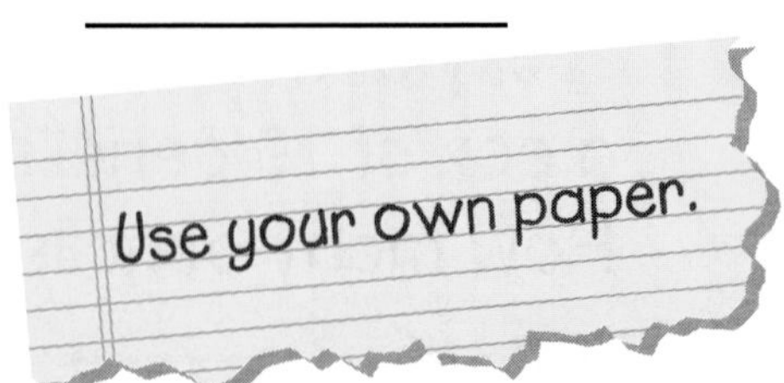

4. Write a problem for your partner to solve.

5. How did your partner solve your problem?

____

At Home: We drew pictures to solve problems. Ask your child to explain to you how to solve Brittany's problem.

Name

Chapter Review

Language and Mathematics

Choose the correct word to complete the sentence.

cube
triangle
sides
fraction
corners

1. A circle has 0 ______________ and 0 ______________.
2. This shape  is a ______________.

Concepts and Skills

Write the name of the shape.

3. 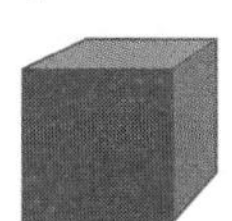 ________
4.  ________

Write the number of sides each shape has.

5.  ________
6.  ________

Draw a line of symmetry.

7. 
8. 
9. 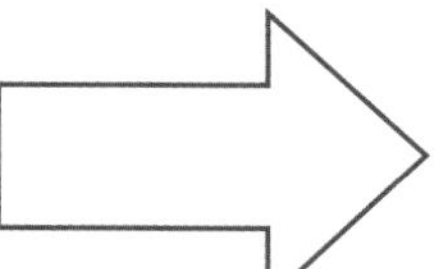
10. 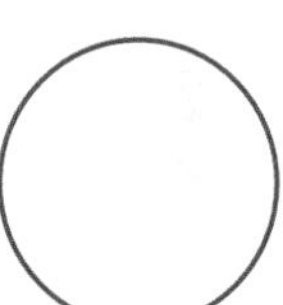

Write the fraction for the shaded part.

11. 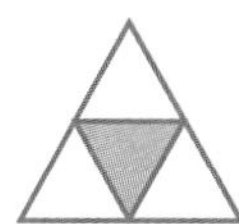 ____
12. 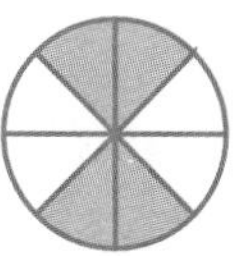 ____
13. 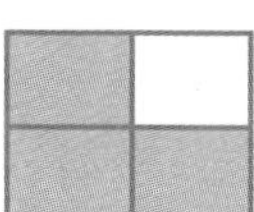 ____
14. 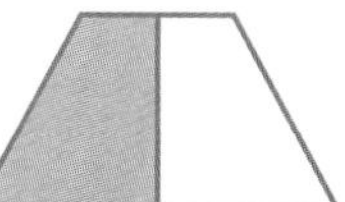 ____

Write the fraction for the part that is green.

15.  ____
16.   ____

Problem Solving

Use a pattern to solve.

17 Kathy makes a picture with 18 shapes.
How many blue shapes will the picture have? ________

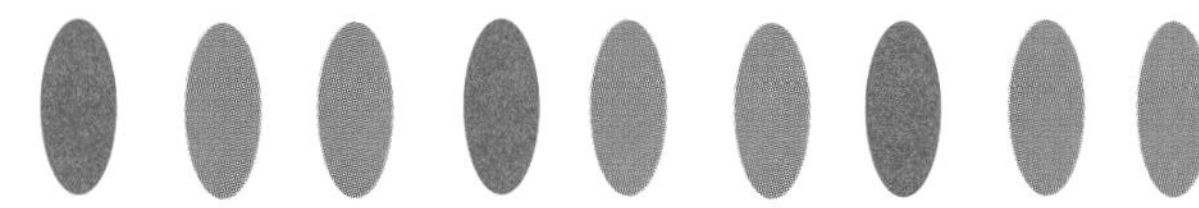

18 Craig's picture will have 16 shapes on it.
How many squares will it have? ________

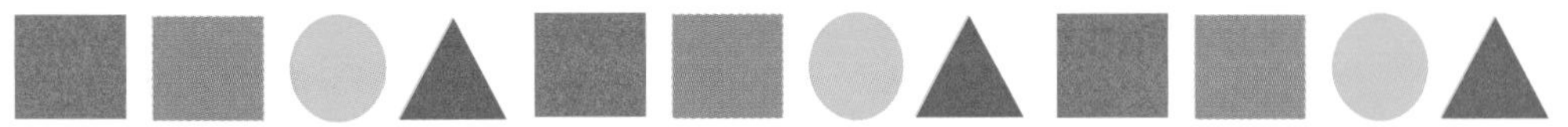

Draw a picture to solve.

19 Tyrell bought a pack of 6 cards. He shares them equally with Gus. How many cards does each child get? ________

20 Lisa and 3 friends share a pie equally. The pie has 8 slices. How many slices does each child get? ________

What Do You Think?

What do you like best about geometry?
☑ Check one.

☐ 2-dimensional shapes ☐ 3-dimensional shapes ☐ Patterns with shapes

Why? ________________________

Journal

Write your name. Use capital letters. Draw arrows to show which letters have lines of symmetry.

ROY

Name

Chapter Test

1. Write the name of the shape.

______

2. Write the number of sides this shape has.

______

Draw a line of symmetry.

3. 

4. 

5. 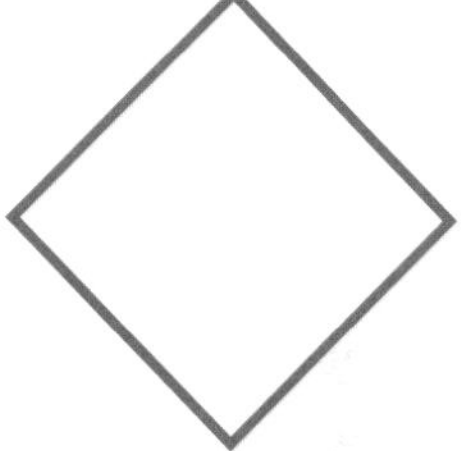

Write the fraction for the shaded part.

6. 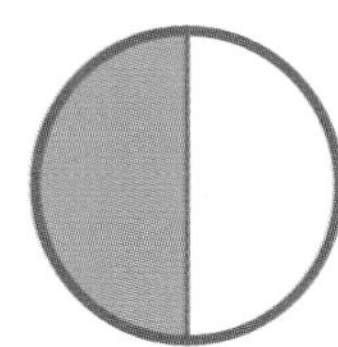

______

7. 

______

Write a fraction for the part that is orange.

8.    

______

9.   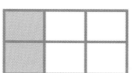

______

Use a pattern to solve.

10. Mandy's picture will have 15 shapes. ○○△○○△○○△○○
How many circles will it have? ______

Performance Assessment

What Did You Learn?

Look at each shape.
Tell what you know about it.

1

2

3

4

You may want to put this page in your portfolio.

Math Connection

Probability

Name ______________________________

Experiment

You and your partner need 1 blue crayon, 1 red crayon, 1 cube, 3 cubes, and a paper bag.

- Put the cubes in the bag and shake.
- Take turns. Pick 1 cube from the bag.
- Color 1 box the same color as the cube you pick.
- Put the cube back in the bag.
- Do this 20 times.

1	2	3	4	5	6	7	8	9	10	11	12	13	14	15	16	17	18	19	20

1. How many times did you pick blue? ____ times out of 20, or $\frac{\quad}{20}$

2. How many times did you pick red? ____ times out of 20, or $\frac{\quad}{20}$

3. What if you picked cubes another 20 times. Are you more likely to pick more blue cubes or red cubes? ________

4. Repeat the experiment. Compare the results.

Technology Connection

Computer

Make a Pattern

PATTERNS You can use a computer to make a pattern.

Continue the pattern until there are 12 shapes.

How many triangles? _____

What fraction of the pattern are the triangles? _____

How many circles? _____

What fraction of the pattern are the circles? _____

How many squares? _____

What fraction of the pattern are the squares? _____

At the Computer

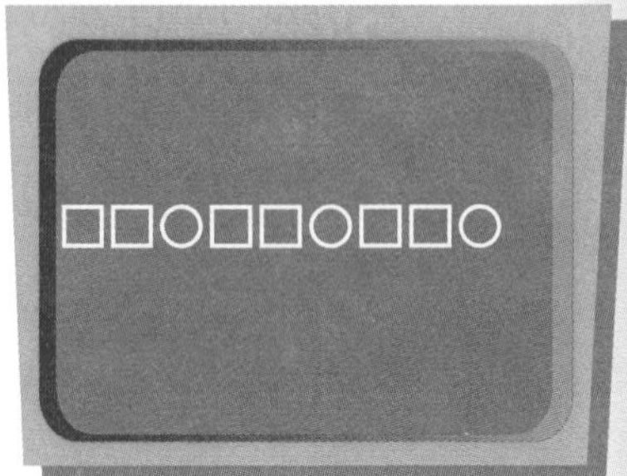

1. Draw your own shapes.
Copy them to make a pattern.

2. Record how many of each shape you use.
Write the fraction of the pattern for each shape.

Name

Cumulative Review

Read each question and choose the best answer.

1. Which is a picture of a square?
   - ⬭ □
   - ⬭ △
   - ⬭ ○
   - ⬭ ▭

2. A puzzle has 75 pieces. Bob put 39 pieces together. Which shows how many pieces are left?
   - ⬭ 75 – 9
   - ⬭ 75 – 39
   - ⬭ 75 + 39
   - ⬭ 75 + 3

3. How much money does Max have?

   - ⬭ 36¢
   - ⬭ 56¢
   - ⬭ 61¢
   - ⬭ 70¢

4. What number is shown?
   - ⬭ 4
   - ⬭ 10
   - ⬭ 45
   - ⬭ 54

5. Mrs. Judd had 51¢. She spent 38¢. Which shows how much money she has now?
   - ⬭ 89¢
   - ⬭ 23¢
   - ⬭ 22¢
   - ⬭ 13¢

6. What is the fraction for the shaded part?

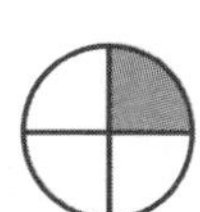

   - ⬭ $\frac{1}{3}$
   - ⬭ $\frac{1}{4}$
   - ⬭ $\frac{1}{2}$
   - ⬭ $\frac{1}{6}$

TEST PREPARATION

TEST PREPARATION

7 What is the time on the clock?

- ⬭ 6:11
- ⬭ 6:55
- ⬭ 7:05
- ⬭ 7:55

8 Thelma has 48 books. She buys 20 more. How many books does she have now?

- ⬭ 28
- ⬭ 38
- ⬭ 58
- ⬭ 68

9
$$\begin{array}{r} 5 \\ 8 \\ +\ 3 \\ \hline \end{array}$$

- ⬭ 16
- ⬭ 15
- ⬭ 14
- ⬭ 13

10 Look at the shape.

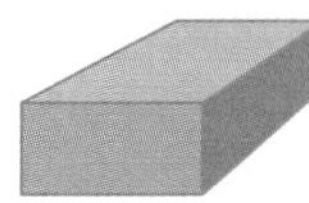

How many faces does this shape have?

- ⬭ 12
- ⬭ 9
- ⬭ 6
- ⬭ 4

11 Tom and 3 friends share 8 pretzels. How many pretzels does each person get?

- ⬭ 4
- ⬭ 3
- ⬭ 2
- ⬭ 1

12 Rita wants to make a pattern with 12 triangles. How many more green triangles does she need?

- ⬭ 3
- ⬭ 4
- ⬭ 5
- ⬭ 6

Home Connection

Chapter 9 Wrap-Up

Name ______________________________

Pick a Fraction

PLAYERS 2

MATERIALS 4 red buttons, 4 blue buttons, paper bag, pencils

DIRECTIONS Put the buttons in the bag. Take turns. Pull out 4 buttons. Name a fraction that tells about the buttons you picked. Ring the fraction you named on your chart below. If the fraction is already marked, skip a turn. Put the buttons back in the bag.

Play until one player marks off all the fractions on his or her chart.

Player 1

$\frac{1}{4}$	$\frac{2}{4}$
$\frac{3}{4}$	$\frac{4}{4}$

Player 2

$\frac{1}{4}$	$\frac{2}{4}$
$\frac{3}{4}$	$\frac{4}{4}$

This game will help your child practice naming fractions that show part of a group.

Dear Family,

I am beginning a new chapter in mathematics. During the next few weeks I will be learning to measure length, weight, capacity, and temperature.

I will also be talking about making and using maps.

Learning About Mapping

Let's talk about how maps can help people. We can make a list.

My Math Words

I am going to use these math words and other math words in this chapter.

Please help me make word cards for the math words. I can use these word cards when I explore measurement.

inch
foot
yard
centimeter
meter
perimeter
area
pound
kilogram
cup
pint
quart
liter

LIBRARY

Your child,

Signature

Measurement

Theme: Mapping Adventures

Prior Knowledge Talk about maps. What do you know about maps? What maps have you used?

Listen to *As the Crow Flies.*

How are the maps in the book like maps that you have used? How are they different?

Name

What Do You Know?

Use (paper clip) to measure each path.

				Estimate	Measure
1		to 		about ____	about ____
2	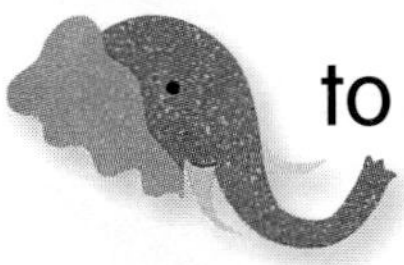	to 		about ____	about ____
3		to 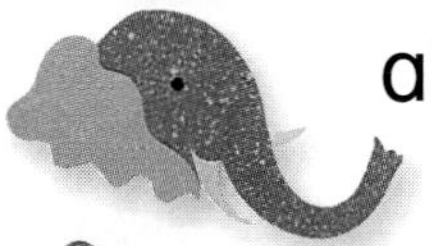		about ____	about ____
4		to 		about ____	about ____

What else could you use to measure? How do you think the measurements would change?

Choose another way to measure. Record.

Measuring Length

Trace around your foot.
Cut out 2 paper footprints.
Measure with the footprints.

Glossary
measure
long
wide

How **long** is your classroom?

Estimate ____

Measure ____

How **wide** is your classroom?

Estimate ____

Measure ____

I foot, 2 feet,
3 feet

Working Together

► You and your partner each use your own footprints to measure.

► Complete the chart.

	Length of chalkboard	Width of hall	Height of door
Estimate	____	____	____
Measure	____	____	____

Why might your measurements be different from your partner's?

Practice!

You need 10 cubes.

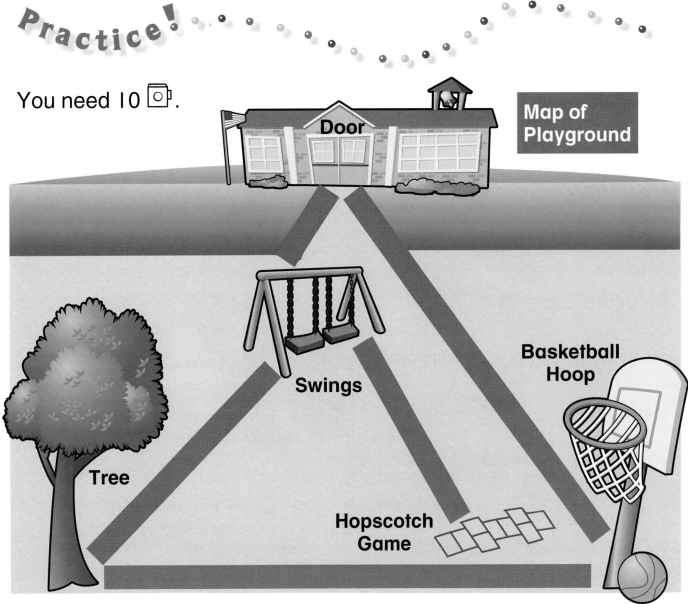

Map of Playground

Door

Swings

Tree

Basketball Hoop

Hopscotch Game

Use cubes to measure each path.

1. tree to basketball hoop — about ____ cubes
2. swings to tree — about ____ cubes
3. swings to hopscotch game — about ____ cubes
4. door to swings — about ____ cubes
5. door to basketball hoop — about ____ cubes

How is measuring with cubes different from measuring with footprints?

At Home: Have your child use a pair of shoes to measure the length of a room.

Name

Inch and Foot

1 **inch** **(in.)**

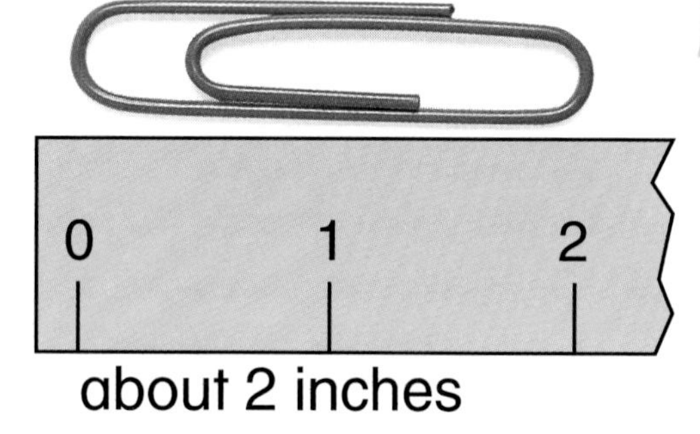

about 2 inches

12 inches equal 1 **foot** **(ft).**

Glossary
inch
foot

You need a [ruler] or some [cubes].

- Find these objects.
- Estimate. Then measure and record.
- Write how many *inches* or *feet*.

		Estimate	Measure
1	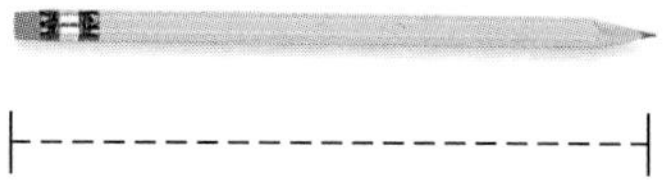 [pencil]	about ______	about ______
2	 [calendar] APRIL	about ______	about ______
3	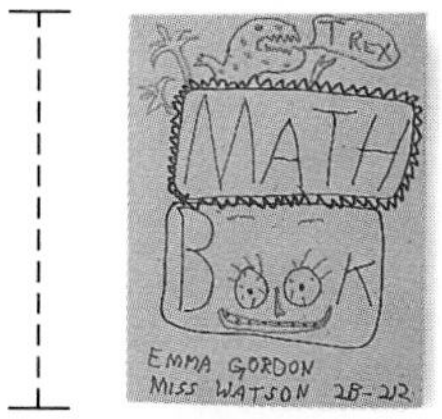 [math book] MATH BOOK EMMA GORDON MISS WATSON 2B-212	about ______	about ______
4	 [chair]	about ______	about ______

Practice!

Use a [ruler] or some [tiles] to measure each path.

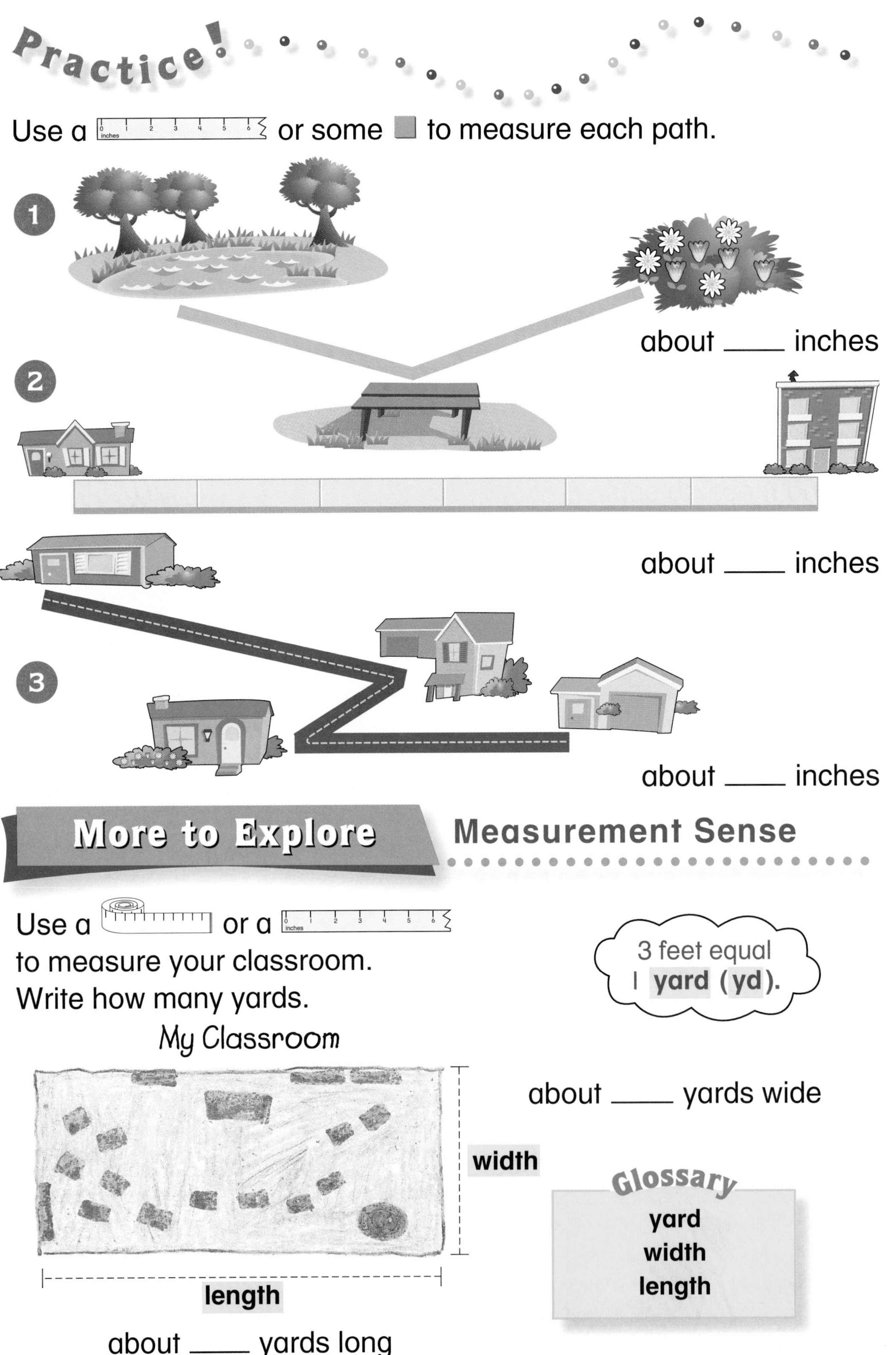

1. about ____ inches

2. about ____ inches

3. about ____ inches

More to Explore — Measurement Sense

Use a [tape measure] or a [ruler] to measure your classroom. Write how many yards.

3 feet equal 1 **yard** (**yd**).

about ____ yards wide

about ____ yards long

Glossary
yard
width
length

At Home We measured in inches, feet, and yards. Have your child show you how to measure with a ruler.

Name ______________________

Centimeter

Glossary

centimeter

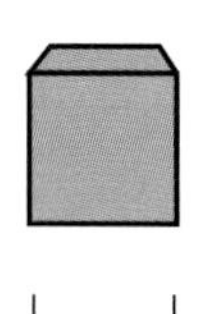

I **centimeter (cm)** about 4 centimeters

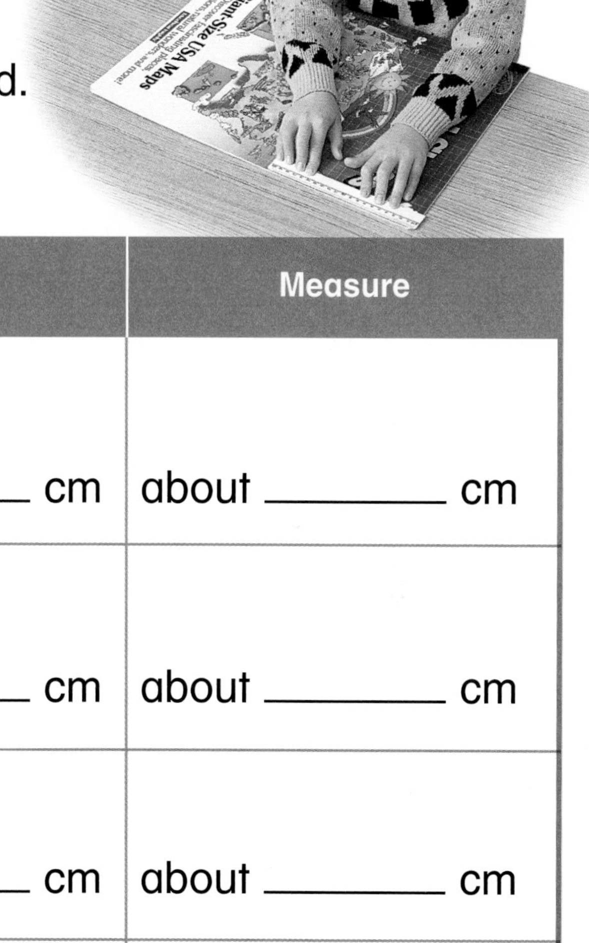

You need a ruler or some cubes.

- ▶ Find these objects.
- ▶ Estimate. Then measure and record.
- ▶ Write how many *centimeters.*

		Estimate	Measure
1		about ______ cm	about ______ cm
2		about ______ cm	about ______ cm
3		about ______ cm	about ______ cm
4 		about ______ cm	about ______ cm

Critical Thinking

How is measuring with centimeters the same as or different from measuring with inches?

Practice!

Use a [ruler] or some [cube] to measure the bug's path.

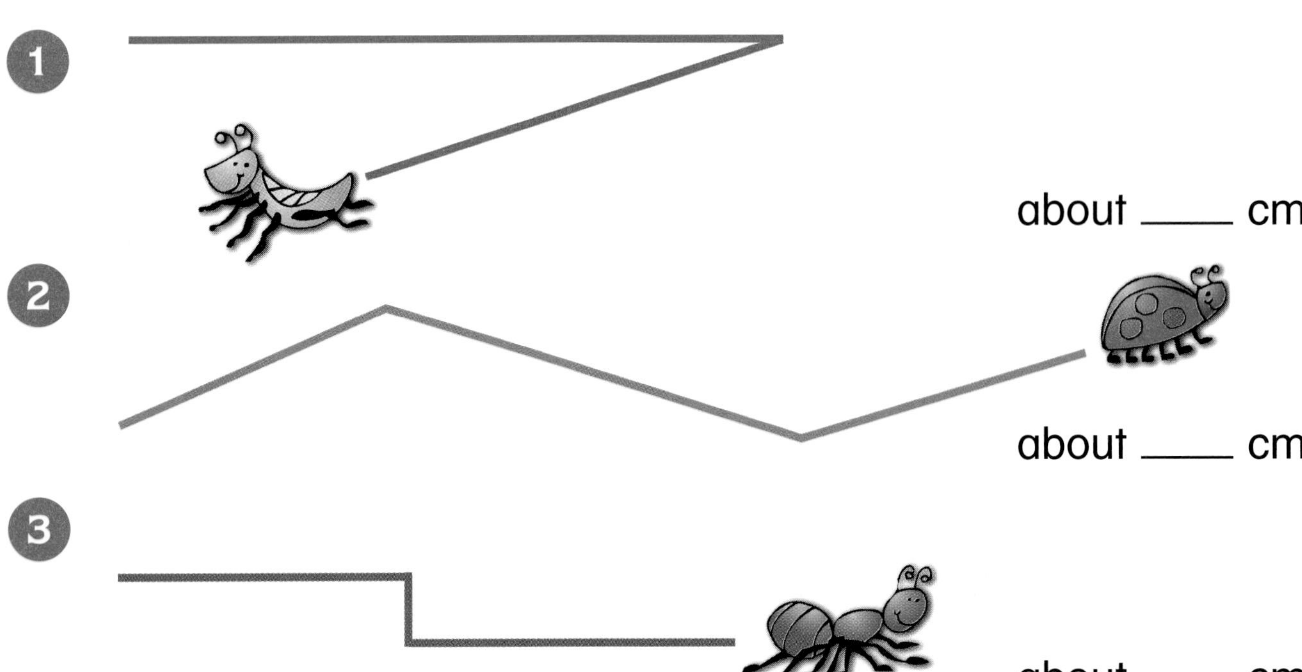

1 about ____ cm

2 about ____ cm

3 about ____ cm

More to Explore — Measurement Sense

Use a [ruler] or a [tape measure].

100 centimeters equal 1 **meter (m).**

Glossary
meter

How many meters long is the chalkboard?

about ____ meters

Choose something to measure in meters.

I measured the ______________________.

It is about ____ meters long.

It is about ____ meters wide.

My bat is about 1 meter long.

At Home: We measured in centimeters and meters. Ask your child to explain how he or she measured in exercise 2 above.

Name

Explore Activity

Perimeter

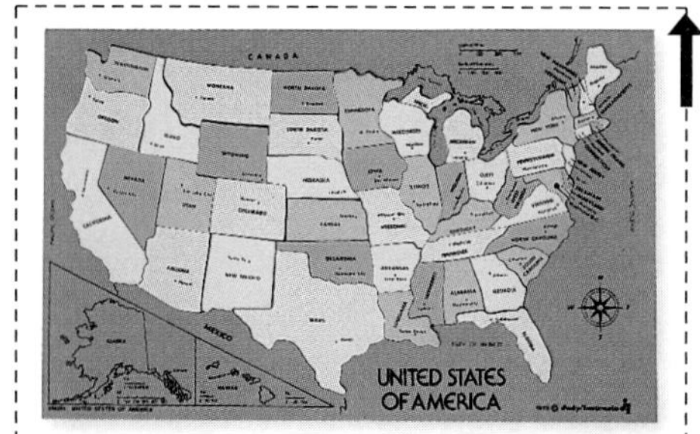

The distance around a shape is called the **perimeter**.

Glossary

perimeter

Working Together

You and your partner need a [ruler, centimeters] or some [cubes].

- Find these objects.
- Measure each side and record.
- Add the sides to find the perimeter.

1

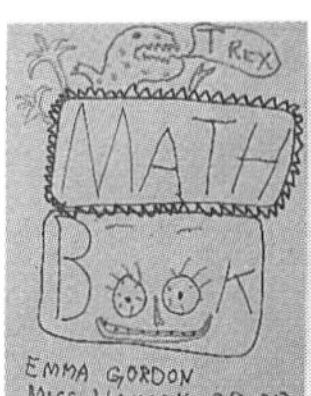

____ + ____ + ____ + ____

The perimeter is about ____ cm.

2

____ + ____ + ____ + ____

The perimeter is about ____ cm.

3

____ + ____ + ____ + ____

The perimeter is about ____ cm.

Tell your partner what you notice about the measures of some sides.

Practice!

Measure. Add to find the perimeter.

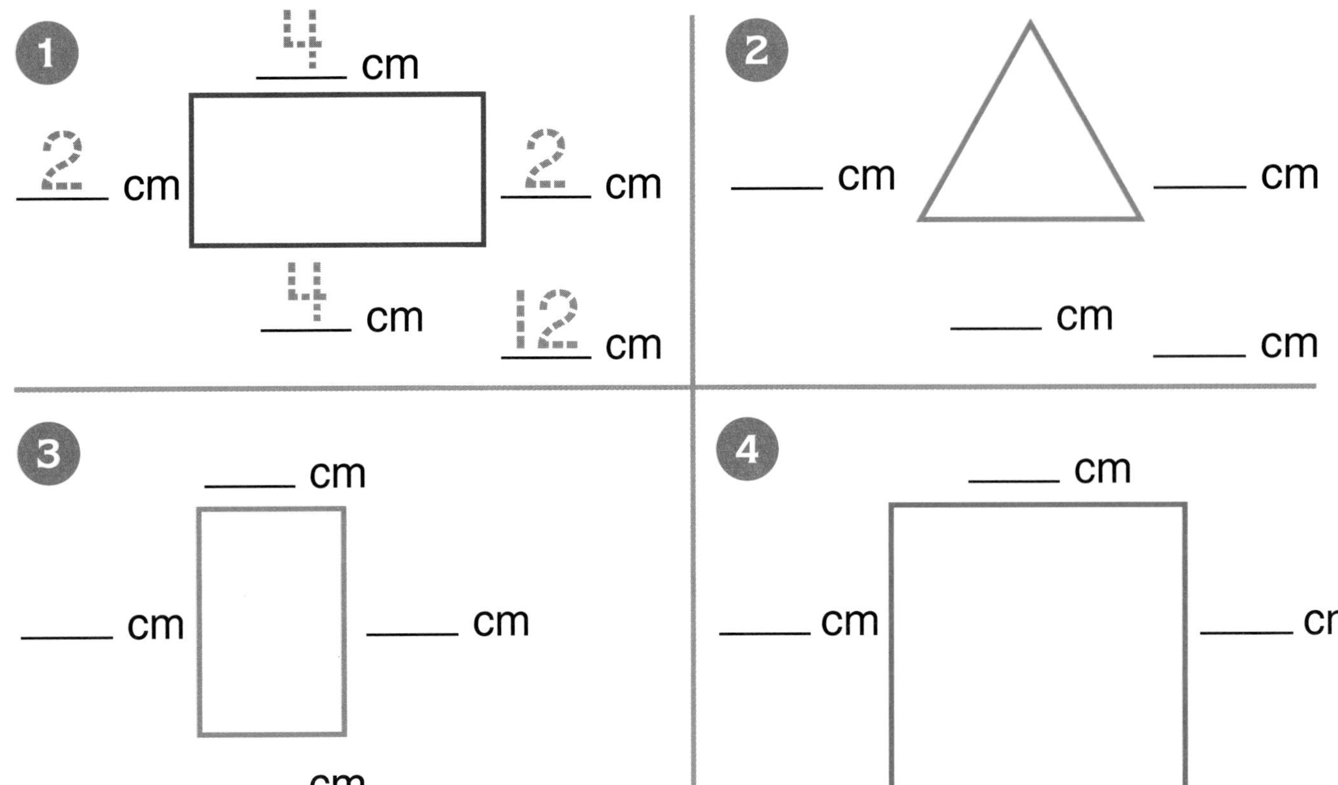

More to Explore Measurement Sense

Trace paths that are about the same length.
Use a different color for each length.

At Home: We explored finding perimeters. Ask your child how he or she solved exercise 3 above.

Name ______________________________

Area

Area is measured in square units.

1 **square unit**

Glossary
area
square unit

 square units

Working Together

You and your partner need 40 paper squares.

- Find these objects.
- Cover each object with squares.
- Count the squares to find the area. Record.

1. 

about ____ square units

2. 
about ____ square units

3. about ____ square units

4. 
about ____ square units

How are perimeter and area different?

Practice!

Color to show the number of square units.

1 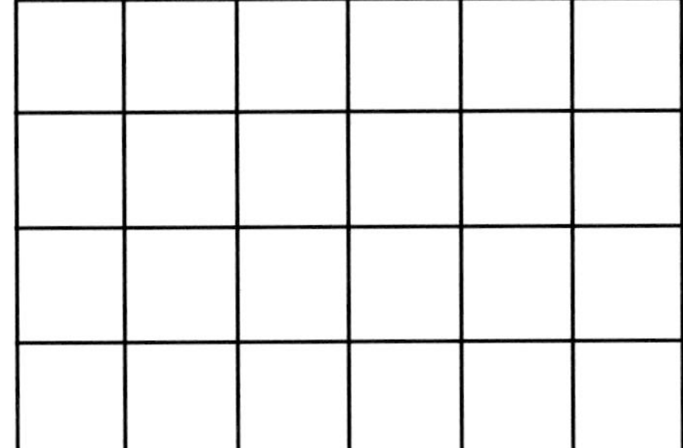

12 square units

2  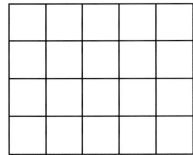

9 square units

Color an area.
Write how many square units you colored.

3 

____ square units

4 

____ square units

Prior Knowledge

Think of an animal. Use what you know about the animal to draw a picture of the animal and where it lives.

Use your own paper.

At Home

We explored finding area. Have your child explain the area shown in exercise 4 above.

Name

Draw a Diagram

Problem-Solving Strategy

Read | Plan | Solve | Look Back

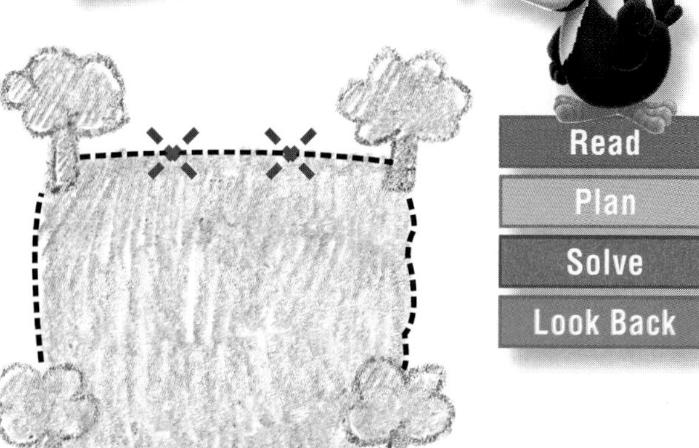

Read Joe planted a tree in each corner of his square garden. He planted 2 bushes between each tree. How many bushes did Joe plant?

Plan What strategy could you use to solve the problem?

Solve Joe drew a **diagram**. Finish it. How many bushes did Joe plant? ____ bushes

Look Back Did you answer the question? Explain.

Glossary
diagram

Draw a diagram to solve.

1. Lu made a map of her street. There is a large house on each corner. There are 5 more houses on each side of the street. How many houses are on Lu's street?

   ____ houses

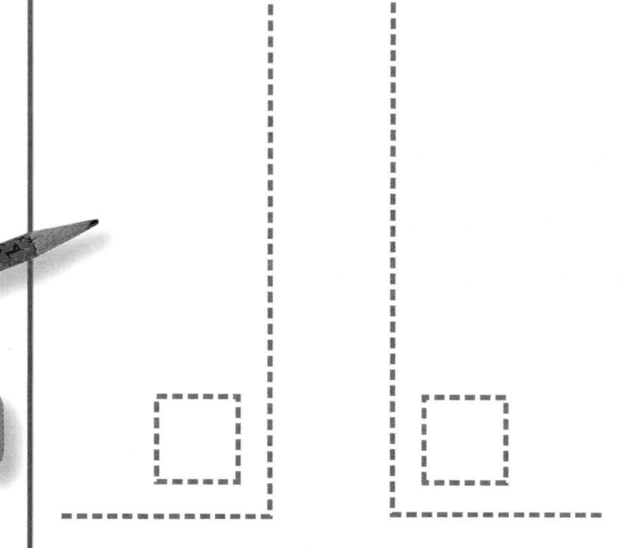

McGraw-Hill School Division

Practice!

Draw a diagram to solve.

1. Sal's garden is shaped like a triangle. There are 6 plants on each side of the garden. How many plants are in Sal's garden?

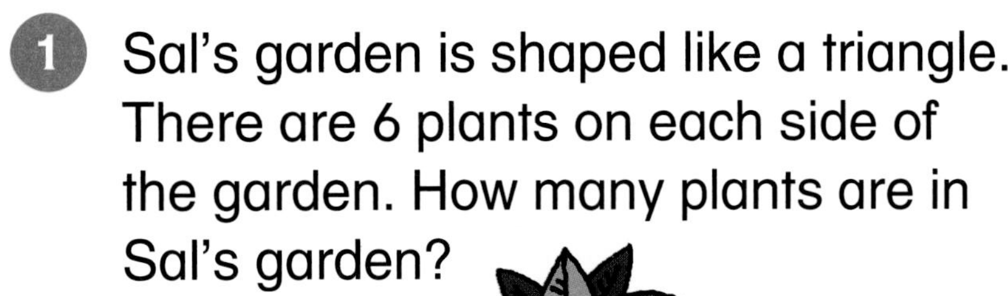

____ plants

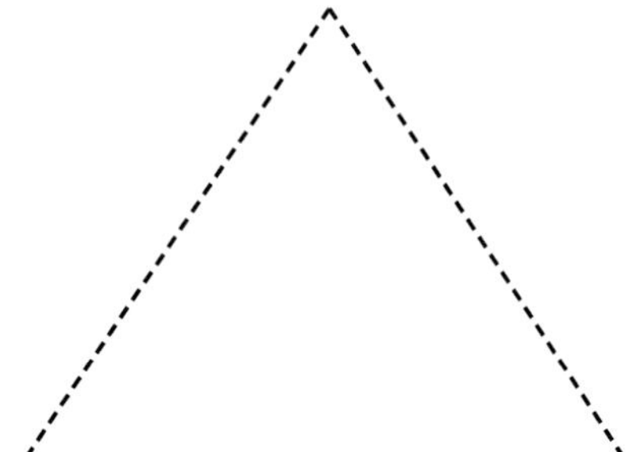

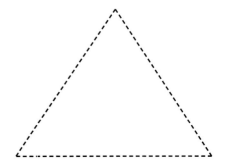

2. Mi made a fence around a pigpen. She used 6 pieces of fence on 2 sides of the pen and 3 pieces of fence on the other two sides. How many pieces of fence did Mi use?

____ pieces

---

3. Juan's map shows each student's desk. He drew 5 rows of desks. Each row has 6 desks. How many desks are on Juan's map?

____ desks

Mixed Review Test Preparation

Subtract.

4.

$$\begin{array}{r} 21 \\ -\ 19 \\ \hline \end{array} \qquad \begin{array}{r} 76 \\ -\ 34 \\ \hline \end{array} \qquad \begin{array}{r} 68 \\ -\ 27 \\ \hline \end{array}$$

Compare. Write $>$ or $<$.

5. 52 ◯ 45   61 ◯ 78

At Home: We drew diagrams to solve problems. Ask your child to explain how to solve problem 3 above.

Name

Midchapter Review

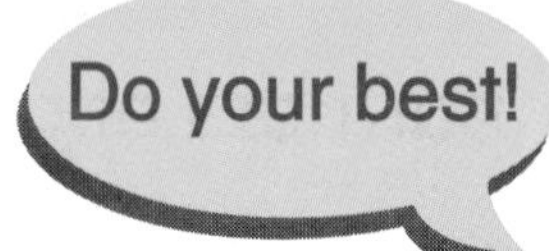

Estimate. Then measure.

		Estimate	Measure
1		about 7 inches	about 2 inches
2		about 1 inches	about 1 inches
3		about 5 cm	about 3 cm
4		about 4 cm	about 4 cm

Measure each path.

5 about 2 inches

6 about 6 cm

Measure. Add to find the perimeter.

7 10 cm

8 8 cm

Draw a diagram to solve.

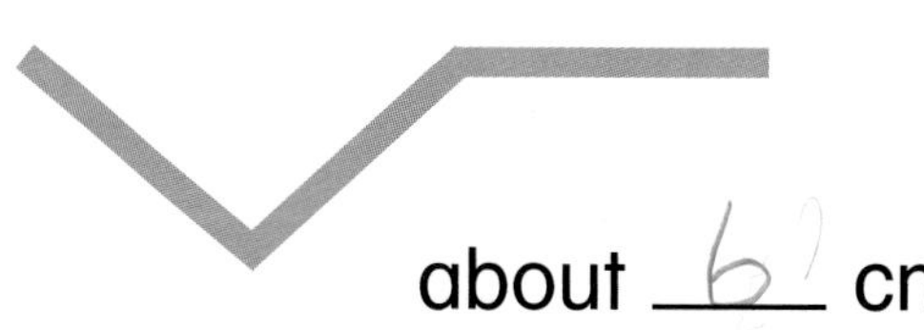

9 A map shows a square garden. There is a big tree in each corner. There are 2 small trees between each big tree. How many trees are in the garden? 2 trees

10 How did you solve problem 9? ______

How do you estimate the length of an object?

Extra Practice

Game!

Scavenger Hunt

You and your partners each need a 0 1 2 3 4 5 6 inches and a 0 1 2 3 4 5 6 7 8 9 10 11 12 13 14 15 16 centimeters.

- Play with other groups.
- Your group must find one object for each measure in the chart.
- Write the name or draw the object on the chart.

The first group to complete the chart wins!

Length	Object we found
about 6 inches long	Pencil
about 1 foot long	
about 12 centimeters long	
about 3 feet long	
about 4 centimeters long	

Real-Life Investigation
Applying Measurement

Name

Make a Map

Listen to *As the Crow Flies*.

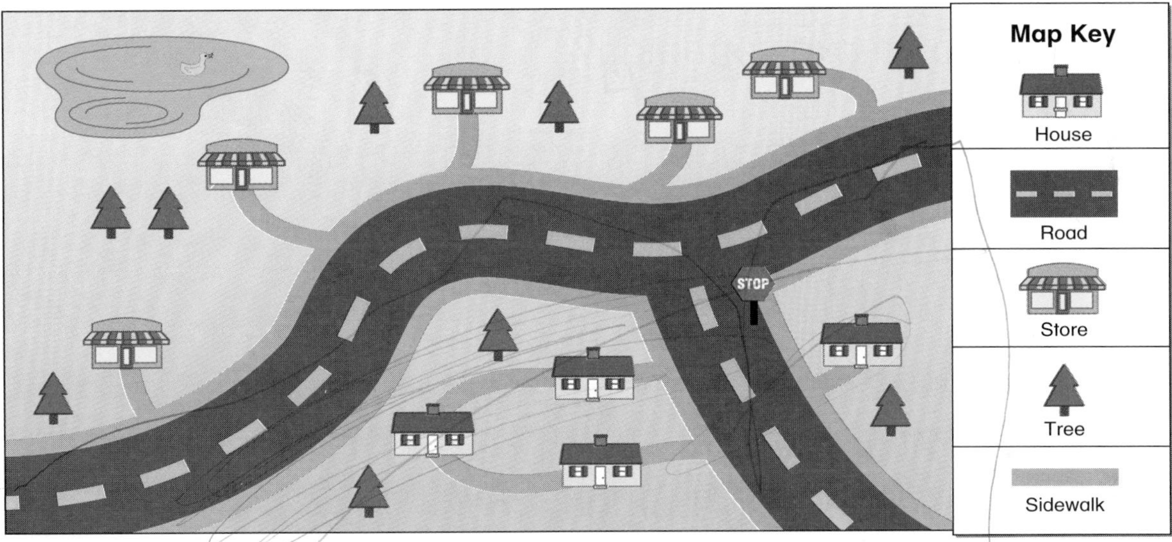

Tell how the **map key** helps you to read the map of this neighborhood.

Glossary
map key

Working Together

Your group will make a map of your school neighborhood.

- Take a walk around your neighborhood. Talk about what you want to show on your map.
- Make notes about the buildings, streets, and other things that you see.

Decision Making

1. What do you want to show on your map and how will you show it?
2. Choose the materials that you want to use, and make your map.

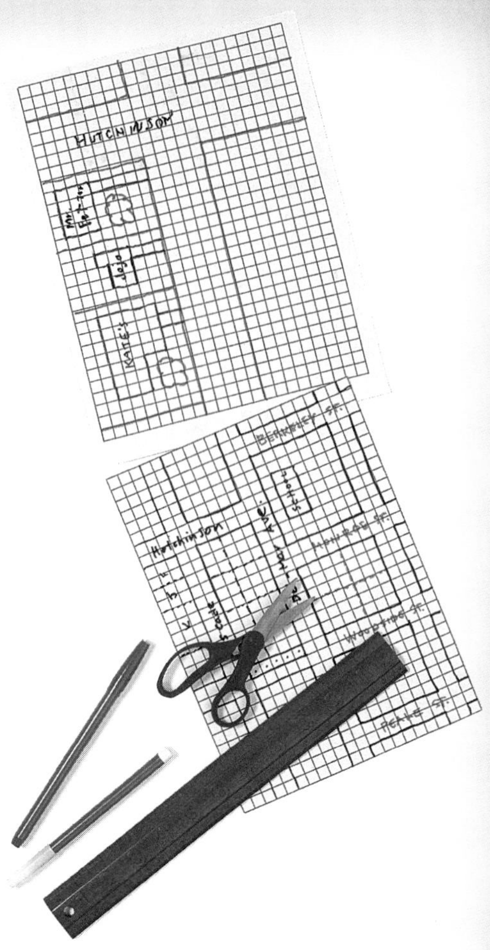

Write a report.

3. Tell what you decided to show on your map.
4. How did you make your map?

More to Investigate

PREDICT What if you made your school neighborhood map part of a bigger community map. Where does your neighborhood fit?

EXPLORE Try it. Make a new map. Show more of the community where you live.

FIND Compare the maps. How are they alike? How are they different?

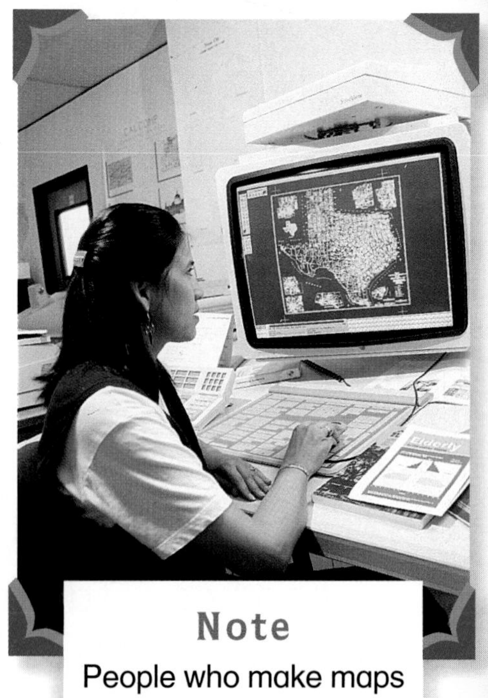

Note
People who make maps are called cartographers. Today mapmakers use computers to sort and arrange the data.

Name ______________________________

Explore Activity
Pound

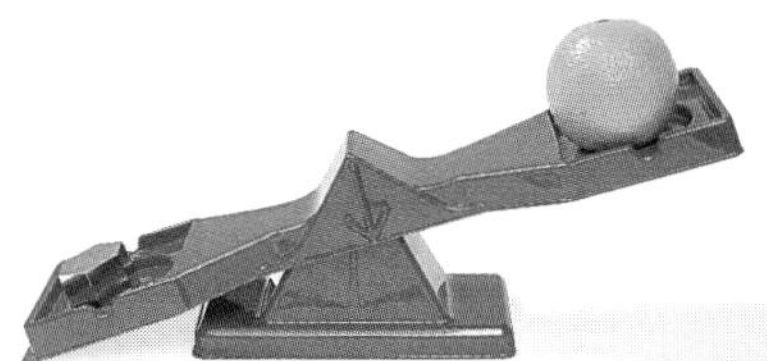

less than 1 **pound (lb)**

1 pound

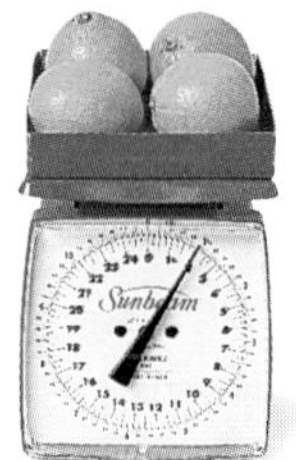

2 pounds

What would the balance look like if you put two oranges on each pan?

Glossary
pound

Working Together

You and your partner need a and a 1 lb.
Take turns.

- Find these objects.
- Hold the 1 lb in one hand and the object in your other hand.
- Estimate. Write *more than* or *less than* 1 pound.
- Measure and record.

	Estimate *more than* or *less than* 1 pound	Measure
		about ____ pounds
		about ____ pounds
		about ____ pounds

Do big objects always weigh more than small objects? Explain.

Practice!

Write *more than* or *less than.*

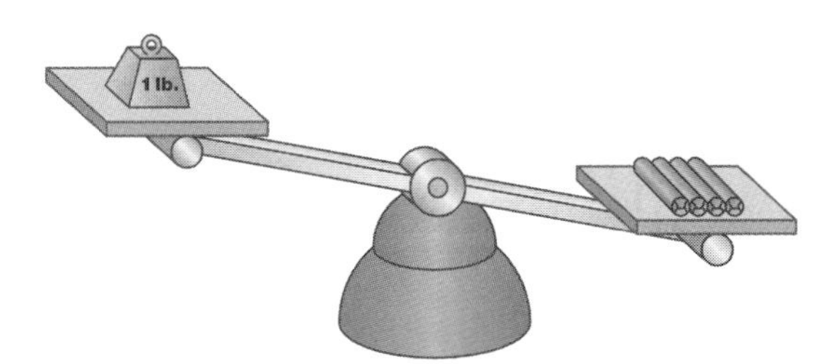

more than I pound

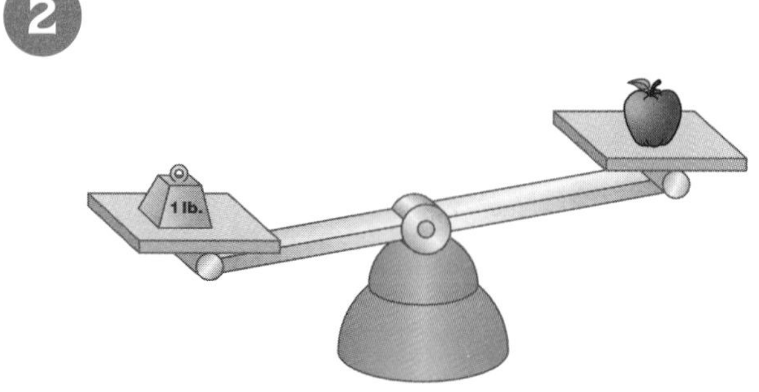

_______________ I pound

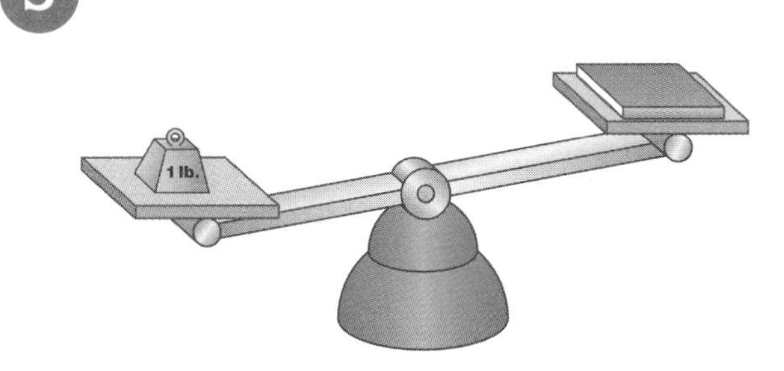

_______________ I pound

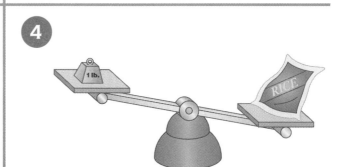

_______________ I pound

How many pounds?

about _____ pounds

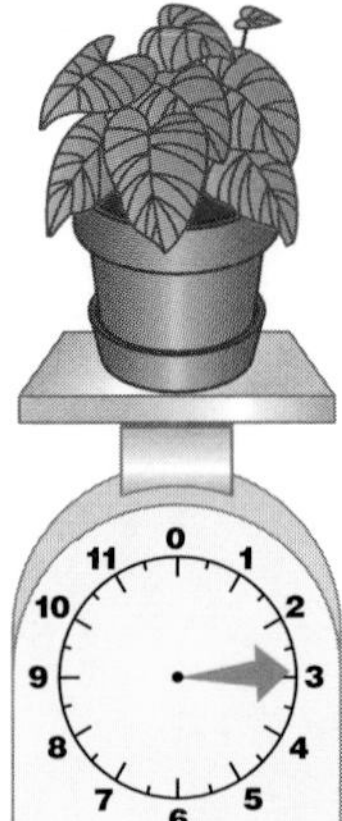

about _____ pounds

Write or draw to show how to find the number of pounds.

Have your child estimate the weight of several objects as *more than* or *less than* I pound.

Name ______________________

Explore Activity

Kilogram

less than 1 **kilogram (kg)**

1 kilogram

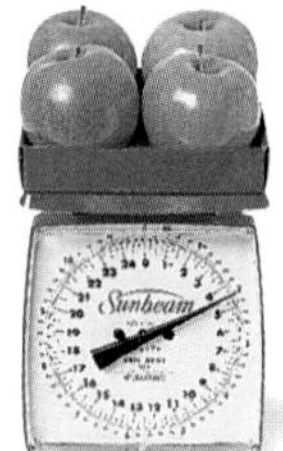

2 kilograms

What would the balance look like if you put 2 kilograms of apples on it?

Glossary

kilogram

Working Together

You and your partner need a and a 1kg.

- Find these objects.
- Hold the 1kg in one hand and the object in your other hand.
- Estimate. Write *more than* or *less than* 1 kilogram.
- Measure and record.

	Estimate *more than* or *less than* 1 kilogram	Measure
		about ____ kilograms
		about ____ kilograms
		about ____ kilograms

Which is heavier: 1 kilogram of rocks or 1 kilogram of feathers? Explain.

Practice!

Write *more than* or *less than*.

1

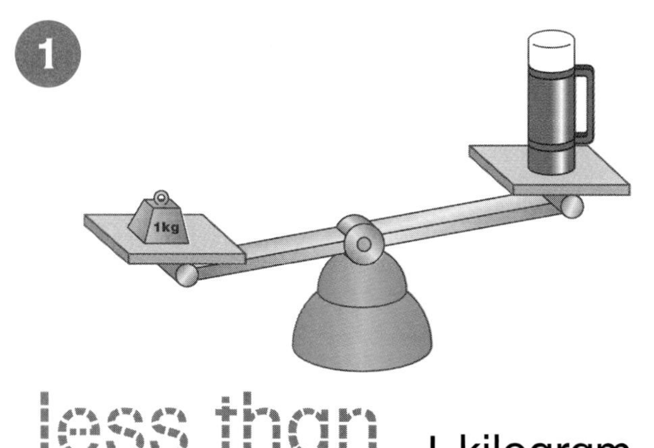

less than I kilogram

2

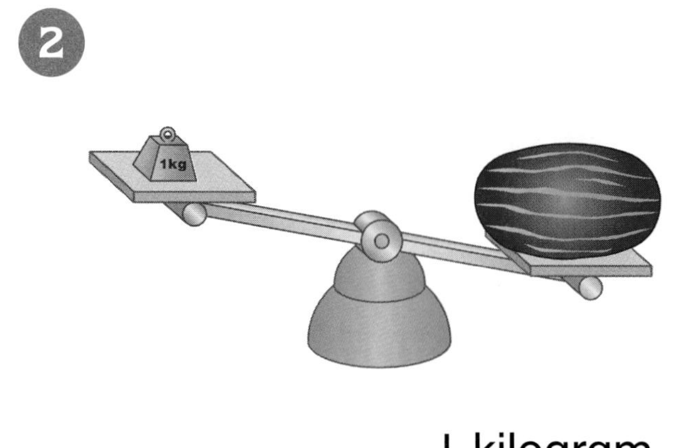

_______________ I kilogram

3

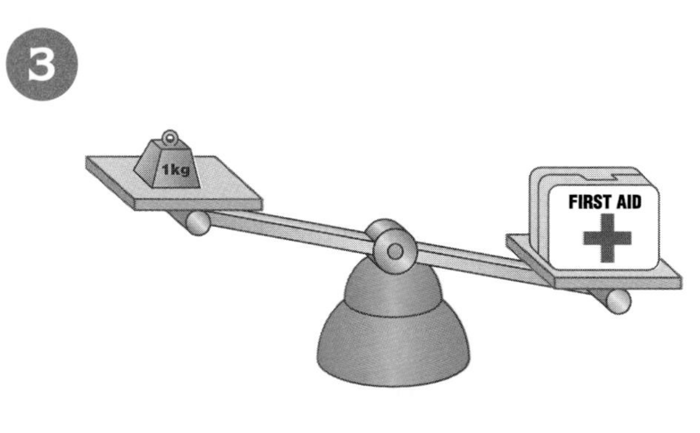

_______________ I kilogram

4

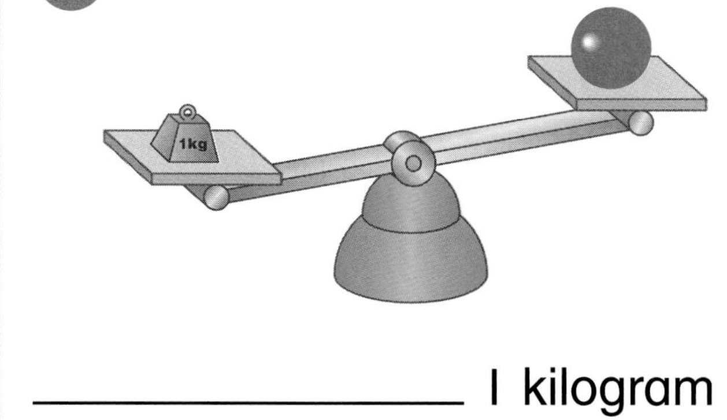

_______________ I kilogram

How many kilograms?

about ____ kilograms

6

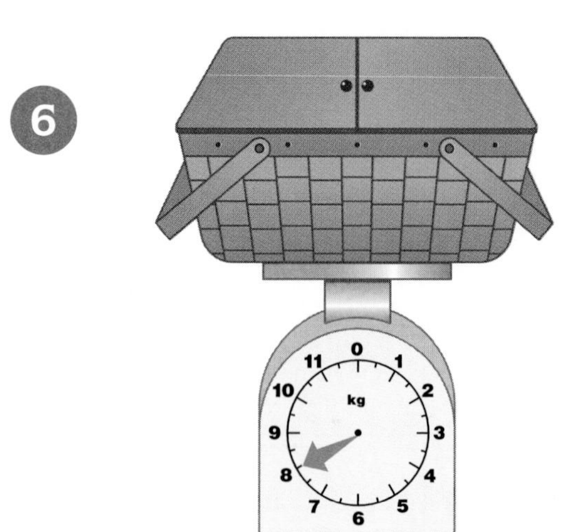

about ____ kilograms

At Home: Have your child estimate the measure of several objects as *more than* or *less than* I kilogram.

Name ______________________

Explore Activity

Cup, Pint, Quart

1 **cup**

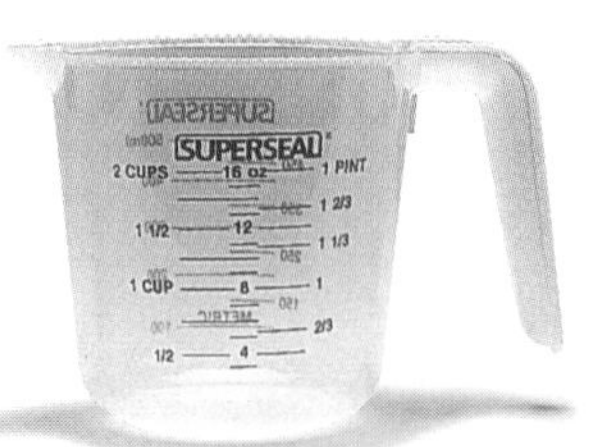

1 **pint**

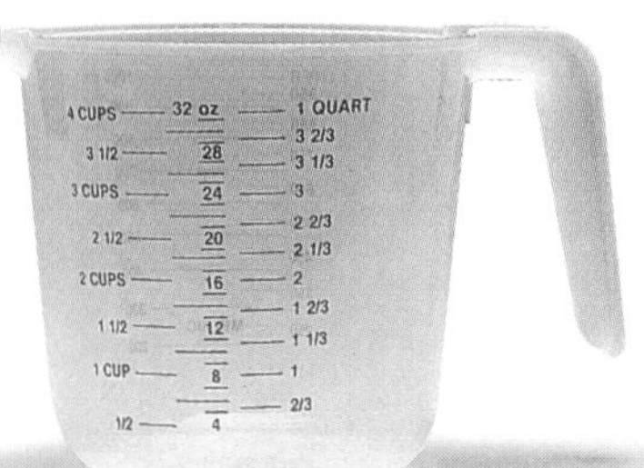

1 **quart**

How can you find how many cups will fill a pint? a quart?

Glossary
cup
pint
quart

Working Together

You and your partner need containers that hold about 1 cup, 1 pint, and 1 quart.

Take turns.

▶ Fill and pour to measure.

▶ Complete the table.

_____ cups = 1 pint

_____ pints = 1 quart

_____ cups = 1 quart

▶ Choose a container.

▶ Estimate how much it will hold. about _______________

▶ Measure to find out. about _______________

Practice!

Choose the better estimate.

1. I cup

more than I cup

less than I cup

2. I pint

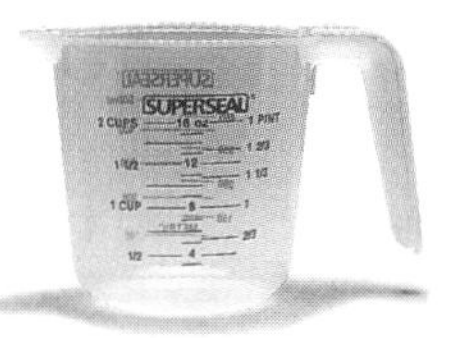

more than I pint

less than I pint

3. I quart

more than I quart

less than I quart

More to Explore Number Sense

Fractions are used to show parts of a cup.

$\frac{1}{3}$ **cup**

Which cup has more?

$\frac{1}{2}$ cup

$\frac{1}{4}$ cup

Which cup has less?

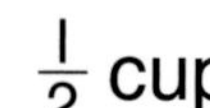

$\frac{1}{2}$ cup

$\frac{1}{3}$ cup

At Home: We measured in cups, pints, and quarts. Ask your child to show you how much $\frac{1}{2}$ cup is.

Name ______________________

This bottle holds 1 liter.

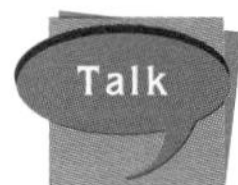

How can you find out if other containers hold more or less than 1 **liter**?

Glossary
liter

Working Together

You and your partner need a container that holds about 1 liter.

The mug holds *less* than 1 liter.

- Choose some containers.
- Estimate if the container holds more or less than 1 liter. Record your estimate.
- Fill and pour to measure. Record the measure.

1. Container ______________
   Estimate ______________
   Measure ______________

2. Container ______________
   Estimate ______________
   Measure ______________

3. Container ______________
   Estimate ______________
   Measure ______________

4. Container ______________
   Estimate ______________
   Measure ______________

Practice!

Choose the better estimate.

1  

more than 1 liter

less than 1 liter

more than 1 liter

less than 1 liter

more than 1 liter

less than 1 liter

Mixed Review Test Preparation

4 Write the fraction for the shaded part.

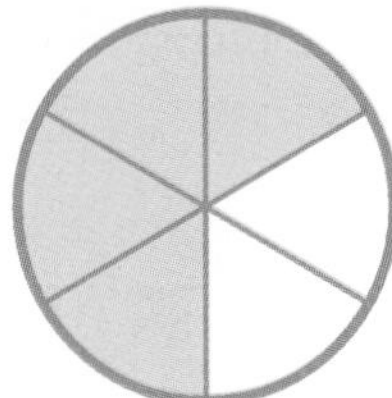 ____

 ____

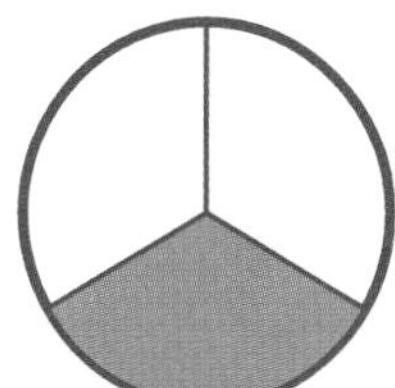 ____

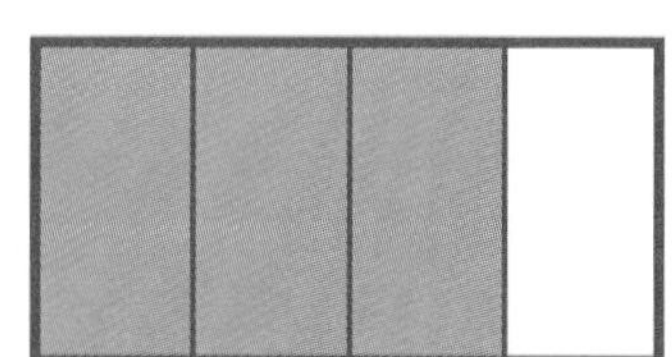 ____

Subtract.

$45	72	50¢	96	39
− 18	− 65	− 26¢	− 53	− 5

At Home: Ask your child to find containers in your home that hold about 1 liter.

Name

Temperature

Temperature can be measured in **degrees Fahrenheit (°F).**

This thermometer shows 24 °F.

Talk

What kind of day is it when the temperature is 24°F?

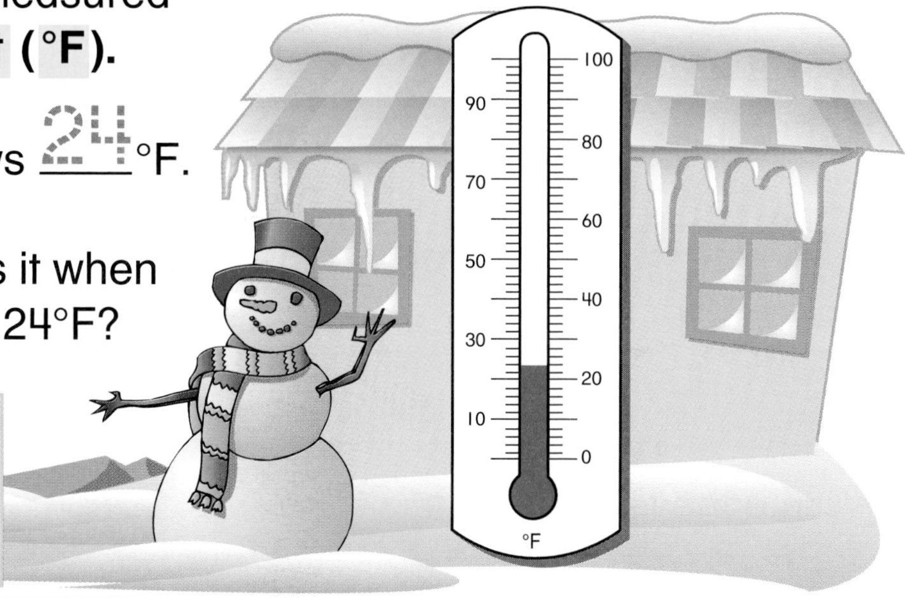

Glossary
temperature
degrees Fahrenheit

Write the temperature. Write *hot, warm,* or *cold.*

1. _____°F

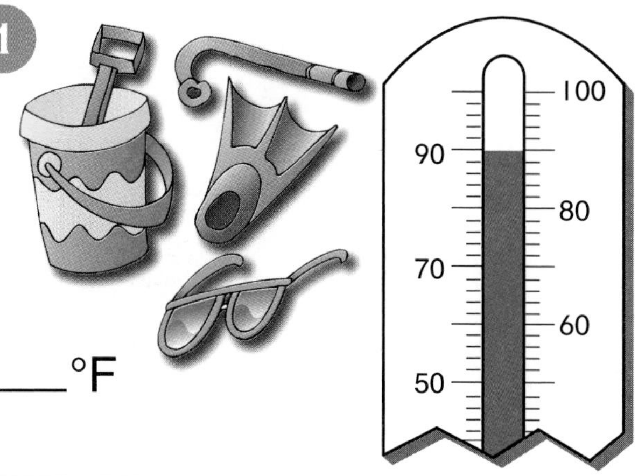

____

2. _____°F

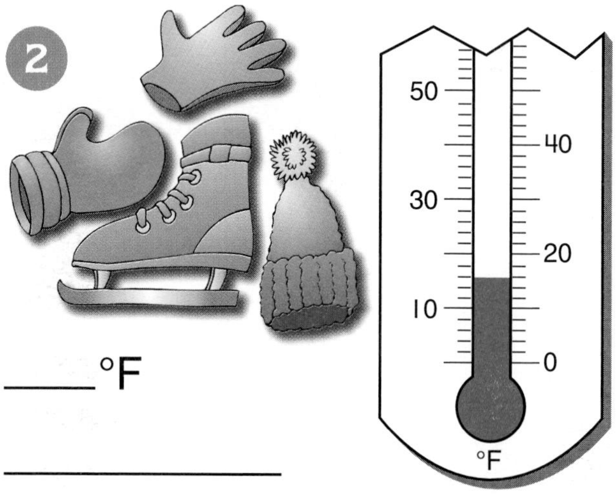

____

3. _____°F

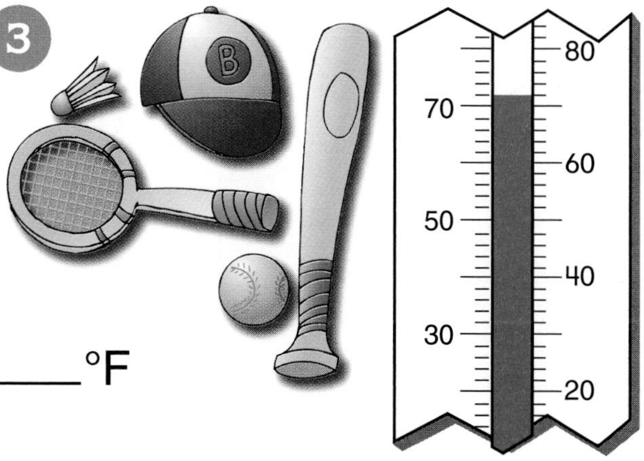

____

4. _____°F

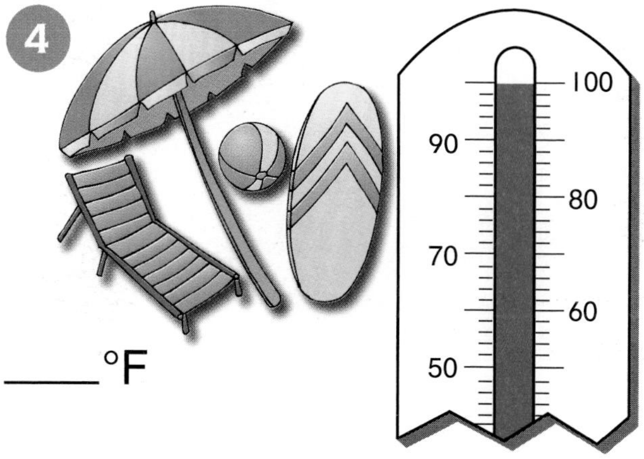

____

What might the temperature be on a hot day? a cold day? a warm day?

Practice!

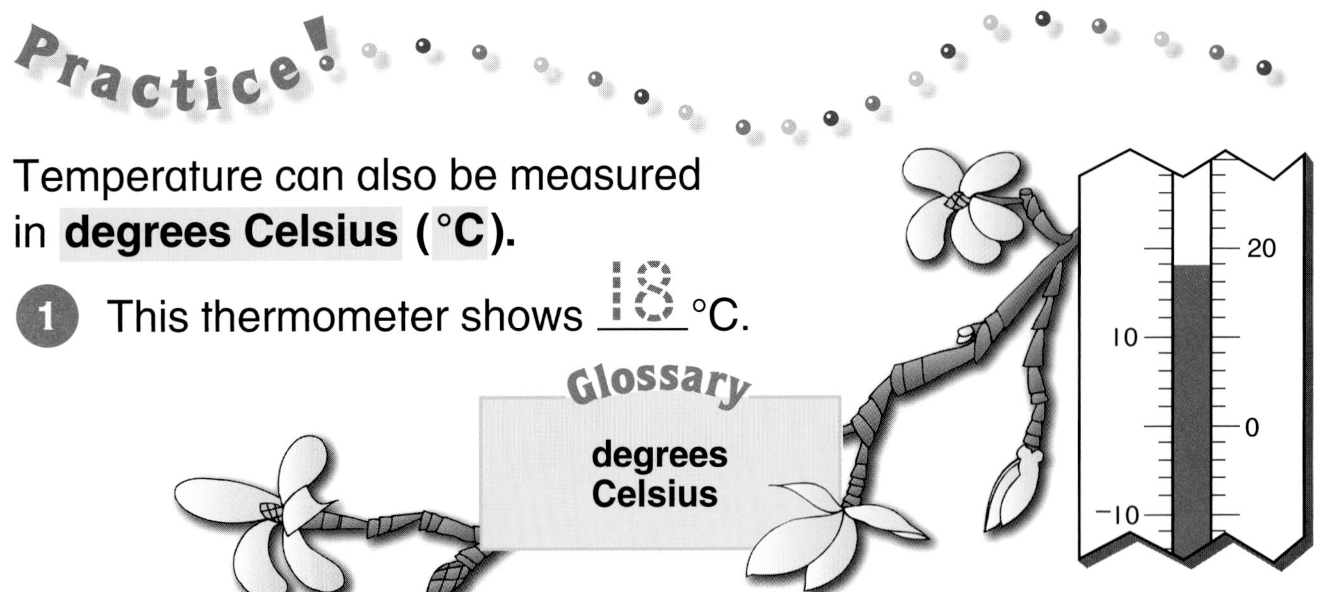

Temperature can also be measured in **degrees Celsius (°C).**

1. This thermometer shows 18 °C.

Write the temperature.

2. ____°C

3. ____°C

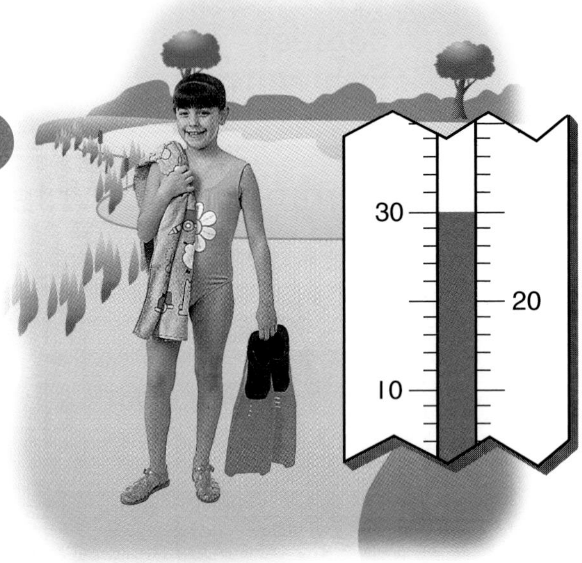

4. ____°C

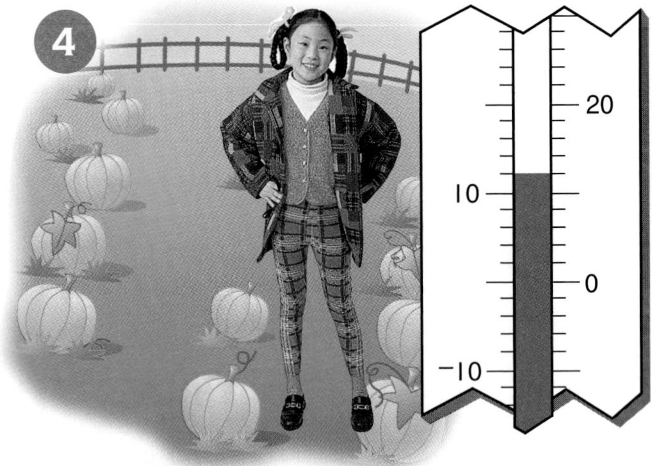

5. ____°C

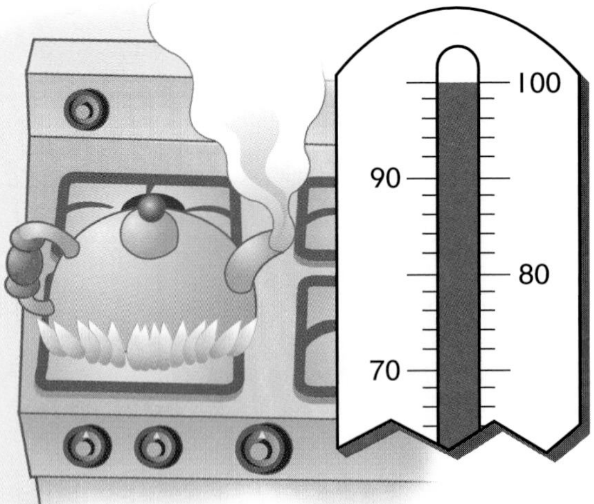

Read a thermometer to find today's temperature. Write about or draw a picture of today's weather.

Ask your child what you might wear if the weather were 20°F.

Name

Measurement Tools

Jenna wants to check how much cereal is left in the box.

Which tool should she use to measure?

Jenna should use a scale.

Choose the tool you would use to measure:

1. how much water is in a fish tank.

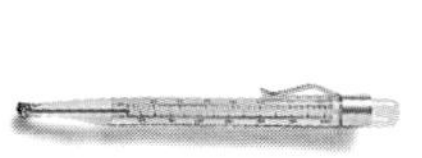

2. how warm it is outside.

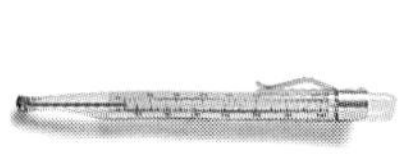

3. how heavy a rock is.

4. how long a lunchbox is.

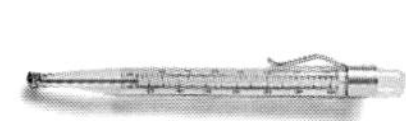

How many ways can you measure a book? Which tools would you use to measure?

Practice!

Match to show which tool you would use to measure:

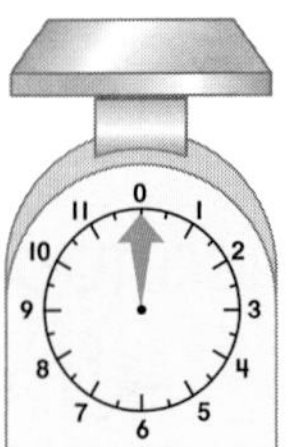

1. how much it holds.

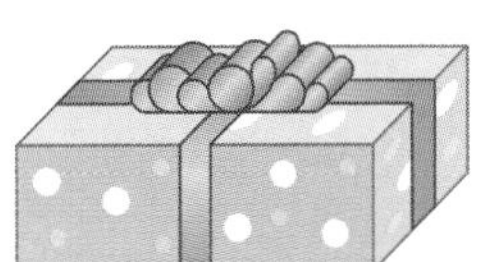

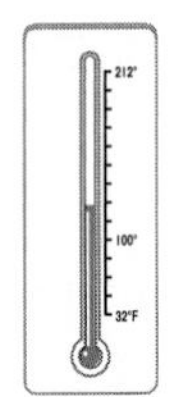

2. how long it is.

3. how heavy it is.

4. how cold it is.

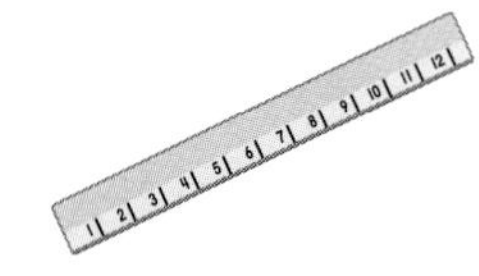

Cultural Connection

African Clay Beads

Make some clay beads.
Mix the ingredients.
Cook until thick.
Let clay cool.

Shape the beads.

Make a hole in each.
Bake 45 minutes at 300°F.

Ingredients

1 cup cornstarch

$2\frac{1}{2}$ cups baking soda

$1\frac{1}{2}$ cups cold water

List the measurement tools you need to make the beads. ____________________

Ask your child to explain which measurement tools he or she would use to measure various household items.

Name

Problem Solvers at Work

Read
Plan
Solve
Look Back

Reasonable Answers

Tori and Jan put a rug
in their tree house.
About how long is the rug?

5 inches   5 feet   15 feet

Which answer makes sense?
Think.

A tree house is smaller than a room in a house.

5 inches is too small.
15 feet is too big.
5 feet makes sense.

Choose the answer that makes sense.

1. Jack reads a thermometer on a warm, sunny day.
About what temperature is it?

8°F   48°F   84°F

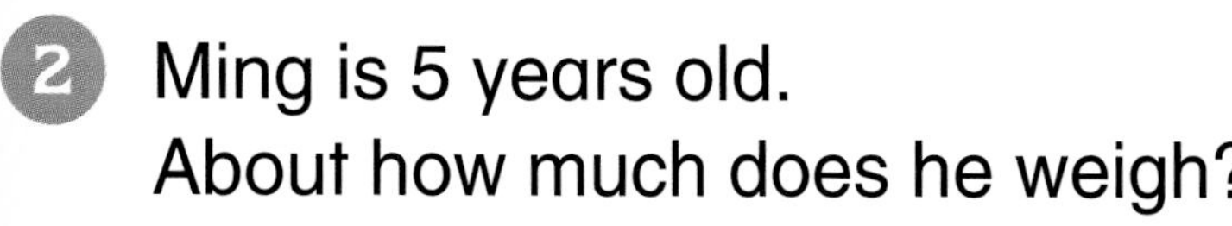

2. Ming is 5 years old.
About how much does he weigh?

4 pounds   40 pounds   400 pounds

Practice!

Choose the answer that makes sense.

1 Kelly makes a container of lemonade for her three friends. About how much does she make?

1 cup   1 pint   1 quart

---

2 Zach measures the length of his room. About how long is his room?

10 inches   10 feet   100 feet

STUDENT TO STUDENT

Write and Share

Dara wrote this problem.

I have a puppy named Lucky. He is small. About how much does he weigh?

5 pounds   50 pounds   100 pounds

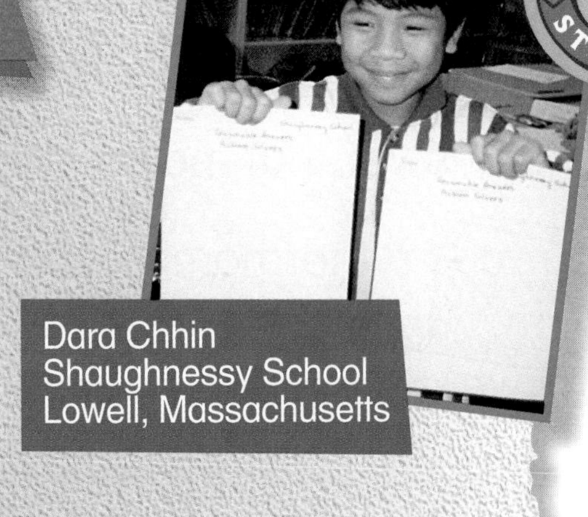

Dara Chhin
Shaughnessy School
Lowell, Massachusetts

3 Solve Dara's problem. ______________________

How did you decide on your answer? ______________________

4 READING ARITHMETIC WRITING **Prior Knowledge** Use what you know about measurement to write a problem. Have a partner solve it.

At Home: Ask your child to explain how to solve the problem that he or she wrote.

Name ______________________

Chapter Review

Language and Mathematics

Choose the correct word to complete the sentence.

perimeter area foot inches

1. 12 __________ equal 1 __________.
2. Measure around a shape to find the __________.

Concepts and Skills

Estimate. Then measure.

		Estimate	Measure
3	▬▬▬	about ___ inches	about ___ inches
4	▬▬▬▬▬▬	about ___ inches	about ___ inches
5	▬▬▬▬▬▬	about ___ cm	about ___ cm
6	▬▬	about ___ cm	about ___ cm

Measure. Add to find the perimeter.

___ cm

___ cm

Choose the better estimate.

more than 1 pound

less than 1 pound

10. 
more than 1 kilogram

less than 1 kilogram

11. 

more than 1 pint

less than 1 pint

more than 1 liter

less than 1 liter

How many pounds?

13 about ____ pounds

How many kilograms?

14 about ____ kilograms

Write the temperature.

15 ____°F

16 ____°C

17 ____°F

18 ____°C

Problem Solving

Draw a diagram to solve.

19 Amy's garden is a triangle.
There is 1 tree in each corner.
There are 3 flowers between each tree.
How many flowers are in Amy's garden? ____ flowers

Use your own paper.

Choose the answer that makes sense.

20 Diana measured her desk.
About how long was it? 2 inches 20 feet 2 feet

What Do You Think?

Which is easier to measure?

☑ Check one. ☐ Inches ☐ Feet ☐ Pounds

Why? ____________________

Journal

Draw a 1-inch line. Tell what you know about inches.

Name

Chapter Test

Estimate. Then measure.

	Estimate	Measure
1	about ___ inches	about ___ inches
2	about ___ cm	about ___ cm

3 Measure. Add to find the perimeter.  ___ cm

Ring the better estimate.

4 
more than 1 pint
less than 1 pint

5 
more than 1 liter
less than 1 liter

Write the temperature.

6 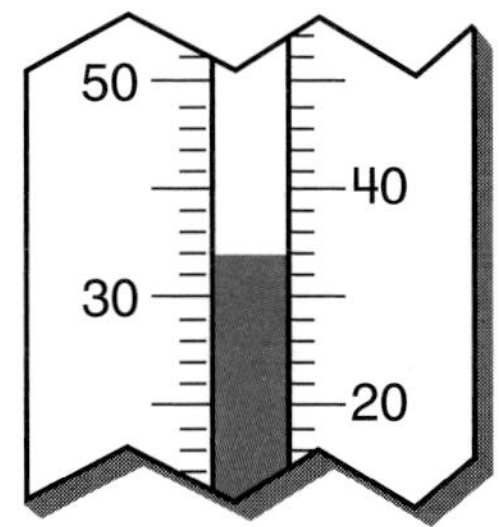

___ °F

7 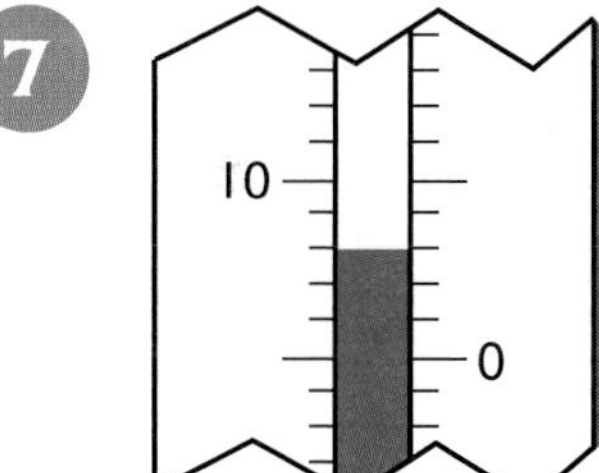

___ °C

8 How many pounds?
about ___ pounds  

9 How many kilograms?
about ___ kilograms 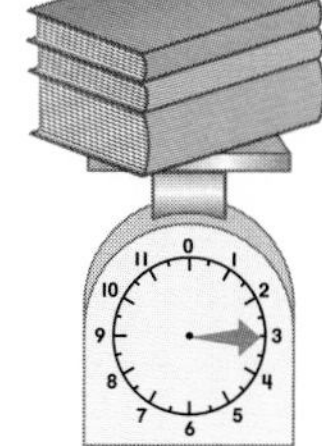

Draw a diagram to solve.

10 Pat used 5 pieces of fence on each of 2 sides of his garden. He used 3 pieces on each of the other 2 sides of his garden. How many pieces of fence did Pat use? ___ pieces

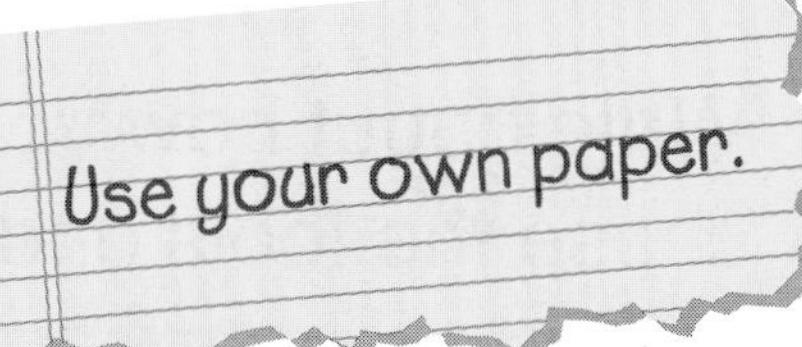

What Did You Learn?

Work with a partner.

Choose two different kinds of objects to measure. Measure each object as many ways as you can. Record the measure and the tool you used.

Object 1:	Object 2:
measure: tool:	measure: tool:
measure: tool:	measure: tool:
measure: tool:	measure: tool:
measure: tool:	measure: tool:

Write about how you measured and why you chose the tools and units you did.

Use your own paper.

You may want to put this page in your portfolio.

Math Connection

Graphing

Name

Coordinate Grids

This grid shows where things are at a campground. How can you find the tent?

- Always start at 0.
- First count across →.
- Then count up ↑.

To find the tent, go across 3 and up 1.

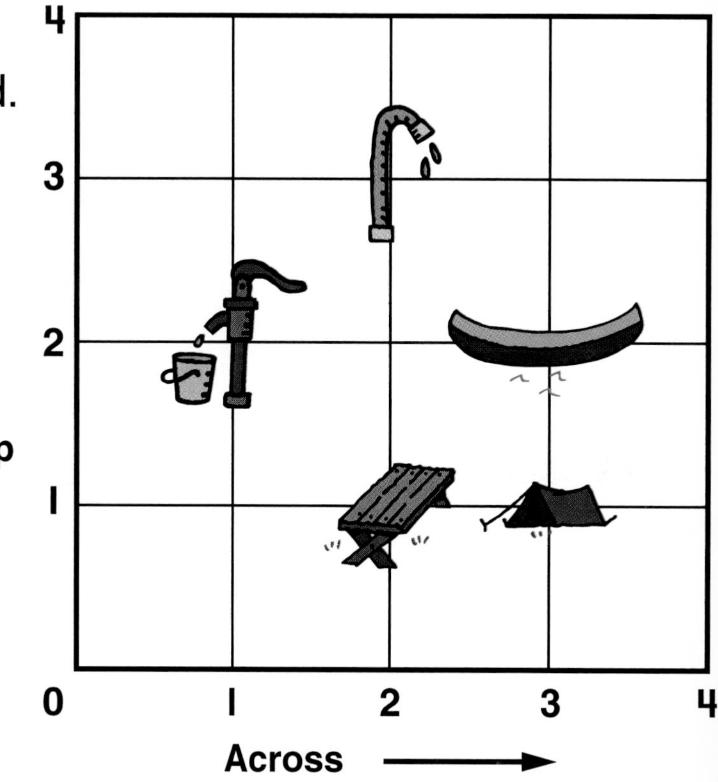

Which things will you find?

	Across →	Up ↑			
1	3	1	tent (circled)	picnic table	water pump
2	2	1	water pump	canoe	picnic table
3	1	2	faucet	water pump	picnic table
4	2	3	water pump	canoe	faucet
5	3	2	canoe	tent	faucet

Technology Connection

Computer

Perimeter

How can different shapes have the same perimeter?

What is the perimeter of this square? ________

At the Computer

1. Draw a rectangle with the same perimeter as the square above.
2. Draw a square with a perimeter of 12 cm. Then draw a rectangle with the same perimeter. Compare your rectangle to those of others.
3. Choose a perimeter. Draw a square with that perimeter. Draw as many rectangles with that perimeter as you can.
4. Draw a triangle with the same perimeter as one of the squares above.

Home Connection

Chapter 10 Wrap-Up

Name ________________

MATERIALS hanger, 2 identical metal clips, 2 identical clothespins

DIRECTIONS Make a balance like this. Find the real objects listed on the chart. Balance them with other objects.

Write the objects you find on the chart.

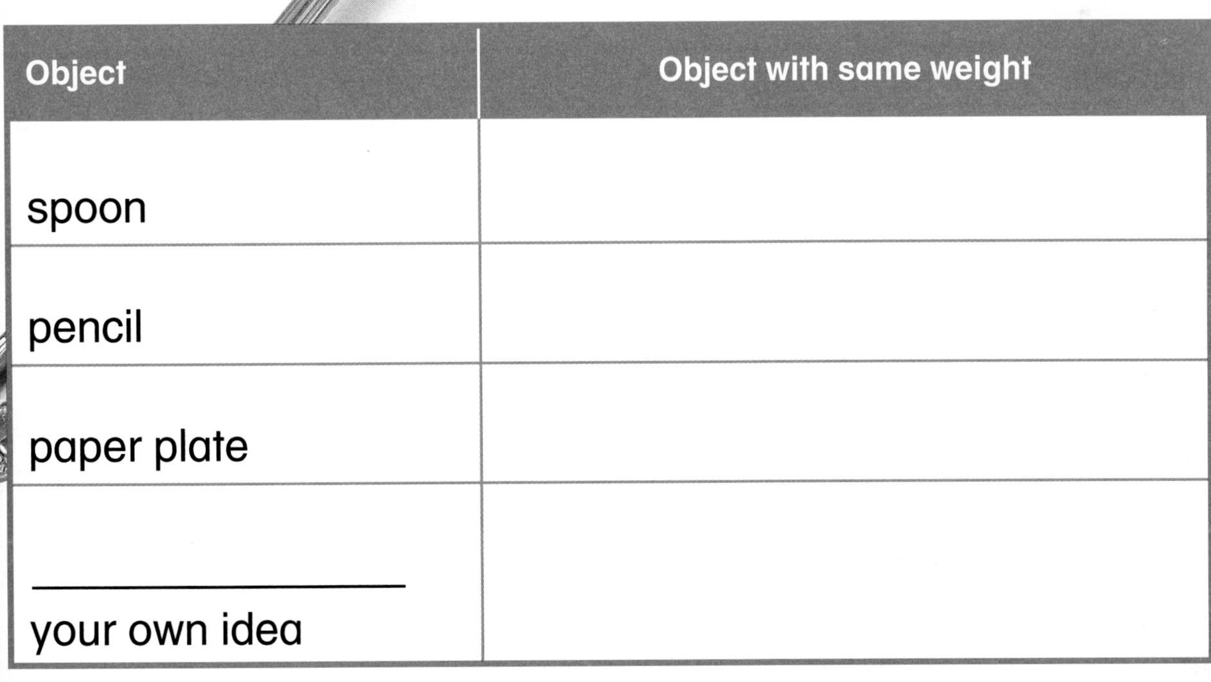

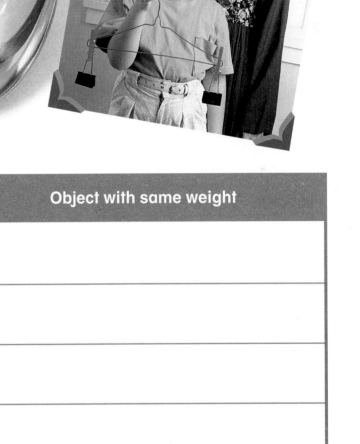

Object	Object with same weight
spoon	
pencil	
paper plate	
________________ your own idea	

This activity will help to develop your child's ability to estimate weight. Point out to your child that on this balance, when neither side of the hanger tips, the objects have the same weight.

At Home

Dear Family,

I am beginning a new chapter in mathematics. During the next few weeks I will be learning about comparing, ordering, adding, and subtracting 3-digit numbers.

I will also be talking about music, concerts, bands, and instruments.

Learning About Music

Let's talk about what kinds of music we like. We can listen to music together.

My Math Words

I am going to use these math words in this chapter.

hundred
3-digit numbers
digit
place
value
compare
Roman numerals

Please help me make word cards for the math words. I can use these word cards when I practice adding and subtracting 3-digit numbers.

Your child,

Signature

Numbers to 1,000
Adding and Subtracting

Theme: Math and Music

CHAPTER 11

Compare/Contrast Listen to the story *The Philharmonic Gets Dressed.*

Talk about parts of the story you can compare.

How is the men's and women's clothing alike? How is it different?

Name ______________________________

What Do You Know?

The orchestra wants to play a concert for the school. The gym will hold only 155 students at a time.

SMITHTOWN SCHOOL	
Grade	**Number of Students**
Kindergarten	85
First	67
Second	78
Third	73
Fourth	59
Fifth	68

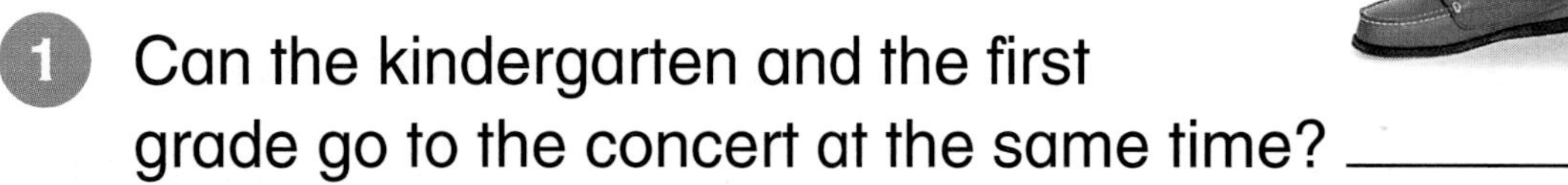

1. Can the kindergarten and the first grade go to the concert at the same time? ________

   Explain. ______________________________

2. Which two grades cannot go to the concert at the same time? ______________________________

   Explain. ______________________________

   ____

Which grades could go together to the concert? How many students could attend each concert?

You may want to put this page in your portfolio.

Name ____________________

Working Together

You and your partners need 10 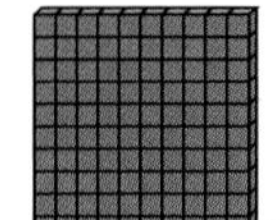.

PATTERNS Take turns.

- Show one more **hundred** each time.
- Write how many hundreds and the number.

Glossary
hundred

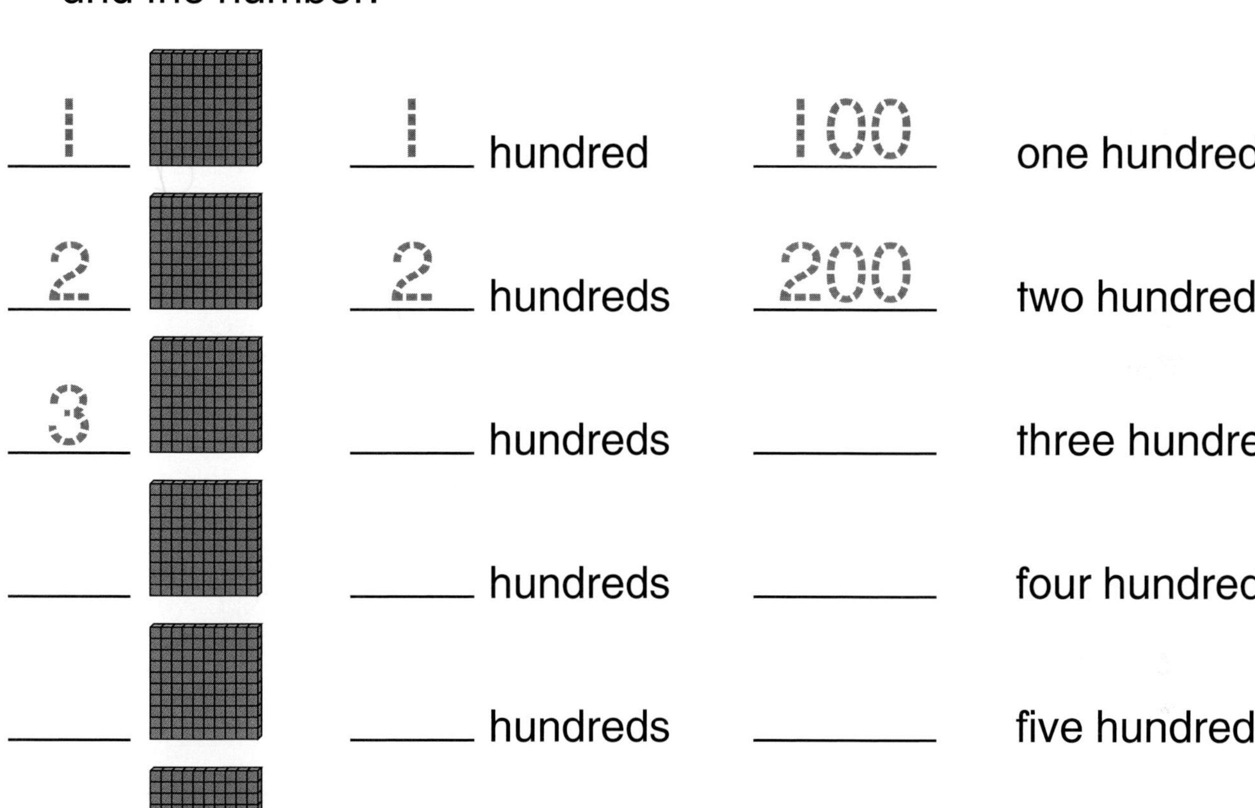
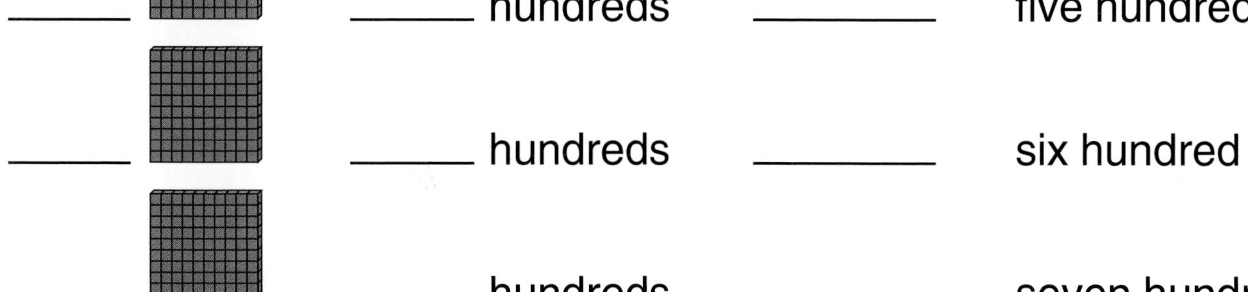

1	1 hundred	100	one hundred
2	2 hundreds	200	two hundred
3	___ hundreds	___	three hundred
___	___ hundreds	___	four hundred
___	___ hundreds	___	five hundred
___	___ hundreds	___	six hundred
___	___ hundreds	___	seven hundred
___	___ hundreds	___	eight hundred
___	___ hundreds	___	nine hundred
___	10 hundreds	1,000	one thousand

Practice!

Write how many hundreds and the number.

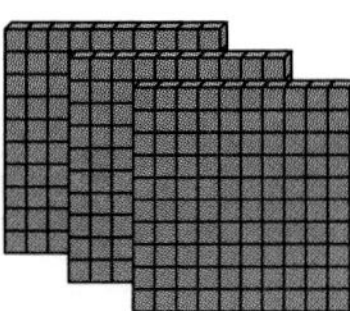

3 hundreds 300

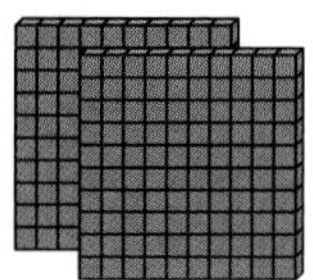

_____ hundreds _____

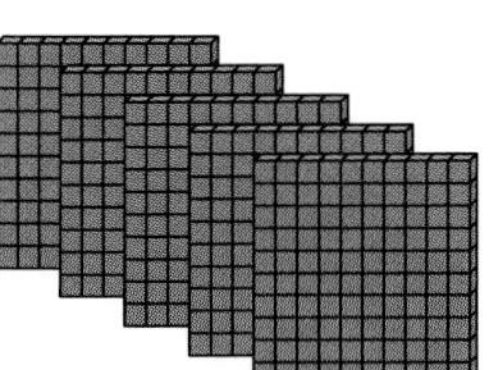

_____ hundreds _____

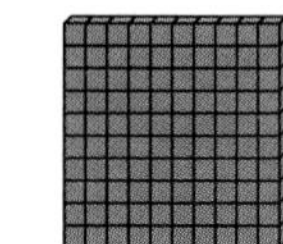

_____ hundreds _____

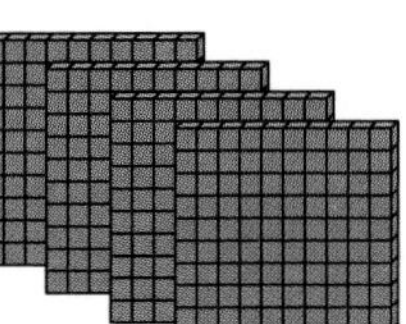

_____ hundreds _____

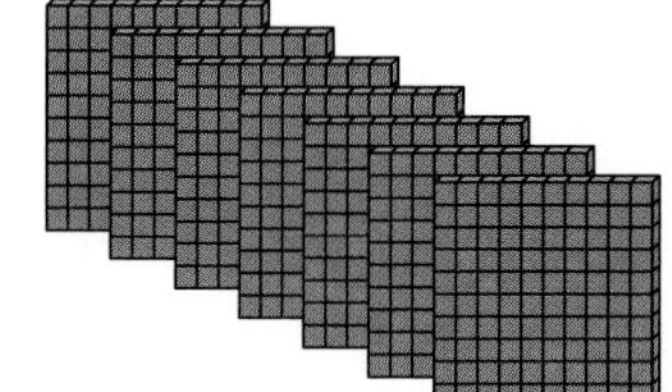

_____ hundreds _____

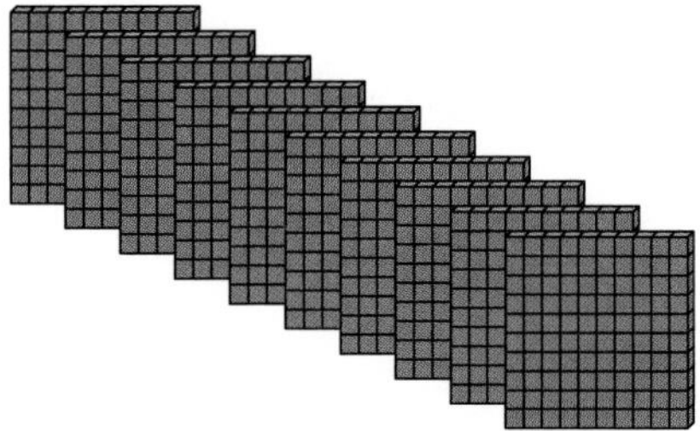

_____ hundreds _____

How is 100 different from 1,000?

We learned about hundreds today. Have your child count by hundreds to 1,000.

Name

Hundreds, Tens, and Ones

Glossary

3-digit number

Working Together

You and your partner need 9 [hundreds block], 9 [tens rod], and 9 [ones cube].

Take turns.

- Pick up some of each model.
- Estimate what **3-digit number** the models show. Then count.
- Your partner writes how many hundreds, tens, and ones and writes the number.

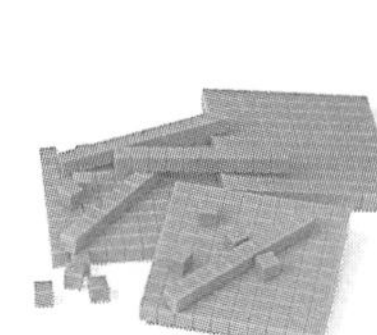

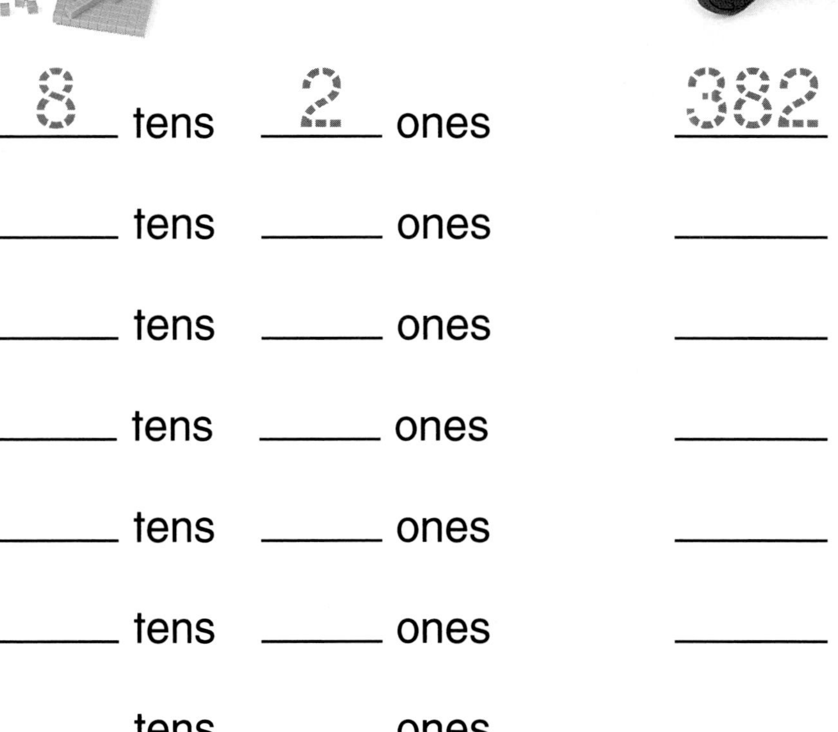

1. 3 hundreds 8 tens 2 ones 382
2. ___ hundreds ___ tens ___ ones ___
3. ___ hundreds ___ tens ___ ones ___
4. ___ hundreds ___ tens ___ ones ___
5. ___ hundreds ___ tens ___ ones ___
6. ___ hundreds ___ tens ___ ones ___
7. ___ hundreds ___ tens ___ ones ___
8. ___ hundreds ___ tens ___ ones ___

What number has 1 ten more than 465? How do you know?

Write how many hundreds, tens, and ones.
Write the number.

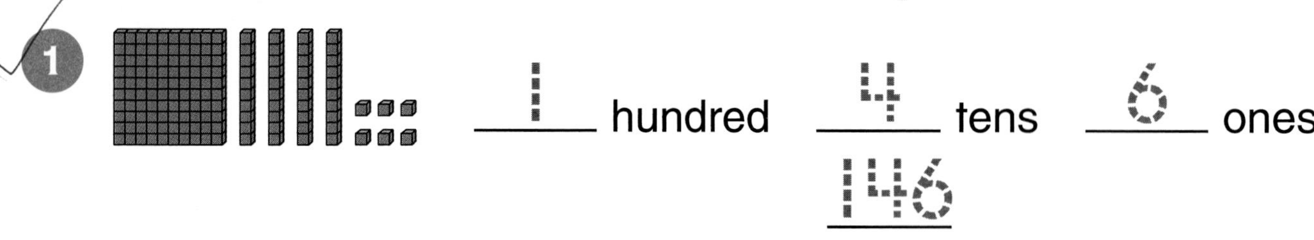

1. 1 hundred 4 tens 6 ones

146

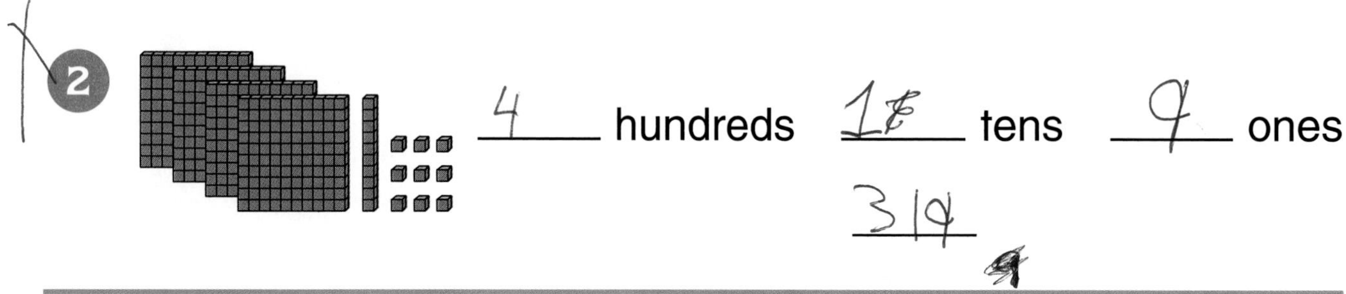

2. ____ hundreds ____ tens ____ ones

____

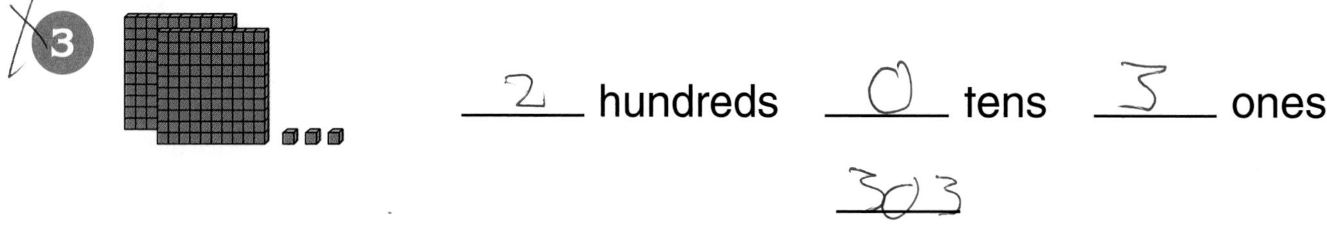

3. ____ hundreds ____ tens ____ ones

____

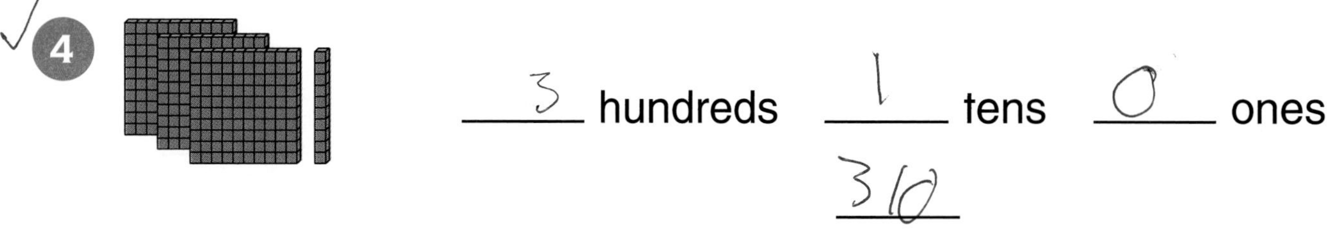

4. ____ hundreds ____ tens ____ ones

____

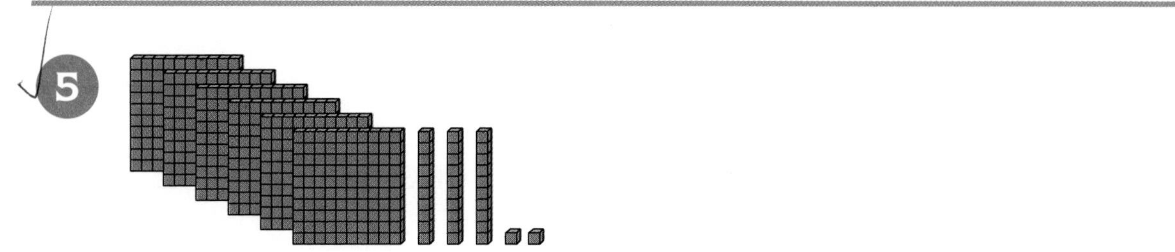

5. ____ hundreds ____ tens ____ ones

____

At Home: Have your child tell you the number of hundreds, tens, and ones for this page number.

Name ______________________

Place Value

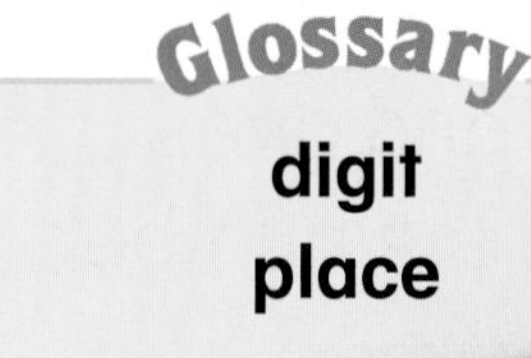

Two hundred six students play in the Parkview High School band.

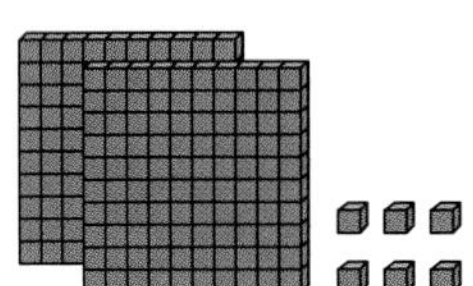

hundreds	tens	ones
2	0	6

206

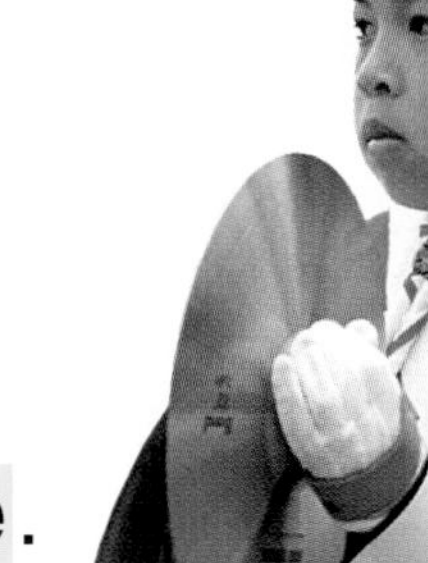

Tell why the **digit** 2 is in the hundreds **place**.
Tell why there is a 0 in the tens place.

Write how many hundreds, tens, and ones.
Write the number.

1. 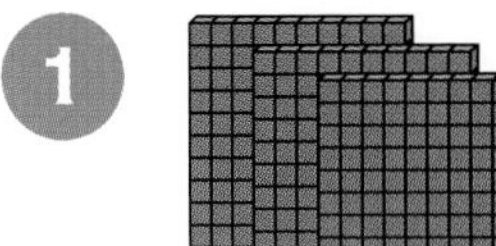

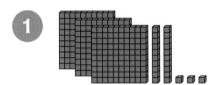

hundreds	tens	ones

______

---

2. 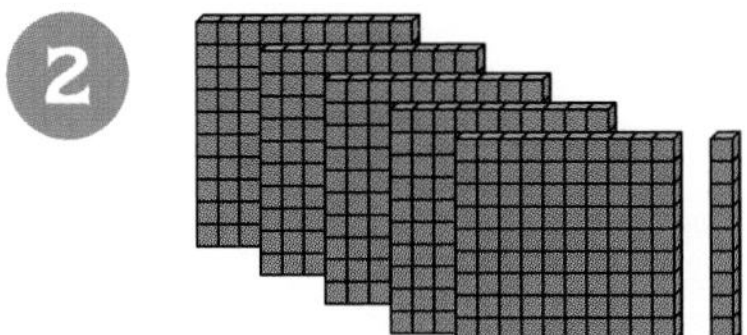

hundreds	tens	ones

______

---

3. 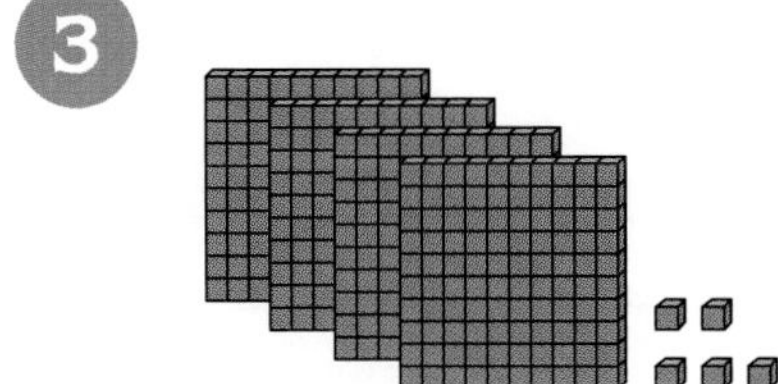

hundreds	tens	ones

______

What is the greatest 3-digit number you can write with the digits 0, 2, and 8?

Practice!

Write a 0 when there are no tens or no ones.

Write how many hundreds, tens, and ones.
Write the number.

1. 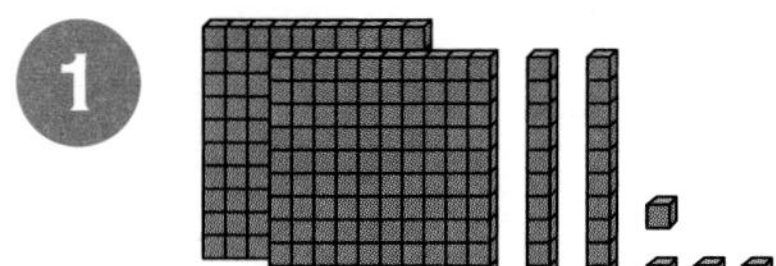

hundreds	tens	ones
2	2	4

224

2. 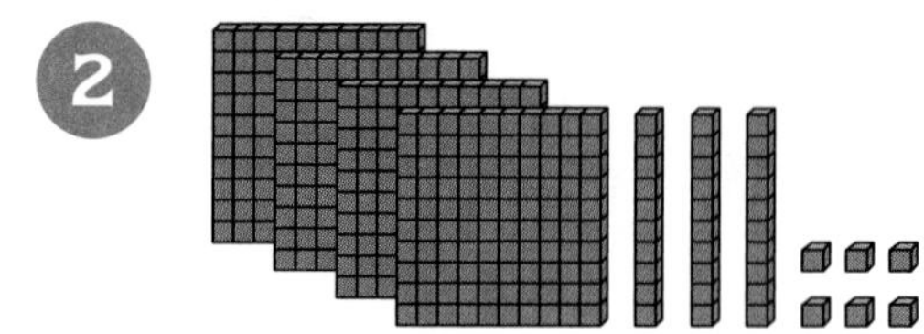

hundreds	tens	ones

______

3. 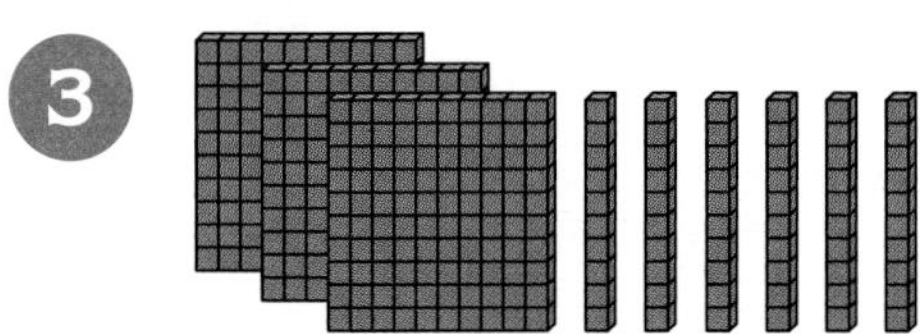

hundreds	tens	ones

______

4. 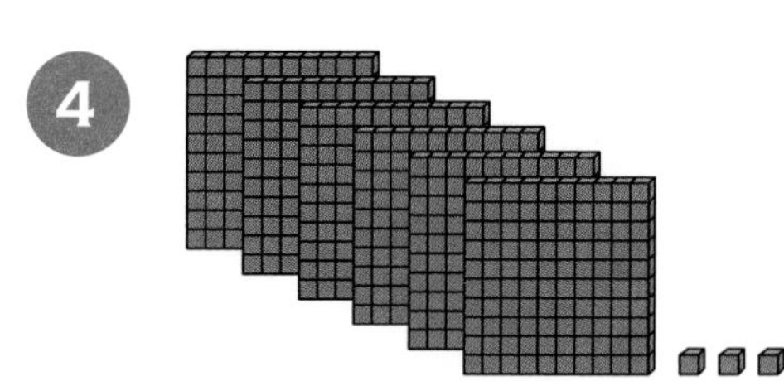

hundreds	tens	ones

______

More to Explore Number Sense

Here is another way to write numbers.

5 hundreds 2 tens 1 one

500 + 20 + 1   521

1 hundred 8 tens 6 ones

____ + ____ + ____   ____

9 hundreds 0 tens 4 ones

____ + ____ + ____   ____

2 hundreds 7 tens 0 ones

____ + ____ + ____   ____

At Home

We continue to work with 3-digit numbers. Ask your child to write the number for 9 hundreds 9 tens 9 ones.

Name ____________________

Explore Activity

Value of a Digit

Glossary

value

There were 452 tickets sold for the school concert.

hundreds	tens	ones
4	5	2

The **value** of 4 is 400.
The value of 5 is 50.
The value of 2 is 2.

In the number 162, how do you know if the 6 means 600, 60, or 6?

Working Together

Take turns.

- Write a 3-digit number.
- Circle one of the digits.
- Your partner writes the value of the circled digit.

	3-digit number	value of circled digit
1	(1)38	100
2		
3		
4		
5		

	3-digit number	value of circled digit
6		
7		
8		
9		
10		

What is the same about 432 and 234?
What is different?

Practice!

Circle to show the value of the underlined digit.

1	3<u>8</u>7	800	(80)	8
2	<u>6</u>92	600	60	6
3	5<u>4</u>	400	40	4
4	8<u>1</u>6	100	10	1
5	14<u>3</u>	300	30	3
6	<u>8</u>0	800	80	8
7	<u>7</u>77	700	70	7

Cultural Connection

Early Arabic Numbers

Early Arabic numbers did not use a zero.
Instead, dots showed what a digit meant.
One dot above a digit meant *tens*.
Two dots above a digit meant *hundreds*.

$\dot{7}2 = 72$ $\ddot{7}\dot{2} = 720$

$\ddot{7}2 = 702$ $\ddot{7}\dot{2}2 = 722$

Write the number.

$\ddot{2}6 =$ 206 $\ddot{8}7 =$ ______ $\ddot{2}\dot{1} =$ ______

$\ddot{1}\dot{7}4 =$ ______ $\ddot{1}\dot{2} =$ ______ $\ddot{6}\dot{1}8 =$ ______

We learned the value of digits in 3-digit numbers. Have your child tell you what the 2 means in 523.

Name ______________________

Extra Practice
Game !

What's My Number?

Play in a large group. Sit in a circle.

- The leader thinks of a secret 3-digit number.
- Each person in turn asks a question about the number.
- The leader answers *yes* or *no*.
- As you hear clues, write them down.

Winner: the player who guesses the number
The winner becomes the new leader.

Is the number greater than 100?

Yes.

Write clues here or use your own paper.

hundreds	tens	ones

Write how many hundreds, tens, and ones.
Write the number.

hundreds	tens	ones

______

2
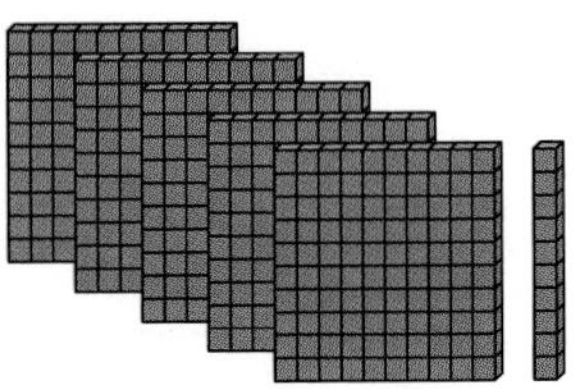

hundreds	tens	ones

______

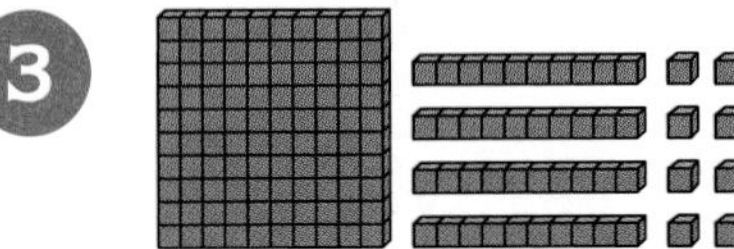

hundreds	tens	ones

______

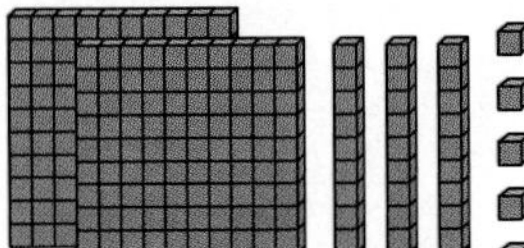

hundreds	tens	ones

______

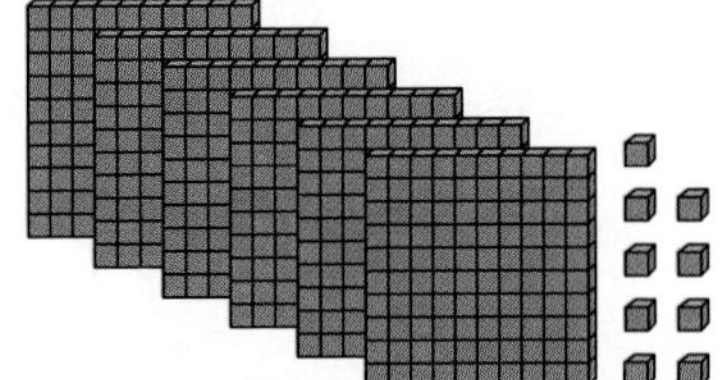

hundreds	tens	ones

______

Circle to show the value of the underlined digit.

6. 970 (7 underlined) 700 70 7

7. 462 (4 underlined) 400 40 4

8. 804 (4 underlined) 400 40 4

9. 153 (1 underlined) 100 10 1

Name ____________________

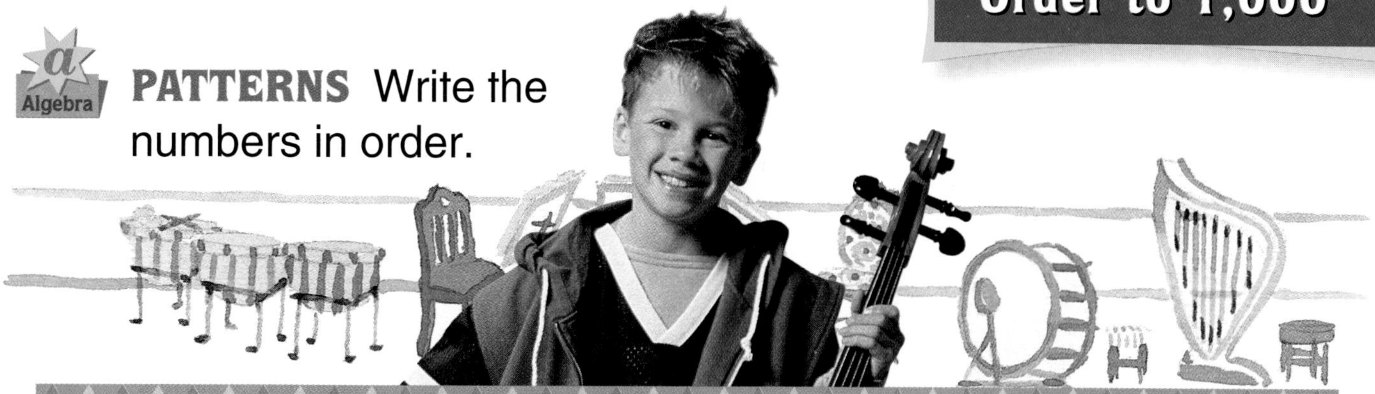

PATTERNS Write the numbers in order.

101	102	103							110
111				115					120
						127			
		133							
				145					
151									
								169	
	172								
							188		
									200

What is the number pattern going across?
What is the number pattern going down?
What is the number pattern going from right to left?

Practice!

Remember the patterns in the chart.

Write the missing numbers.

1. 412, 413, 414, 415, 416, 417, 418

2. 994, 995, 996, ____, ____, 999, ____

3. 279, 280, 281, ____, ____, ____, ____

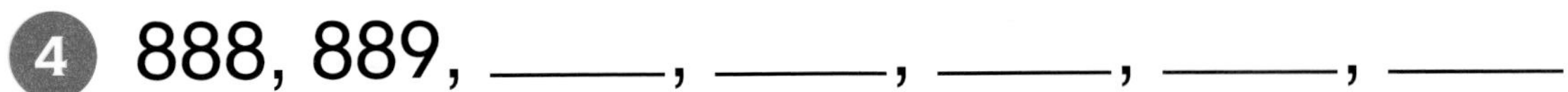

4. 888, 889, ____, ____, ____, ____, ____
5. 327, 326, 325, 324, 323, 322, ____
6. 683, 682, 681, ____, ____, ____, ____
7. 748, 747, ____, 745, ____, ____, ____
8. 560, 559, ____, ____, ____, ____, ____
9. ____, 263, ____, 265, ____, ____, ____

More to Explore Patterns

PATTERNS Skip-count to connect the dots.

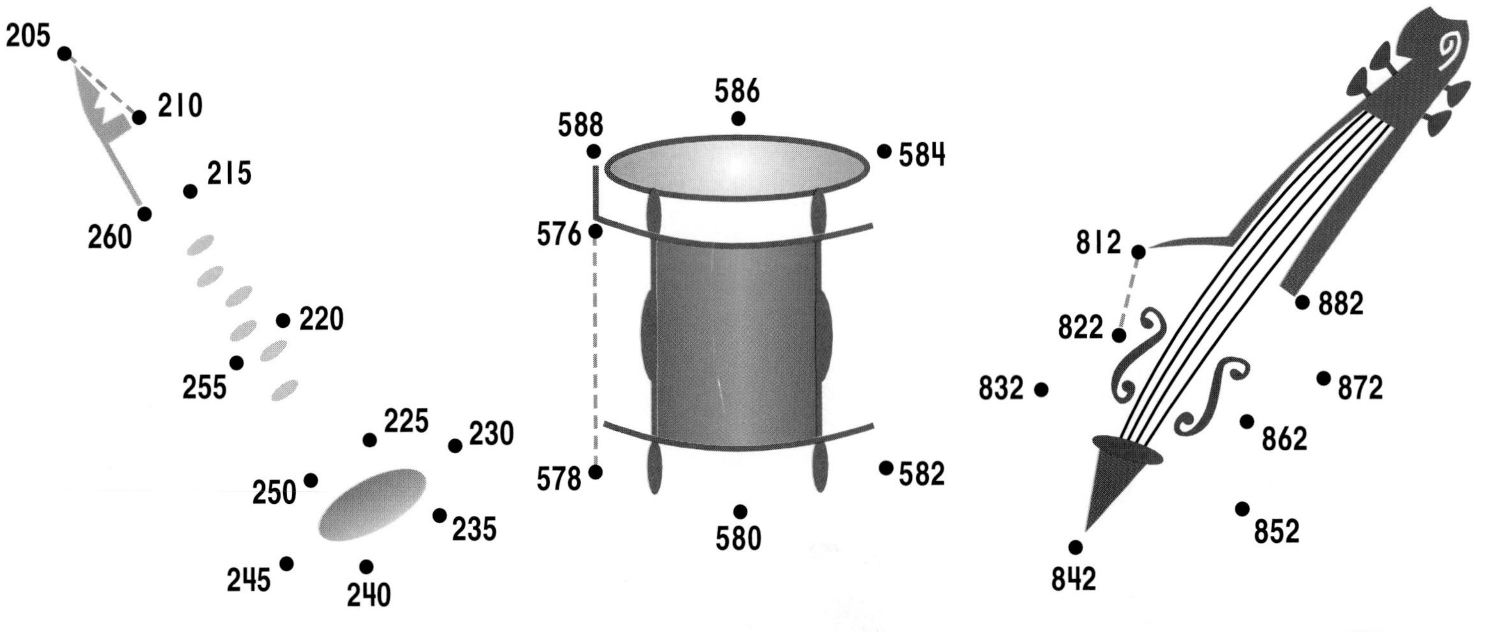

We counted in order to 1,000. Ask your child to count from 950 to 1,000.

Name

Before, After, Between

Peter put his numbered sheets of music in order from least to greatest.

284
285
286
284 is just before 285.
285 is between 284 and 286.
286 is just after 285.
287

Write the number that is just after.

1. 697 698 | 202 ___ | 439 ___

2. 755 ___ | 170 ___ | 999 ___

Write the number that is just before.

3. 562 563 | ___ 888 | ___ 390

4. ___ 941 | ___ 427 | ___ 775

Write the number that is between.

5. 816 817 818 | 188 ___ 190

6. 633 ___ 635 | 945 ___ 947

Practice!

Write the number just after, just before, or between.

1.  806 ___ ___ 799

2. 158 ___ 160 806 ___ ___ 637

3. 339 ___ 951 ___ 953 ___ 400

4. 674 ___ 676 289 ___ 291

5. 554 ___ 831 ___ 833 ___ 262

Mixed Review Test Preparation

Add or subtract.

6.

59	34	83	24	52	67
+ 37	− 8	+ 6	+ 24	− 19	− 36

Write how many equal parts.

7. 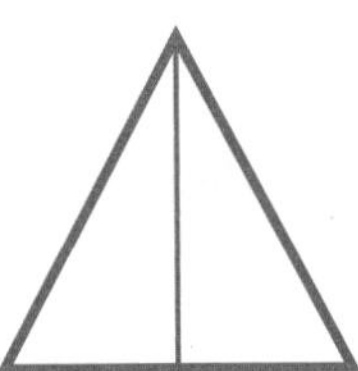 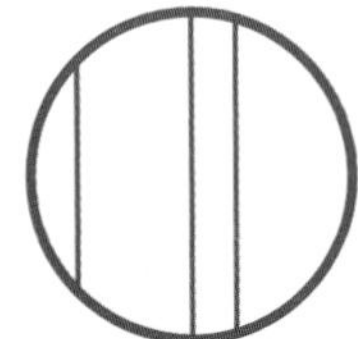 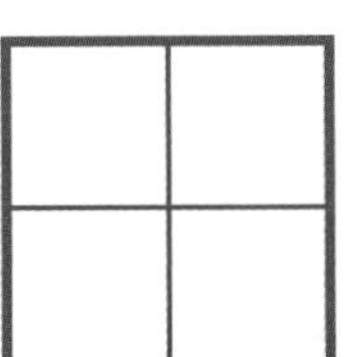

___ ___ ___

At Home: We learned more about ordering numbers to 1,000. Ask your child to tell you the number that comes just after 600.

Name ______________________

Compare Numbers to 1,000

Glossary
compare

A music store has 118 opera CDs. It has 135 jazz CDs. Which kind of CDs does the store have more of?

Compare 118 and 135 to find out.

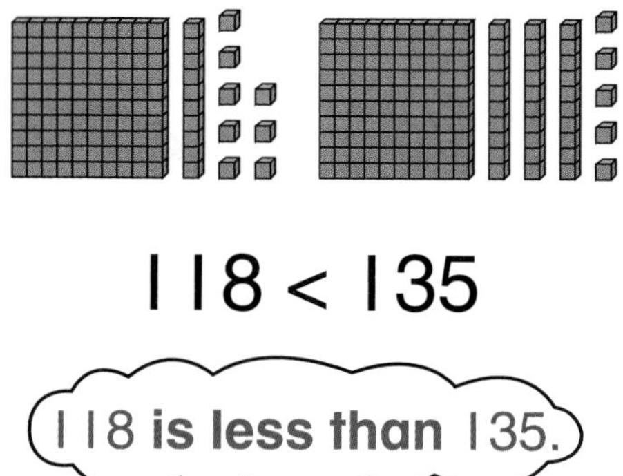

118 < 135

118 **is less than** 135.

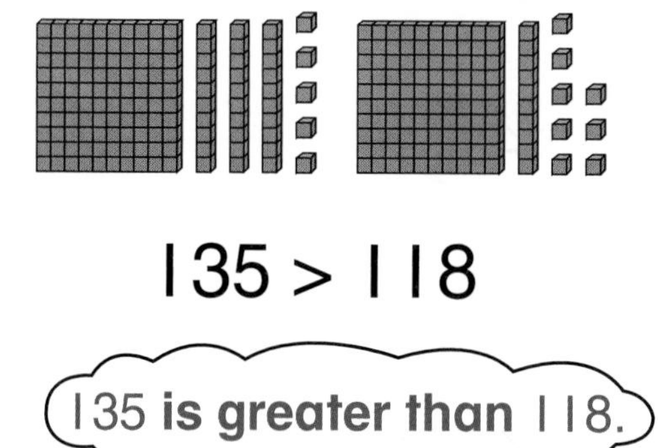

135 > 118

135 **is greater than** 118.

The store has more jazz CDs.

Working Together

You and your partner need 10 hundreds, 18 tens, and 18 ones.

Take turns.

- You show a 3-digit number with models.
- Your partner shows a different 3-digit number.
- Write the numbers below.
- Compare. Write > or <.

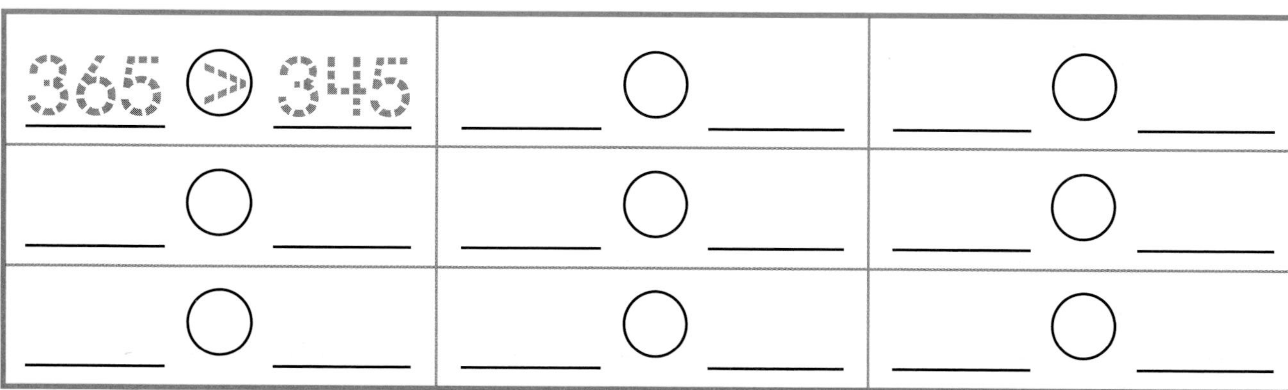

365 (>) 345	____ ○ ____	____ ○ ____
____ ○ ____	____ ○ ____	____ ○ ____
____ ○ ____	____ ○ ____	____ ○ ____

Practice!

Compare. Write $>$ or $<$.

Remember:
$>$ means *is greater than.*
$<$ means *is less than.*

1	341 $>$ 241	194 ○ 199	673 ○ 623
2	556 ○ 159	978 ○ 987	480 ○ 380
3	179 ○ 279	747 ○ 737	255 ○ 329
4	908 ○ 897	499 ○ 498	84 ○ 174
5	470 ○ 475	283 ○ 224	636 ○ 549
6	264 ○ 363	219 ○ 608	933 ○ 930
7	838 ○ 818	147 ○ 347	
8	335 ○ 330	421 ○ 428	

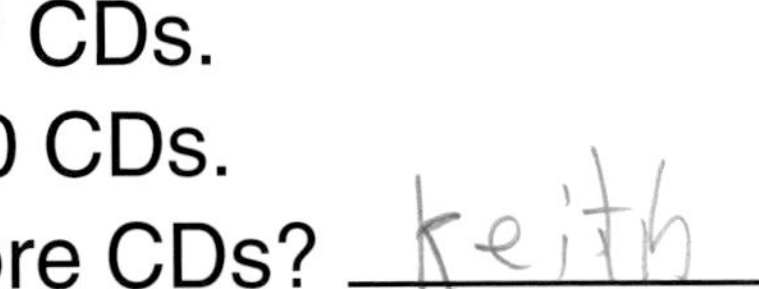

Solve.

9. Mimi's family has 139 CDs.
Keith's family has 160 CDs.
Whose family has more CDs? ______

10. Choose two 3-digit numbers.
Use them to write a word problem about comparing. Then solve it.

Write how to put these numbers in order from least to greatest.

347	385
147	305

At Home: We used the symbols $>$ and $<$ to compare numbers. Ask your child to tell whether 987 is greater than or less than 798.

Name ______________________________

Extra Practice
Game!

Get to the Concert!

You and your partner need 2 game markers, a spinner, and a number cube.

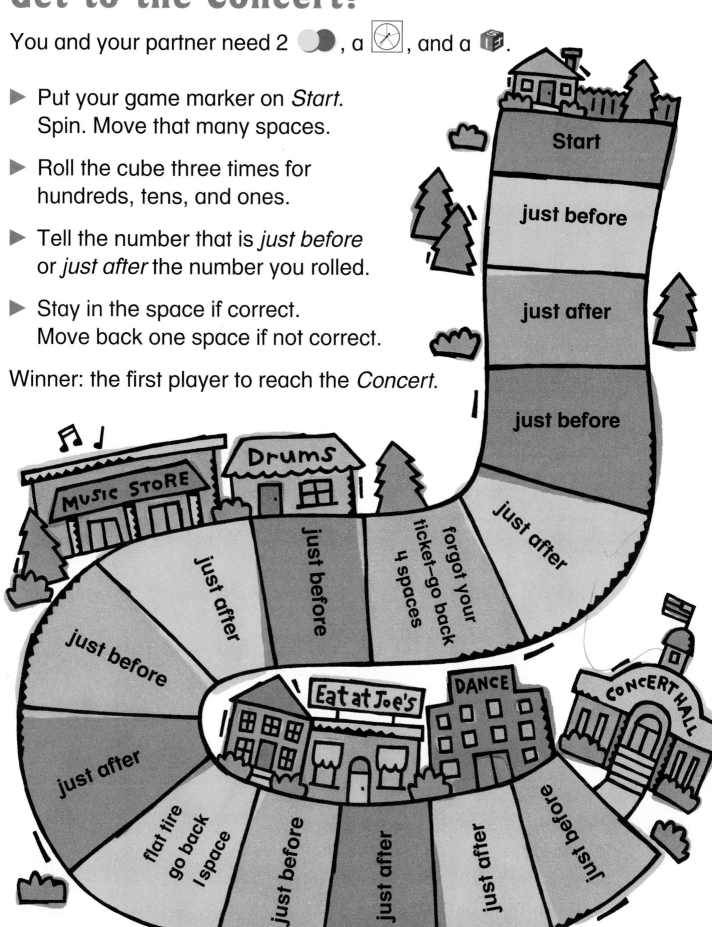

- Put your game marker on *Start*. Spin. Move that many spaces.
- Roll the cube three times for hundreds, tens, and ones.
- Tell the number that is *just before* or *just after* the number you rolled.
- Stay in the space if correct. Move back one space if not correct.

Winner: the first player to reach the *Concert*.

Start
just before
just after
just before
just after
forgot your ticket–go back 4 spaces
just before
just after
just before
just after
flat tire go back 1 space
just before
just after
just after
just before

MUSIC STORE
Drums
Eat at Joe's
DANCE
CONCERT HALL

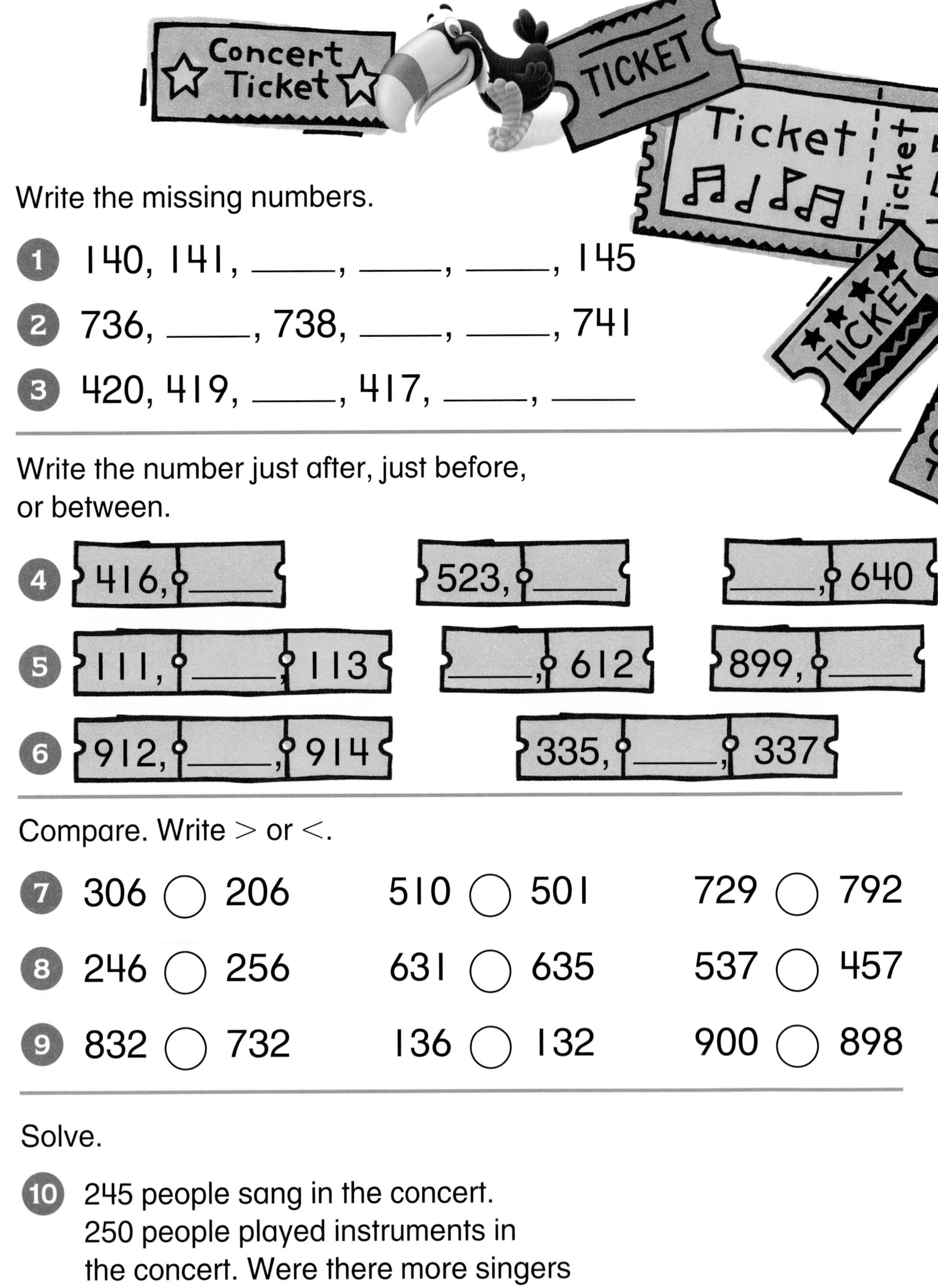

Write the missing numbers.

1. 140, 141, ____, ____, ____, 145
2. 736, ____, 738, ____, ____, 741
3. 420, 419, ____, 417, ____, ____

Write the number just after, just before, or between.

4. 416, ____   523, ____   ____, 640
5. 111, ____, 113   ____, 612   899, ____
6. 912, ____, 914   335, ____, 337

Compare. Write $>$ or $<$.

7. 306 ◯ 206   510 ◯ 501   729 ◯ 792
8. 246 ◯ 256   631 ◯ 635   537 ◯ 457
9. 832 ◯ 732   136 ◯ 132   900 ◯ 898

Solve.

10. 245 people sang in the concert. 250 people played instruments in the concert. Were there more singers or instrument players? ____________

Name ______________________________

Midchapter Review

Write how many hundreds, tens, and ones. Write the number.

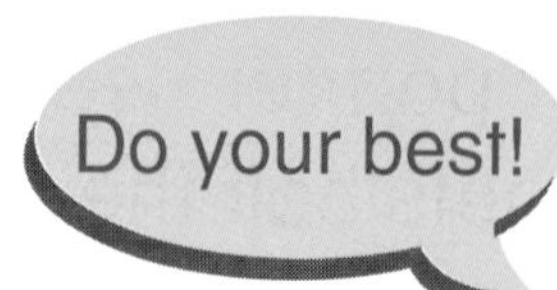

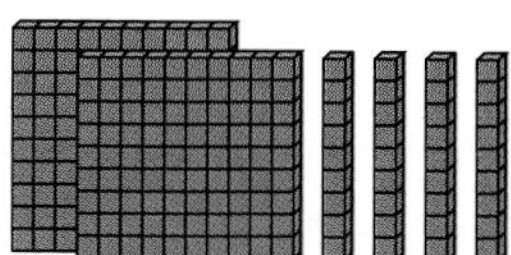

_____ hundreds _____ tens _____ ones

_____

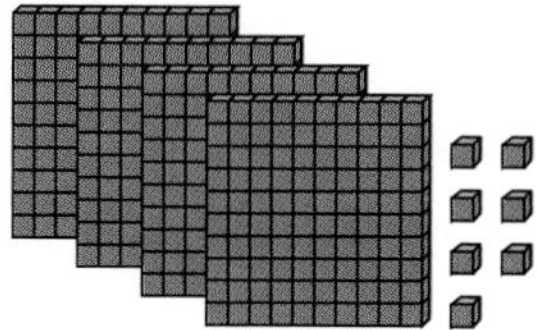

hundreds	tens	ones

_____

3. What does the digit 7 mean in 674?

   How do you know? ______________________

Write the missing numbers.

4. 937, 938, 939, _____, _____, _____

5. 603, _____, 605, _____, _____, _____

Write the number just after, just before, or between.

6. 198, _____, 200
7. 575, _____
8. _____, 611

Compare. Write > or <.

9. 329 ◯ 368
10. 897 ◯ 743

Tell how you compare 3-digit numbers.

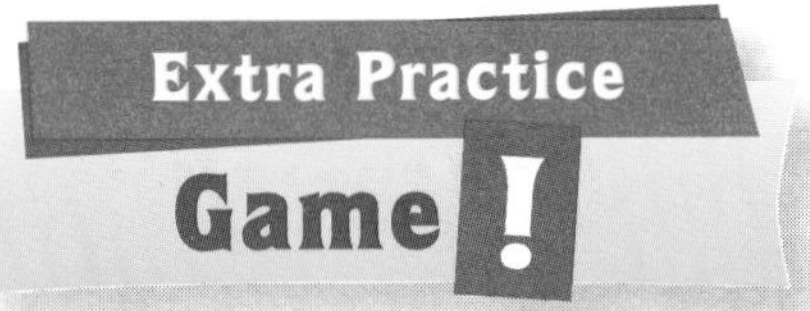

Comparing Cards

You and your partner need number cards. Each player gets half the cards.

- You and your partner each show the top three cards in your pile.
- Make the greatest 3-digit number that you can. Compare your numbers.
- The player with the greater number wins all six cards.

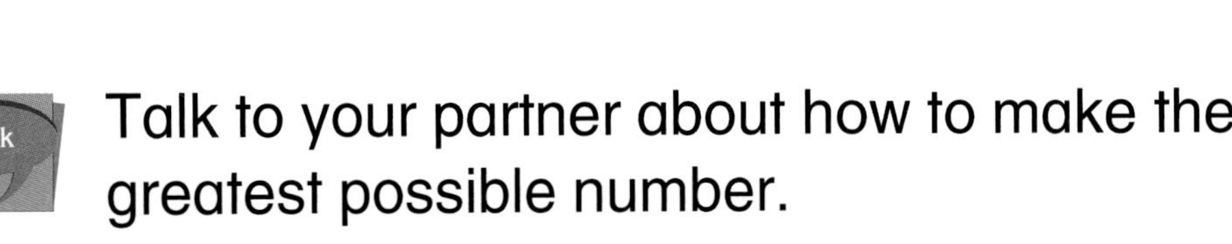

Talk to your partner about how to make the greatest possible number.

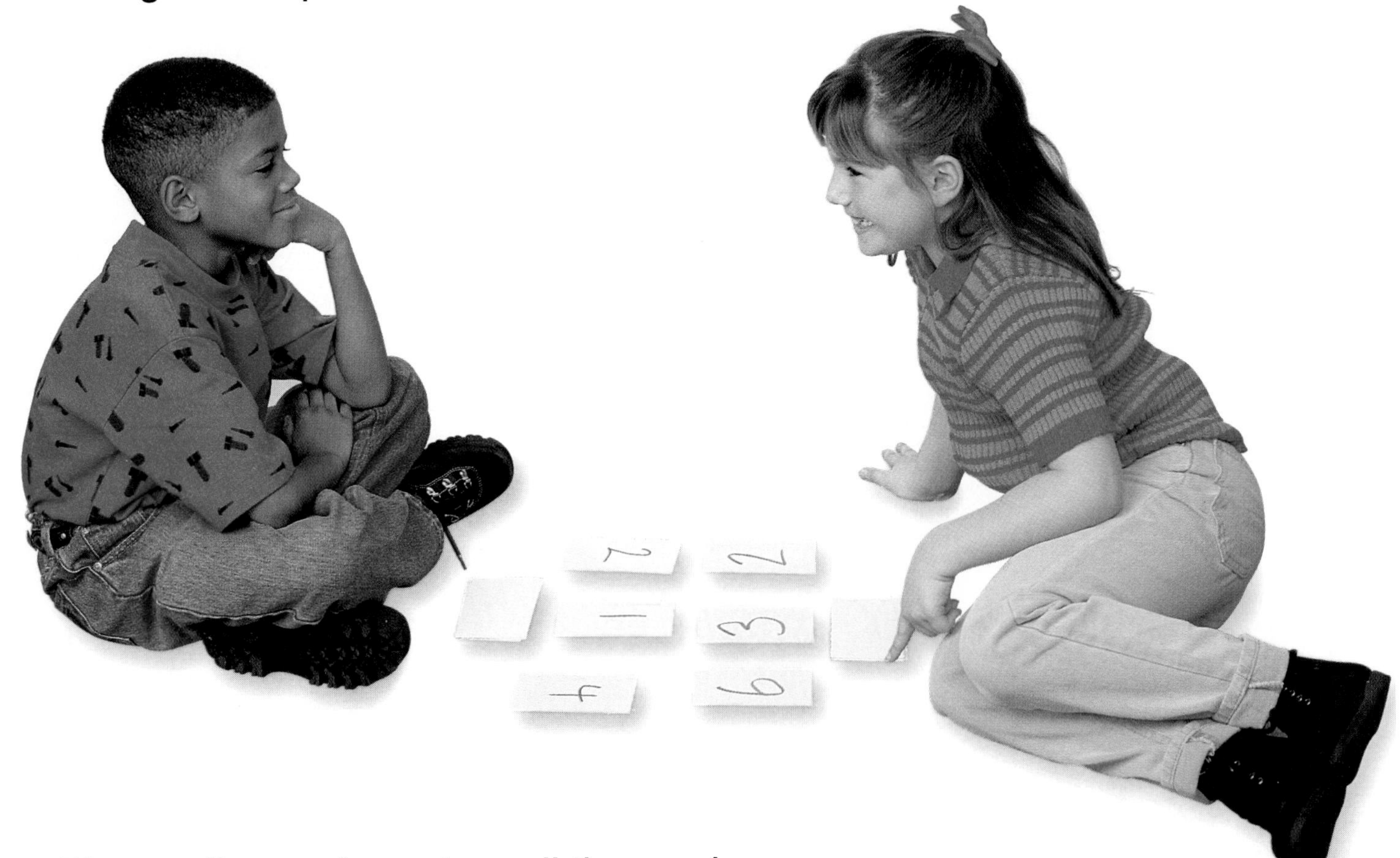

Play until one player has all the cards.

Play again. Make the least possible number.

Name ____________________

A Music Tour

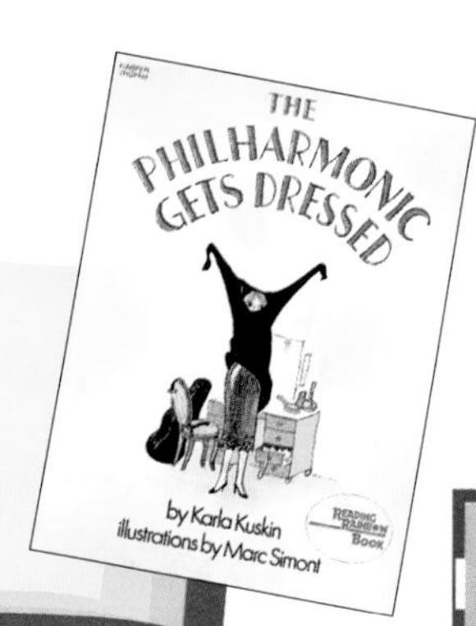

Listen to *The Philharmonic Gets Dressed.*

Each year the New York Philharmonic tours for 1 month.

The tour director is planning a short tour. The orchestra will visit six cities.

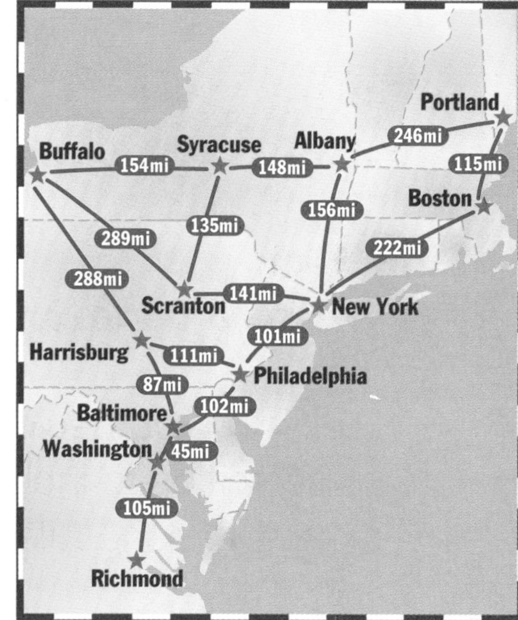

***mi* stands for miles**

Working Together

- Your group will make a tour schedule for the orchestra.
- Look at the map. Choose six cities.
- Decide on the order of cities to visit. Find the shortest route.

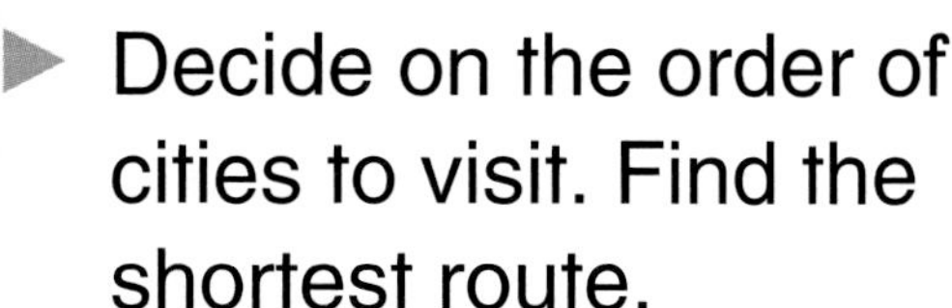

- Make notes for what you decide.

Decision Making

1. Decide what to include on your schedule. Think about what the orchestra needs to know.

2. Make a schedule.

Write a report.

3. Tell how you decided which cities to include on your tour schedule.

4. Explain how you found the shortest route for the tour.

More to Investigate

PREDICT What if the tour director only wants to travel 1,000 miles on the tour. Would you have to change your schedule?

EXPLORE 

Try different methods for finding the total miles.

FIND Compare your total miles to 1,000. Show how you could change your schedule.

Name

Working Together

You and your partner need 6 [hundreds block] and 20 [tens rod].

- You show some tens.
- Your partner shows some tens.
- Complete the table.

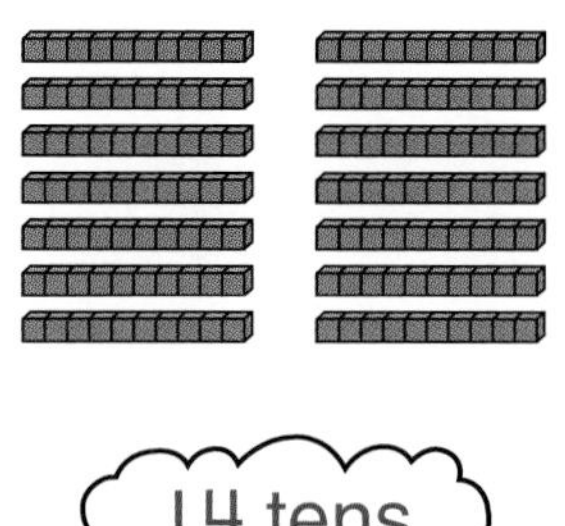

Regroup 10 tens as 1 hundred.

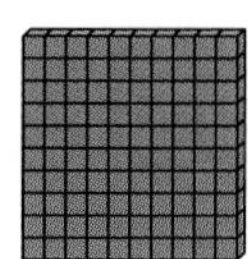
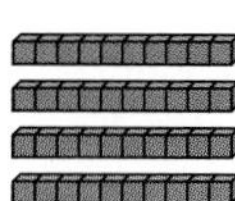

14 tens

1 hundred

4 tens

	How many tens?	Can you regroup?	How many hundreds and tens?
1	14 tens	(yes) no	1 hundreds 4 tens
2	____ tens	yes no	____ hundreds ____ tens
3	____ tens	yes no	____ hundreds ____ tens
4	____ tens	yes no	____ hundreds ____ tens
5	____ tens	yes no	____ hundreds ____ tens
6	____ tens	yes no	____ hundreds ____ tens
7	____ tens	yes no	____ hundreds ____ tens

When can't you regroup?

Practice!

Use models. Show the hundreds, tens, and ones. Regroup when you can. Write the number.

1. 3 hundreds 11 tens 6 ones

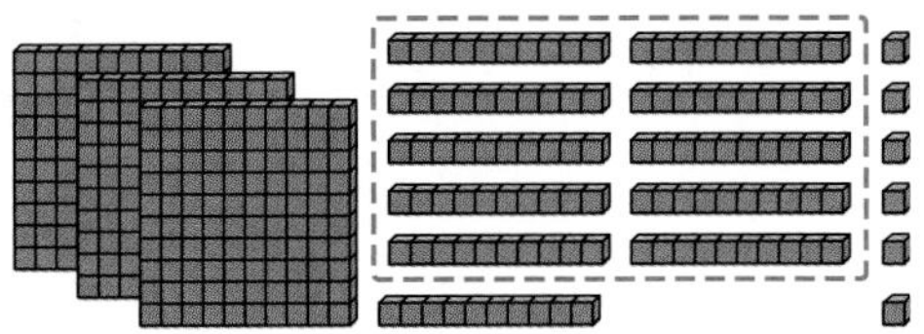

hundreds	tens	ones
4	1	6

2. 6 hundreds 2 tens 9 ones

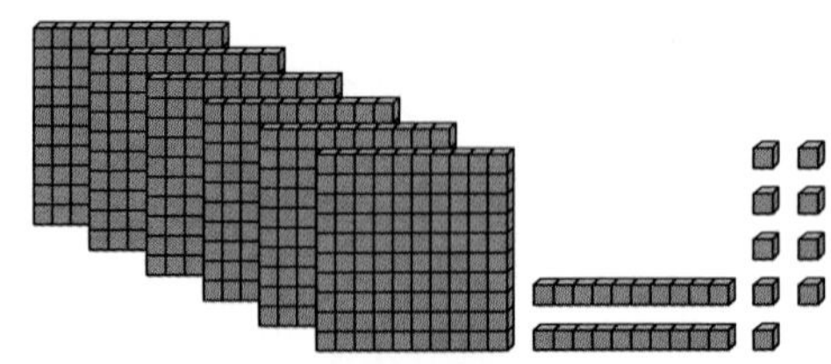

hundreds	tens	ones

3. 5 hundreds 15 tens

hundreds	tens	ones

4. 1 hundred 18 tens 3 ones

hundreds	tens	ones

5. 2 hundreds 9 tens 1 one

hundreds	tens	ones

6. 4 hundreds 16 tens 2 ones

hundreds	tens	ones

More to Explore — Number Sense

Without adding, which sums will be greater than 100? Ring them.

$\begin{array}{r} 49 \\ +\ 83 \\ \hline \end{array}$ $\begin{array}{r} 27 \\ +\ 21 \\ \hline \end{array}$ $\begin{array}{r} 68 \\ +\ 78 \\ \hline \end{array}$ $\begin{array}{r} 43 \\ +\ 33 \\ \hline \end{array}$ $\begin{array}{r} 38 \\ +\ 72 \\ \hline \end{array}$ $\begin{array}{r} 40 \\ +\ 53 \\ \hline \end{array}$

At Home We regrouped 10 tens for 1 hundred. Ask your child how to regroup 15 tens.

Name ____________________

Add 3-Digit Numbers

You need 9 [hundreds], 20 [tens], and 20 [ones].
Add 156 + 273.

Add the ones. Regroup when you can.

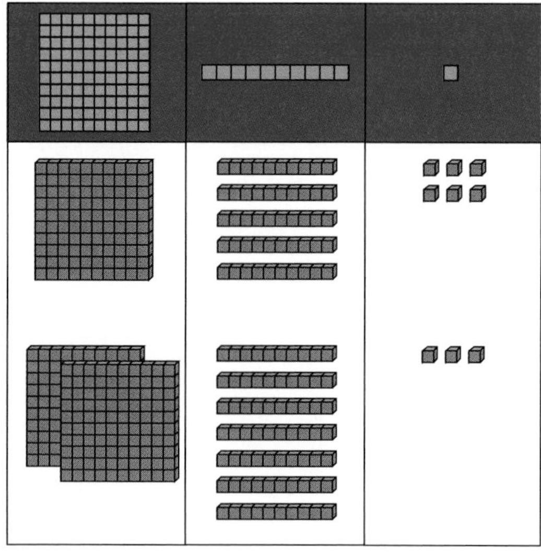

	hundreds	tens	ones
	☐	☐	
	1	5	6
+	2	7	3
			9

9 ones

Add all the tens. Regroup when you can.

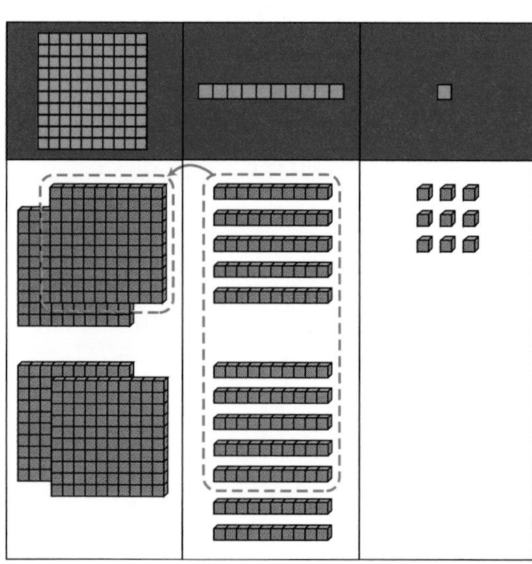

	hundreds	tens	ones
	1	☐	
	1	5	6
+	2	7	3
		2	9

12 tens
1 hundred 2 tens

Add all the hundreds.

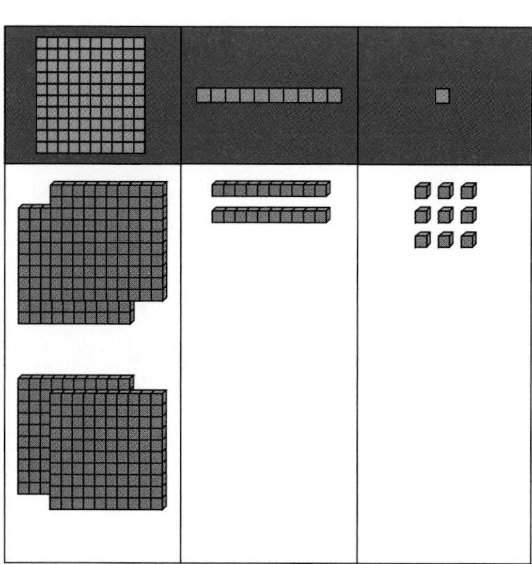

	hundreds	tens	ones
	1	☐	
	1	5	6
+	2	7	3
	4	2	9

Practice!

Add. Use hundreds, tens, and ones models to help.

1

	hundreds	tens	ones
	3	2	9
+	1	3	8
	4	6	7

	hundreds	tens	ones
		7	5
+	6	7	1

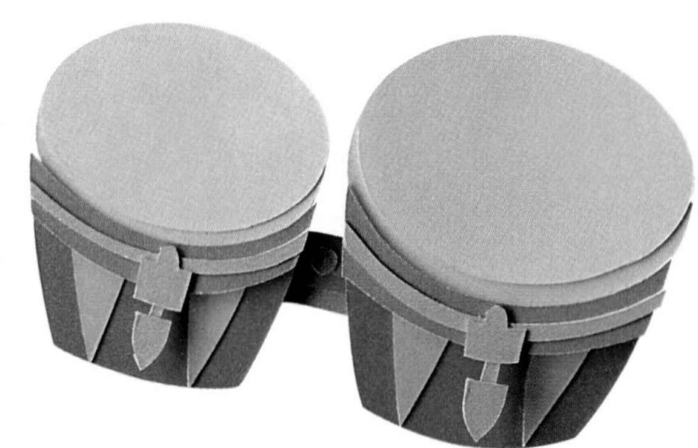

2

	hundreds	tens	ones
		5	2
+	5	6	3

	hundreds	tens	ones
	4	2	8
+	1	3	4

	hundreds	tens	ones
	2	0	4
+	3	7	5

3

	hundreds	tens	ones
	4	3	1
+			9

	hundreds	tens	ones
	1	4	9
+	2	7	0

	hundreds	tens	ones
	6	4	6
+		5	2

4

	hundreds	tens	ones
	3	8	7
+	4	9	0

	hundreds	tens	ones
	5	3	7
+	1	3	9

	hundreds	tens	ones
	6	1	2
+	1	9	4

At Home We began adding with 3-digit numbers. Ask your child to tell you about adding 329 + 138.

Name ________________

More Adding 3-Digit Numbers

The band sold 368 CDs last year.
This year they have sold 185 CDs.
How many CDs has the band sold?

Add the ones. Regroup when you can.	Add all the tens. Regroup when you can.	Add all the hundreds.
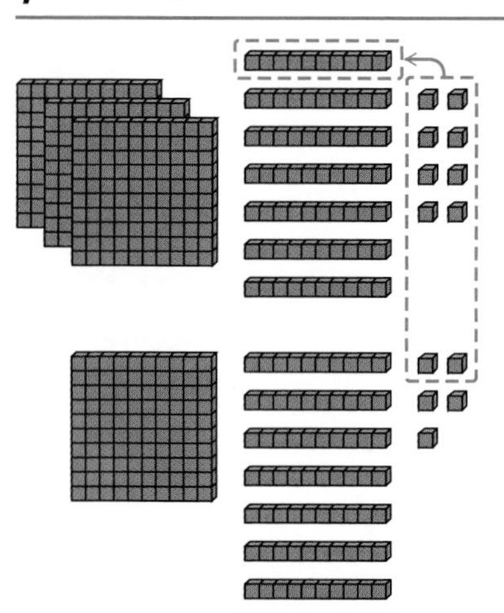	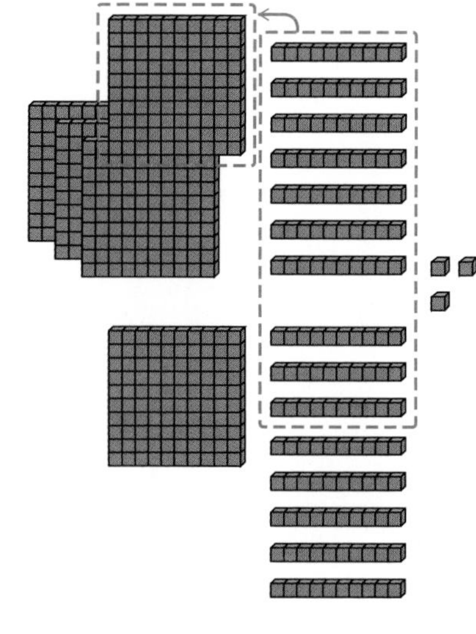	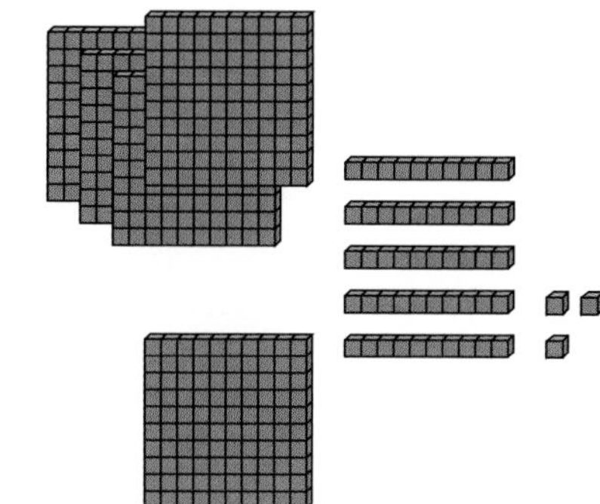
$\begin{array}{r} \square\,1 \\ 368 \\ +\ 185 \\ \hline 3 \end{array}$	$\begin{array}{r} 1\,1 \\ 368 \\ +\ 185 \\ \hline 53 \end{array}$	$\begin{array}{r} 1\,1 \\ 368 \\ +\ 185 \\ \hline 553 \end{array}$
13 ones 1 ten 3 ones	15 tens 1 hundred 5 tens	5 hundreds

The band sold 553 CDs.

Add.

1. $\begin{array}{r} 1\,1 \\ 349 \\ +\ \ 63 \\ \hline 412 \end{array}$ $\begin{array}{r} 195 \\ +\ 606 \\ \hline \end{array}$ $\begin{array}{r} 427 \\ +\ 231 \\ \hline \end{array}$ $\begin{array}{r} 564 \\ +\ \ \ 8 \\ \hline \end{array}$ $\begin{array}{r} 79 \\ +\ 312 \\ \hline \end{array}$

Practice!

Add.

1. $\begin{array}{r} 297 \\ +\ 315 \\ \hline 612 \end{array}$ $\quad$ $\begin{array}{r} 48 \\ +\ 468 \\ \hline \end{array}$ $\quad$ $\begin{array}{r} 670 \\ +\ 126 \\ \hline \end{array}$

2. $\begin{array}{r} 175 \\ +\ 473 \\ \hline \end{array}$ $\quad$ $\begin{array}{r} 847 \\ +\ 151 \\ \hline \end{array}$ $\quad$ $\begin{array}{r} 325 \\ +\ 85 \\ \hline \end{array}$

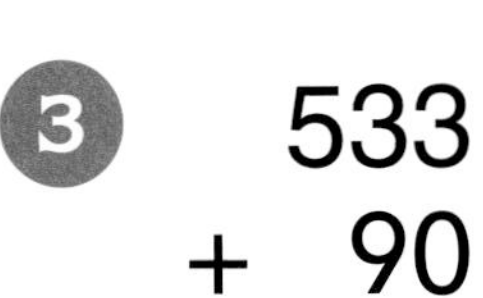

3. $\begin{array}{r} 533 \\ +\ 90 \\ \hline \end{array}$ $\quad$ $\begin{array}{r} 488 \\ +\ 286 \\ \hline \end{array}$ $\quad$ $\begin{array}{r} 172 \\ +\ 69 \\ \hline \end{array}$ $\quad$ $\begin{array}{r} 394 \\ +\ 7 \\ \hline \end{array}$ $\quad$ $\begin{array}{r} 406 \\ +\ 422 \\ \hline \end{array}$

Solve.

4. There are 379 rock-and-roll cassettes.
There are 452 classical cassettes.
How many cassettes are there? _____ cassettes

5. One bin in the music store had 68 CDs. Another bin had 256 CDs. How many CDs are in both bins? _____ CDs

6. 

Write a word problem.
Use the numbers 273 and 685.
Have a partner solve the problem.

Use your own paper.

We continue to add with 3-digit numbers. Ask your child to explain how to add 394 + 27.

Name ______________________________

Extra Practice
Game!

Reach 999!

Each team needs 9 , 20 , 20 , and a .

Teams take turns.

- Start with 8 and 6 . Write 86 in the chart.
- Throw the cube three times to get hundreds, tens, and ones. Write the number in the chart. Show the number with models.
- Combine the new and old models. Regroup when you can. Write the new number.

Winner: the first team to reach or pass 999

	hundreds	tens	ones
		8	6
+			
+			
+			
+			
+			
+			
+			

Add.

1	430 + 84 = 514	257 + 686	375 + 149	6 + 508	347 + 383
2	291 + 456	711 + 4	38 + 338	425 + 172	268 + 693
3	24 + 580	432 + 389	8 + 146	304 + 76	257 + 256

Compare/Contrast

Use the chart to answer the questions.

	West Band	East Band
Bugle Players	138	126
Drummers	46	46
Flute Players	0	10

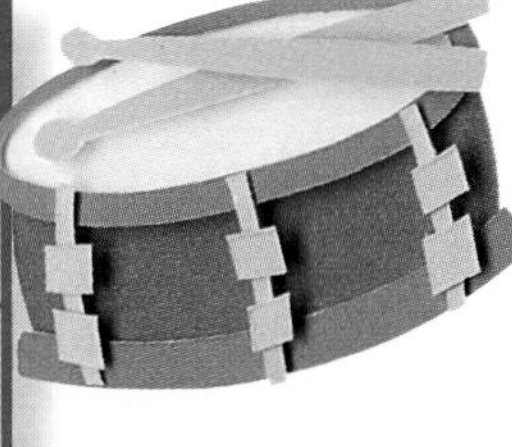

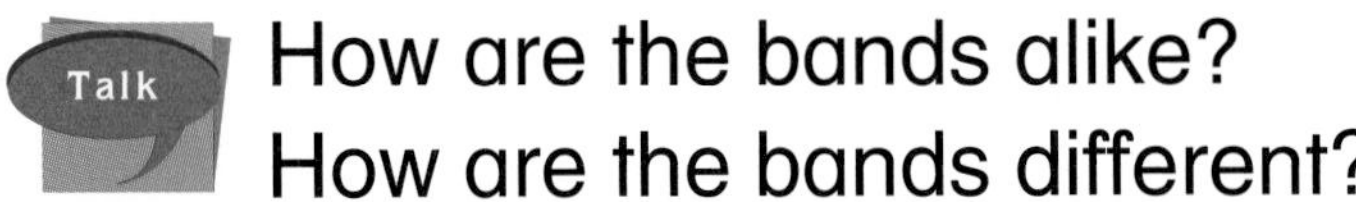

How are the bands alike?
How are the bands different?

Write a word problem that compares the two bands. Have a partner solve it.

Use your own paper.

Name ____________________

Explore Activity

Regrouping for Subtraction

Working Together

You and your partner need 7 [hundreds], 20 [tens], and 9 [ones].

Take turns.

- Your partner shows hundreds, tens, and ones.
- You regroup if needed. Take away hundreds, tens, and ones.
- Write the number that is left.

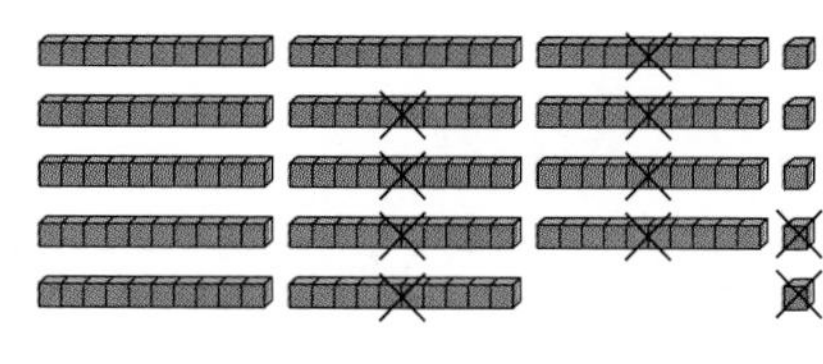

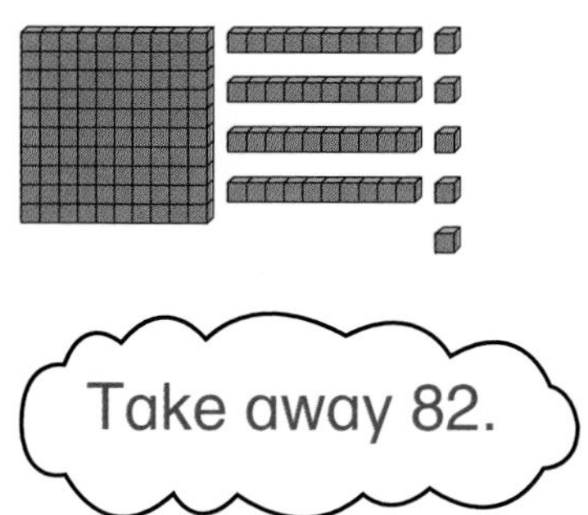

	Show.	Take away.	Did you regroup?	Number left.
1	145	82	(yes) no	63
2	284	144	yes no	
3	205	184	yes no	
4	132	51	yes no	
5	507	95	yes no	
6	328	217	yes no	
7	459	166	yes no	

Practice!

Use [hundred block], [ten rod], and [one cube] to show the number. Complete the chart.

	Show.	Take away.	Did you regroup?	Number left.
1	641	250	(yes) no	391
2	397	172	yes no	
3	436	63	yes no	
4	308	154	yes no	
5	122	71	yes no	
6	659	447	yes no	
7	275	65	yes no	

Mixed Review Test Preparation

Choose the tool you would use to measure:

8 how tall a bottle is.

Use mental math to add or subtract.

9 18 + 20 = ____ 10 + 80 = ____ 42 + 2 = ____

10 50 – 20 = ____ 33 – 30 = ____ 75 – 15 = ____

At Home: We regrouped I hundred as 10 tens. Ask your child how to subtract 429 – 60.

Name ____________________

Subtract 3-Digit Numbers

You need 9 hundreds, 20 tens, and 20 ones.
Subtract 318 − 165.

**Look at the ones.
Regroup if you need to.
Subtract the ones.**

	hundreds	tens	ones
	☐	☐	☐
	3	1	8
−	1	6	5
			3

3 ones left

**Look at the tens.
Regroup if you need to.
Subtract the tens.**

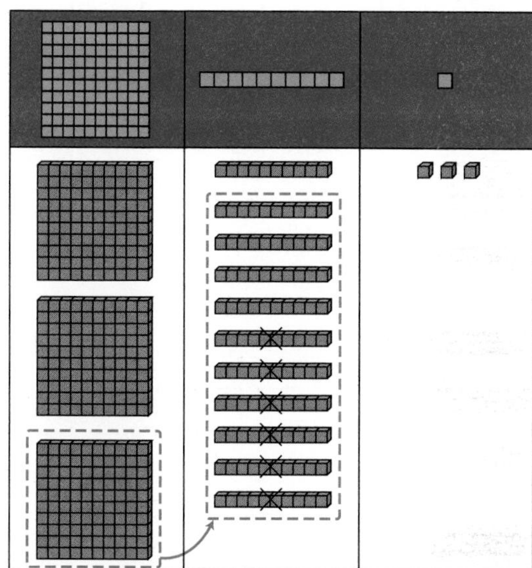

	hundreds	tens	ones
	2	11	☐
	~~3~~	~~1~~	8
−	1	6	5
		5	3

5 tens left

Subtract the hundreds.

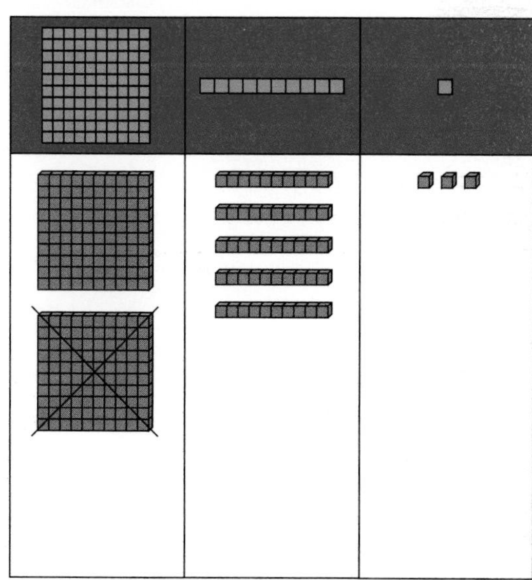

	hundreds	tens	ones
	2	11	☐
	~~3~~	~~1~~	8
−	1	6	5
	1	5	3

1 hundred left

Practice!

Subtract. Use hundreds, tens, and ones models to help.

1

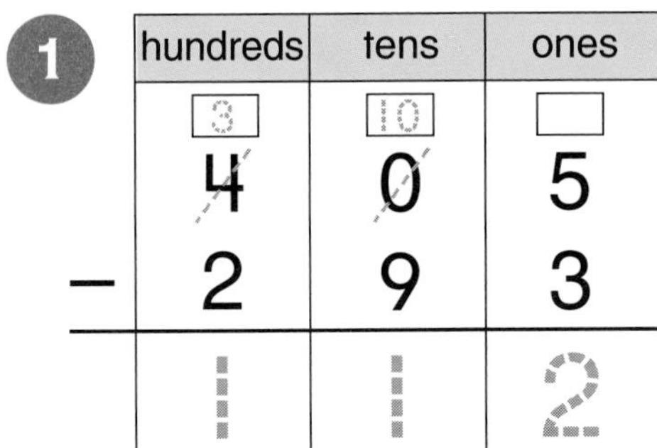

	hundreds	tens	ones
	3	10	
	4	0	5
−	2	9	3
	1	1	2

	hundreds	tens	ones
	8	6	4
−	3	7	1

2

	hundreds	tens	ones
	5	4	6
−		8	3

	hundreds	tens	ones
	8	7	7
−	6	0	4

	hundreds	tens	ones
	4	1	7
−	1	3	5

3

	hundreds	tens	ones
	3	2	1
−	2	6	0

	hundreds	tens	ones
	6	6	4
−	1	7	2

	hundreds	tens	ones
	2	0	9
−		1	8

4

	hundreds	tens	ones
	9	2	9
−	4	3	7

	hundreds	tens	ones
	7	3	8
−			6

	hundreds	tens	ones
	6	3	1
−	3	7	0

At Home: We began subtracting with 3-digit numbers. Ask your child to tell you about subtracting 405 − 293.

Name

More Subtracting 3-Digit Numbers

The drama club had 143 students try out for parts in a musical.
109 students did not get parts.
How many students got parts?

Look at the ones. Regroup if you need to. Subtract the ones.	Look at the tens. Regroup if you need to. Subtract the tens.	Subtract the hundreds.
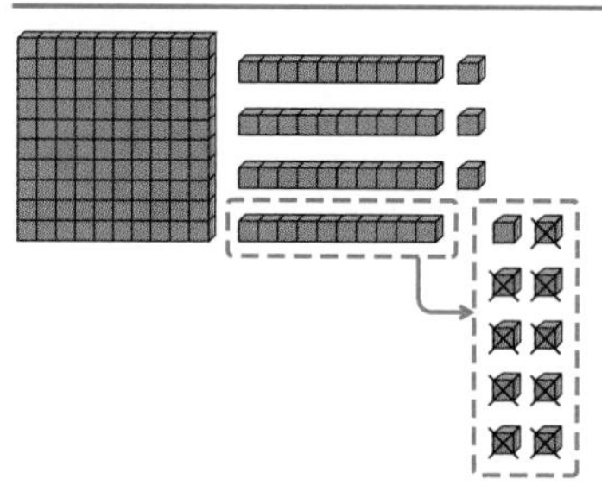	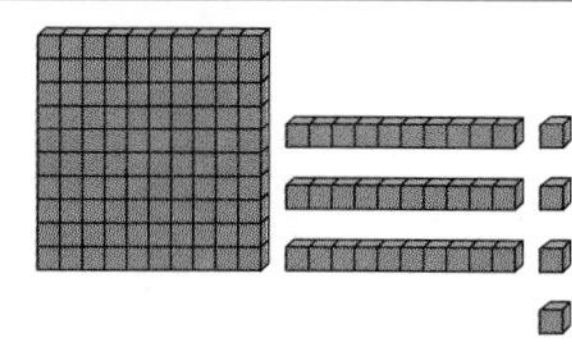	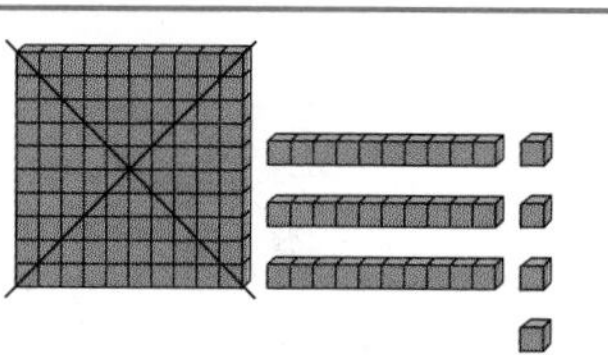
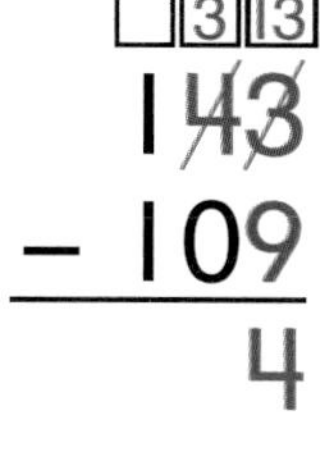 143 − 109 = 4	143 − 109 = 34	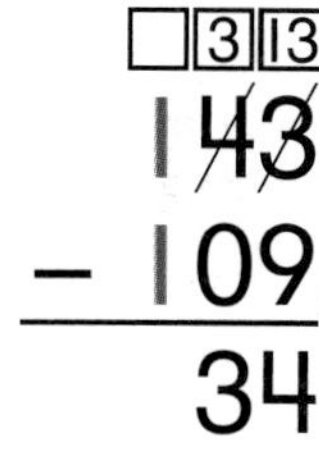 143 − 109 = 34
 4 ones	3 tens	0 hundreds

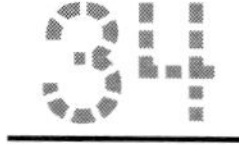 34 students got parts.

Subtract.

1. 895 − 407 = 488   462 − 138   531 − 325   227 − 164   739 − 6

McGraw-Hill School Division

Practice!

Subtract.

1	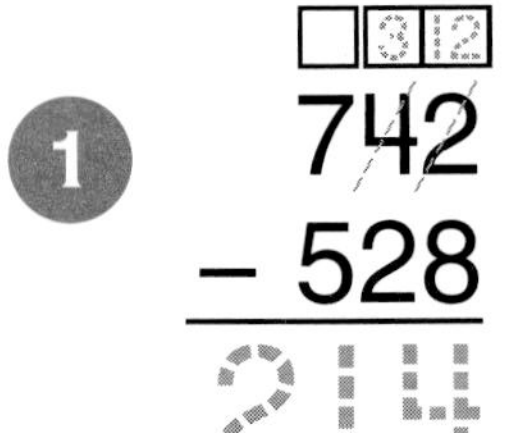 742 − 528 = 214	528 − 383	254 − 32		
2	416 − 173	399 − 268	860 − 435		
3	657 − 234	270 − 180	768 − 475	444 − 313	993 − 567

Solve.

4. The auditorium has 328 seats.
53 seats are empty during the play.
How many seats are filled?
_____ seats

5. 390 people went to the musical on Monday.
287 people went on Tuesday. How many more people went to the musical on Monday than Tuesday?
_____ people

6. Write Use the numbers 527 and 182 to write a word problem.
Have a partner solve the problem.

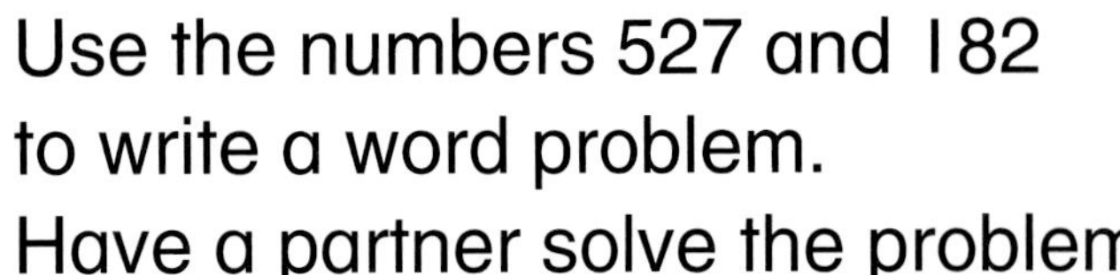

We continue to subtract with 3-digit numbers. Ask your child to explain how to subtract 993 – 567.

Name

Subtraction Action

You and your partner need 2 .

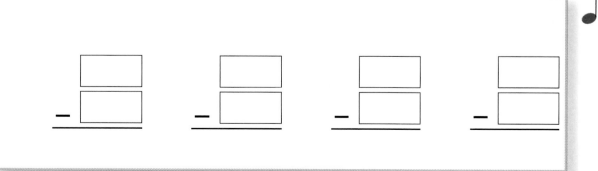

Take turns.

- Drop a counter on each sheet of music. Write the subtraction.
- Subtract.

Starting number

382	967	439	553	875
545	694	833	729	387
929	736	689	418	896

Number to subtract

307	191	5	204	60
91	129	215	13	382
8	353	82	271	160

Subtraction exercises

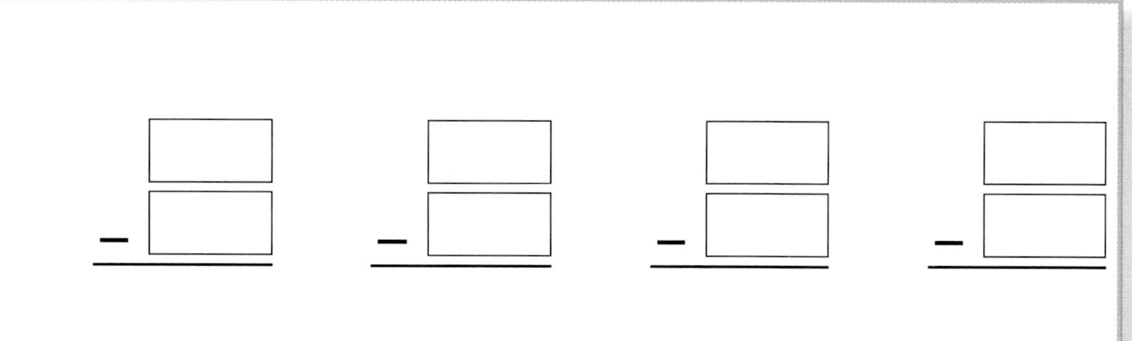

Subtract.

1	4 12 ~~5~~ ~~2~~ 8 − 463 65	851 − 339	374 − 7	643 − 220	967 − 685
2	230 − 28	589 − 412	438 − 293	724 − 13	152 − 136
3	987 − 656	360 − 112	138 − 98	827 − 384	577 − 268

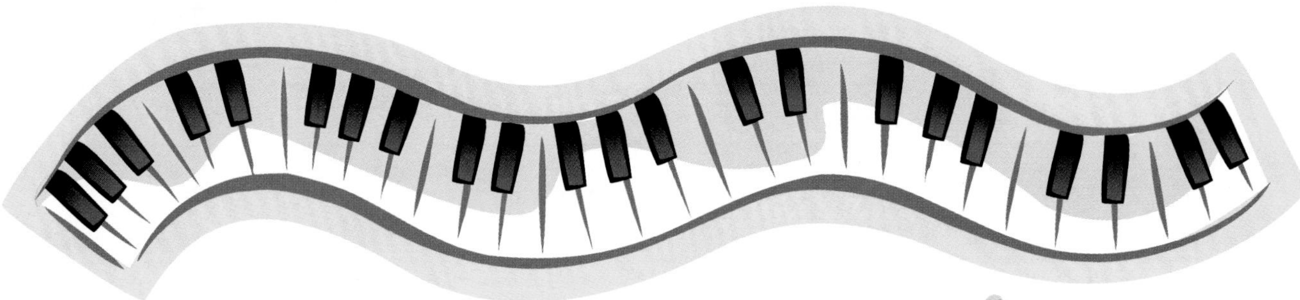

Solve.

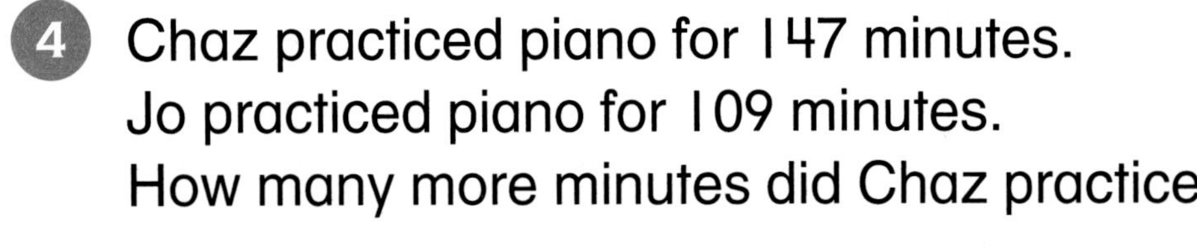

4 Chaz practiced piano for 147 minutes.
Jo practiced piano for 109 minutes.
How many more minutes did Chaz practice?

_____ minutes

5 The band room has 219 brass instruments.
There are 56 fewer stringed instruments.
How many stringed instruments are there?

_____ stringed instruments

Name ______________________________

Solve a Simpler Problem

Problem-Solving Strategy

Read | Plan | Solve | Look Back

Read A rock band traveled 336 miles on Monday. They traveled 428 miles on Tuesday. How many miles did the band travel during the 2 days?

Plan You can make the problem simpler.

Solve Think: 3 miles and 4 miles
How many miles?

You can add.

Add:
$$\begin{array}{r} 336 \\ +\ 428 \\ \hline 764 \end{array}$$

The band traveled ______ miles.

Look Back Does the answer make sense? Explain.

Solve.

1. The band sold 120 T-shirts. They also sold 239 posters and 385 tapes. How many more posters than T-shirts did the band sell?

____

What numbers did you think of to make problem 1 simpler?

Practice!

Solve.

1. Cheri travels 85 miles for her singing lesson. Then she travels 85 miles back home. She does this 2 times a week. How many miles does Cheri travel each week?

   ____

2. Sid played the song on page 327 of his songbook. He turned back 109 pages and played a second song. On what page was the second song?

   ____

3. A piano has 52 white keys and 36 black keys. How many more keys are white than black?

   ____

Cultural Note
Jazz is a mix of African, Latin, and American music. It began in New Orleans.

At Home We solved problems by thinking of simpler or easier numbers. Have your child explain how to solve problem 2 above.

Name

Add and Subtract Money

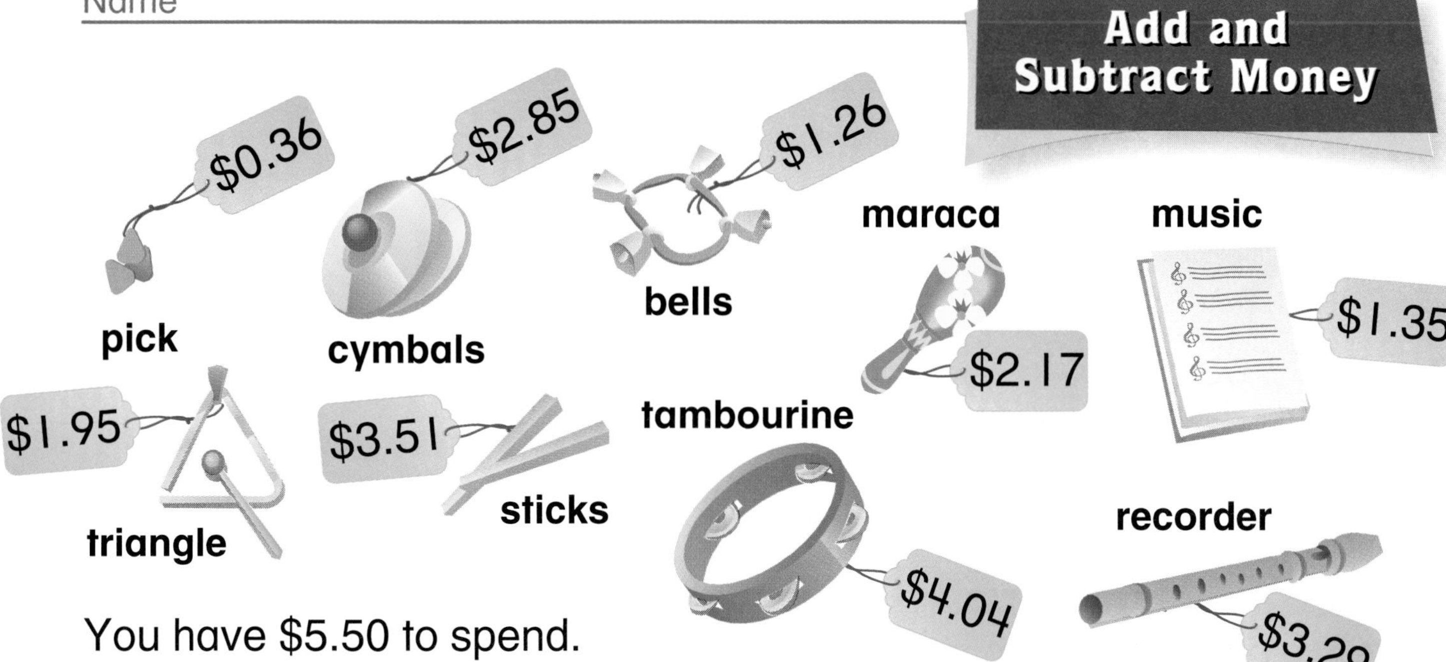

You have $5.50 to spend.

- Choose two different items to buy.
- Find the total cost.
- Find how much money you have left.

	Items	Total Cost	Money Left
1	maraca bells	\$2.17 + 1.26 \$3.43	\$5.50 − 3.43 \$2.07
2	______ ______		
3	______ ______		

Which two items can't you buy? Explain.

Practice!

CD $6.80

computer game $4.39

tape $3.75

video $5.56

Solve.

Workspace

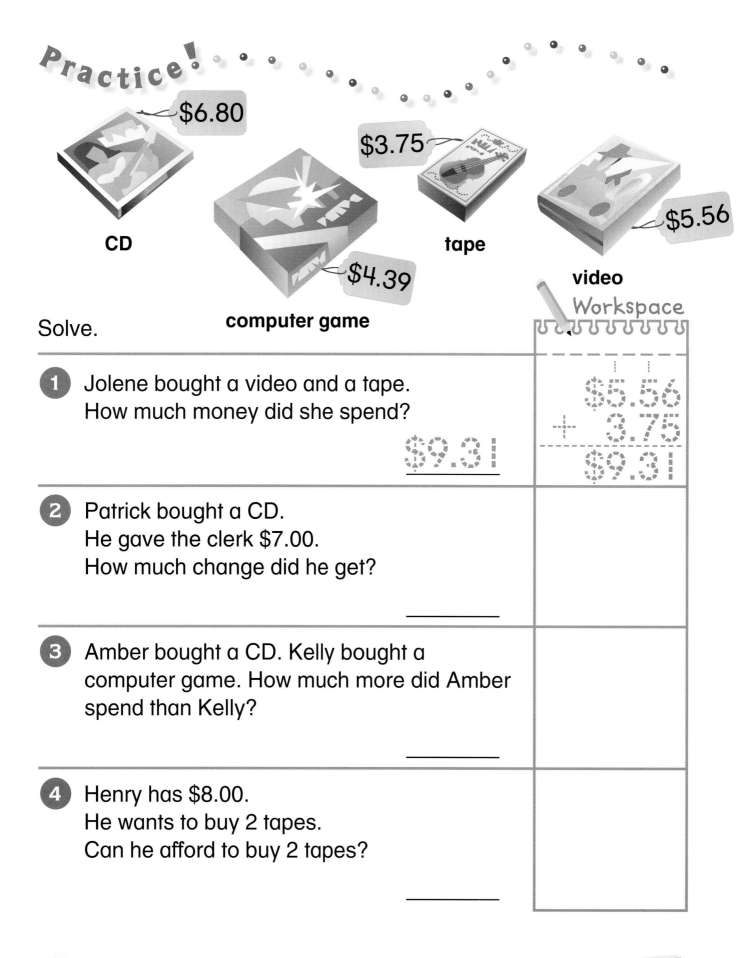

1 Jolene bought a video and a tape. How much money did she spend? $9.31	$5.56 + 3.75 = $9.31
2 Patrick bought a CD. He gave the clerk $7.00. How much change did he get? ______	
3 Amber bought a CD. Kelly bought a computer game. How much more did Amber spend than Kelly? ______	
4 Henry has $8.00. He wants to buy 2 tapes. Can he afford to buy 2 tapes? ______	

5 
Write
Write your own money problem.
Have a partner solve it.

Use your own paper.

At Home: We added and subtracted money amounts. Have your child find the total price of two items from a supermarket flyer.

Name ______________________

Choose the Method

When an orchestra travels, so do many instruments. The chart shows how much the instruments weigh.

Instrument	Weight
drum set	124 pounds
tuba	45 pounds
harp	239 pounds
double bass	52 pounds
piano	648 pounds

Solve. Choose the best method for you.

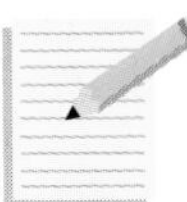

1. How much do the tuba and harp weigh together? ______ pounds

How did you solve the problem? Which method did you choose?

---

2. How much more does the piano weigh than the harp? ______ pounds

3. Which two instruments are the heaviest? ________________

4. How much do the two heaviest instruments weigh altogether? ______ pounds

Practice!

drum set	124 pounds
tuba	45 pounds
harp	239 pounds
double bass	52 pounds
piano	648 pounds

1. A truck can hold 600 pounds more. How many harps can fit?

   ____ harps

   How many more pounds can the truck hold now?

   ____ pounds

2. Which instruments would you put in a truck that could fit 600 pounds more? ______________________

   ____

Explain how you solved problem 2.

Write and Share

Meghan wrote this problem.

How much do the heaviest instrument and the lightest instrument weigh together?

Meghan Petchell
Northwest School
Howell, Michigan

3. Solve Meghan's problem. ______________________

   What method did you choose? ______________________

4. READING ARITHMETIC WRITING **Compare/Contrast** Write a problem that compares instruments. Use information from the chart. Have a partner solve it.

   Use your own paper.

   What method did your partner use? ______________________

At Home: Ask your child to tell you how to solve the problem he or she wrote.

Name

Chapter Review

Language and Mathematics

Choose the correct word to complete the sentence.

digit
hundred
value
3-digit number

1. The ______________ of the digit 4 is 400 in the number 415.

2. You can regroup 1 ______________ as 10 tens.

Concepts and Skills

Write how many hundreds, tens, and ones.
Write the number.

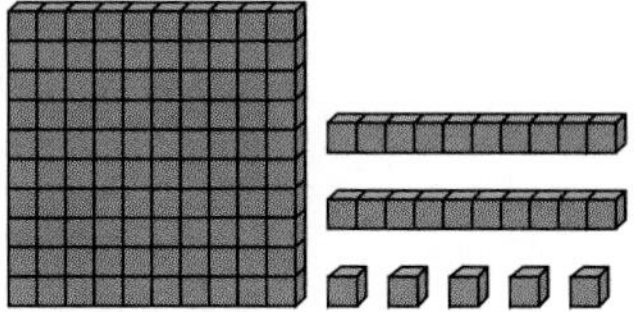

hundreds	tens	ones

______

125 ______ hundreds ______ tens ______ ones

4. 9 hundreds 3 tens 7 ones ______

Write the number just after, just before, or between.

5. 287, ______ 454, ______, 456 ______, 800

Compare. Write > or < .

6. 734 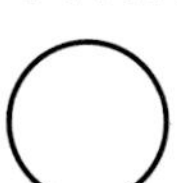 750 387  378

Add or subtract.

7.

$$\begin{array}{r} 677 \\ +\ 43 \\ \hline \end{array} \qquad \begin{array}{r} 442 \\ -\ 18 \\ \hline \end{array} \qquad \begin{array}{r} \$8.76 \\ -\ 5.47 \\ \hline \end{array} \qquad \begin{array}{r} \$1.95 \\ +\ 4.76 \\ \hline \end{array}$$

Problem Solving

Solve.

8. A songbook has 173 folk songs, 46 marches, and 126 jazz songs. How many more folk songs than jazz songs are there?

   _______ folk songs

9. Dino bought popcorn for $1.75 and juice for $2.15. What should his change be from $5.00?

   ____

10. Meg had 217 tapes. She bought 36 more. How many tapes does she have now?

   _______ tapes

What Do You Think?

Which is the quickest way to subtract 261 from 523?
☑ Check one.

☐ 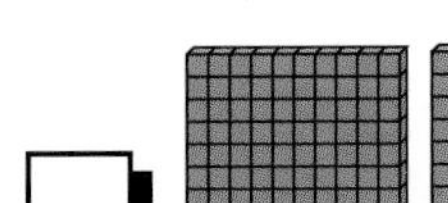 ☐ 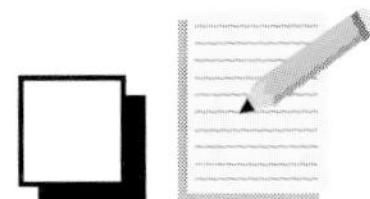 ☐ 

☐ 

Why? ________________________________

Write these exercises in your journal. Find the sums. Explain which is easier to add.

$$\begin{array}{r} \$1.04 \\ +\ 5.86 \\ \hline \end{array} \qquad \begin{array}{r} 369 \\ +\ 255 \\ \hline \end{array}$$

Name ______

Chapter Test

Write how many hundreds, tens, and ones.
Write the number.

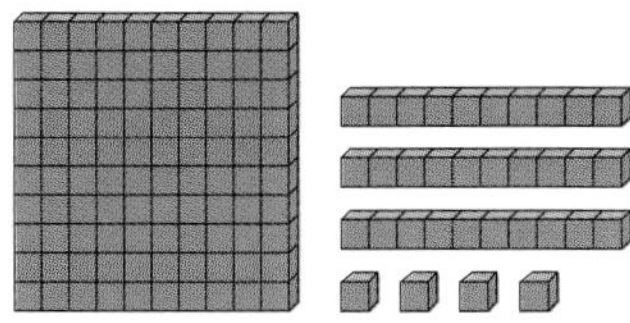

hundreds	tens	ones
1	3	4

______

2 620 ____ hundreds ____ tens ____ ones

3 8 hundreds 6 tens 5 ones ____

4 Write the number just after, just before, or between.

408, ____, 410   ____, 700   365, ____

5 Compare. Write > or <.

> means *is greater than.*
< means *is less than.*

831 ◯ 854   762 ◯ 759

Add or subtract.

6 561 + 372 = ____

7 $382 − 167 = ____

8 $292 + 365 = ____

9 893 − 268 = ____

Solve.

10 The band sold 225 tapes.
They also sold 109 CDs and 352 posters.
How many more tapes than CDs did the band sell?

____ tapes

Performance Assessment

What Did You Learn?

$3.95 harmonica

$5.05 piano

$6.42 drum

$4.63 trumpet

$3.63 flute

$6.88 xylophone

$2.57 violin

$4.90 music book

You have $9.00 to spend.
Which two toys could you buy?

Show as many combinations as you can.

____

____

____

____

You may want to put this page in your portfolio.

Math Connection

Calculator

Name ____________________

Compute with Greater Numbers

You can use a calculator to add and subtract greater numbers.

1,987
+ 4,530
6,517

Press these keys.

To add or subtract dollars and cents, you need to use the [•].

$5.53
− 2.89

Press these keys.

Use a calculator to add or subtract.

1. 5,241 − 3,875 = 1,366 $69.23 + 89.67 $17.30 − 6.82   2,348 + 5,629

2. 848 + 929 $52.18 − 24.75   9,200 − 4,867 $3.86 + 9.59

3. 700 − 433   6,009 − 3,667 $35.46 + 3.95   658 + 885

Curriculum Connection

Social Studies

Roman Numerals

The Romans of long ago used letters to name numbers.

To read **Roman numerals**, you need to add or subtract.

Roman Numeral	Our Numeral
I	1
V	5
X	10
C	100

XXX — Add letter values together. 10 + 10 + 10 = 30

XVII — Add letter values together. 10 + 5 + 1 + 1 = 17

IV — Subtract when a letter with less value comes just before a letter with greater value. 5 − 1 = 4

Glossary
Roman numerals

Write the number for each Roman numeral.

1. XC = 90
2. CCC = ______
3. IX = ______
4. VII = ______
5. CX = ______
6. XXII = ______

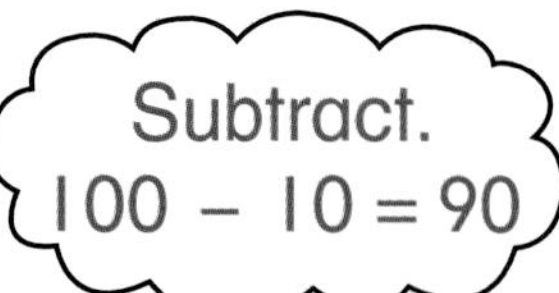

Write Roman numerals for each number.

7. 105 = CV
8. 33 = ______
9. 200 = ______
10. 101 = ______

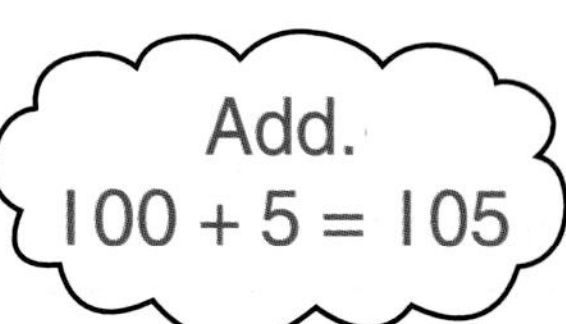

Home Connection

Chapter 11 Wrap-Up

Name

High Number, Low Number

PLAYERS 2

MATERIALS 3 sets of cards for 0 to 9

DIRECTIONS Each player picks 3 cards. Lay the cards faceup to show a 3-digit number. Compare the numbers. The player with the greater number takes all 6 cards. Play until all the cards are picked.

The winner is the player with the most cards.

This card game will help your child practice comparing two 3-digit numbers. Make 3 sets of cards for 0 to 9 from construction paper. A variation of the game would be to play rounds where the lesser number wins.

Dear Family,

I am beginning the last chapter in our mathematics book. I will be learning about multiplication and how to find how many groups and how many in each group.

3 groups of 2

$3 \times 2 = 6$

I will also be talking about food, especially vegetables.

Learning About Vegetables

Let's talk about different kinds of vegetables. We can tell about our favorite vegetables.

My Math Words

I am going to use these math words in this chapter.

Please help me make word cards for the math cards. I can use these word cards when I explore multiplication and division.

- multiply
- product
- factor
- make a table
- divide
- division sentence
- multiplication sentence

Your child,

____

Signature

Exploring Multiplication and Division

Theme: Vegetables

CHAPTER 12

JUNE 29, 1999

DAVID WIESNER

READING ARITHMETIC WRITING

Ask Questions You may have questions when you hear a story.

Listen to *June 29, 1999*. Then write one question about the story.

Ask a partner to answer your question.

Name ______________________

What Do You Know?

You and your friends are having a picnic.

This is what is in the basket.

Find out how many in all for each item. Show your work.

1. 4 bags with 2 sandwiches in each ______________________

____

2. 2 bags with 8 carrots in each ______________________

____

3. 2 packages with 5 plates in each ______________________

____

4. 4 bags with 3 cookies in each ______________________

____

5. 3 packages with 2 juice boxes in each ______________________

____

Add something else to the basket. Show how many in all.

Name ______________________

Explore Activity

Multiplication

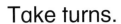

Working Together

You and your partner need 25 counters, a ,

and a workmat.

Take turns.

▶ You spin to find how many groups to make.

▶ Your partner spins to find how many counters in each group.

▶ Show the groups of counters on your workmat. Complete the chart.

I made 3 groups of 2. That is 6 in all.

How many different ways can you and your partner find the total number of counters?

	Number of groups	Number in each group	Number in all
1	3	2	6
2			
3			
4			
5			

Practice!

Use counters and . Complete the chart.

	Number of groups	Number in each group	Number in all
1	5	3	15
2	2	4	
3	3	1	
4	3	4	
5	4	5	
6	1	2	

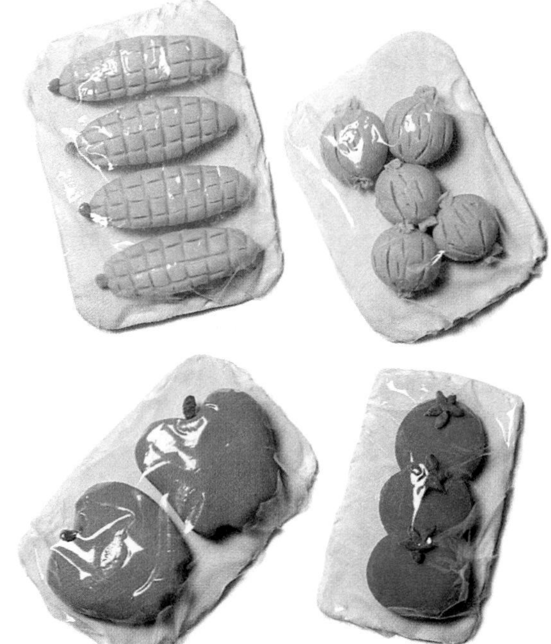

Cultural Connection

India

In Bombay, India, some merchants use fingers to show numbers.

Each finger of the right hand stands for a group of 5.

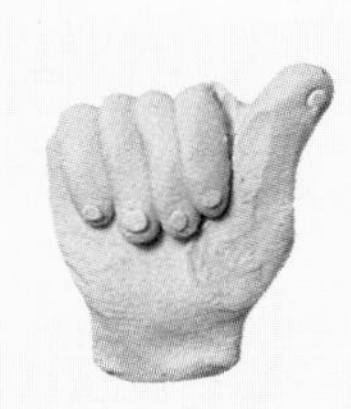

1 group of 5

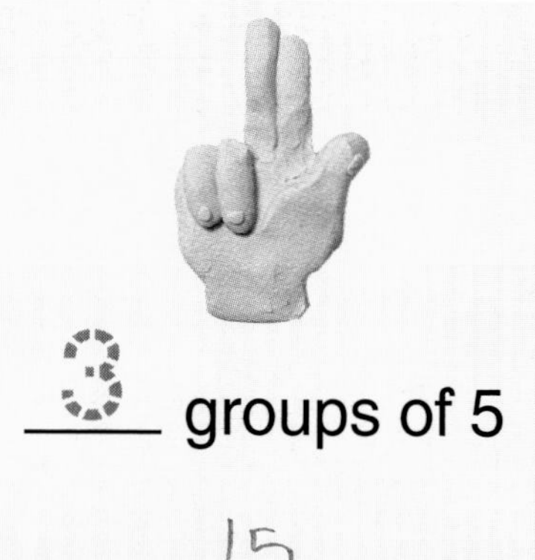

3 groups of 5

15

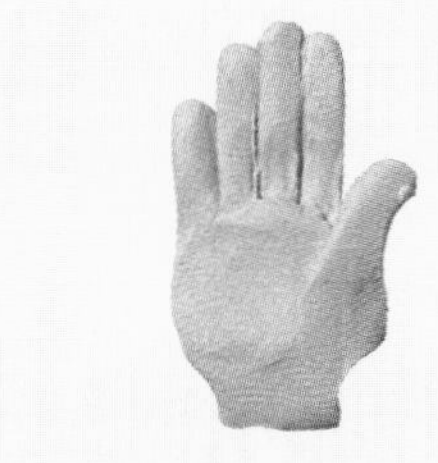

5 groups of 5

25

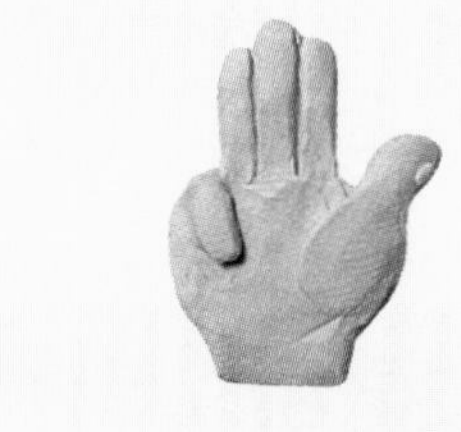

4 groups of 5

20

We explored making equal groups. Ask your child to find the total for 5 groups of 4.

Name ______

Explore Activity

Multiply by 1, 2, and 3

You can **multiply** to find how many ears of corn in all.

4 groups of 2 8

$4 \times 2 =$ 8

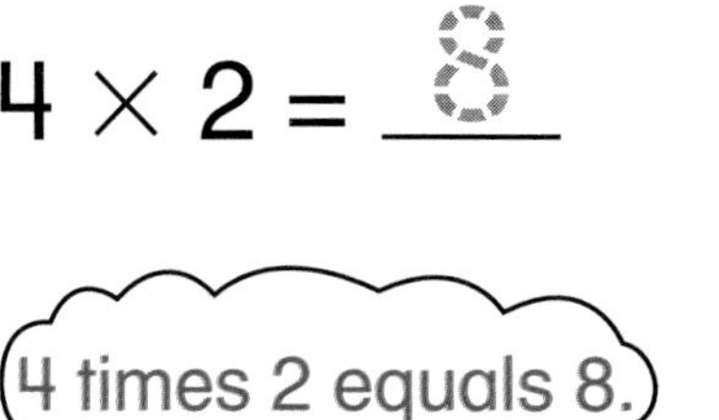

There are 8 ears of corn.

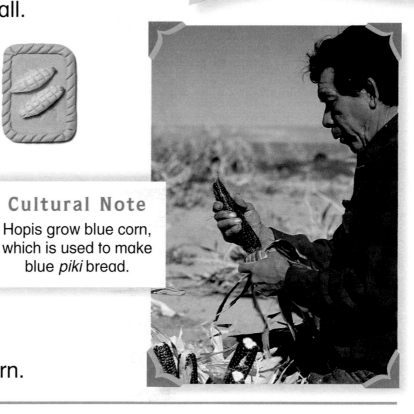

Cultural Note

Hopis grow blue corn, which is used to make blue *piki* bread.

Working Together

You and your partner need 15   and 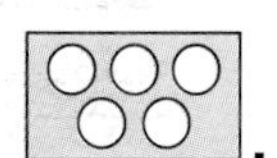.

Glossary

multiply

- Use counters to make the groups.
- Draw dots to show the groups you made.
- Write how many in all.

1. 4 groups of 3 12

   $4 \times 3 =$ ____

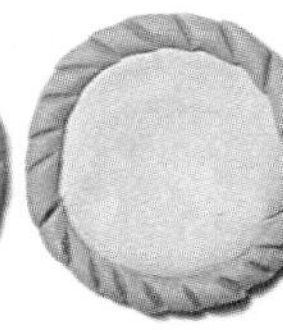

2. 5 groups of 1 ____

   $5 \times 1 =$ ____

What does 5×3 mean?
How do you find how many in all?

Practice!

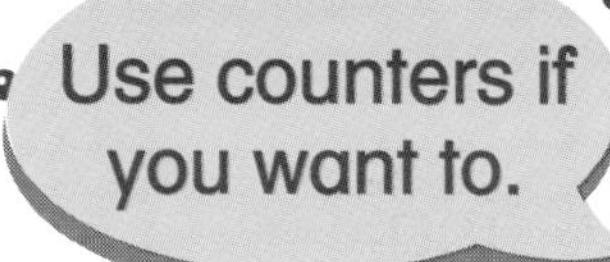

Use counters if you want to.

Multiply.

1 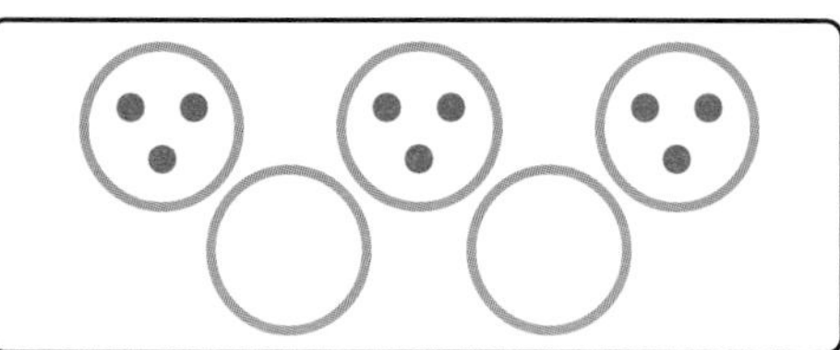

3 groups of 3 9

$3 \times 3 =$ ___

2 

5 groups of 2 ___

$5 \times 2 =$ ___

3 

3 groups of 1 ___

$3 \times 1 =$ ___

4 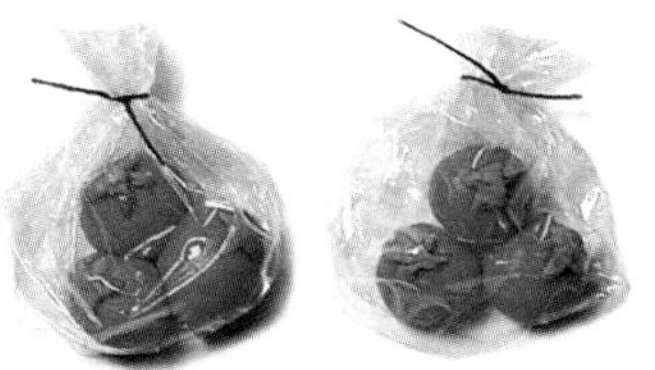

2 groups of 3 ___

$2 \times 3 =$ ___

Mixed Review Test Preparation

Write the fraction for the shaded part.

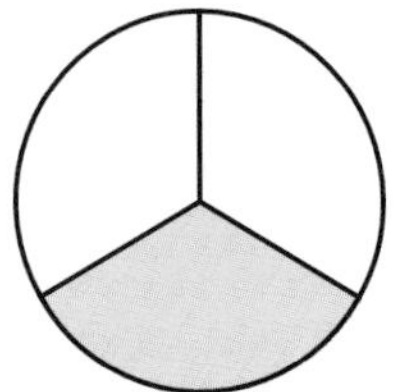 ___

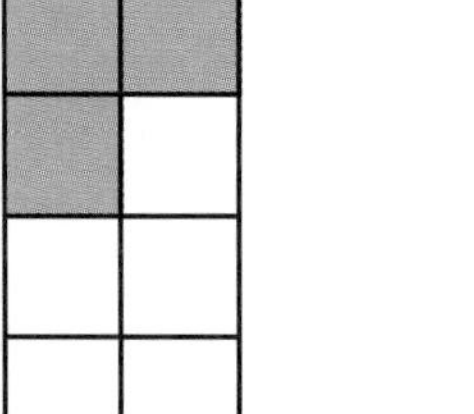 ___

 ___

Measure each path.

about ______ inches

about ______ cm

At Home

We multiplied by 1, 2, and 3. Ask your child to show 4 groups of 3 and find how many in all.

Name ______________________

Explore Activity

Multiply by 4 and 5

Write a **multiplication sentence**.
Find how many jars of salsa Elena made.

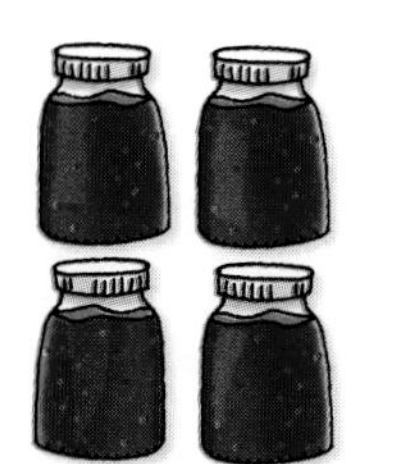  

3 groups of 4

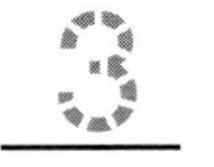 × 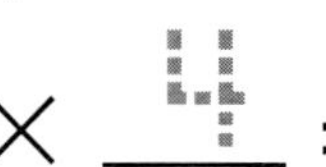 = 

Elena made 12 jars of salsa.

Working Together

You and your partner need 25  and 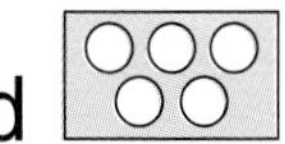.

- ▶ Use counters to make the groups.
- ▶ Draw dots to show the groups you made.
- ▶ Write the multiplication sentence.

Glossary
multiplication sentence
product

1. 2 groups of 5

____ × ____ = ____

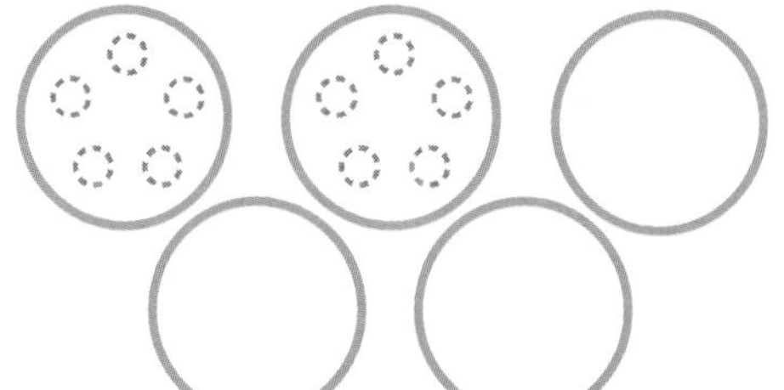

2. 5 groups of 5

____ × ____ = ____

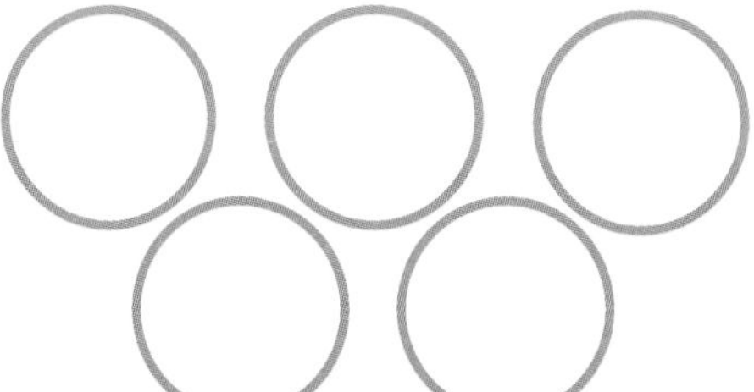

3. 5 groups of 4

____ × ____ = ____

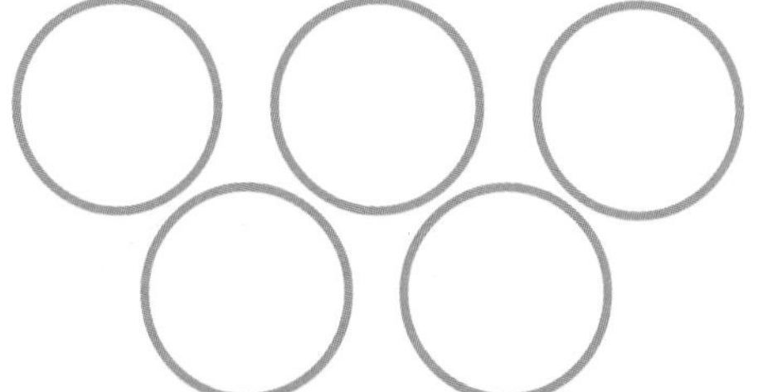

Practice!

Use counters if you want to.

Write the multiplication sentence.
Find the product.

1 group of 5

1 × 5 = 5

2 groups of 4

___ × ___ = ___

4 groups of 4

___ × ___ = ___

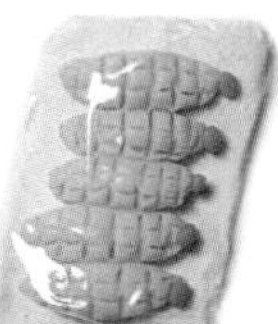

3 groups of 5

___ × ___ = ___

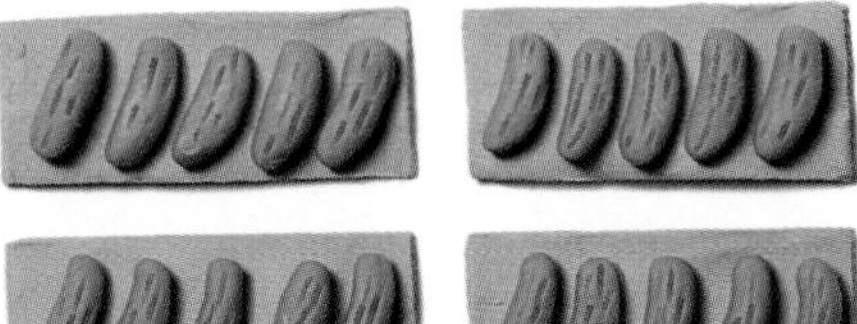

4 groups of 5

___ × ___ = ___

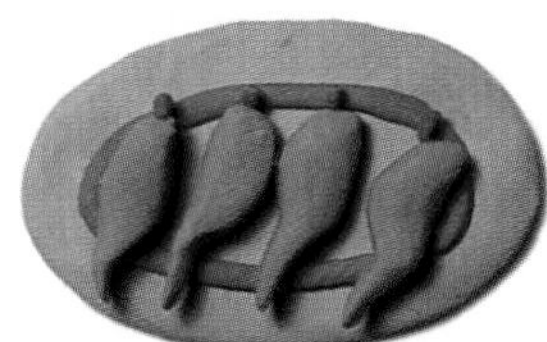

1 group of 4

___ × ___ = ___

7. You need 4 tomatoes to make 1 jar of salsa. How many tomatoes are needed for 3 jars of salsa?

___ tomatoes

Write about how you multiply to find the product.

At Home

We multiplied by 4 and 5. Ask your child to show 2 groups of 5 and find the product.

Name ______________________

Explore Activity

Multiplication Patterns

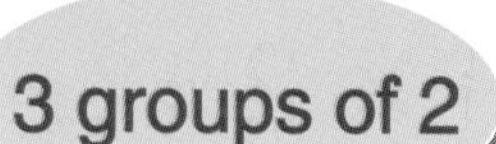

$2 \times 3 = \underline{6}$ $3 \times 2 = \underline{6}$

factor factor product   factor factor product

What happens to the product if you switch the order of the **factors**?

____

Glossary

factor

Working Together

You need 25 counters and a workmat.

- ▶ **PATTERNS** You use counters to find the first product.
- ▶ Your partner uses counters to find the second product.
- ▶ Compare your work.

1 $3 \times 5 =$ ____ $4 \times 1 =$ ____ $4 \times 5 =$ ____

$5 \times 3 =$ ____ $1 \times 4 =$ ____ $5 \times 4 =$ ____

2 $5 \times 1 =$ ____ $3 \times 4 =$ ____ $2 \times 1 =$ ____

$1 \times 5 =$ ____ $4 \times 3 =$ ____ $1 \times 2 =$ ____

When 1 is a factor, what do you notice about the product?

Practice!

Multiply.

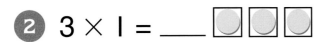

1. $4 \times 2 = \underline{8}$

   $2 \times 4 = \_\_\_$

2. $3 \times 1 = \_\_\_$

   $1 \times 3 = \_\_\_$

3. $5 \times 2 = \_\_\_$ 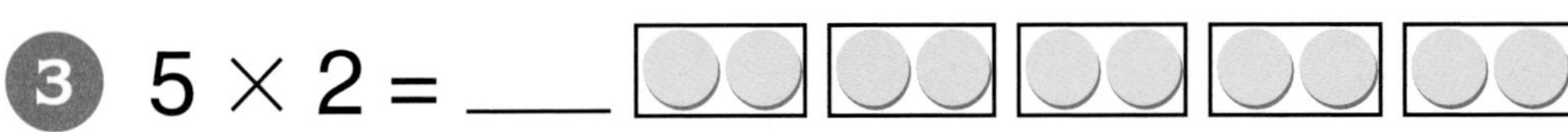

   $2 \times 5 = \_\_\_$

4. $4 \times 3 = \_\_\_$

   $3 \times 4 = \_\_\_$

More to Explore — Algebra Sense

Look at the factors. Look at the products.

$0 \times 1 = 0$	$1 \times 0 = 0$
$0 \times 2 = 0$	$2 \times 0 = 0$
$0 \times 3 = 0$	$3 \times 0 = 0$
$0 \times 4 = 0$	$4 \times 0 = 0$
$0 \times 5 = 0$	$5 \times 0 = 0$

What do you notice about the factors and the products? Write about it.

At Home Ask your child to tell you why 2×3 and 3×2 have the same product.

Name ______________________

Extra Practice
Activity !

Oh, Beans!

You and your partner need 25 beans and 2 counters.

Take turns.

- Place 1 counter on a number in each row.
  This shows how many bowls and how many beans.
- Put that many beans in that many bowls below.
- Write the multiplication sentence.

Number of bowls	1	2	3	4	5
Number of beans for each bowl	1	2	3	4	5

___ × ___ = ___ ___ × ___ = ___

___ × ___ = ___ ___ × ___ = ___

___ × ___ = ___ ___ × ___ = ___

Find the product.

1 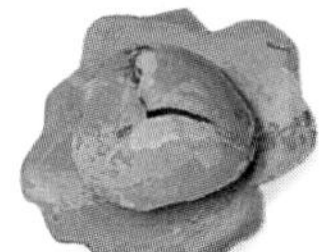 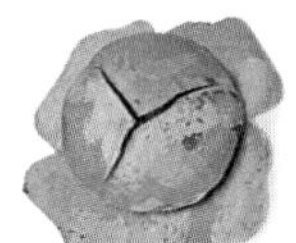 

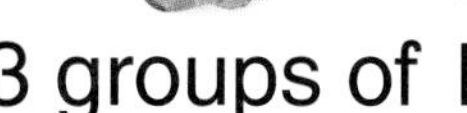

3 groups of 1

$3 \times 1 =$ ____

2 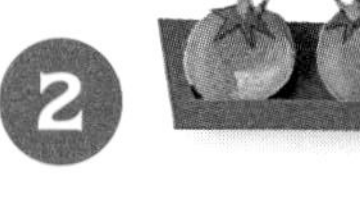 

3 groups of 4

$3 \times 4 =$ ____

   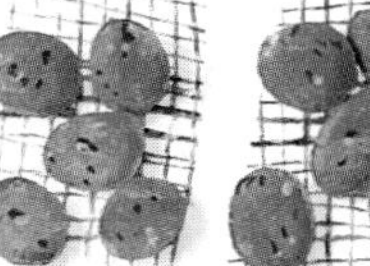

4 groups of 5

$4 \times 5 =$ ____

  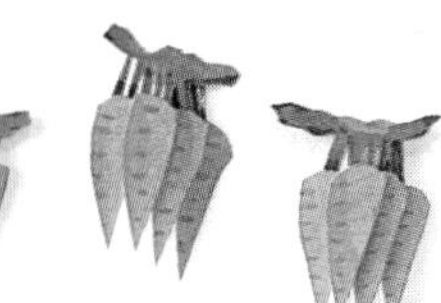

5 groups of 4

$5 \times 4 =$ ____

   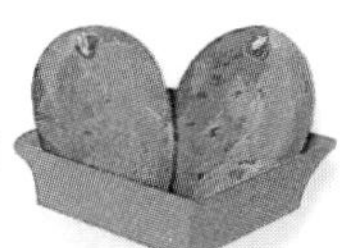

3 groups of 2

$3 \times 2 =$ ____

1 group of 2

$1 \times 2 =$ ____

 $2 \times 4 =$ ____ 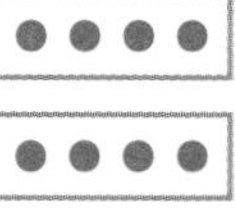

$4 \times 2 =$ ____ 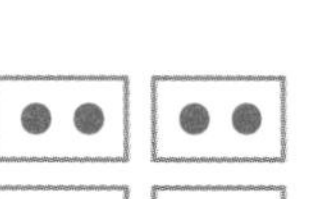

 $5 \times 2 =$ ____ 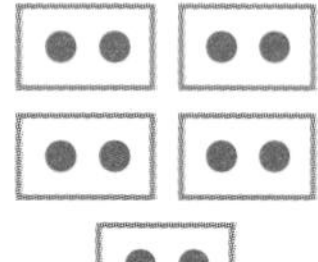

$2 \times 5 =$ ____ 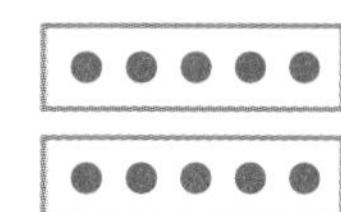

Ask Questions

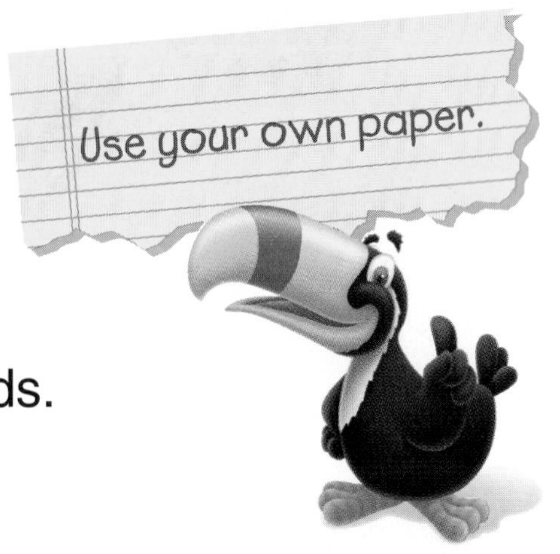

What other information do you need to know to solve this problem?

A farmer finds 3 giant carrots in each of his fields. How many giant carrots does he find in all?

Write a question about what you need to know.

Name

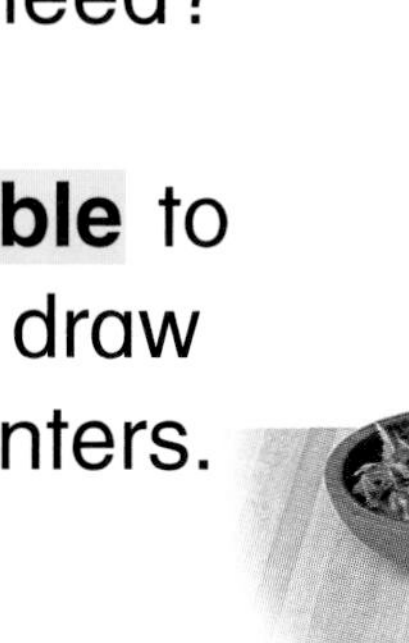

Problem-Solving Strategy

Read
Plan
Solve
Look Back

Make a Table

Read Gabe is making 7 salads. He puts 3 cherry tomatoes in each salad. How many tomatoes does he need?

Plan You can **make a table** to solve. You can also draw a picture or use counters.

Solve Make a table.

Salads	1	2	3	4	5	6	7		
Tomatoes	3	6	9	12	15	18	21		

Gabe needs 21 tomatoes for 7 salads.

Look Back Did you answer the question? Explain.

Glossary
make a table

PATTERNS Make a table to solve.

1. Tess cooks 2 potatoes for each person. There will be 6 people at dinner. How many potatoes should Tess cook? ____ potatoes

People	1	2	3						
Potatoes	2	4							

2. What if 8 people came to dinner. How many potatoes should Tess cook? ____ potatoes

Make a table to solve.

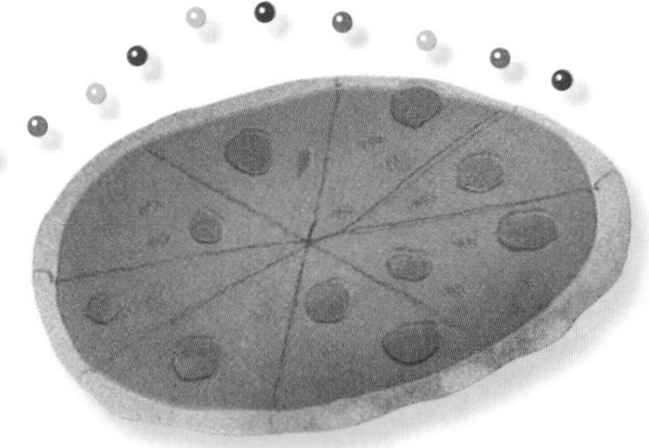

1. Marla makes 9 pizzas.
She slices 2 tomatoes for each pizza.
How many tomatoes does Marla need? ________ tomatoes

Pizzas	1	2							
Tomatoes	2	4							

2. Tony buys 6 eggplants.
He cuts each eggplant into 4 pieces.
How many pieces does Tony have? ________ pieces

Eggplants	1	2							
Pieces	4	8							

3. Louis uses 3 crates of lettuce each week. How many crates does he use in 8 weeks? ________ crates

Weeks	1								
Crates	3								

4. 

Write your own problem.
Have a partner solve it.

Use your own paper.

We made tables to solve problems. Ask your child to explain how to solve problem 3 above.

Name

Midchapter Review

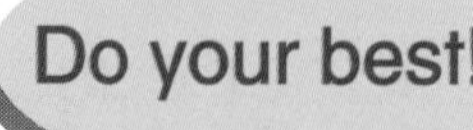

Multiply.

1 2 groups of 5 ____

2 $2 \times 5 =$ ____

3 4 groups of 4 ____

4 $4 \times 4 =$ ____

5 1 group of 3 ____

6 $1 \times 3 =$ ____

7 $4 \times 2 =$ ____

8 $2 \times 4 =$ ____

Make a table to solve.

9 Casey buys 6 boxes of peppers.
Each box has 3 peppers.
How many peppers does Casey buy? ____ peppers

Boxes										
Peppers										

10 What other way could you solve problem 9? ____________________

____

How are 3×4 and 4×3 the same? How are they different?

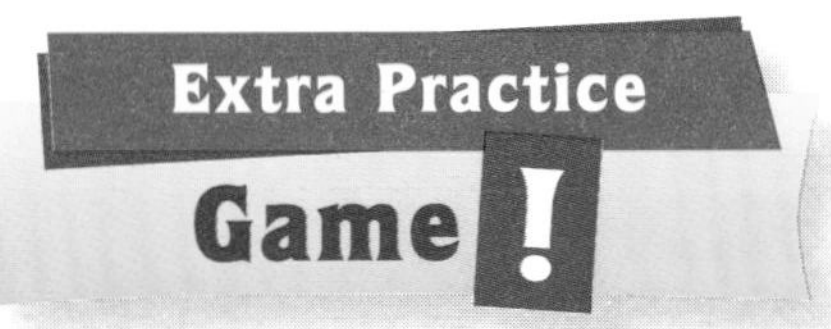

Multiplication Table

You and your partner each need your own color and 1 .

Take turns.

- Toss your counter on the multiplication table.
- Find the product for that space. Write it. Your partner checks.
- Color that space if you are correct. Your partner colors the space if you are wrong.

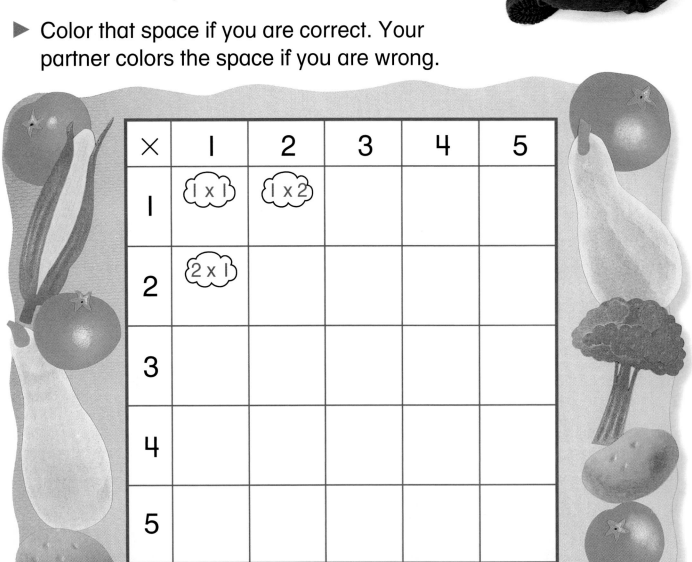

×	1	2	3	4	5
1	1 x 1	1 x 2			
2	2 x 1				
3					
4					
5					

The winner is the player with more spaces colored.

Name ____________________

Plan a Garden

People in cities sometimes plant community vegetable gardens.

Then people share the vegetables they grow. The greater the yield, the more they have to share.

Algebra

Find the yield for two kinds of vegetable plants.

BUSH CUCUMBERS										
Plants	1	2	3	4	5	6	7	8	9	10
Yield each week	2	4								

TOMATOES										
Plants	1	2	3	4	5	6	7	8	9	10
Yield each week	3	6								

Decision Making

1. Plan a vegetable garden. Decide what vegetables to grow.
2. Find the yield for each kind of vegetable or choose a reasonable number.
3. Draw a map of your garden.

Write a report.

4. Tell how you decided what to plant and how many plants you chose.
5. Explain your garden plan and tell how you will share the vegetables.

More to Investigate

PREDICT Choose a vegetable to grow. How long do you think it will take before you have a vegetable to pick?

EXPLORE Plant some seeds. Watch them grow.

FIND Keep track of the days until the first vegetable appears. Keep a record of the yield.

Name

Explore Activity

How Many Groups?

How many groups of 3 can you make from 12 counters?

4 groups of 3

Working Together

You and your partner need 16  and .

- Use counters to make the groups.
- Draw dots to show the groups you made.
- Write how many groups.

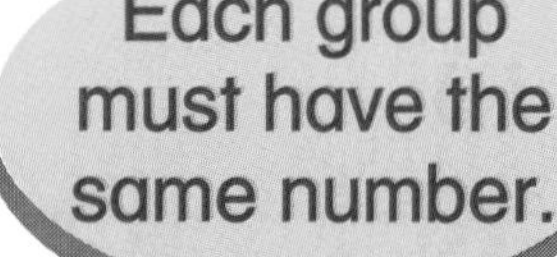

1. Use 6 counters. Make groups of 2.

____ groups of 2

---

2. Use 9 counters. Make groups of 3.

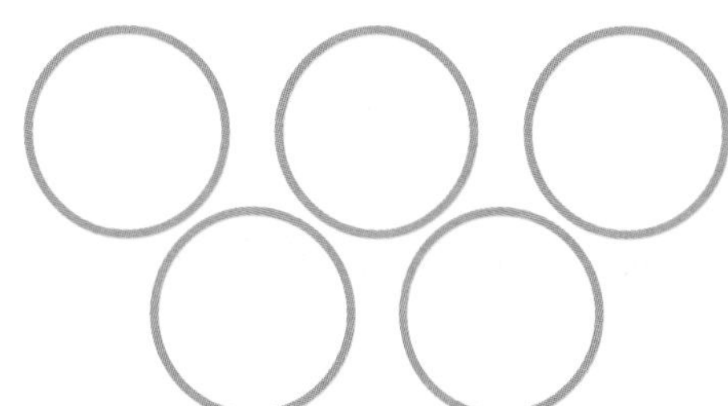

____ groups of 3

---

3. Use 16 counters. Make groups of 4.

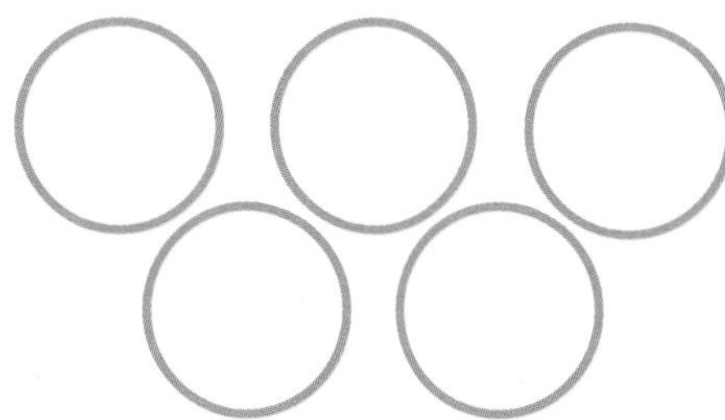

____ groups of 4

How can you check your answer?

Practice!

Each group must have the same number.

Use counters to make groups.
Draw dots to show the groups.
Write how many groups.

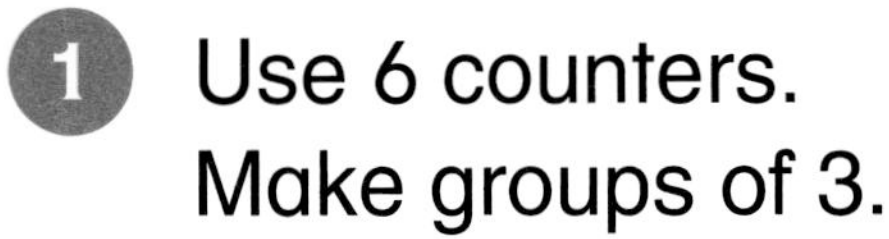

1. Use 6 counters.
   Make groups of 3.

   ____ groups of 3

2. Use 10 counters.
   Make groups of 5.

   ____ groups of 5

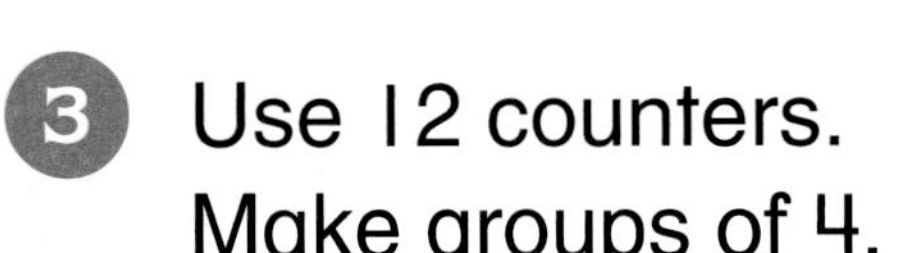

3. Use 12 counters.
   Make groups of 4.

   ____ groups of 4

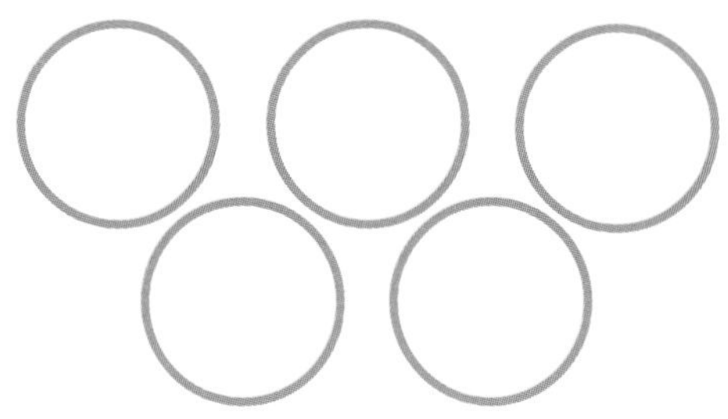

More to Explore Number Sense

You have 24 counters.

Number in each group	Can you make equal groups?	How many groups?	How many left over?
2	Yes.	12	0
5			
3			
7			

At Home

We made equal groups today. Ask your child to explain exercise 3 above.

Name ________________________________

Explore Activity

How Many in Each Group?

There are 12 crates to put in 3 trucks.
Each truck gets the same number of crates.
How many crates go in each truck?

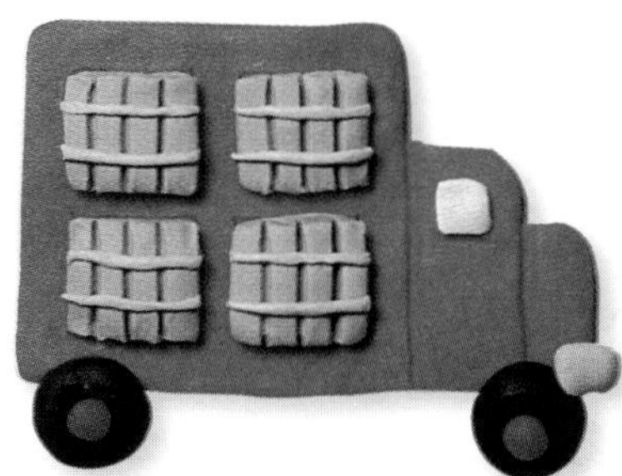
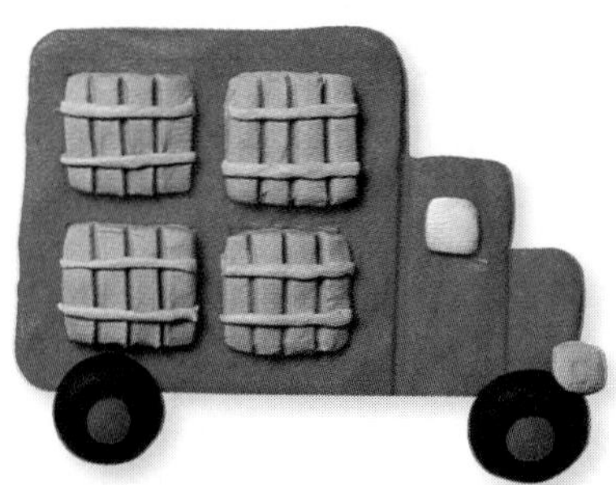

There are __4__ crates in each truck.

Working Together

You and your partner need 16  and 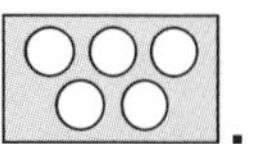.

- Use counters to make the groups.
- Draw dots to show how many counters in each group.
- Write how many in each group.

1. Use 8 counters.
   Make 2 groups.

   _____ in each group

2. Use 15 counters.
   Make 5 groups.

   _____ in each group

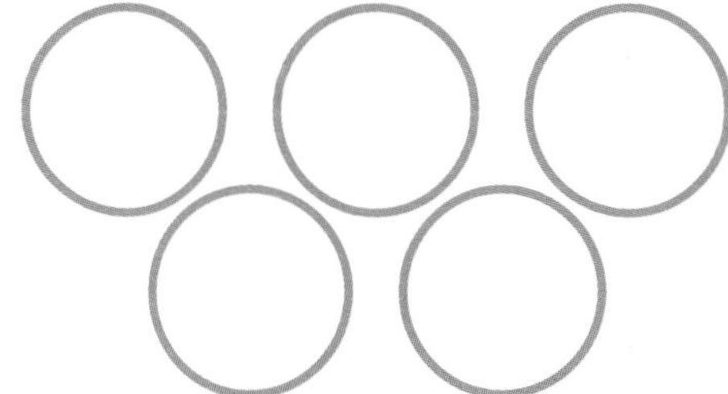

How do you make the groups equal? Share your ideas.

Use counters to make the groups.
Draw dots to show the groups.
Write how many in each group.

1 Use 6 counters.
Make 2 groups.

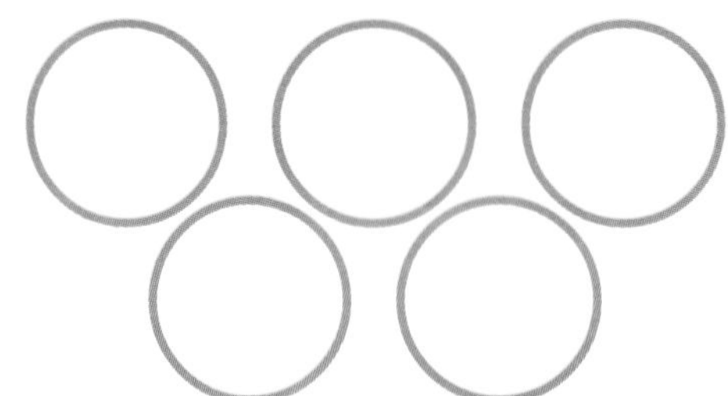

____ in each group

2 Use 12 counters.
Make 2 groups.

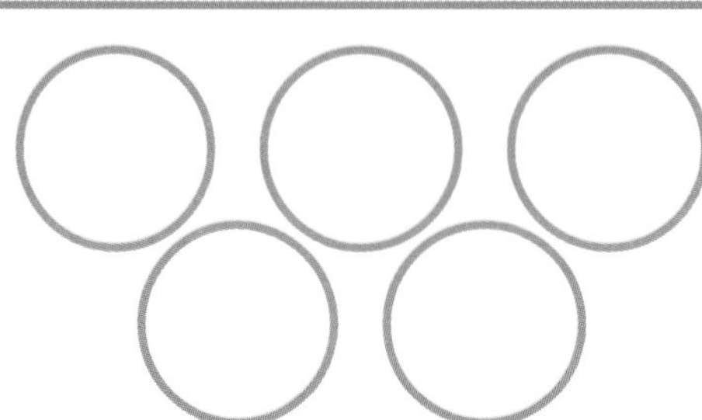

____ in each group

3 Use 10 counters.
Make 5 groups.

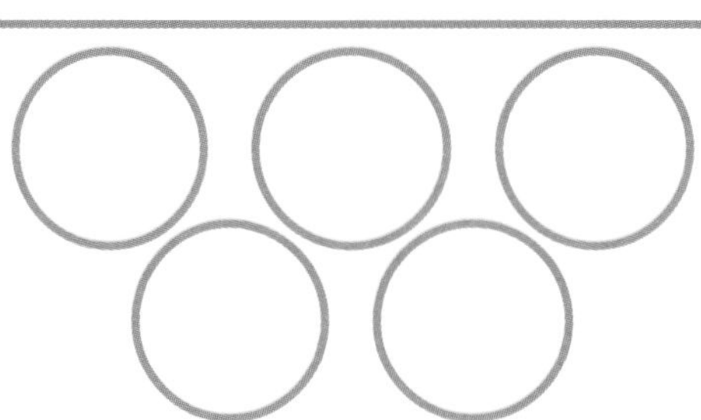

____ in each group

Mixed Review Test Preparation

Add or subtract.

4				
571	36	$1.45	362	525
− 329	+ 377	+ 4.90	− 9	+ 299

Write the fraction for the shaded part.

5  ______

6 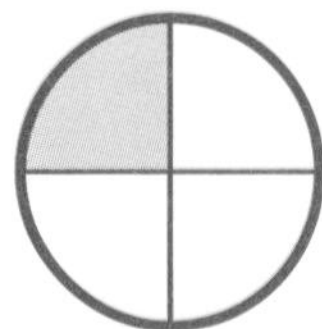 ______

7 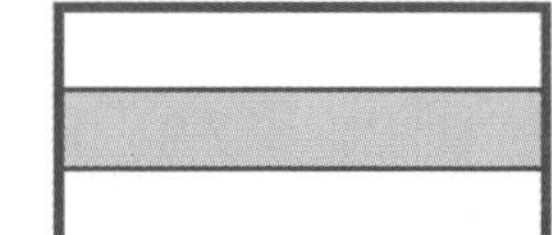 ______

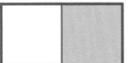

At Home: We made equal groups of counters. Ask your child to explain or show how to solve exercise 3 above.

Name ______________________

Divide and Counters

You need 20  and 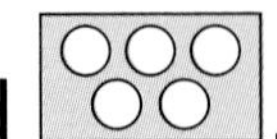.

PATTERNS Complete the table.

	Number of children	Number of teams	Number of children on each team
1	15	5	3
2	15	3	5
3	6	2	2
4		2	3
5	20		4
6		4	5
7	8	2	
8		4	2
9	12		4
10		4	3
11	16	2	
12		8	2
13	10		5
14		5	2

Draw dots to show the counters.
Write how many groups.

1 8 counters
Make groups of 2.

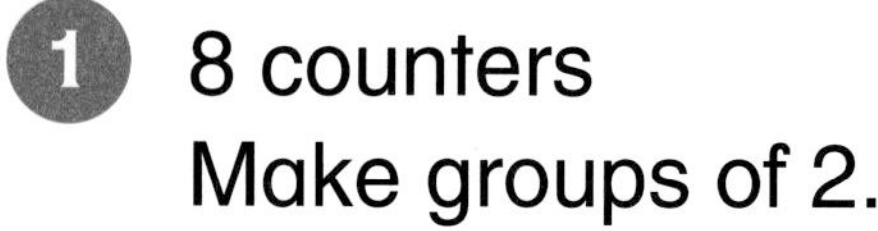

____ groups of 2

2 20 counters
Make groups of 5.

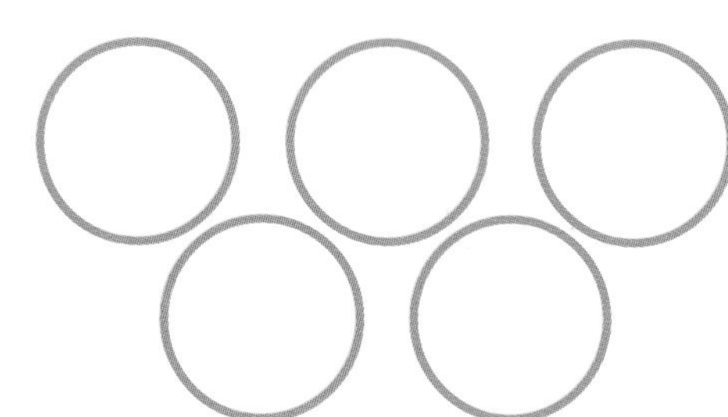

____ groups of 5

Draw dots to show the counters.
Write how many in each group.

3 4 counters
Make 4 groups.

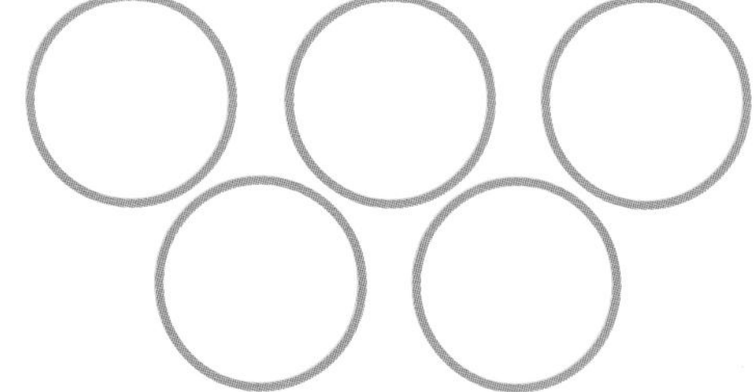

____ in each group

4 9 counters
Make 3 groups.

____ in each group

5 20 counters
Make 5 groups.

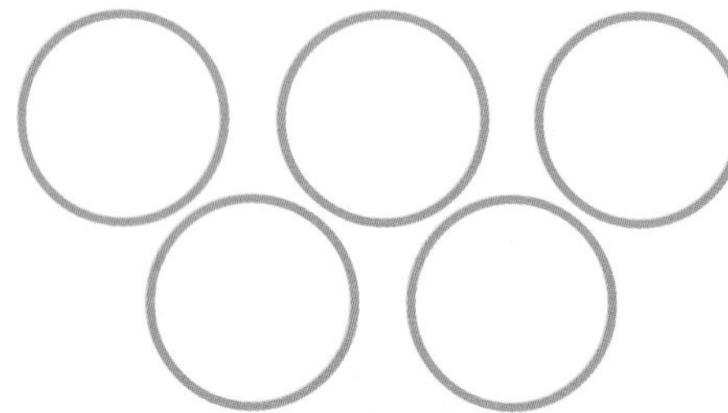

____ in each group

Name

Use Models

Ellen picked 20 little pumpkins.
She wants to **divide** them equally among herself and 3 friends. How many pumpkins will each person get?

Read
Plan
Solve
Look Back

You can use models to show groups.

Each person gets __5__ pumpkins.

Tell about another way to solve the problem.

Glossary
divide

Use models to solve.

1. The farmer has 20 red peppers. He puts 4 peppers in each bag. How many bags of peppers can he make?

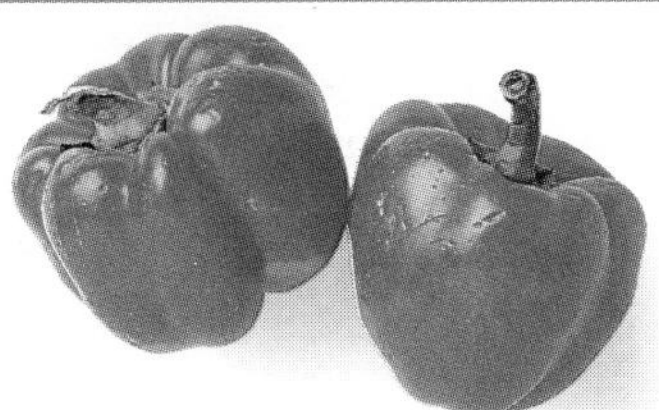

____ bags

2. The farm has 10 crates of onions. Each van can carry 5 crates. How many vans are needed to carry the 10 crates of onions?

____ vans

3. Each box holds 6 heads of cabbage. There are 3 boxes of cabbage. How many heads of cabbage is that in all?

____ heads

Practice!

Solve.

1. Tim picks 16 carrots. He puts them into 4 equal bunches. How many carrots are in each bunch? _____ carrots

2. What if Tim puts 8 carrots in each bunch. How many bunches would he make? _____ bunches

Write and Share

Nico wrote this problem.

The farm has 5 crates of apples. Each car carries 5 crates. How many cars carry the 5 crates of apples?

Nico Mooduto
P.S. 144
Forest Hills, New York

3. Solve Nico's problem. __________

   What strategy did you use? ____________________________

4. READING ARITHMETIC WRITING **Ask Questions** Write a question to finish the problem. Have a partner solve it.

Each box holds 6 big beets.
There are 3 boxes of beets.

We used models to help solve problems. Ask your child to explain how to solve the problem he or she wrote.

Name ___

Chapter Review

Language and Mathematics

Choose the correct word to complete the sentence.

factors
product
multiply
divide

1. You can ___ 3 x 2 to find the ___.

2. 4 x 1 is the same as 1 x 4 because the ___ are the same.

Concepts and Skills

Find the product.

3.  

2 groups of 5

$2 \times 5 =$ ___

4. $3 \times 5 =$ ___ 

$5 \times 3 =$ ___ 

Draw dots to show the counters. Complete.

5. 9 counters
Make groups of 3.

___ groups of 3

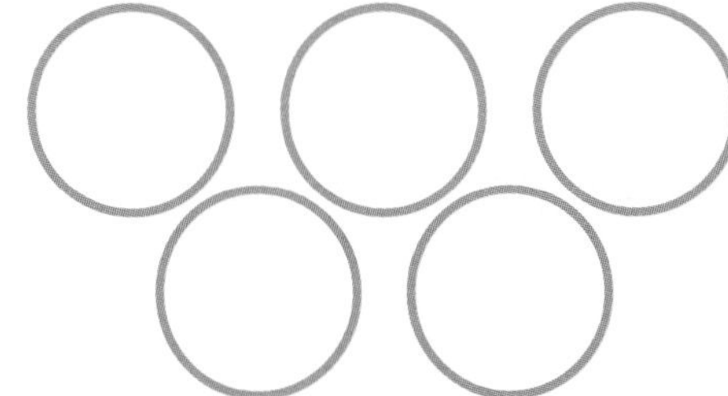

6. 12 counters
Make 4 groups.

___ in each group

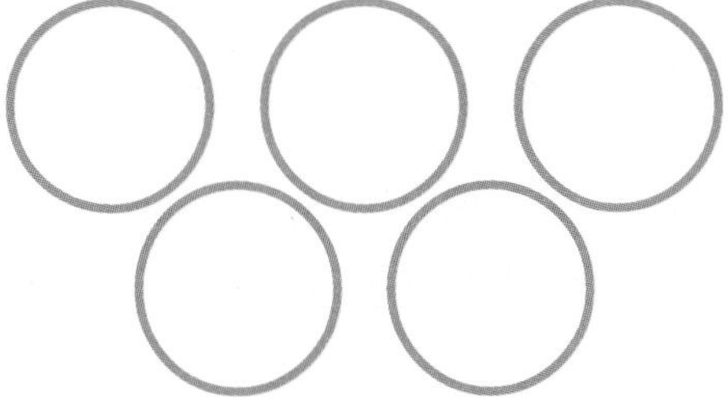

Problem Solving

Make a table to solve.

7 A farmer fills 3 crates of corn each hour.
How many crates can he fill in 5 hours? _____ crates

Hours	1								
Crates	3								

8 How many crates could the farmer fill in 7 hours? _____ crates

---

Solve.

9 Each truck holds 5 crates of corn.
How many crates can 4 trucks hold? _____ crates

10 A farmer picked 16 carrots.
She put them into 2 equal bunches.
How many carrots were in each bunch? _____ carrots

What Do You Think?

Which strategy would you use to find 3 groups of 2?
☑ Check one.

☐ Use counters. ☐ Draw dots. ☐ Draw a picture.

Why? ____________________

Journal: Write and show how to find how many in each group.

Name

Chapter Test

1 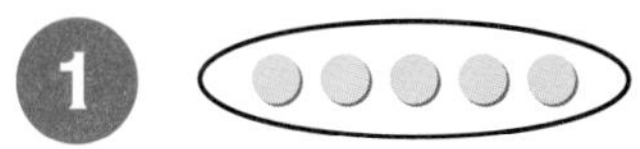

I group of 5

$1 \times 5 =$ ____

2 

2 groups of 4

$2 \times 4 =$ ____

3 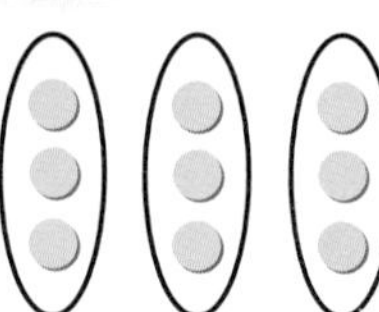

3 groups of 3

$3 \times 3 =$ ____

4 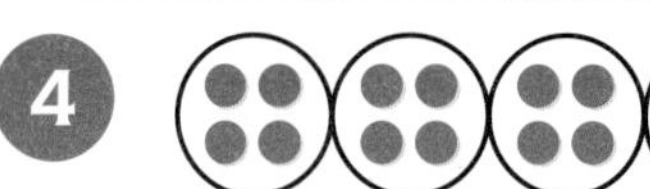

4 groups of 4

$4 \times 4 =$ ____

5 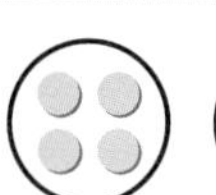 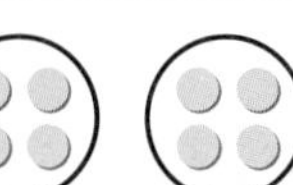 

$3 \times 4 =$ ____

6 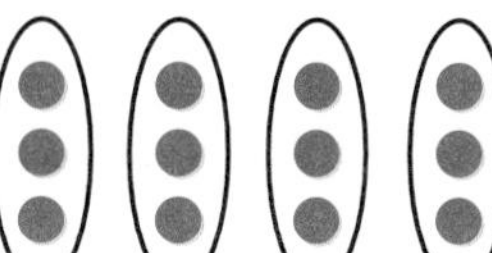

$4 \times 3 =$ ____

Draw dots to show the counters. Complete.

7 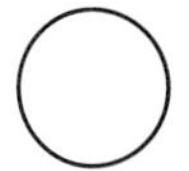 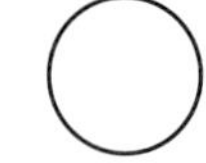 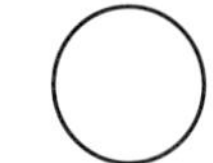 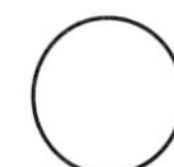 

10 counters
Make groups of 2.

____ groups of 2

8   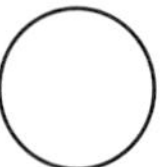 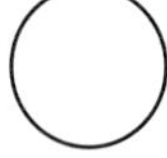    

12 counters
Make 4 groups.

____ in each group

Make a table to solve.

9 Jed makes 8 pizzas.
He puts 2 meatballs on each pizza.
How many meatballs does Jed need? ____ meatballs

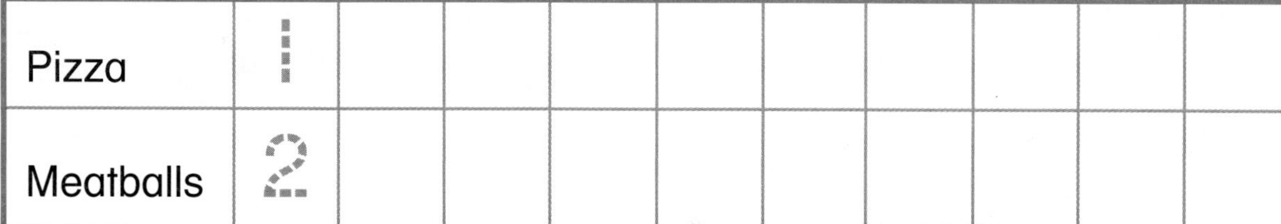

Pizza	1									
Meatballs	2									

10 What if Jed makes 10 pizzas.
How many meatballs does Jed need? ____ meatballs

Performance Assessment

What Did You Learn?

Work with a partner. You need .

You have 2 bags with 9 ears of corn in each. You want to share the corn with some friends. Give each friend the same number of ears of corn.

Show how many ears of corn each friend gets.
Draw a picture or write a sentence.

What if you have more friends. Is there another way you can share the corn equally?

You may want to put this page in your portfolio.

Math Connection

Name

Division Sentences

Sal makes sauce with 14 tomatoes. He uses 2 pots. He puts the same number of tomatoes in each pot. How many tomatoes go in each pot?

14 tomatoes in 2 equal groups

$14 \div 2 = 7$

14 divided by 2 equals 7.

Draw dots to show equal groups of tomatoes. Complete the **division sentence**.

Glossary
division sentence

1. 8 tomatoes
   Make 2 groups.
   $8 \div 2 =$ 4

2. 12 tomatoes
   Make 3 groups.
   $12 \div 3 =$ ____

3. 12 tomatoes
   Make 2 groups.
   $12 \div 2 =$ ____

4. 9 tomatoes
   Make 3 groups.
   $9 \div 3 =$ ____

Curriculum Connection

Health

Healthful Snacks

Here is a healthful snack your class can make.

Double the recipe so that you will have enough.

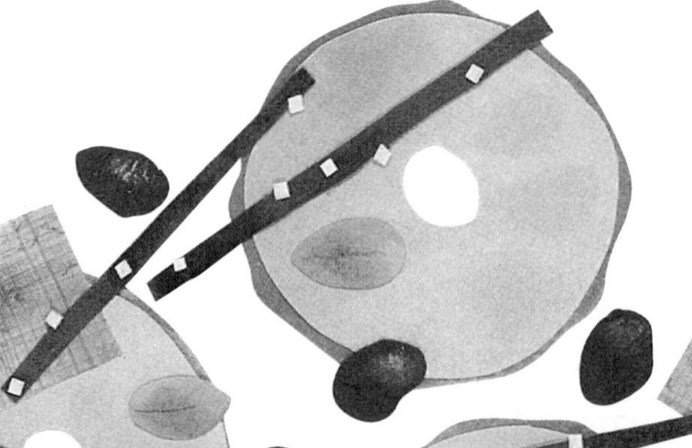

Party Mix

2 cups Wheat Chex ____________________

3 cups pretzel sticks ____________________

$1\frac{1}{2}$ cups peanuts ____________________

$\frac{1}{2}$ cup raisins ____________________

$\frac{1}{2}$ cup dried sliced apples ____________________

What else could you add to the party mix? How much would you add?